BROMP

BICYCLE

EXCELLENT BOOKS

EXCELLENT BOOKS
5 VIKING AVENUE
EMLEY
WEST YORKSHIRE HD8 9SE
07762 545 543
www.excellentbooks.co.uk
2nd edition updated and revised printed 2017

Text © David Henshaw 2009-2017
Photographs and illustrations © David Henshaw / Brompton Bicycle Ltd / Richard Peace except where indicated otherwise

ISBN 978-1-901464-25-2

Front cover design: Diana Powell dianampowell@googlemail.com
Rear cover photo: Once Bromptons only came in red - today's colour range is vast
Frontispiece: Electric Nano-Brompton with SP trailer bike and child seats

With thanks to: Will Butler-Adams Brompton Bicycle MD, Alan Clarke of Sturmey-Archer
Europe BV, Steve Grosvenor, Tim Guinness, Tony Hadland, Adam Hart-Davis, Gary Lovell,
Juliane Neuß, Tim Reeves and Andrew Ritchie
And to photo contributors:
Paul Bader, Andy & Sue Black, Vincent Burgeon, Tony Castles, ETS Design,
Dave Holladay, Marcus Jackson-Baker, Carl Kamenzind, Paul Lenton, Phil O'Connor,
Tony L. Oliver, Philipp Onori, Olivier Pascaud, Antoine Pethers, Len Rubin, Mark Sanders,
Andrew Stevenson, Jos Vromen, Thomas Wiegold and Ken Yanoviak
Thanks to David Walker for retouching work on the inside rear cover photo

Author's Dedication:
To Julian Vereker, who would
have enjoyed a Brompton book.

The Brompton won Best Product award
at Cyclex in 1987 - a big step forward
for the company at the time. Julian's
delight is obvious.

Contents

Foreword

During the 1990s I presented a television series called Local Heroes, in which I cycled around this country (and a few others), mainly on a mountain bike, talking about dead scientists and inventors, and showing what they had done. We transported the mountain bike from Land's End to John O'Groats (literally) – and beyond – and were constantly aware that it might come to grief (or get nicked) and leave us stranded; so I decided to acquire a standby machine – and a folding bike was the obvious choice.

I can't remember who pointed me in the direction of the Brompton, but it may well have been David Henshaw; I met him and his wife Jane at some bike event. Anyway, I persuaded Andrew Ritchie to make me a pink-and-yellow machine for the TV series; I rode it to an early meeting of the Folding Society at Weymouth, and it travelled with me and the TV crew for many thousands of miles, appearing on television in Sicily (where I broke the back axle at the top of Mt Etna), in Egypt (where I used it to show how Eratosthenes had measured the size of the Earth) and in sundry other exotic locations. I even rode it round the demonstration desk at the Royal Institution and through the corridors of the BBC offices at White City.

Sadly that lovely machine was stolen. I was invited to be interviewed about folding bikes on Radio 4's *You and Yours* programme at Broadcasting House in London. The producer told me not to bring my Brompton into the studio, which was cramped, but to lock it up outside. I did as I was told, but when I came out again it was gone. Now I have a smart green one with only two gears, which is fine, because this is my London transport, and London has no hills (well, almost none).

The Brompton is an ideal bike for any city and for commuting. It folds easily and quickly, and can go in a train, the tube, or a bus; it's not too heavy to carry, and it's a good ride. The really important thing is that I can take it in with me; it is welcome at the British Library, the Science Museum, the Royal Society, and even the Dog and Duck, and once inside a building it is unlikely to be stolen.

I find the Brompton the most reliable way to get around London; regardless of traffic, strikes, or security threats, I know just how long it will take me to get from A to B, and I can easily carry what I need in the bag on the front.

This book is splendid; David writes clearly and amusingly, and I was delighted to find out about the tortuous history of this superb bicycle. I have visited Andrew Ritchie and been shown around the factory, but he is modest about his achievements, and tends to hide his light under a bushel. I hope this book will go some way to hauling it out again. In any case I am sure you will enjoy reading it.

Adam Hart-Davis 2009

The Author and his Brompton

I can honestly say the Brompton changed my life. In the early 1990s, my wife Jane and I were house-sitting - generally in London and the busy southeast - and filling spare moments writing books and articles about cars and trains. But like many people at the time, we were becoming concerned about the way transport was going - Twyford Down, Bathampton, the news seemed to be full of stories of apparently unwanted trunk roads being foisted on unwilling communities. Working much of the time in London, and driving a fairly high mileage, we started to look for ways of reducing our car mileage, with the rather vague idea that if everyone did the same, the need for new roads would be reduced and we'd all be happier.

The rail network, despite being ravaged by politicians of all shades, is generally competitive with car journeys between city centres, but what about those awkward journeys ten miles from the nearest railhead? I began sketching ideas for a personal transport machine on the back of an envelope. Some sort of bicycle seemed to fit the bill, but it would need to fold to go on trains and buses, be light enough to carry, and strong enough to transport one person and enough luggage for six weeks for maybe ten miles.

I didn't know it at the time, but I had sketched a Bickerton, a British invention of the 1960s and in many ways the granddaddy of the modern folding bike. The Bickerton was good enough, but it was wobbly and idiosyncratic to ride, and no doubt my invention would have been even wobblier. While leafing through *New Cyclist* (a new and vaguely avant-garde cycle magazine) early in 1991, I came across an advertisement for a neat and compact folding bike. I happened to be in London the following week, and called at Cyclecare Olympia, the shop that had placed the advertisement, and one of very few cycle shops stocking the Brompton at the time.

It turned out to be an amazing machine, and capable far beyond my wildest dreams. A bit heavy perhaps, but neat, easy to fold after a few trial runs, and eminently practical for rail commuting, with clip-on luggage that made light work of 10kg loads, and equipped with other sensible things like mudguards and lights.

I bought a Brompton on the spot and rode it the short distance to Kensington Olympia station, folding it behind a pillar to avoid any embarrassing folding faux pas. I still have that Brompton L3, although like a well-used vintage motor car, there aren't many original parts on it after 40,000 miles. That same night, I threw away the back-of-an-envelope sketches and became an enthusiastic Brompton owner. It was too good to be made in the Far East. Perhaps it was American? The brochure said Brentford. I popped out there a few weeks later, and instead of a distribution warehouse I found a couple of railway arches, a charming intellectual-looking chap, two men in blue overalls, and an office girl. At the time, that *was* Brompton Bicycle. If the product was so fantastic, why was the company so small? The world, it seemed, had yet to discover the Brompton, but eventually it did.

Within a year we had established The Folding Society, nominally a forum for all folding bikes, but built around our enthusiasm for the Brompton, and the folding bike club gradually grew with the bike manufacturer. By October 1993, the Folding Society had its own magazine, which became The Folder, and metamorphosed in August 1997 into *A to B* magazine. It was much the same - similarly tongue-in-cheek, but with a broader transport base, touching on bike carriage by rail, sea and air, and later electric bikes too, but always coming home to the folding bike concept.

Writing in 2017, I still edit *A to B*, and I still ride that original black L3 Brompton, and both have shaped my life. In a quarter of a century, Brompton has changed too, from a tiny workshop under a railway arch to a major British exporter, and one of the biggest industrial employers in West London. Back then, ownership of a Brompton was considered to be either absurd, or faintly elitist, depending on your point of view, but today the little bikes have become everyday transport for everyman and everywoman, and quite right too.

The Brompton really was years ahead of its time in 1991. Back then, most trains still offered luggage space, and the concept of folding bike commuting was a new and rather radical idea. Brompton fought for years to get cycle shops on side, and even longer to win round sceptical rail companies, but it all came right in the end. For me, this look back at the development, and ultimately the triumph, of the Brompton folding bicycle is something of a personal pilgrimage. If it wasn't for the Brompton, I might still be writing books about historic motor cars. Something I would never have guessed in 1991 is that I might one day write a book about an iconic bicycle.

David Henshaw 2017

A Short History of Folding Bikes

Top - An early spur to development of folding bikes was the concept of military use. Here pre-WWI French troops experiment with folding bikes. Their high command was said to be quite receptive to the idea, hoping the bikes would make troops more mobile in any forthcoming conflict.

Above - C.H. Clark's tiny-wheeler of 1919 reportedly spawned some folders in the US.

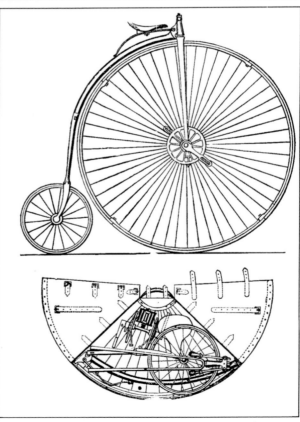

Above - the Grout Portable attempted to overcome the obstacle to folding that large wheels posed, with a front wheel that split down into four quadrants.

A Short History of Folding Bikes

"The idea of putting a bicycle into a bag is, indeed, a queer one, but of considerable value for all that, in these days of high railway charges."
Henry Sturmey   'The "Indispensable" Bicyclist's Handbook' 1881

The 19th Century to WWII

Folding bicycles (and indeed tricycles) have existed at various levels of sophistication since bicycles first appeared. The bicycle was a revolutionary machine in the late 19th century, but relatively cumbersome, and many inventors would try to reduce its size for transport or storage. When cyclists today talk about restrictions on carrying bicycles by train, they tend to treat this as a modern phenomenon, but bicycles were just as unwelcome aboard trains in Victorian times. In the mid-1880s, it typically cost a shilling (£4.90 today[1]) to carry a bicycle 50 miles by train, but in south-east England, the price could be twice that. To take a bike 250 miles by train could cost from 3 shillings and 6 pence to a whopping 7 shillings (£17.05 to £34.10 today[1]). Clearly, a Brompton would have paid for itself very quickly, had it been available!

Before the invention of the compact chain-driven 'safety' bicycle in the 1890s, bicycles had a huge driven wheel of anything up to 150cm in diameter. These 'high bicycles' (popularly known as penny-farthings) were big, heavy and awkward to transport.

A recurring theme with folding bikes is small wheels, because no matter how clever the folding mechanism, the final folded height can never be less than the diameter of the wheel. As the high bicycle was little taller than its enormous front wheel, the only way to produce a smaller package for transport was to 'fold' the wheel itself, something that was achieved in 1878 by one William Grout, inventor of the Grout Portable. The Grout was a clever design, the front wheel separating to produce four quadrants that packed together in a bag, together with the rear wheel, cranks, saddle, folded handlebars and frame. The latter split into two parts, which fitted neatly into the bag with everything else. Little is known about the Grout, not even its weight, which must have been considerable, but at £19 to £23 (£1,660 to £2,010 today[1]) - when a skilled craftsman earned less than £2 a week - it was expensive, and it took a claimed ten minutes to fold, probably a good deal longer in practice. It was not a success, and no examples are thought to survive.

In any event, the Grout Portable was rendered obsolete within a few years by the arrival of the safety bicycle. This innovation put the pedal cranks in the middle of the frame, linked to a relatively small back wheel by a chain or (rather less successfully) a belt. A 'safety' could be ridden just as fast as a high bicycle because the chain drive allowed higher gearing, so the same comfortable pedal speed would spin the back wheel faster, giving the advantages of a large wheel without the inconvenience. Much later, the same technique would be applied to even smaller wheels on ever more compact folding bikes, but in the 1880s the safety bicycle settled down with wheels of 26 to 30 inches in diameter, and was to remain more or less unchanged until the modern era. The remarkable longevity of the classic diamond-frame safety bicycle helps to explain why acceptance of small-wheeled folding bikes a century later was a little reluctant. The bicycle had hardly changed for four generations, making bicycle shops rather conservative establishments, but in reality the modern small-wheeled folding bike was simply a radical application of the 'safety' principles - that is, smaller wheels with more extreme gearing.

---

[1] See text note on page 192

1

Small wheels took a long time to arrive, but manufacturers continued to experiment with folding frames, generally doing the obvious thing and putting a vertical hinge in the middle of the main frame tube, allowing the wheels to fold around and sit side-by-side. One of the first was the Faun, patented in 1896. This was quite a neat 'fold in half' design, producing an acceptably compact folded package that wouldn't look out of place on a commuter train today. But these early folders were expensive. The Faun cost 28 to 30 guineas (£3,070 to £3,290 today[1]), a considerable sum, making it accessible only to the very wealthy.

At the time, all bicycles were expensive, but within a few years, the price of a no-frills non-folding machine had tumbled, thanks to mass production and growing demand, although they remained expensive by modern standards. Folding bikes cost even more to make, and their limited sales made it difficult to realize the economies of scale available to manufacturers of simpler, cruder machines - nothing has changed! In the late Victorian era, a folding bicycle would have been extremely useful for a working man commuting by rail or tram, but the high prices meant they were only within reach for the wealthy, who generally had carriages - increasingly of the horseless variety - to get to and from the station. For these reasons, the market remained very limited.

By the early 20th century, the folding bicycle had become little more than a curiosity, though several attempts were made to revive the genre, principally for military use. In the days when soldiers slogged their way forward on foot, military theorists reasoned that a folding bike could be carried easily across rough ground, and unfolded for rapid advancement (and, of course, retreat) when the opportunity presented itself.

The most interesting machine of this type was the Dursley-Pedersen, produced by Mikael Pedersen, a Danish engineer who had settled in England. The Pedersen was constructed of a light, rigid lattice of steel tubes, with a suspended hammock-like seat. Most models didn't fold,

but in 1900, at the height of the second Boer War, Pedersen introduced a separable version with a detachable front wheel and steering assembly. Sadly, it was ignored by the military top brass, and sold only fitfully to the public, before being withdrawn five years later.

With the demise of Pedersen's folder, the trail goes cold until the advent of the First World War, when armament (and bicycle) manufacturer BSA was instructed to produce a folding bike for military use. These were heavy, unsophisticated machines, folding in half around a vertical bar mid-frame. Quite how many went into service and how useful they proved in combat is not known, but BSA went on to produce another folding machine during the Second World War. This was a rather more elegant design, with twin curved

WWI saw folding bikes developed as (theoretically) a mobility aid on the battlefield, though those demonstrated on the left by the high-mobility Italian Bersaglieri corps appear more of a hindrance to quick movement when mounted on the back for carrying over rough terrain.

[1] See text note on page 192

The unusual Pedersen (above) was aimed at Boer War
troops but largely ignored by those in power.
The BSA (below) was most certainly used in WWII - but
exactly how and where remains unclear.

© Pinkerton Collection

frame tubes fitted with hinged joints mid-way, the joints being secured by wing-nuts. This time, the folding bicycle did at last seem to have found a genuinely useful role.

According to military vehicle expert Colin Stevens, analysis of the serial numbers indicates that over 70,000 BSA folders were manufactured during the Second World War. Though often referred to as "parabikes" by collectors, this term more properly applies to a non-folding postwar model, sold to the public and trading on wartime mythology as a marketing tool - actual training manuals tended to refer to the original military folder as the "airborne bicycle".

Contemporary military instruction manuals show how the 'airborne' really did become airborne. Used independently of individual soldiers, the bikes could float to earth under their own mini-parachutes that were released in flight. Alternatively, and seemingly highly perilously, they could also be attached to the parachutist by suspension lines (see below left), and accompany him on his descent. The potential for serious injuries or worse from entanglement, or actually landing on the bike itself, don't seem to have been at the forefront of the military planners' minds.

BSA's WWII 'airborne' folder certainly looked the part strapped to a parachutist (far left) or ridden in the 'drop zone' (near left.).

In reality many were hauled through the uninviting waters of the English Channel in the face of fierce German resistance - as the D-Day battle scene (left) shows. Here the folder's main advantage was to make best use of the storage space in the landing craft. Apparently many were abandoned within a few miles of going ashore.

Folding Bikes in the US - the 19th Century to WWII

The early history of folding bikes in the US appears to have been the realm of lone inventors and small-scale manufacturers rather than mass market orientated companies - despite the fact that the country was in the midst of a well-documented bicycle craze in the late 19th century. One of the largest early US manufacturers of bikes, the Pope Manufacturing Company, built nearly 50,000 bikes in 1881, yet seems to have totally overlooked folders.

And so it fell to an individual to introduce folders to America's bicycle hungry populace in the late 19th century. In 1893 Michael B. Ryan patented a folding bicycle and a New York Times entry from 1897 makes it clear the bicycles were already in very limited production; 'a decided novelty at the show was the display of military folding bicycles, made by the Dwyer Folding Bicycle Company of Danbury Conn...a ladies folding bicycle is also shown and will be sure to attract much attention from the women'. Despite the newspaper terming the bikes 'military', the US military seem to have shown little interest in folders at this time, in stark contrast to many contemporary European armed forces.

In 1919 Scientific American magazine featured 'a new model of bicycle invented by Mr C.H. Clark...whose wheels had apparently shrunk to the size of a dinner plate.' The bike was claimed to have held its own against conventional bikes in a New York City race, though reportedly losing some ground due to difficulty cornering. The tiny small-wheeler was taken in a lift into the offices of Scientific American. Although the bike didn't fold, a later, tantalisingly undated report on the 1919 article states 'One can still spot these "city bicycles" today, now made with the advantage of being able to be folded for easier storage.'

A photo from Scientific American in 1919 shows C.H. Clark's groundbreaking use of small wheels.

Around half a century after their first appearance in the US the military placed its first official order for folding bicycles - or more accurately demountables; in 1941 Westfield-Columbia Compax 'folding' bikes were delivered to a Paramarines training camp in Lakehurst, New Jersey. With US-Japanese tension mounting, the Westfield-Columbia Manufacturing Company had seemingly foreseen a future need for a military folder and designed what the 1940 patent calls a 'collapsible bicycle'. As sales catalogues from the time make clear, the initial version of the Compax was aimed squarely at civilians who wanted all the advantages of a bike that packed down quickly, which the Compax (actually branded the Compax Sports Traveler for the non-military market) appears to have done. A single-bladed wing nut allowed the handlebars to swing down to one side of the frame whilst a wing-nutted collar held the two halves of the single mainframe together. Quick the process may have been, but the disassembled package appears to have lacked any means of holding the two halves together and adverts from the time show the two sections being carried separately. A single-speed rear hub featured coaster braking. Though there are no recorded sales figures during peacetime for what was claimed to be 'America's first folding bicycle' it seems safe to assume - with an effective sales period of only six months before wartime austerity brought an end to such fripperies - that the figures were relatively small. The first urgent shipments of bikes to the military still bore the civilian paint job, but this was later changed and the spec beefed up to include balloon tyres amongst other things. Despite the Paramarines being the first to take delivery of the bikes there is no recorded evidence of them arriving in a war zone by parachute. Indeed, the exact use of US military folding bikes in action remains cloaked in mystery, despite the evidence suggesting the military took delivery of several large shipments.   .

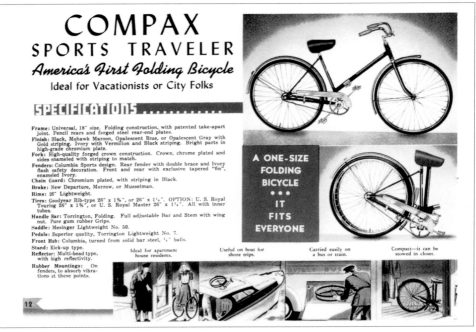

The Compax was aimed initially at civilians, with marketing suggesting use in boats and trains. However, true mass production only became feasible with large contracts to supply the military.

Post WWII - the Moulton Era

Clearly civilian folding bikes remained rare in the first half of the 20th century, and it was not until the 1960s, with the arrival of the Moulton, that the technology began to find its feet. Moultons are often described as folding bikes, but in fact Dr. Moulton never produced a folding machine. Most were completely rigid, although the Stowaway variant split in two with the application of an Allen key to a central joint. Even that was a car boot job, and certainly not the sort of thing you would carry on a commuter train or in a small boat.

Dr. Alex Moulton was an engineer specialising in automotive suspension, and as such, he did a great deal of work for British car manufacturers, principally developing rubber and rubber/gas suspensions. But his expertise in suspension technology also led Moulton to challenge the orthodoxy of the 26-inch wheel safety bicycle, reasoning that a bicycle with suspension could give an acceptable ride with wheels about half the normal size.

Why use small wheels if the bicycle was not to fold? There is a popular misconception that small-wheeled bicycles are wobbly, slow and hard to ride, but that is by no means always the case, and Moulton soon realized that smaller wheels brought a number of key advantages: the wheels were lighter, increasing acceleration and - assuming the bicycle had decent suspension - reducing unsprung weight, beneficial to both ride and handling. A small wheel also offered a smaller frontal area, reducing wind resistance, and the shorter spokes produced less turbulence, both factors making the bike easier to pedal at speed. And where most of a conventional bicycle is unusable dead space, a small-wheeled machine offered plenty of room front and rear for carrying luggage.

The downside of small wheels is increased tyre rolling resistance. There are two main reasons for this - smaller wheels tend to be deflected up and down on bumps and holes more than big wheels, producing energy-sapping vibration (this can be largely solved with suspension), and the sharper radius of the small tyres results in a greater degree of flexure where the tyre meets the road. Quite simply, the road is flat, and the tyre curved. As the tyre revolves it is continually being deformed and springing back into shape, flexure that absorbs quite a bit of energy. The smaller the wheel, the greater the deformation and the greater the loss of power. In a series of experiments, Dr. Moulton succeeded in minimizing this effect, chiefly by utilizing high tyre pressures, reducing the size of the 'flat' area where the tyre hits the road.

Using his considerable influence, Moulton persuaded Dunlop to develop improved high pressure bicycle tyres, and although he might not have realized it at the time, by choosing the existing 16" x 13/8" (ISO 37-349mm) tyre, Moulton had set the pattern for the future development of the folding bike. The 349mm tyre was primarily used on children's bikes, but, more or less by chance, it was close to ideal for use on a folding bike - small enough to produce a low folded package, but large enough to deal with potholes, particularly when aided by suspension, of course.

By the postwar period, bicycle tyre sizes, like many international standards, had developed into a haphazard mishmash of imperial and metric sizes. Traditionally tyre sizes were measured in either metric or imperial in terms of overall diameter and width, so a 16" x 13/8" would be roughly 16 inches tall by 13/8 inches wide (in practice most examples are closer to 17 inches tall).

Put a Moulton stowaway in your boot!

Courtesy of Paul Grogan

All images © Moulton Developments

Although the classic Moulton didn't fold, the Stowaway variant broke in two for carriage in a car boot, as above. This Stowaway version of the smaller Moulton Mini was the nearest Dr. Moulton ever came to producing a compact folding bike, but although it appeared in the 1967 brochure, it never went into production. Also note the bike is being placed in the boot of a Morris 1100 with Moulton Hydrolastic suspension

The classic Moulton design (bottom right)- small wheels with their own unique suspension system, meaning plenty of luggage room front and rear

However, this system tells us nothing about the rim diameter the tyre will fit, and by the 1950s, the bicycle tyre trade was collapsing into farce, with different countries offering different rims and different systems of measurement, so that an apparently over-size tyre might prove too small for a given wheel rim, and vice-versa.

Some sanity arrived with the formation of the European Tyre & Rim Technical Organization, or ETRTO, in 1964. ETRTO introduced a metric 'bead seat diameter' system, which was later adopted by the International Standards Organization. The tyre code (sometimes described as ETRTO and sometimes ISO) classifies a tyre by its width, and the diameter between the two opposing sides of the 'bead' - the steel or nylon cables in the root of the tyre that secure it over the wheel rim. To prevent the tyre falling off, the ISO size is slightly smaller than the rim diameter, which is nominally 360mm on the Moulton or Brompton tyre. Dr. Moulton went on to develop an even better 17-inch (ETRTO 369mm) tyre in cooperation with Dunlop, based on a pre-existing tubular racing tyre, but this size remained something of an oddity, used only on Moulton bikes. It is for his work in proving and developing the 37-349mm tyre that Dr. Moulton will be remembered in the folding bicycle world.

The Moulton bicycles were extremely clever machines, giving a conventional riding position, improved performance (thanks to the inherent advantages of 16-inch wheels and suspension) and better load-carrying. There have been few transport revolutions quite as complete as the advancement (and subsequent retrenchment) of the Moulton bicycle in the 1960s. From a standing start in 1963, sales peaked at 1,000 a week in 1965, making Moulton the second biggest single brand cycle manufacturer in the country. Quite by chance, this radical 'mini' bicycle had caught the mood of the times, becoming as much an icon of the swinging '60s as the miniskirt and the mini car. The stratospheric sales curve caused utter panic among established manufacturers, still producing bicycles whose appearance and technology had changed little since Edwardian days. There followed a wild stampede to introduce rival small-wheelers, most of which were knocked out in a few weeks by unwilling draughtsmen, who knew little of the technological principles involved and - one suspects - cared less.

Despite its small wheels, the Moulton's clever design kept the riding position and much of the bike's geometry in a similar layout to the standard big wheelers - giving a reassuringly comfortable yet fast ride

As Moulton had the patents on suspension, his rivals had to find other means of giving their bikes a compliant ride. Dawes chose a larger tyre size, opting initially for a wide, low-pressure metric 500A tyre, of about 20$1/2$ inches in diameter, with a bead seat diameter of 440mm. The Dawes Kingpin, launched in 1964, proved quite a successful machine, although only about 10% were true folders with hinged frames, the resulting package being arguably more cumbersome than the rigid bike.

But although heavy and cumbersome, the Kingpin was well made, and stayed in production well into the 1980s. On some versions, such as the Newpin, Dawes used the British format 20" x 1$3/8$", or 451mm tyre. Where the 349mm tyre was the ideal basis round which to build a compact folding bike, the 500A and 451mm sizes were particularly well suited to larger fold-in-half machines, and this general layout evolved into the standard folding bike of the 1960s and early '70s. British bikes, such as the Raleigh 20 range, tended to use the 451, whereas European machines were typically fitted with 500A. Some export Raleigh

The Raleigh RSW Compact, illustrated in a Swiss retail catalogue from the time. Even in its folded form it occupies much of the Mercedes' capacious boot.

20s were fitted with the North American 406mm rim and the BMX craze later introduced this slightly smaller tyre to the UK. Subsequently most 20-inch wheel bikes have used the 406mm tyre. Unfortunately, most bikes of this type were heavy, undergeared and - lacking the Moulton's sophisticated geometry and suspension - hard work to ride. Increasingly produced in Eastern Europe and the Far East and sold through popular magazines, the 'shopper' turned a generation against folding bikes. When the Brompton arrived twenty years later, bicycle shops would - reasonably enough - argue with Andrew Ritchie, its designer, that if the 20-inch shopper was poor, logically his 16-inch machine would be even worse.

This jaundiced view was reinforced by Raleigh, which had actually been involved in the Moulton bicycle project in the early days, but pulled out prior to the launch. Desperate to get a bit of the small-wheel action, Raleigh developed a 16-inch Moulton-esque bicycle, known as the RSW16. To get round the suspension patent, the company opted for wide low pressure tyres, which gave a soft ride and appalling rolling resistance. Raleigh came to the party a bit late, launching the RSW16 in July 1965, but it spent £100,000 on publicity, and took many sales from Moulton.

Like the Moulton, the original RSW16 didn't fold, but it was soon joined by the Compact variant, possibly the worst folding bike ever produced. The RSW Compact hinged upwards mid-frame, bringing the two wheels together, while the handlebars hinged down. Almost 100cm long when folded, it really was easier to transport when unfolded, especially when the sinew-challenging weight of 18kg (40lb) was taken into account. The RSW Compact was an absurd bike, but thanks to Raleigh's marketing muscle and national dealer network, it stayed in production until 1968, while the slightly more practical non-folding version was still available in 1974, albeit with slimmer tyres.

The cheap and cheerful 20-inch shopper bikes and dreary RSW did terrible damage to the reputation of small wheels. Within a few short years, all the good work done by Moulton had been undone, the folder becoming synonymous with shoddily made, short-range bicycles. The public soon forgot that Dr. Moulton's 16- and 17-inch machines held a number of speed and endurance records, some of which remain unbeaten to this day.

The public might have been put off, but the poor riding and folding performance of contemporary folding bikes brought about a number of new designs, all - interestingly enough - aimed at the car boot rather than rail commuter, cars being very much the modern thing in the late 1960s. One early example was the Newland, designed by engineering lecturer David Newland. He set out to produce a bike that would fit in the boot of a Mini and weigh around 9kg (20lb). In practice, the 'productionized' prototype built by Raleigh weighed 12.9kg (28$1/2$lb), but although it was ready for production by 1967, a downturn in small-wheeled sales, and Raleigh's subsequent purchase of Moulton, scuppered the project. As the Moulton itself had been extinguished within a few years, one gets the distinct impression that Raleigh was only interested in folding bikes to the extent of protecting its traditional territory. With the Moulton out of the way, Raleigh's big-wheel diamond-frame bicycles (and the Raleigh 20 fold-in-half machine) would not be seriously challenged for another twenty years. Although it didn't even reach production, the Newland is important in any history of the folding bike because it pointed the way to the future by folding in three places. Admittedly all the folds were in the same plane, so the resulting package was rather large at 127cm x 91cm x 33cm, with a volume of 381 litres (13$1/2$ cubic feet), but it is said to have folded and ridden well, despite diminutive 12-inch wheels.

The Bickerton

In the 1970s, the folding bike finally hit the big time in terms of sales, if not rideability, with the arrival of the Bickerton. Harry Bickerton was an aeronautical engineer who had learnt his craft squeezing horse-power out of the Spitfire's Rolls-Royce Merlin engine, and keeping the plane one step ahead of the Messerschmidt. It was arguably one of the most critical jobs undertaken by anyone in the Second World War.

After a varied post-war career, he found himself banned from driving in the late 1960s after an accident in Dorset. To help stay mobile, Harry bought a Puch Pic-Nic, a reasonably competent 20-inch shopper of the day, but he detested the machine, describing it as 'a heap of scrap iron'. Like all good engineers, he decided that he could do better, and set about designing himself a smaller, lighter bicycle that could be used to link or 'integrate' other forms of transport. The Bickerton didn't share many traits with the Merlin engine, but Harry's aeronautical background made itself felt in his use of light alloys, and bolts, dowels or resin bonding in place of welds. As so often before and since, this completely fresh approach to what a bicycle should do, and how it was made, was to yield some interesting results.

Like David Newland, Harry Bickerton aimed high with the specification - a bike that would fit in the boot of a Mini and weigh 8.2kg (18lbs). In the event, it satisfied the first requirement, but weighed a little more - 9.1kg in single-speed form, 10kg for a 3-speed version, and 10.4kg for the Sturmey 5-speed model. Like the Moulton, the Bickerton was built around the excellent 37-349mm tyre, or at least the back wheel was, the front being a smaller 14-inch tyre, also used by Dr. Moulton on his 7/8-size Mini Moulton range.

The Bickerton horrified conventional cyclists by flexing and wobbling like a jelly, but if you adopted a smooth riding technique it went quite well and could be ridden considerable distances. If you rode with gusto, something usually broke, as many riders found to their cost. Harry, who seems not to have minced his words, emphasized in an early brochure that the bike was, 'designed for intelligent, competent human beings - not gorillas'. For all its failings, the Bickerton folded into a compact package reasonably quickly and was lighter than anything that had come before. And so it was that Harry's driving ban kicked the folding bike industry into gear. The engineer had needed a machine light and compact enough to carry by bus and train, and his little bike pushed the technology far beyond its 'chuck in a car boot' brethren to achieve this.

Like many other folding bikes, the Bickerton had a single mainframe tube, although in this case, it was made of rectangular aluminium alloy rather than steel tube, with a folding joint roughly midway, allowing the rear wheel to fold around to meet the front wheel. Before this could be done, the handlebars had to be realigned by loosening four quick-release joints, allowing the grips to twist inwards and the whole assembly to turn through 90°, ending up sandwiched between the two wheels. Another quick-release allowed the saddle to be dropped, but if you really wanted a compact package, the saddle and pillar had to be removed and squidged in with the other bits.

There were several howling disadvantages to this arrangement. The frame and tall spindly handlebars flexed all over the place, and if you forgot to tighten any of the many joints and clips, you could end up in a heap on the ground. Unlike most folders, the oily chain was sandwiched between the frames when the bike was folded, but it still protruded far enough

A Bickerton Classic - with its trademark huge handlebars and angular mainframe.
It folded down surprisingly compactly and quickly - certainly better than anything that had come
before, and in this respect was groundbreaking.

to smear the clothes and luggage of fellow travellers on the train. And as the frame halves and handlebars didn't clip into place, the bike was liable to unfold while being carried. The Bickerton was launched in 1970, and sales grew rapidly, until the small company was producing more than 500 bikes a year. Still very small beer to the likes of Raleigh and Moulton, but respectable enough.

In 1975, Bickerton licensed production to engineering company TCK, but in generally gloomy economic conditions, the new licence-holder went bankrupt just two years later in 1977. The rights were transferred once again to an Australian company, which went on to build another 50,000 bikes in the next few years, but in 1982, this company also got into difficulties, and being owed £60,000, Harry Bickerton took the rights back. The wheel then turned full circle, Harry Bickerton teaming up with his son Mark and former MD of TCK Steve Rowlinson to set up a folding bike factory of their own. The Bickerton-Rowlinson years were the most stable for the Bickerton, but it was by now an elderly machine, and after Harry's retirement in 1987, Mark found himself in control of a shrinking business selling a single ageing product, and surrounded by new and much better folding bikes. Although the Brompton wasn't yet being manufactured in big numbers, it was very much on the scene, as was the cruder, but mass-market Dahon, fresh in from Taiwan. Mark responded by introducing the Bickerton Country, a larger, heavier variant, equipped, rather absurdly, with knobbly 406mm BMX tyres to appeal to a younger audience.

A Bickerton Californian - Bickerton effectively ditched the 'wobbly wonder' that was their original creation and went with the more rigidly engineered style of Dahon.

14

All the Country succeeded in doing was ditching the Bickerton's only strengths, its compact size and light weight. In 1989, Mark Bickerton made a last desperate attempt to develop a completely new bike, teaming up with the National Engineering Laboratory in East Kilbride. The project got underway, but for various reasons, Mark decided to pull the plug before the bike went into production and the factory was closed in 1991. Bickerton-Rowlinson was already marketing a 'badge-engineered' Dahon model as the Bickerton Dahon (later the Californian). Badge-engineering - the production of a 'new' model by rebadging a machine made by someone else - was still rare, but it would become an increasingly common route for product-starved British manufacturers. Mark Bickerton went on to sell Klein mountain bikes for a few years, but came back to folding bikes in 1995 as Dahon's UK agent.

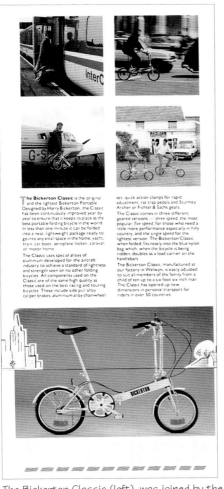

The Bickerton Classic (left), was joined by the Country (right) in the late 1980s. Aimed at a younger off-road market, it added weight, but little else, to the original Bickerton design.

Dahon

There are probably more myths surrounding the Dahon than any other folding bike. From its first stirrings with the Grout Portable to the 1960s, the folding bike story had been a predominantly British affair. From the 1960s to the 1980s, European manufacturers had joined the party, mass-producing fold-in-half bikes in large numbers, but the Dahon was to turn the folding bicycle into a global phenomenon.

First, the myths: Dahon might be an anagram of Honda, but only by chance! It is actually a contraction of the name of David Hon, the founder of the company. Hon was a physicist working for the Hughes Aircraft Corporation in America, and a specialist in laser technology, with several patents to his name. He is also credited with designing the NASA moon buggy, which appears not to be true, although he certainly had some involvement with the moon landings, as part of the general mobilization of the US scientific community. Another myth has it that the Dahon is a US-made machine, but it has always been made in the Far East, the Stars & Stripes on the frame referring rather tenuously to the country in which it was designed.

The turning point for Dr. Hon came with the Arab oil embargo of the early 1970s, and the ensuing oil supply crisis that almost brought the car-based US transport system to its knees. Might a bicycle not offer an alternative? Not the heavy, bulky bicycles of Hon's youth, but light, foldable machines that could be carried by bus, train or car. Designing a prototype took several years, and it was not until 1982 in the wake of the second oil crisis provoked by the Iranian revolution, that Dr. Hon finally introduced a bike.

Hon had hoped to hand the design over to a manufacturer, but as with the Bickerton (and as we shall see, the Brompton), things didn't work out quite so smoothly, and he was shown the door by all the major bicycle manufacturers. Undaunted, Hon gathered together $3 million in venture capital backing and set up a factory in Taiwan to produce the bike himself, the first machines appearing in 1983, two years behind the Brompton, but in much greater numbers.

Dahon today produces an almost bewildering variety of bikes - but at the heart of most models is a mid-frame hinge dating back to Dahon's earliest designs - still no rival to the Brompton's compact 'fold-in-three'. Here are some of their more varied recent offerings:

* Helios SL - At 7.6kg claimed to be the 'lightest production line folder in the world' - at the time. In fact, the Panasonic Traincle was much lighter and produced in fair numbers for Japan.

* Curve - touted as a 16" wheeled, sub-10kg competitor to the Brompton

* Cadenza - a fast 26" wheeled road bike

* Ciao - an easy to ride town bike, complete with rack and dynamo lights

* Jack - big tyres and rigid construction for town and trail

On the face of it, the Dahon was a simple fold-in-half bike, built around 16 x 1³/₄" (ISO 44-305mm) tyres. Although nominally 16 inches like the British 349mm, this was in reality closer to 15 inches in overall diameter, which helped to produce a lower folded package, but increased the rolling resistance of the tyres proportionately. Unlike the clumsy 20-inch fold-in-half bikes of the 1960s, the Dahon featured a folding handlebar stem, and was quite compact (if a little long) and easy to fold. Early models were quite heavy, but Hon and his team gradually refined the bikes, going on to produce around two million in 25 years and dominating the folding bike market.

Most Dahons have the trademark fold-in-half frame, in a variety of wheel sizes, from 305mm to full-size, but the company came to specialize in 20-inch (406mm)-wheeled bicycles. As well as producing its own machines, Dahon also developed (or in some cases, 'badge-engineered') bikes for other major bicycle manufacturers, while licensing its older technology to cut-price Far Eastern manufacturers. But we're jumping some years ahead of our story, because Dr. Hon was not the only inventor working on a folding bike in the 1970s. In London, the Brompton was already taking shape.

The bike is one of the 16-inch wheel prototypes, P3 or P4, Although the cow horn handlebars and clunky frame hinge look ungainly, it's clearly a Brompton, especially when part- or fully-folded.

18

Getting Brompton Off the Ground
1973-1977

"The plastic seat sleeve was made of old drainpipe, because I couldn't afford a mould."
ANDREW RITCHIE

Personal Background

On 15th March 1947, in Newdigate, Surrey, Andrew Ritchie was born, the youngest of three children, after Caroline and Jamie. Although the Ritchies were in many ways an archetypical English upper middle class family, Andrew's mother Sybilla (better known as Moppy throughout her life) was German, with the added complication that his maternal great grandmother had been Australian. Mary Beauchamp (a cousin of writer Katherine Mansfield) had - rather improbably, but romantically - fallen in love with a Prussian aristocrat, Count Henning von Arnim, while undertaking the fashionable Italian tour with her father.

Mary married the Count in 1891, and Elizabeth von Arnim, as she became known, went on to become a successful author, publishing a string of titles in the early years of the 20th century. The couple had five children, the third of whom (sometimes referred to as 'the April Baby') was Andrew Ritchie's grandmother.

Continuing in this rather exotic vein, Elizabeth later had an affair with H G Wells, and after the Count died in 1910, went on to marry John Francis Stanley Russell, the 2nd Earl Russell (and elder brother of Bertrand Russell), before fleeing to America from what seems to have been a deeply unhappy marriage.

Andrew's father, WIlliam (Bill), came from an equally interesting line. His grandfather Charles Thomas Ritchie was Scottish, and held high office in the Conservative government of 1900-1905, first as Home Secretary, then - from 1903-1905 - as Chancellor of the Exchequer. He is best known for introducing to parliament the Local Government Act, which established the County Council administrative system. He was made a peer when the government resigned in 1905, but sadly lived only another few days. Charles' brother, Alderman Sir James Thomson Ritchie, became Lord Mayor of London in 1903.

With characteristic precision (and indeed modesty), Andrew Ritchie simply describes himself as $3/8$ths German, half English and $1/8$th Australian, "quite a mixture". Whether the Scottish political nous, German aristocratic blood, and artistic flair of these forebears have had any influence on the engineering of the folding bicycle is a matter for conjecture!

Set against the flamboyance of the Edwardian literary set, Andrew Ritchie's father Bill Ritchie seems to have led a quiet and respectable life as an area manager for Barclays Bank, before joining stockbroker Galloway & Pearson as an analyst. Home life for the children followed a comfortably Betjemanesque pattern of parties, rugger matches and public school. For an intelligent young man from his social class, Cambridge University was more or less an assumption, and Andrew graduated in 1968 with a 2.1 Degree in Mechanical Sciences. At this time, engineering as a career was hardly a sexy option, and many of Ritchie's contemporaries (including Tim Guinness, who was later to play a pivotal role in the Brompton story) opted for jobs in the financial world, while the more adventurous chose the embryonic field of computing, the path taken by Andrew Ritchie.

In the late 1960s, of course, computers were very large, very expensive and fiendishly difficult to programme and operate. But the computer world was at the cutting edge of Harold Wilson's 'white heat of technology', and for a young engineering graduate of the day, arguably the engineering of the future.

Ritchie soon found himself in Borehamwood, Hertfordshire, working for Elliott Automation, a company that produced computers and computer programmes, mainly for government, the table-sized machines performing a variety of roles, including air traffic control and - with advancing miniaturization - avionics and military applications. By modern standards, where millions of transistors can be printed on a wafer the size of the proverbial pin head - these were clunking great machines, with laughably modest computing power, typically 16kb of memory at the time Andrew Ritchie joined the firm.

Trained in a rather different discipline, Andrew spent the first eight months getting to grips with the architecture and structure of the computer, time that seemed wasted to an ambitious youngster, but the exercise no doubt served to refine an already logical and analytical mind. With computers being such a new field, Elliott Automation was a little unsure how to recruit potential programmers, and what to do with potential recruits once it had found them. Some bright spark in the personnel department ("ex-army, affable, and pretty useless," according to Ritchie), came up with the idea of sending the young graduates to Colchester Technical College to study metal working for four months.

One might assume that a Cambridge graduate engineer would know all there was to know about engineering, but - in those days at least - graduates were sent out into the world with only the barest of practical skills, such as welding and lathe work. Graduates like Ritchie were the young technocrats who would design the roads, bridges and turbocharged boys' toys of the Thunderbirds era. They knew plenty about the theory of engineering - thermodynamics, the stresses and strains imposed on structures, and the behaviour of materials - but virtually nothing about the practice of metal-bashing.

And so it was, quite by chance, that Elliott Automation not only gave Andrew Ritchie a grounding in computers, but some essential 'hands on' mechanical skills. He could never have guessed it at the time, but these apparently unconnected multi-layered skills - engineering design, computer design, and practical metal bashing - were to serve him well in later years.

Ritchie seems to have enjoyed himself at Colchester, sharing a house with two Cambridge friends sent on the course by their respective employers, one of whom was Marcus Agius, an engineer destined to take the commercial route to fame and fortune, winding up as chairman of Barclays Bank.

Back at Borehamwood, Ritchie soon got itchy feet, and moved to Engineering Solutions, a software development company based in Croydon. The cold logic of software design seems to have suited him, and he soon became immersed in the development of an automated drawing machine for the civil engineering industry. Today, a £50 laser printer attached to a home PC could do the same job in a few seconds, albeit on a smaller scale, but for the chunky 16kb mainframes of the late 1960s, the idea was somewhat ahead of its time. Despite writing everything in basic machine code rather than memory-hungry high level language, and wrestling with the task for eighteen months, Ritchie left the company without producing a workable program, a rare failure that still rankles today. At the time, 32kb machines were just appearing, but to use something so sophisticated in a drawing machine would not have been economic. The episode might appear to have been a dead end, but after the high-flying theory of Cambridge, and 'money no object' government projects at Elliott Automation, the period at Engineering Solutions was Ritchie's first brush with the economics of the market place. For the first time, he had worked with the constraints of cost very much in mind. His next move was to take him even further down the entrepreneurial road.

The Pot Plant Era

Quite why some people settle into a steady career, while others exhibit a certain restlessness, is not always clear. Andrew Ritchie had shown a flair for engineering design, but chose to move into computers; he had a talent for computer programming, but moved into the world of commerce.

At the age of 24, Ritchie left the computer industry, never to return, choosing instead to sell pot plants door-to-door. Why would anyone with such marketable skills opt for a career that many less qualified people could have mastered? After three years in large organizations, Ritchie seems to have felt the need for some independence, and he had been seduced by the profit potential, intrigued that a plant bought for £1 at 5am in Covent Garden could be sold a few hours later for £2 in Putney. It seemed like money for old rope, but perhaps only a Cambridge graduate engineer could have been naive enough to think that the world of market trading could be that simple.

With a Morris Minor van, Ritchie would drive to Covent Garden every morning, then west against the commuter flow, to "flog the plants to pretty housewives in Wimbledon, Putney and Barnes". Initially, Ritchie worked single-handedly with a single van, but with an injection of £3,000 of capital from his friend Tim Guinness, now doing rather well in the financial world, London House Plants briefly flourished. Within a couple of years the company had a fleet of five ex-GPO vans, and more than a dozen employees:

"I'd get up at 4.30am every morning to go to the market, then armed with a peddler's licence, hawk plants to the housewives of Barnes and Wimbledon. Then one thing led to another. Somebody said, 'Could you do a lawn?' I hadn't a clue how to lay turf or put up a trellis, but we ended up creating some biggish London gardens, doing displays in hotels and looking after pot-plants for all sorts of people, including the great and good of the day. There was plenty of opportunity."

1975: Andrew Ritchie and Tim Guinness with one of the ex-GPO London House Plants vans

But London House Plants was hardly marketing a unique product, and despite boundless youthful enthusiasm, Andrew seems to have rather lost interest in the scheme as his fertile mind began to burst with new and more exciting ideas. After four years ("chaos" according to Ritchie), the goodwill was sold off for next to nothing, Tim Guinness got most of his £3,000 back and London House Plants melted quietly away. But the retail experience had added another crucial talent to Ritchie's growing range of abilities, and by this time he was thinking much bigger thoughts.

At its height, the houseplant company had spawned a retail shop in Dawes Road, Fulham, and most days Ritchie would share a lunchtime pint with his friend and landlord Robert Newall, owner of a printing works in the same premises. Despite a brief flirtation with motorcycling, Andrew was a regular cyclist, the germ - as for so many graduates - being planted during his university days. One lunchtime the talk turned to bicycles: "Wouldn't it be wonderful if you had a bike which went with you wherever you wanted to go?", said Ritchie. This was in about 1973. It was the sort of light pub chatter that is soon forgotten, but Ritchie didn't forget, and his thoughts began to turn towards the problems of bicycle storage and use.

Other ideas came and went as London House Plants ran its course. One was an idea for a thermostatic shower mixer tap, something quite common today, but a leap of the imagination then. Ritchie decided that there were too many technical issues, and in any event, most people were perfectly happy with the ordinary mixer design, but the bicycle idea was to come back into focus after a chance meeting.

The Brompton Takes Shape

At this time, in 1975, Andrew's father Bill was working for city stockbrokers Galloway & Pearson, and it was there that he was approached by Bill Ingram, an Australian who had become involved with the Bickertons. Harry Bickerton was still building small numbers of folding bikes from a garage in Welwyn Garden City, and Bill, who was captivated by the principle of a portable bike, was trying to raise capital to expand the business. It's not entirely clear how he ended up at Bill Ritchie's door, but nevertheless, he did, and Bill Ritchie suggested a meeting with his son. We can't be sure quite how and why Ritchie senior thought Andrew's input would be helpful. His son was interested in engineering, and at something of a loose end at the time. In any event, it was to be a fateful meeting:

"Bill Ingram fetched up at my flat in 1975 with a Bickerton under his arm, and I thought on the one hand, 'Wow! Here's somebody who's done something about it', and then, 'Gosh, that's not a particularly clever approach'. After a chat, Bill went, but it seems we had established something of a rapport, because later he said, 'Do you think I should back you, with your intellect, and a foetal idea which doesn't even exist, or Harry Bickerton who's actually got a concrete thing, which works, and is there? Which way do I jump?'"

Ingram decided to go with the faintly Heath Robinson folding bike he knew, rather than back an enthusiastic young engineer who had yet to demonstrate a workable design. It was an understandable decision, but it turned out to be a big mistake. Even as the Australian left the flat above the Brompton Road, Ritchie was, unwittingly, embarking on what was to be a lifetime career. A folding bicycle seemed to be the ideal project: he recognised that he worked well on his own, and a folding bicycle was a modest enough undertaking to be managed by one person, rather than a team of engineers. Designing a folding bike would give him the independence he cherished, and make good use of the various skills he had acquired during his short, but peripatetic working career.

Andrew Ritchie was now 28, and convinced that he had at last found his niche. He scribbled down a few notes. Four things, he wrote, unavoidably have to stick out from a bicycle: the front wheel, back wheel, handlebars and saddle. The task was to fold these elements down quickly, safely and repeatably. This apparently straightforward problem had exercised some formidable minds, but for all sorts of reasons, Andrew Ritchie seems to have been the ideal man to finally solve it.

He immediately dismissed the long-established fold-in-half option, because it only partially solved the four folding objectives. A design where all four elements came into the middle made a lot more sense, but the key folding breakthroughs would take some time to arrive.

The first problem was money. London House Plants was still alive, working out a few long-term contracts in the hands of Tim Guinness's wife Beverley, but Ritchie would need backers if he was to spend months, or perhaps years, designing a folding bicycle from scratch. He talked the options through with a few friends, and one, Richard Goode, agreed to undertake a whip round among their mutual friends, persuading ten fledgling shareholders to put up £100 apiece. The long-suffering Tim Guinness was given an opportunity to come on board, but this time - in the nicest possible way - he refused to invest any money himself, and although the pair were to remain close friends, he was to have no further involvement in Brompton for nearly a quarter of a century: "I said to Andrew, 'You're not a businessman!'", Guinness later recalled, "and I think he agreed. That's why his plan was just to develop the prototype Brompton, outsource it and receive a royalty."

The directors of the company were Andrew Ritchie, Ritchie Senior, Richard Goode, George Brooksbank of Debenhams and Robert Woods (later a CBE and Chief Executive of P&O). The ten shareholders would later be joined by two more, and in time Andrew would return to the group to call in another couple of thousand pounds, but the trust of those first ten backers was instrumental in getting the project off the ground. It helped, of course, that Ritchie had some fairly well-off friends with an investment philosophy and ready cash to risk a punt.

The prospectus, grandly entitled 'A Project for the Development of an Advanced Folding Bicycle' also included an early drawing of the Brompton design, sadly undated, but probably produced in early 1976. This sketch is interesting because it demonstrates the depth of detail Andrew had already put into the design. Although superficially very different to the Brompton, it included a few key features that would survive into production.

The bicycle was expected to have 18-inch wheels (although Ritchie suggested that more common 20-inch wheels would be feasible, if bulkier) and a 104cm wheelbase, which was pretty much as it ended up. By contrast, weight, with aluminium construction, was projected at 15 to 20lb (6.8 - 9.1kg), which represented a considerable degree of wishful thinking.

The handlebars and seat pillar were both to have telescopic sections, so as to reduce their height for folding, the collapsed pillar then folding forwards, and the front bars folding sideways to sit alongside the front wheel, a feature that would survive, as would the Moulton-style rubber block suspension, on the back at least.

Folding was interesting. The rear wheel would hinge forward to nestle between twin mainframe tubes, a trick made possible by lifting the bottom bracket bearing up and out of the way as the seat pillar folded. The front wheel/fork assembly was fitted with an angled (or asymmetrical) hinge, to fold under and back alongside its partner, with the folded handlebars on the outside. The various elements, including the bottom bracket, would be spring-loaded into the closed position and linked by a steel 'Bowden' cable, so that raising the seat pillar

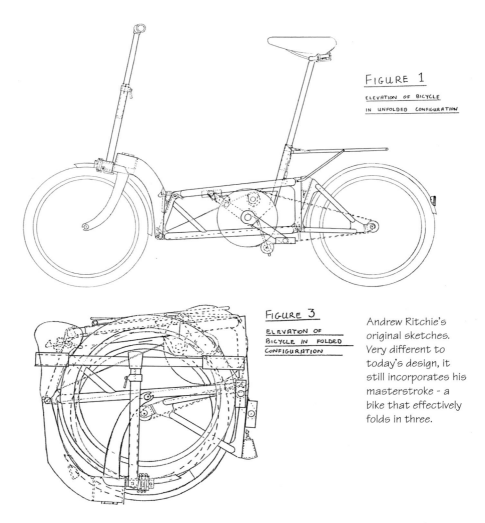

FIGURE 1

ELEVATION OF BICYCLE
IN UNFOLDED CONFIGURATION

FIGURE 3

ELEVATION OF
BICYCLE IN FOLDED
CONFIGURATION

Andrew Ritchie's
original sketches.
Very different to
today's design, it
still incorporates his
masterstroke - a
bike that effectively
folds in three.

would cause everything to pop into place, and lowering it would (rather alarmingly) cause everything to collapse, including the rear rack, which folded neatly in from behind.

Unlike the basic fold-in-half bikes of the day, this was, in effect, a bike that folded in three equal portions rather than two, and this means of reducing the length of the folded package was to be Ritchie's first masterstroke.

There wasn't enough money to fund even the most basic premises to build this machine, but with some rudimentary tools, Andrew began work on the first prototype in his flat. Stories about the man who designed and built a folding bicycle in his bedroom soon spread amongst friends and acquaintants. According to one early shareholder, Andrew allowed a mutual friend to take girls back to the flat when he wasn't at home, and on one memorable occasion a young lady fled in horror after discovering metal swarf in the bed!

The first prototype bicycle, P1, seems to have come together quite quickly. It was similar

24

to the drawing, but differed in some key respects. The neat one-piece handlebar/stem assembly had been replaced with clever, but complicated, 'cow horn' bars that folded down either side of the front wheel. The front wheel assembly was similar to the drawing, folding under with an asymmetrical hinge to place the wheel alongside the frame tube, while the rear wheel folded under, but it now came up below a single large mainframe tube, rather than fitting between two thinner tubes, a crucial step forward.

The proposed Bowden cables survived onto P1, pulling the various elements apart when the seat pillar was raised, but it soon became clear that the idea was a non-starter: "...the cables broke pretty quickly under the considerable loads. I rode it a few times, but it was pretty wobbly! It eventually went into a skip." With the folding elements now falling more easily to hand, the need for the weight and complication of the cables was already looking questionable. It was one of those ideas that looked obvious on paper, but worked less well when translated into hardware. The idea was to make a reappearance on the Bike Friday Tikit, but only with respect to the simpler function of locking the handlebar stem clamp when the rear wheel was unfolded.

With its big 18-inch wheels, the prototype was not yet obviously a linear ancestor of the Brompton, and it was heavier, but it was inching in the right direction.

On the second prototype, P2, the front end was completely redesigned, the suspension and skewed horizontal hinge being replaced with a vertical hinge, allowing the wheel to fold sideways to nestle against the mainframe. The handlebars were much simpler, but still rather ungainly, comprising two tubes which folded down either side of the front wheel. The steel cables had gone, and in most other respects, it was now looking quite Brompton-like.

The P2 prototype

One innovation was to become a quintessential Brompton feature. Instead of tipping forwards to fold, the seat pillar now telescoped straight down behind the folded rear frame, automatically locking the folded package together.

The rack was now firmly attached to the rear frame, and a nice touch was a couple of spring-loaded rollers from which two panels of cloth could be drawn up to enclose the folded package.

Quite when the Brompton name evolved is unclear, but Ritchie chose it because his flat was situated in the Brompton district of West London, with an eagle's eyrie view up and down the Cromwell Road and across to the Brompton Oratory. A mile or two east or west and the machine could have become the Kensington, the Belgravia, or even the Pimlico. Brompton - by pure chance - was an inspired choice. It had a timeless British ring to it, but without the implied snobbery of better-known West London addresses. It was smart, yet workaday. Ideal for a folding bike designed to appeal to everyday users.

The Brompton company was formally established in June 1976, registered to an address in Bowerdean Street, London SW6. Andrew Ritchie signed away his rights to the design in exchange for two thousand £1 Ordinary shares in the new company, a holding big enough to give him a controlling interest.

Even without the Bowden cables, the Brompton remained a complex design, but Ritchie set about refining and simplifying the machine, producing two more prototypes in his bedroom workshop by 1977. There were still many detail differences from the modern Brompton, but in terms of geometry and function, the identical prototypes P3 and P4 were effectively much the same as today's machine. The final crucial element was that both were built around the smaller 16-inch (349mm) tyre size, enabling the bike to pack even smaller, without compromising the wheelbase.

The company filed a provisional patent in 1976, and was granted a full British patent on 6th May 1977, the drawings showing a bicycle identifiably similar to the final product, with two important omissions: the handlebars still separated and folded down either side of the front wheel, and the front wheel still pivoted right around until it faced backwards, lying alongside the rear wheel, much the same as P2. But most of the other features were there: the rear wheel that folded under the frame, the rear suspension, the seat pillar locking the package together, and the chain tensioner taking up slack as the bike folded. These elements were successfully safeguarded in the 1977 patent, plus one or two other Brompton trademarks, including the rear rack that became a 'stand' under the bike when folded.

The design process had taken two and a half years, from conception to practical reality, and arguably could not have happened without the unique range of skills Andrew Ritchie had picked up in the preceding decade. He had produced a timeless classic, and from the reaction of friends and strangers alike, it was a consumer product that would take little selling. He could never have guessed that the battle to commercialise the bike was to be far more challenging.

Cold-shouldered by Industry

The board of Brompton Bicycle was split on the question of whether to establish a factory to build bicycles, or simply sell the design to an established manufacturer. The two big corporation men, Brooksbank and Woods, rather fancied the idea of setting up a small manufacturing plant as a diversion from the day-to-day tedium of running big business. The more pragmatic Richard Goode argued that it would be less risky, and more logical to pay Andrew to use his skills to design it, and put together a prototype or two to demonstrate the principles to a third party manufacturer with the tooling, financial muscle and skills to put the machine into production. The board would then sign a licensing agreement, and enjoy a steady flow of royalty payments as reward for setting the enterprise in motion.

It might have sounded a logical and sensible scenario, but for all sorts of reasons, it just wasn't going to work. British industry was going through hard times in the mid-1970s, and although one or two innovative products were inching into production, manufacturers were extremely wary. Lotus engineer Ron Hickman had developed the Workmate - a folding workstand with integral clamps - but his attempts to licence the product to either Stanley or

The early Bromptons - P2, in blue, retains the 18-inch wheels and Bickerton-style handlebars, but the green P3 (top right) is much more Brompton-like, with 16-inch wheels. The only key elements still to be developed are the one-piece fold-down handlebars and the final piece in the puzzle, the geometry that enabled the front wheel to keep pointing forwards while the bike was folded - elements shown on the Mark 1 and Mark 2 bikes in red and black respectively.

Black & Decker had failed. It was only after Ron had found the capital to put the Workmate into limited production himself that Black & Decker eventually courted him, mass-producing the product from 1973, and ultimately turning Ron into a millionaire. Even for such an obvious and intuitive DIY product, targeted precisely at Black & Decker's existing customer base, getting the manufacturer on side had been an epic struggle. And bicycles were very much yesterday's news in the 1970s. The Moulton had injected some excitement into the genre a decade before (and briefly made small wheels respectable too), but it had peaked early and was now on the point of disappearing altogether.

In many ways, the Brompton was ahead of its time. Car boots were still reasonably cavernous, air travel far from commonplace, trains had guards vans, and bicycle theft was nowhere near as widespread or as sophisticated as it is today. Andrew Ritchie would be the first to admit that he was no salesman, leaving the Brompton to sell itself, rather than making a pitch to enthuse reluctant investors. But in 1977 even the most enthusiastic salesperson would have had trouble conjuring up an image of ranks of commuters unfolding their bikes at London Bridge station and riding into the city. A quarter of a century later it became fact, but in 1977 it would have been very hard to imagine such a scenario. Several potential manufacturers reacted positively to Andrew's demonstrations but none were willing to offer backing or to build the bike under licence. The key targets were Raleigh - then still the British cycle industry's biggest brand - Dawes, another household name, and Black & Decker - not an obvious choice product-wise, but a company that had demonstrated innovation by championing the Workmate, albeit rather grudgingly.

Ritchie first contacted I H Phillips, the then Managing Director of Raleigh on February 8th 1977, offering to 'demonstrate and discuss the product'. The letter was duly passed to the desk of Mr A P Oakley, the Design Director, but Oakley was on an overseas tour and did not consider the offer until early March. It was not until Friday 1st April that Ritchie actually travelled up to Nottingham, demonstrated the prototype, and left it with the Raleigh engineers for a two-week examination. On the following Monday he wrote offering a few additional thoughts for Raleigh to digest, including the rather far-sighted observation that a battery-powered version might be feasible. This prediction might have seemed somewhat far-fetched in 1977, before the principle of electrically-assisted bicycles had even become enshrined in law, but again, it was to come true.

In due course, the prototype was returned to London, followed by a rejection letter on 21st April. According to Mr Oakley, the rejection was made on two counts: the Brompton would 'require a considerable degree of redesign', and - more damningly - Raleigh was 'not convinced that the device could open up a market of sufficiently high volume at the price it would have to be sold at.'

This caution might have been influenced by Raleigh's unhappy entanglement with Moulton. The manufacturer had initially rejected the design, then watched in horror as Dr. Moulton went it alone, taking a large slice of the declining bicycle market. Raleigh had then tried to spoil the market with its own inferior small-wheeler, and finally bought Moulton out, eventually phasing the machine out of existence.

In 1977, this expensive and troublesome foray into small wheels was still fresh in the minds of Raleigh's sales and marketing executives. Of course, by rejecting the Brompton, there was always the risk that Ritchie, or one of Raleigh's competitors, would do exactly what Moulton had done and swamp the market with an innovative new design. Mr Oakley must have been absolutely convinced that the Brompton had no widescale commercial merit whatsoever.

Interestingly, Andrew had approached Dr. Moulton while building the prototypes, and Moulton had been interested enough to make the long trek up from Bradford-upon-Avon to have a look. It must have been quite a meeting, the chauffeur-driven Bentley purring up to the pavement, and the guru of small wheels stepping out, and climbing the long flight of stairs to the flat where the young engineer was working on one of the prototypes. According to Dr. Moulton, Andrew asked straight out if he would consider building it, to which the reply was a flat "No". At this time, long after selling out to Raleigh, Moulton no longer had suitable production facilities, although he was considering going back into small-scale manufacture himself, the spaceframe AM series Moulton being launched a few years later. Both men were highly motivated, skilled engineers, but apart from the wheel size, their design philosophies were quite different. "I wouldn't have done it that way", says Moulton, "but I said, 'go on with it and do it yourself'. In no way did I discourage him from doing it." The two were not to meet again for some years, but they seem to have developed a mutual - if rather wary - respect. With a growing pile of rejection letters, Andrew Ritchie started to consider small-scale production along the lines suggested by Brooksbank and Woods. This resulted in a split among the Brompton board, and as they (and indeed most of the other shareholders) were close friends, Richard Goode decided the best course of action was to resign, but he stayed close to Brompton, and remained a shareholder.

The plan now was to get enough venture capital behind the project to start production. After approaching several other firms, Brompton Bicycle began negotiations with venture capitalists ICFC (now known as 3Is), who eventually found some potential investors in Jersey. As the talks dragged on, Andrew stopped work on the project and took a delivery job with courier firm Fleet Street Flyers, using one of the old London House Plant delivery vans. He kept a bicycle in the back to reach congested parts of the city: "Whenever I had a run through Soho, I would just park the van - parking wasn't quite so onerous then - pop the bike out and do the errands while one's peers were still floundering in a traffic jam!" He was driving the van through Mayfair when the fateful message came through that after 18 months of negotiation, the ICFC deal had finally collapsed, and he was right back where he had started.

It was a major blow, but Andrew went back to work on the project, and in quite a short space of time made the final and decisive changes to the Brompton. The breakthrough was to re-engineer the fold so that the front wheel folded back on itself by pivoting around the headset bearings as the frame hinged back.

© Brompton Bicycle Ltd

This was a brilliant bit of lateral thinking. The head bearings were already there, so there was no extra weight or complication involved, and the concertina-style double fold reduced the distance the wheel folded back, while increasing the distance it folded out.

This eliminated the offset rear hinge, because the front wheel would now fit neatly against a centrally positioned rear wheel. The double fold also allowed the frame hinge to be moved back, reducing the length of the folded bike.

The final element in the Brompton design was the unique 'hinge, swivel and hook' system, where the front wheel kept pointing forwards instead of turning to face backwards, as it had done on the fold-in-half machines. It was a masterstroke - the front wheel now nestled comfortably against the rear wheel, with the chain sandwiched between the two, and the handlebars clipped against the outside.

The next logical move was to eliminate all the Bickerton-style quick-releases from the handlebars, put a single hinge at the base of the handlebar stem at 45° to the front wheel and fit a rigid bar/stem assembly that folded down against the outside of the front wheel. This made the package lighter, simpler and more compact. The skewed handlebar stem hinge was later patented in America by Dr. David Hon, although Andrew's early drawings seem to confirm that he had thought through this innovation first.

More or less by chance ("Careful design and good luck!", according to Ritchie), it emerged that the double fold and cantilevered handlebars suited the 16 x 13/8" tyre size almost perfectly. With frame elements scaled to suit a typical adult (not a tall one, but this would come later), the bike now folded down into a package little larger than its wheels and well under 30cm across. The folded Brompton had shrunk to a size that no-one had previously imagined possible, but without compromising the weight or strength of the bike.

"My heart sank in 1979 after the ICFC failure", said Ritchie, "but it was one of the best things that could have happened to Brompton. If I had got an institutional investor behind me and proceeded with an ill-thought through product, it would have sunk without trace." In the event, those few crucial extra months of design work had made all the difference.

Barring a few detail design changes, the Brompton was now equipped with all the innovations that would make it such a unique, practical and long-lived commercial product. It folded quickly and easily into a tiny package. Once folded, it was safe and clean to manoeuvre, as the chain and sprockets were on the inside, shielded between the wheels. Unfolded, the wheelbase was a generous 102cm - not quite up to conventional full-size bike standards, but almost miraculous from something that seconds before had been so small. The Brompton was more conjuring trick than folder, yet the generous wheelbase and rear suspension gave it excellent ride characteristics too. It was an engineering classic, but would it ever be built?

Steve Grosvenor's wife, Frances, demonstrates rather elegantly one of the keys to Brompton's success: portability. Whilst some subsequent folding bike designs were lighter or even folded to a smaller package, few were easy to carry when folded.

The first Bromptons were born partly out of a perceived need to combine bike use with cars - indeed Andrew Ritchie's business plans emphasised this as a more ready market than coach and train travellers.

As these early publicity photos demonstrate, the Mark 1 Brompton coped well in both situations. As it happened, neither car boots nor coaches were to be as important as the bike/rail commuter market. While Andrew Ritchie does the folding, the bike is carried and ridden by Frances Grosvenor.

Going it Alone and the Mark 1 Bike Though the original plan was to sell the Brompton idea to a large scale manufacturer, inventor Andrew Ritchie found himself taking the lead role in producing the bikes almost single-handedly. It seems this was a stroke of luck, for in the process he was able to iron out initial weaknesses, ensuring the bike stood up well to the stresses and strains of daily use.

Going it Alone and the Mark 1 Bike
1978-1983

Brompton Goes it Alone

In 1978, while searching for capital and expertise to get the Brompton project underway, Andrew had been recommended to visit Lawrence-Tune, a company that built racy car conversions from premises in Ravenscourt Arches, Hammersmith, a few miles west of Brompton. The company wasn't able to help, but Andrew became friendly with Lawrence-Tune engineer Tim Reeve, a chance meeting that would prove significant later on.

If the mid-70s wasn't a very good time for launching a bicycle, it was a rotten time for selling souped-up sports cars. After the OPEC oil embargo of 1973-74, the writing was on the wall for firms like Lawrence-Tune, and soon after Andrew Ritchie arrived at the door, Chris Lawrence closed the business and started again in California, where he initially did rather well, trading as Lawrence-Tune West Inc.

Meanwhile, several of the bright young team of British engineers decided to branch out on their own. Tim Reeve and Steve Grosvenor set up an engineering design business in Barleymow Passage, Chiswick, while Nick Ouroussoff established an engineering workshop in nearby Kew. Ouroussoff was a designer too, but he had ended up with enough space to build things, and as the two companies often worked closely together, Grosvenor-Reeve tended to do the design and Nick Ouroussoff the engineering. These small West London engineering works were to play a significant role in getting Brompton off the ground.

Right from the start, Andrew Ritchie built his own jigs. In this early picture the steel tubes of a rear frame are held in position in the jig while being brazed. The techniques have changed little today.

After the collapse of the ICFC deal, Ritchie began to do occasional work for Grosvenor-Reeve and Nick Ouroussoff, who had recently left Lawrence-Tune. It is, perhaps, typical of Andrew Ritchie that his first move was to commission Ouroussoff to build a rig testing machine to endurance test the folding bikes, Brompton Bicycle thus paradoxically becoming Ouroussoff's first customer, at the same time as Andrew Ritchie became his first employee!

With the folding bike project more or less ready to go, and space available in Nick Ouroussoff's workshop, Ritchie scraped together basic funding by pre-selling a small batch of 30 bikes to shareholders for £250 a time. Building 30 machines would provide something tangible for his long-suffering investors, with a few demonstrators left over, plus a bike or two for Ritchie to test to destruction himself.

Building those first bikes in 1981 was a painfully slow process. Ritchie had little in the way of tooling, so most of the specialist parts had to be painfully crafted by hand. But there's no better way to improve and polish a product than to build a batch of 30 single-handedly. The 12 months allotted for the pre-production batch eventually stretched to 20 months and 50 bikes, but Ritchie admits that he learnt a tremendous amount in this period. Two relatively minor flaws came to light. The first 30 had plastic headset bearings: "I saw them in a catalogue and thought, 'If they're being marketed they must be all right. They were rubbish: all spongy and wobbly." Headset bearings were easily replaced. More problematic were the hinge assemblies, beautifully crafted eccentrics that gently pulled the frame and seat pillar sections together. Building 50 by hand proved very time-consuming, and they were just too complex for full production. A much simpler, more 'Brompton-style' solution would fall into place later on...

Despite a few niggles, the first bikes seem to have worked well and delighted their owners. Andrew Ritchie went on to ride 5,000 miles on his own machine before something cracked,

Ritchie's initial batch of bikes lined up in Nick Ouroussoff's workshop

revealing that further materials changes would be required on the next batch.

With no obvious prospect of a licensing agreement, Ritchie began to think a little bigger. The first small run had helped iron out production problems, and generate enough cashflow to produce some rudimentary jigs and other tooling. What if he found bigger premises from which to build and sell a decent batch of bikes? Several hundred? Brompton was moving slowly and inexorably towards manufacture in its own right, but there was still a feeling that production of a bigger batch might encourage Raleigh or one of the other big players to invest.

Andrew Ritchie and his band of shareholders scraped together capital: £4,000 from a government-backed loan guarantee scheme and a further £8,000 of share capital, something that would probably not have been possible if the shareholders hadn't received their shiny new bikes! £12,000 wasn't much, but it was enough to buy basic machinery, produce some tooling and order stock.

Premises would have been a huge expense, and money was something Brompton Bicycle had very little of. But Ritchie still had his engineering know-how, and it was a very marketable asset. Having built a small number of bikes in Nick Ouroussoff's workshop, he moved back in with Tim Reeve and Steve Grosvenor, the design arm of the former Lawrence-Tune engineers, who had now moved from the cramped rooms at Barleymow Passage to the Old Powerhouse near Kew Gardens railway station, a substantial building with plenty of room to spare.

The agreement seems to have been that Ritchie would pay rent while building the batches of bikes, but there is some confusion over whether cash actually changed hands in practice, because Andrew also did quite a bit of design work for the company. Suffice to say, it was a friendly and amicable arrangement and it allowed Andrew to build bikes on a production line scale.

From their origins in designing souped-up motorcars, Grosvenor-Reeve was carving out a niche as a specialist engineering company - specialist in that many of its products were one-offs, and it was willing to talk to clients about anything. The deal worked out well for all concerned. Ritchie got the premises he needed, and Grosvenor-Reeve won the services of a designer with a flair for specialist engineering. According to Steve Grosvenor, "He even came with his own drawing board! He's a Cambridge graduate engineer, and the work he did for us was pretty impressive."

Ritchie designed a number of machines for Grosvenor-Reeve. Some, like the Turkish hazelnut skinning machine, have become the stuff of Brompton legend, but there were more mundane things too, like a machine for pressing plasterboard wall panels. The most interesting was a four-wheeled machine for loading and inspecting blast furnaces. This was normally front wheel drive and rear steer, enabling it to trundle up to the furnace, but at the flick of a switch all four wheels would swing through 90°, enabling it to move sideways, using, for example, the left pair of wheels for steering and the right for propulsion. The machine had a long manipulating arm that could be fitted with various tools and perform different functions under the control of a joystick, enabling it to take samples from the furnace, or skim impurities from the molten metal with some dexterity. This complex and sophisticated machine was controlled entirely by hydraulics, the drive system being designed by Andrew Ritchie. In the end, three were made, one going to Newcastle, and the others exported to Australia and New Zealand.

Left: Today the Old Powerhouse has an air of well-heeled luxury about it - a far cry from the brutish conditions in the early stages of Brompton production.

© www.etsdesign.co.uk

© www.etsdesign.co.uk

Above and left: Arguably Andrew Ritchie's most successful design whilst at Grosvenor-Reeve; the very complex drive system on this four-wheeled machine for loading and inspecting blast furnaces. This was normally front wheel drive and rear steer, enabling it to trundle up to the furnace, but at the flick of a switch all four wheels would swing through 90°, enabling it to move sideways, using, for example, the left pair of wheels for steering and the right for propulsion.
See **www.etsdesign.co.uk** for more detail.

Intriguingly, he also worked on an electric traction motor designed by a young London engineer called Cedric Lynch. The motor was an unusually compact and efficient design, and the Greater London Council helped to fund basic tooling for a pre-production run, the tooling - including a machine for soldering the armature - being designed by Andrew Ritchie. For all its brilliance, the Lynch motor seems to have been rather ahead of its time. It was made for a while in the UK, then by Agni Motors in India. The turning point came when a Lynch motor powered an electric motorbike to victory in the inaugural Zero Emission Isle of Man TT race in 2009. In 2015, Agni Motors merged with Agility Global, and the resulting company, the Saietta Group, is firmly at the cutting-edge of electric motor design, with Cedric Lynch still very much involved.

The Lynch Motor tooling was just one job of many, and between bouts of design work upstairs, Andrew Ritchie would be in the downstairs workshop building bikes. To help with the production of Bromptons, he had taken on his first employee, a dour Scot and occasional alcoholic, called Patrick, whose hours of work and behaviour could be a bit unpredictable. Employing Patrick - considered by less charitable souls to be unemployable - was a typically philanthropic Ritchie move, but his faith was to be well rewarded. Patrick might have been a bit morose with others, but he stayed loyal to Brompton Bicycle, brazing frames for the next twenty years, and becoming a slightly irregular fixture in three different factories.

Andrew *needed* a brazer as tough as Patrick at the Powerhouse. The winter of 1981-82 included the coldest December of the 20th century, with three weeks of bitter cold and snow. The workshop at the Powerhouse was on the ground floor, and rather poorly insulated. The ensuing Dickensian scenes made an impression on Steve Grosvenor:

"During that period Andrew hired Patrick. I remember one day when it was snowing and blowing a gale. Patrick was downstairs next to the big iron doors, wrapped up in scarves and a woolly hat, standing in a snowdrift which had come under the door, brazing up frames." Grosvenor, obviously impressed, added "I've never known anyone with as much determination as Andrew Ritchie". Tim Reeve was less complimentary, but equally impressed with Andrew's drive and abilities: "I tried hard to persuade him to stop wasting his time on the bloody bicycle! I thought, 'this is a really clever engineer and this obsession is damaging his career.' "

Andrew recalled the Powerhouse days with a mixture of affection and frustration:

"The snow came in under the doors at the Powerhouse and lay three feet deep in the brazing area. We got cracking and made batches of a hundred. Patrick was brazing, but he turned up fairly irregularly, and I was rushing around dealing with customers, organizing suppliers, and trying to find painters who wouldn't fill the thing with shot-blast grit. If it wasn't that, it was too much chrome on the cranks, wrongly bent tube or whatever. Plenty of problems, and endless grinding and trimming. I toiled away listening to Radio 4, but I could have done without the repeats..."

Short-lived Boom

Despite the apparent chaos, bikes were being shipped out, and they were rather good. The Brompton cost £207 in 1982 (about £660 at 2016 prices) for a basic 3-speed hub-geared model, with options of a rather chunky dynamo lighting set for an extra £12.65, a front luggage carrier for £11.50 and a cover for £23. The luggage carrier was a simple platform, not Brompton's trademark luggage system, which was still some way off.

At this stage, Brompton received its first serious press coverage, with a favourable article in the *London Evening Standard*, and a major spread in the *Financial Times* by Nico Colchester. Then Foreign Editor of the *FT*, Colchester was the first of many opinion formers to be attracted to the Brompton, and his favourable 3/4-page article in the Saturday 'How to Spend' column proved to be a turning point for Brompton Bicycle. From selling by word of mouth to friends of friends, the bikes were actually being sought out by an eager public. Brompton even persuaded Fulham Cycles on the Fulham Road to act as a retail outlet, at the relatively low mark-up of 20%. This arrangement was something of a coup, giving Brompton a local showroom and at least a veneer of respectability. The outlet accounted for nearly a quarter of those early sales.

In May 1982, Andrew got back in touch with Raleigh, explaining that the Brompton was much improved and in limited production. His letter to Michael Boughton, the chairman of parent company Tube Investments, brought a polite reply to the effect that the information and enclosures (including copies of the *Evening Standard* and *FT* articles) would be forwarded to Raleigh in Nottingham.

Whether the Raleigh executives simply filed it under 'P' for potty, or gave serious thought to the much improved design and favourable reviews, we shall never know, but when Mr Boughton wrote back in June, the tone was cold and final. Raleigh considered the Brompton 'most ingenious', but once again, the stumbling block was cost and limited sales potential. "In the circumstances", concluded Boughton, " I feel it right... to decline your offer to discuss this with us further."

Whether Raleigh could have made a success of the Brompton then or now, is an interesting question. In 1982 the company was in the throes of a major reorganization. It had lost its Nigerian and Iranian markets and had recently been the subject of a Monopolies & Mergers Commission report that criticised certain anti-competitive practices. The company was also setting out on the long and painful road away from manufacturing that would soon result in its frames, then whole bicycles, being made in the Far East. The Brompton was a complex and sophisticated bicycle that would have required a great deal of input from the engineers and designers that Raleigh was in the process of shedding. Then there was the spectre of Moulton...The company didn't want the Brompton, and it's hard to imagine the relationship working out if it had taken it on. Andrew Ritchie was later to buy components through Raleigh's Parts & Accessories division, but the 1982 rebuff was to be his last communication with the manufacturing side of the company.

With little capital available for tooling, many parts were being crafted by hand, including the plastic handles and other small items. One of the few exceptions were the folding pedal cranks, which were sub-contracted out after Andrew had painstakingly cut the first 100 on a semi-automatic lathe. No matter how buoyant the demand, mass manufacture without capital is something of a Catch 22 situation: without tooling, unit costs remain high and volumes low, leaving little profit to buy tooling to reduce costs and increase output. Without an injection of serious capital, Brompton was unable to escape from the trap.

The final crunch came when the supply of hinge forgings dried up. Andrew had replaced the complex eccentric device (hand-crafted onto the pre-production machines) with a neater, simpler hinge similar to the system used on the junior version of the Dawes Kingpin. This used a pair of forged plates, one brazed to each tube, joined together by a hinge pin, with a simple C-shaped plate to pull the two forgings - and thus the frame halves - together. It was cheap to make, relatively foolproof, and self-adjusting to a degree, even eliminating play in the hinge pin as it was tightened, but each hinge required two forgings, so four were needed per bike. As Patrick and Andrew started work on the fourth batch of 100 bikes, the French supplier of the hinge forgings announced that production had ceased. With Brompton unable to fund the considerable set-up costs to produce its own, further progress was out of the question.

If conditions had been difficult before the hinge forgings ran out, production of the last hundred bikes was to turn into a nightmare, with Andrew sitting at a milling machine for three months, cutting hinge plates from blocks of solid steel. "I couldn't see any other way to do it", he said later.

Ironically, word was getting out that the Brompton was an excellent product, and further favourable press coverage, including a piece in *Design* magazine, was generating a steady stream of sales. The bikes (unofficially referred to since as Mark 1s) were almost identical to the modern Brompton, but identifiable by a sharper dog-leg curve in the mainframe tube, because Ritchie had been forced to use a standard pipe bending tool, as the company couldn't afford the custom tooling to produce a smoother curve.

At 14.1kg, the bikes were a little heavier than today's machines, but not outrageously heavy for the time. The foldability and riding characteristics were widely praised, but reviews in those early days were not universally favourable. In early 1983 *Cycle* magazine tested the Brompton against the Airframe (still under development at that time), the long established Bickerton, and the by now long-in-the-tooth Dawes Stowaway. Summing up, *Cycle* - which presumably put more emphasis on weight than foldability or rideability - ruled out the Brompton as being too heavy (although acknowledging its sturdiness), whilst praising the Bickerton. This might seem odd, but cyclists can be a conservative bunch. The Bickerton might have been a wobbly horror, but it was a known quantity and easy and cheap to repair when things fell off. At the time, the Bickerton was grudgingly accepted as the default public transport machine. Both bikes cost a shade under £200, more or less twice as much as the conventional fold-in-half models from Raleigh and Dawes.

By the time this test was published in February 1983, production had already halted. In late 1982, after 18 months of production, Andrew reluctantly paid Patrick off and brought the brief run to a halt. Six months later, the last hand-made hinge plate had been fitted and the last machine sold.

The failure to find a licensee or sufficient funding to continue production seemed a major blow at the time, but with the benefit of hindsight, Andrew Ritchie feels it was another stroke of good fortune, allowing a breathing space to perfect the design. The steel handlebars had been welded to the stem, resulting in a potential failure point (although none seem to have broken in practice), but some of the frames actually did break:

"Those bikes were not right, and I had to repair maybe 60 of them. There were no real safety issues, but they developed a little crack around the seat clamp slot in the mainframe. At the very worst, the saddle would have sagged a bit. The slot was very short and it went down at an angle of 45° and it was in tension, so it opened up. The plastic seat sleeve was made of old drainpipe, because I couldn't afford a mould. It had a little ridge cut into it to prevent it coming out of the frame, so every time I took these apart to braze the frame, I had to make another seat sleeve. The whole thing was wonderfully inefficient."

Repairing 60 bikes was a nuisance, but a product recall involving 600 or 6,000 would have been a disaster. It might not have seemed it at the time, but the limited production run of 400 bikes was an ideal number for sorting out the practical difficulties that inevitably arose as a design was translated from hand-manufacture to the mass market.

© Marcus Jackson-Baker

Brompton Mark 1s in action. The example to the left boasts the front luggage rack, later dropped in favour of an unobtrusive mounting block.

Mark 1s show a number of tell-tale design features - the shopping trolley rear rollers on a black tubular rack, folding left-hand crank arm, steel handlebars, hefty hinges, chrome headlight and perhaps most distinctive of all, the sharp bend in the 'mainframe' which was smoothed out on subsequent Marks.

Yet the Mark 1 still folded to a size virtually the same as today's Bromptons.

Although production had ceased, Brompton Bicycle was by no means moribund. Andrew was busy redrawing certain bits, and the company continued to take out patents to cover key territories, to prevent earlier applications from lapsing. A US patent had followed close on the heels of the UK application in January 1980, with Japan being granted in May 1983, and Europe the following year. Despite the detail changes in the intervening years, these patents were all identical to the original one filed in the mid-1970s.

In 1983, Andrew Ritchie had no clear idea if or when his bicycle would go back into production, but he now knew that he had perfected an attractive, saleable, and easily manufactured bicycle and the innovative parts of the design were now well covered, should anyone try to pirate it. This was fortunate, because it would be five long years before another Brompton was made.

Left: Caroline Gibbs (later Caroline Reekie) would play a crucial role by introducing Julian Vereker to the Brompton.

Below: Andrew Ritchie and Frances Grosvenor demonstrating the Mark 1 Brompton, this time outside Kew Gardens railway station. The Mark 1 bike was in a class of its own, riding better than most of its contemporaries, yet folding into a package little bigger than its wheels.

Mark 2 Bikes In the early days, the Brompton fascinated people wherever it went. In 1996, this Mark 2 caught the attention of the guard on the Southwest Chief at a stop somewhere between Chicago and Los Angeles. This same bike would later be stripped and rebuilt as a lightweight special, then be reborn later still as the Junior Brompton (page 175), proving that old Bromptons never die!

Mark 2 Bikes
1984-1993

"*The point is that it is a machine that will sell to non-cyclists and thus expand the market.*"
NEIL MURRAY

Julian Vereker's Influence

One of the most enthusiastic early advocates of the Brompton was businessman Julian Vereker. Vereker was in some ways the antithesis of Andrew Ritchie, but in other ways, their aims and achievements were strikingly similar. Something else they shared in common were tenuous aristocratic links, Vereker being the great-great grandson of the third Viscount Gort, patriarch of a distinguished Anglo-Irish family, whose title came to a rather confused end following the creation of the Irish Free State in 1922. The English arm of the family included Lord Gort, the sixth viscount, who won the Victoria Cross in the First World War, later leading the British Expeditionary Force into France in 1939, and saving his reputation by leading most of them safely home again a few months later. He rose to become Chief of the Imperial General Staff - effectively the head of the army - and was widely liked and respected.

The son of Charles Vereker, a professor of Political Theory at Durham University, young Julian seems to have been something of a rebel, leaving school with few academic qualifications, but like Andrew Ritchie, a love of, and instinctive empathy for, engineering. For a while, he became well known in the car tuning world, with particularly close links to the Austin Mini, racing minis (cars with Moulton-designed suspension of course!) with some success towards the end of the 1960s. For lesser intellects, this might have been career enough, but Julian Vereker sparkled with a restless energy, and by 1969 he had moved into electronics, designing an industrial sound-to-light unit, which was hired out to film companies.

Vereker went on to develop all sorts of entrepreneurial ideas over the years, but his primary interest was to be audio amplifiers, and Naim Audio, the company he established in 1973, is today a global business with a £25 million annual turnover. He had a fine ear for music, but couldn't play himself, something that might have been a frustration, but Julian turned to recording live music for friends. In echoes of Andrew Ritchie and the folding bike, he was appalled by the quality of commercial amplifiers, and in time-honoured tradition set about making something better. This quest to reproduce music with the utmost fidelity was to be the driving force behind Naim Audio, then and now.

At a time when the Japanese electronics giants were cutting a swathe through the global audio industry, Naim was (and remains) a remarkable enigma. A small British company, with headquarters in Salisbury, Wiltshire, Naim was able to compete with the big global players through the sheer quality of its products. Julian Vereker went on to add a classical music label, again applying the very highest standards to the genre.

A successful businessman by the age of 40, he had no need to get involved in new projects, and could have sat back to enjoy his growing wealth. But Julian was a born salesman, and he was also a perfectionist. That desire to champion the best product in its class made him a natural Brompton ally, and just what the company needed in the mid-1980s. Vereker also had a passion for sailing, commissioning and designing several yachts, and it was whilst cruising in northern France in 1982 that he first came across the Brompton.

Like many yachtsmen, Julian kept a couple of cheap folding bikes on board. The marine market has always been a valuable one for folding bike manufacturers, as yachtsmen are liable to find themselves with no practical means of onward transportation. Land at a remote harbour in western France or the Mediterranean, and the local eatery might be five miles up the road. That's a long walk under a hot sun, but easy with a bike, especially one that can be carried part way by taxi or public transport. Yachtsmen, realizing that a folding bike could open up the hinterland beyond the marina in a magical way, had always been enthusiastic users.

Moored alongside another yacht at a harbour on the Cherbourg peninsula, Julian Vereker got talking with a pretty girl on board. The girl was Caroline Gibbs, an old friend of Andrew's, who had appeared in the early brochure with Steve Grosvenor's wife, Frances, so she knew the bike well. When the subject turned to the inadequacies of folding bikes, Caroline told Vereker that her friend made much better bikes - why not give him a ring? Many would have forgotten the conversation, but Vereker was a man of his word. He was also a self-taught engineer, well aware of the failings of the cheap bikes he kept on deck, and something of a perfectionist in matters mechanical. As soon as the opportunity arose, he phoned Ritchie, visited the factory, and bought a pair of bikes on the spot.

Vereker went on to develop a real passion for the Brompton. It was neater and cleverer than anything he had seen before, and it rode better too. Ever the salesman, he cajoled friends and acquaintances into buying the bikes, and his enthusiasm had soon produced around a dozen sales.

The yachting community was to prove vital to Brompton.

Meanwhile, Andrew was winding down production, and renewed attempts to find new finance were failing. In three years, several venture capitalists had paid a visit and inspected the bike (and, more importantly, the business plan), but none had taken the bait. Despite the production of 400 Mark 1 Bromptons, and clear interest from press and public, the answer was always the same:

"There was the same level of interest. All these people arrived and loved the Brompton, but when it came to actually signing a cheque and putting their shareholders' money into a risky business, they backed away. They would obviously have been putting other people's money into it. Everyone says the banks are mean, but they're actually looking after your dosh!"

A couple of leads seemed to be going somewhere, but they were all destined to fall by the wayside. An approach from an engineering company in Redditch looked promising, as the company had contacts in China, but the deal fell through. In 1984, the Brompton project was still ticking along, but Andrew was working for Grosvenor-Reeve with increasing regularity.

At about this time, Julian Vereker rang up to order some more bikes and was surprised to hear that production was at an end. He must have made an impression, because Andrew Ritchie rang him back, the pair agreed to meet, and with characteristic enthusiasm, Julian offered to get involved. In September 1985, when all avenues seemed to be exhausted, Andrew wrote asking for help, and Julian was soon on board. The plan was to forget the licensing option, and go it alone, but with a third party subcontracted to manufacture the frame.

Andrew Ritchie and Julian Vereker became business partners and good friends, with Vereker purchasing a significant 20% shareholding in Brompton Bicycle. He was an ambitious man, but he was shrewd, realizing that the company would only flourish if Andrew retained control, while he gently guided from behind the scenes. The two met regularly to discuss prospects over a meal, often at La Pappardella on Brompton Road. After exploring the venture capital option and discounting a fresh but derisory offer from 3Is (later described by Vereker as 'financial theft') the pair came up with a workable financial package that would enable them to go it alone. Using all his undoubted charm and selling techniques, Julian Vereker helped Andrew persuade other shareholders to come on board, from both the Vereker and Ritchie camps. Crucially, he also personally guaranteed a £40,000 overdraft with his bank.

These initiatives yielded only 60% of the capital Andrew Ritchie felt the company needed, but it was enough to fund modest premises, tooling and stock, including that elusive order for frame hinge forgings. "It was", said Vereker, "the most amazing joint venture - a lot of chance and some friends with money". Incredible it might have been, but it worked. Brompton now had two directors, 40 shareholders, modest funding, and a proven, patented product.

A New Lease of Life

Andrew wasted no time in stockpiling tools and equipment at the Powerhouse, foraging around London in one of the life-expired London House Plants Morris Minors, which even hauled back a sturdy old flypress, one of several historic - but very effective - machines still in use today, albeit under constant threat from Health & Safety legislation. By late 1986, he had resumed full-time work on the project.

Brompton was creeping towards full-scale manufacture, but even at this late stage, the directors were hoping to outsource the frame manufacture to Haden Brothers, a Midlands engineering company. This would have much simplified the London operation, removing the heavier engineering - the tube work, jigging and brazing - at a stroke. Haden's went on to become one of many suppliers to Brompton, but in the end, Andrew decided not to go ahead with the subcontracting deal. It had only been considered because the Brompton shareholders didn't have the faith that a small workshop in West London could build the frames with sufficient quality. The arrangement ultimately fell through because Andrew didn't have the faith to entrust the work to anyone else. The frames were complex assemblies that required very precise jigging to work:

Andrew Ritchie was always a hands on boss! This is one of several flypresses salvaged by Andrew in the 1980s. Although threatened by modern Health & Safety legislation, several remain in use today.

"I didn't really trust Haden's in the organization of frame making: the jigging, the alignment, making sure the material was up to the right strength, and all the massive engineering to make the thing work. But the failure to reach an agreement with Haden's turned out to be a stroke of good luck, because if I had had subcontractors building the frames, they might have been wrong, and we would have had three bike assembly men standing around with nothing to do, or we would have taken what they'd done and it would have broken."

It was the third crucial stroke of luck that would set Brompton on the road to mass-production, but the last minute change of plan meant producing the tooling, including substantial brazing jigs, setting the project back 18 months. But it was certainly the right thing to do. When Brompton did start building bikes it was able to respond quickly and decisively to quality control issues in a way that would have been impossible had the frames been built by a subcontractor in Birmingham, or indeed China.

While the production was delayed, Julian - ever the marketing man - recommended launching the Brompton at the annual Cyclex trade show in April 1987. At that time, production was still some way off, but Andrew stripped and rebuilt a couple of the pre-production machines to produce bikes representative of the new design. The principal changes were those custom-made hinge forgings, aluminium handlebars, a new chain tensioner, and of course, the elimination of the sharply kinked mainframe tube.

The Brompton won the Best Product award, although it was indicative of the conservatism prevalent in the bike world at the time that the judges were split, one complaining that it was a sad sign of the times when the top prize had to go to a machine which 'you fold up and chuck in a car boot'. Such grumbles did nothing to dampen the spirit of the two Brompton directors who had gambled everything, and won this prestigious award at their first attempt. One wonders how the win went down on the Raleigh stand, where it must have reawoken echoes of the Moulton's spectacular success twenty years before.

According to Neil Murray, one of the Cyclex judges, the front runners were the Peugeot Comete, a traditional lightweight racing machine, and the Brompton:

"The point is that it is a machine that will sell to non-cyclists and thus expand the market. In a nutshell, there are other machines in the mould of the Comete which, if you stripped off the graphics, resemble it. There's nothing like the Brompton, so the Brompton won."

Cyclex was a turning point. Cycle shops weary of impractical, gangly, even dangerous folding bikes were forced to look again. It would be more than a decade before the shops were actually hammering at Brompton's door, but several key outlets signed up at Cyclex, the first being York Cycleworks, followed by Bicycle Doctor in Manchester, and a further four in London: Cyclecare Olympia, Condor Cycles, Ealing Cycles and Simpsons in Kentish Town. It was a very modest dealer network, and the handful of shops would have to wait a while for their bikes, but as the directors shook hands at the end of the show, they knew they had the nucleus of a dealer network up and running.

Winning Best Product award at Cyclex in 1987 was a great step towards acceptance of the Brompton by a wary cycle trade. It must also surely rank as one of Julian Vereker's and Andrew Ritchie's proudest joint achievements.

What they didn't have were bikes or even a factory, but both problems were soon to be remedied. In November 1987 a truck arrived at the Powerhouse to take away the big equipment, carrying it a few miles north to a former railway arch in Brentford. The railway had been part of a Great Western freight line to wharves on the river Thames, cut back a few years before, leaving four arches isolated beside a branch of the Grand Union canal, next to London Road, Brentford.

Two of the arches were being used by a car trader, Bird Autos, while the other two were let to 'Charlie' who dealt in Volkswagen Beetles. Finding himself behind on the rent, Charlie had been evicted from one of the arches, leaving behind a tangle of VW spares, and it was in this 1,000 square feet of leaky, insalubrious workspace that Brompton found its first home. The rent was a bit high for what it was, but the arch was perfect for a small manufacturing operation.

For Andrew Ritchie, the prospect of setting up the factory brought mixed emotions. As he later recalled, it was 'dead frightening', but they were exciting days too, and he set to work with enthusiasm. Once the arch had been tidied up, the ancient machinery was wheeled in with some difficulty and bolted to the floor, a rudimentary office established above, and Brompton Bicycle was ready for business:

"There was all this new tooling to prove, and I just started making bits. There were hundreds of new tools... which ones would work? Most of them did, which was extraordinary."

In March 1988 the first Brompton was delivered to York Cycleworks, the very first dealer, signed up at Cyclex almost a year before. Production of this 'Mark 2' machine ramped up gradually from a trickle to 60 a month, which wasn't bad going for a factory then employing only three staff. Andrew had brought in Sonny, a full-time brazer, and had been persuaded to employ a salesman, Charles 'Chuck' Shepherd. In the early days, Shepherd helped around the factory, but once he had bikes to demonstrate, he was sent out on the road to tackle unwilling bike shops. This small team were soon joined by an office girl, Esther Chubb, but she somehow never quite gelled into the team and didn't stay long.

Generally speaking, the relationship between Julian Vereker and Andrew Ritchie was harmonious in those early days, but there were occasional tensions that exposed the sharp differences in their underlying philosophies.

One element of Brompton manufacture that has barely changed is brazing. Here Sonny is turning out a rear frame at the Arches. Note the line up of main frames and rear frames in the foreground.

The Mark 2 bikes had a new, smoother frame curve and were produced in red with black extremities, or all-over black, both options being available in 3- or 5-speed form, although 3-speed bikes were usually red. There were two models, the 'L', or lightweight (above) and the 'T' or touring model (below), which came with a steel rack (upgraded to aluminium by the time this photo was taken) and dynamo lights. Note that the 'T' type is fitted with the front carrier block, while the 'L' is not, but it has a fitting to accept the block which was optional at the time.

Andrew expected customers to come to him, and he saw no reason why he shouldn't produce bikes in a single colour: red with black extremities for the Mark 1, but with the addition of an all-black option for the Mark 2, initially only on the more expensive models. If customers wanted a folding bike, he reasoned, they would seek out a dealer, and once they had ridden the Brompton and found it to be the best available, they would buy one. It was a charmingly low-key approach, and the product was good enough for it to work by and large, but it was quite at odds with Julian Vereker's more flamboyant marketing philosophy.

Julian knew that many more people would buy the bike if they were educated in Brompton theory and practice. True, a handful of early adopters knew exactly what they wanted, but the majority of potential customers didn't yet know they wanted a Brompton. They hadn't yet discovered that a Brompton could change their lives for the better!

Both men were right in a way of course, and Brompton's subsequent development was to take a middle path between these two extremes, the company growing at a steady, but unspectacular rate, largely without advertising or pressure from sales reps. Back in 1988, Andrew wasn't happy with the principle of employing a sales rep, and Chuck Shepherd's time with the company would be relatively short. There wouldn't be another.

Meanwhile, Julian was working out his sales addiction by publicizing the Brompton at shows and exhibitions, particularly boat shows, where his slick, hard-sell routine always drew a crowd. As a yachtsman, Julian could talk to sailors in their own language. He knew the harbours of the English Channel and he knew from personal experience that - for example - a Brompton could carry a crate of wine back from an interesting vineyard, just out of reach for the average yachtsman. At caravan and camping shows, Vereker sometimes struggled, but with yachtsmen and pilots he excelled, helping to establish a niche market that Brompton has profited from ever since.

His early efforts resulted in a steady stream of sales for the growing band of dealers, whose proprietors were delighted to have had the hard work done for them. The bike trade often argued that the margins were poor on the Brompton, but the bikes soon gained a reputation for working straight out of the box, and Brompton made a point of never undermining the dealers with anything as vulgar as direct sales.

The company rapidly developed a slightly superior image that went down a storm with the yachtsmen and middle-class commuters who were the primary customers in those early days. The only real competition at this time was from the Taiwanese Dahon, sold rather half-heartedly through a motorcycle dealership in Ruislip, and never quite able to match the Brompton's effortlessly classy appeal.

Luggage & Gearing Develops

When Ritchie and Vereker launched the Brompton at Cyclex in 1987, dealers were told that the bike would cost from £210, but in an era of high inflation, this estimate was bound to rise. The increases were modest at first: the early machines seem to have sold for £220, but by May 1989 the price had edged up to £235.75 (£529 at 2016 prices), an increase of 15%, or 3% above inflation. But for the next two years, the basic price of the Brompton rocketed, hitting £270 in 1990 and £320.78 (£621 at 2016 prices) the following year; a whacking 36% increase in two years, twice the rate of inflation. To Raleigh, it must have looked as though its caution had been vindicated, but prices never increased as sharply again, and the revolutionary Brompton continued to find eager buyers.

These were basic prices, but the spec was still relatively simple, with 3-speed or 5-speed

Sturmey-Archer hub gears, the two colour options, and a steel rear rack. On the Mark 1 machine, the rack had been integral to the rear frame, but it was now a chromed steel option, resulting in two models, the basic red 'L' or Lightweight without a rack, and the black 'T' or Touring model. This was exactly the same, but fitted with the steel rear rack and dynamo lights at a premium of about £50.

Either of the bikes could be fitted with Brompton's superb front pannier system. This involved a plastic block that bolted to the frame, making good use of the dead space where a 26-inch wheel would normally go. The 'T' type in particular was quite a prodigious load carrier, rather after the style of the Moulton, and with the rack and pannier bag mounted so low, it was also a very stable load platform.

At first there were three custom bag options: a steel frame that could be bolted to the rider's briefcase, another frame that could be bolted to a standard Spencer wire basket, and a Carradice pannier bag. All could be clipped on and off the mounting block on the bicycle headtube. It looked as though the load moved with the steering, but it was actually rigidly attached to the frame, and thus had little adverse effect on handling.

The briefcase frame was not a success and was soon dropped, and the wire basket was later replaced by a clever folding basket aimed at the same shopping and leisure market. This stayed in production, but it wasn't a spectacular success either, accounting for only 20% of bag sales over the years. On the other hand, the cloth pannier - although expensive at nearly £70 - went on to become something of a sales phenomenon, and an iconic badge of ownership, bringing together early-adopter Brompton owners. In the early 1990s, if you were carrying a Brompton pannier, you were clearly a clubbable sort of chap, and thus might find yourself in conversation with captains of industry, celebrities, or even MPs, whilst waiting at the traffic lights.

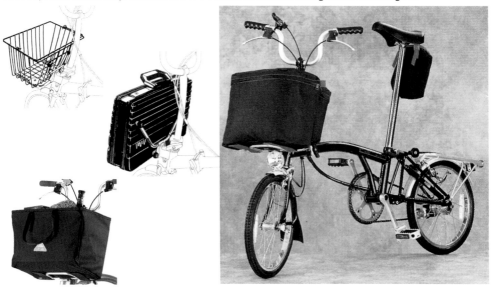

The Carradice bag went on to become something of a sales phenomenon, surviving almost unchanged until 2009. The folding basket (bottom left) succeeded the wire basket (top left). Neither of these options was a big success but the folding basket is still available today. The briefcase frame (centre left) and wire basket were soon dropped.

51

Feedback from the press and public continued to be positive, but there were one or two grumbles. The steel wheel rims were a bit heavy, and the chromed steel finish resulted in the braking effect more or less evaporating in wet weather. The brakes were poor anyway, and some riders felt the front of the bike was a bit flexible. All these issues would be dealt with, but the complaints about high gearing were not to be addressed for some years.

At this time Andrew Ritchie was riding into the factory on a Brompton most mornings. This sort of hands-on daily commuting was a logical move for a bicycle designer trying to iron out minor problems, and in some ways the key to the bike's success, but it could result in the machine being rather tailored to the terrain the designer was familiar with. Andrew had specified a 50-tooth chainring and 13-tooth rear sprocket, giving gears of 46", 62" and 82" with the 3-speed hub. Gearing is always a compromise, and as compromises go, this was spot on for West London, but a bit ambitious for hillier regions.

The 5-speed machine used the Sturmey-Archer 5-Star hub. This gave more gears and a bigger overall gear range than the 3-speed, but it was a rather odd device utilizing two gear levers. One lever gave three distinct gears like any other Sturmey 3-speed gear lever, while the other effectively switched between close ratios and wide ones. In practice, this lowered first gear and raised top gear, but left the direct-drive middle gear unchanged. Difficult enough to explain, it was tricky to adjust, and even more difficult to use effectively, and it's probably fair to say that many owners never fully grasped the concept.

The gear steps of -33%, -21%, direct, +25% and +50% seemed a useful bonus over the 3-speed model, but as there was some extra internal resistance in the more extreme gears, it wasn't much better at climbing hills. Nevertheless, the 5-speed was soon well established, appealing as much to those who naturally gravitated to the most expensive variant as those living in hilly areas.

Magazine testers and customers continued to grumble about the high gearing for years, but the standard ratios remained stubbornly unchanged. Eventually, a smaller chainring was offered as an option, but this cost more, and you needed to know that you wanted it before making the purchase. Somehow, these departures from Andrew's chosen script were

5-speed models were fitted with early Sturmey-Archer 5-speed hubs, controlled by two shifters via twin cables - a heavy and rather complex solution. The first Mark 2s were fitted with the S5/2, but this was soon replaced by the very similar 5-Star , which lasted until the single-cable Sprinter arrived in 1994.

always offered a bit grudgingly. It was the sort of 'nanny knows best' attitude to marketing that often had Julian Vereker jumping up and down with frustration, but it did nothing to upset sales, which continued to grow steadily. By the end of 1988, the little factory was producing 90 bikes a month, and when Charlie was finally given the boot from the adjoining arch in 1991, Brompton was quick to absorb the extra space, doubling the size of the factory. Staff levels gradually increased, and the following year, Andrew's original employee Patrick - who had found gainful employment as a security guard in the intervening years - answered an advertisement, and was soon back on the team.

The 5-speed certainly proved profitable for Brompton, selling for £368.95 in early 1991, against £320.78 for the 3-speed. These 'to the penny' prices were an Andrew Ritchie idiosyncrasy, and for a few years were to become as much a feature of the bikes as the neat fold and limited colour range. With luck, the price might come out at a low-sounding £499.83, but a Brompton might just as easily be priced at £501.01, which didn't sound half as good. Some dealers were perplexed by this deliberately 'non-marketing' approach. Others jokingly displayed the exact price, while a few - even more tongue in cheek - made a big show of discounting the bike by 78 pence or whatever the surplus might be. Brompton, incidentally, always took a hard line on discounting or profiteering by dealers. It was all part of Andrew's sales philosophy that the bike was being sold at a fair price and dealers and customers could take it or leave it; and although Andrew Ritchie would never admit it, this strict adherence to pricing had a vaguely socialist ring to it. The enforced level playing field helped the small shops selling a Brompton or two a month to compete with the big ones turning over half a dozen a week. The big shops were angling hard for a superior discount to match their more aggressively successful sales, but Ritchie always resisted this too, staying loyal to the small shops that had shown confidence by placing orders at Cyclex 1987 and soon after. Brompton's refusal to allow discounting was later referred to the Office of Fair Trading by a disgruntled dealer in Yorkshire. The OFT subsequently found against Brompton, forcing it to make a humiliating apology to the cycle trade in press advertisements, but Ritchie still had the last word. Thereafter, the fledgling sales team would simply inform discounters very sweetly that the order book was full...

Getting dealers on board had been critical to the Brompton's early success, and the first shops had soon been joined by a handful of others: Avon Valley in Bath, Peddlers in Worcester, Drakes in Cambridge, Spa in Harrogate and Warlands in Oxford. These were quite small shops in the main, but they were mostly situated in cycling areas, which perhaps gave a little more leeway to experiment than those in less bike-friendly towns and cities.

Resistance to folding bikes was understandable. Older traders had witnessed the Moulton's spectacular rise and fall, while others had been scared off by the Bickerton. Production of the Bickerton had nearly ceased by this time, but many shops had been left with unsaleable stock, vowing never to touch 'portables' again. In practiced hands, the Bickerton wasn't at all bad, but it needed an engineer's delicate touch to perform well, and the dealers were consequently having a hard time with warranty claims.

It was against this backdrop that Andrew Ritchie - and for a limited period, salesman Chuck Shepherd - sometimes had difficulty getting a foot in the door, let alone demonstrating the bike. Resistance to the Brompton was strongest in working class and depressed areas, and even after sales had taken off in the south it would be some years before the bike fought its way out from a couple of strongholds in the North, and the single dealer covering the whole of Scotland.

Rapid Expansion

By 1991, Brompton had an impressive 56 outlets in the UK (18 in London alone), and was starting to make big inroads into Europe. The most important markets were Germany, where the bikes were distributed by Hans Voss, a specialist cycle manufacturer and distributor, and The Low Countries, which were handled by a slightly eccentric bicycle enthusiast called Simon Korn. Eccentricity has never been a significant stumbling block in the Brompton orbit of course, and Korn went on to do extremely well. Within a year of the Brompton's launch, half the output was being exported, mainly to The Netherlands and Germany, and by year two, exports were accounting for two-thirds of production, and have remained more or less at that level ever since.

Exports brought extra complications in terms of lights and reflectors to satisfy local legislation, and this together with a steady stream of orders from the British shops, meant the little office in the upper storey of the Arches was close to being overwhelmed.

Brompton had been started by an inventive engineer, who had been joined by a marketing guru, but what the tiny company now needed was a steady hand to bring order to its administrative affairs. Almost exclusively masculine up to this time, it also needed a woman's touch, and so it was that a third key character entered the story.

Nicola McGregor was the daughter of a Scottish doctor. Born in Africa, her early years were largely spent in the Middle East, where her father was employed by an oil company. Nicola went on to graduate from St Andrew's University with a 2:1 in Zoology, and to start a PhD in microbiology at Oxford. But temperamentally unsuited to research, she left before acquiring any further academic qualifications. Following a short stint with the National Enterprise Board, through luck and a sense of adventure, she found herself back in the Middle East, now in the banking sector, enjoying the prosperity and ostentatiousness of the 1980s boom years.

This was brought to an end by Saddam Hussein's invasion of Kuwait, and Nicola, by now a product manager with an international financial information company, was moved back to the London office, but not before she had fallen for a US marine. By early 1991 the war was over, but with the Middle Eastern financial markets shattered, Nicola followed her marine back to the US. The relationship soon foundered and she returned to her parents' house in Scotland, effectively back to square one. It was in this somewhat downcast state that she contacted Penny Naylor, an old Oxford University acquaintance, now married to a Brompton shareholder. During the conversation it emerged that Esther Chubb was leaving, and Andrew was seeking a 'Girl Friday' to help bring the administration under control.

After a call to Andrew (who with typical financial caution, agreed to a meeting if she was willing to travel down from Dundee at her own expense!), Nicola made the long journey south and was soon on board, initially lodging with friends in Barnes, a comfortable cycle ride from the Brentford factory. Nicola fitted the Brompton mould to perfection: like Ritchie and Vereker she had a considerable intellect allied to a streak of non-conformity.

Another interesting and rather far-sighted element to Andrew Ritchie's management philosophy was that everyone who worked for Brompton must first learn to build the bike. This was fair enough while he was taking on engineers and brazers, but a slightly tall order for young Miss McGregor, whose CV had been varied, but always some distance from engineering. Nevertheless, after some initial trials, she had soon built her own bike, and as Andrew hoped, the experience gave her enough expertise to hold her own with the cycle shops, and ultimately gain the respect of hardened engineers on the shop floor.

But when Nicola sat down on her first day, she surveyed the cramped office with a mixture of dismay and a growing sense of excitement at the challenge ahead:

"It was really an organisational problem - letting shops have the bikes they wanted when they wanted them. It didn't require any extraordinary talents, but it needed someone who was independent and logical."

The office was packed with secondhand filing cabinets, the unisex toilet (which the 'Girl Friday' had to clean!) was a lean-to in the yard, the bin was a cardboard box in the corner, and rats and foxes were occasional visitors, but gradually Nicola took the administration in hand. In the early days, each bike had been given a job card, four cards being laboriously cut from sheets of A4 paper with a Stanley knife on a block of wood. Gradually the systems were improved, and matters like the payroll and tax paperwork were brought in-house and computerized (often with a programme and/or programmer from Julian's long list of friends and associates).

Always keen to enhance the marketing side of the company, Julian suggested that Nicola be given a marketing role, but such was the rate of growth in the company, this never formally happened, although she did effectively oversee Brompton's low-key and rather gentlemanly 'marketing department' for many years.

'Girl Friday' Nicola McGregor also played a pivotal role in marketing. After several fruitless attempts to engage the railway companies, Brompton was finally permitted to position a small stand at Marylebone station, by Chiltern Trains, one of the most forward-looking of the new rail franchisees. This stand, designed and made by Andrew Ritchie was a folding design and could be carried in the panniers of the display bikes!

The mid-90s were a period of rapid expansion for Brompton, and the company found it difficult to keep up with demand. Marketing may have played a role: Julian Vereker always enjoyed demonstrating the bike at shows, here testing a Brompton-mounted trailer!

As Brompton found its feet in the late 1990s, the company began to undertake some tentative marketing. Here the Brompton is identified with another London icon, the red bus, an association that has stuck ever since.

Meanwhile, Andrew was busy refining the bike, introducing a number of key innovations in the first few years of production, mostly aimed at reducing the weight and enhancing the bike's rigidity. The steel wheels were replaced by aluminium in 1991, saving a few grams and improving wet-weather braking. In late 1992, the chain tensioner was strengthened, and at about the same time a cast alloy rack replaced the tubular steel rack on 'T' models. This was one of many small improvements made possible by the increased output. The steel rack had been expensively brazed together by hand, whereas the alloy rack was cast in one piece by a sub-contractor. It was lighter, and cheaper to make, but only possible once the factory was in a position to place the large orders that made casting cost-effective. Later that year, the diameter of the handlebar stem was increased, and the headset enlarged from 1 inch to $1\frac{1}{8}$ inch, a move that added little or no weight, but greatly beefed up the front end, improving the feel of the bike on the road.

There would be many, many changes in the years to come, but this machine, on sale from the spring of 1992 was the definitive Brompton. In a short, frenetic period, the bike had been brought to production and refined until most of the early criticisms had been overcome. It was still on the heavy side compared to the Bickerton, but it was much lighter than the Raleigh, Dawes and cheap Far Eastern fold-in halves, and apart from a degree of small-wheel twitchiness, it rode superbly. Andrew Ritchie's slightly gawky brainwave had outshone its peers. It wasn't just a folding bicycle, it was a timeless classic, and although market penetration remained patchy, sales were starting to take off.

The Taiwanese Brompton

Soon, the two arches were bulging at the seams, but it looked as though salvation had already arrived in the shape of a call from the Far East. Out of the blue, late in 1991, Andrew had taken a call from Peter Wang of Eurotai in Taiwan. The Brompton had come to their notice and they wanted to build it under licence:

"Peter Wang said 'I think you've got the best folding bike there is, and I'd love to build it under licence'. I told him to piss off, but he came back several times and really seemed to mean business, and after talking it over with Julian, we said, 'OK, let's talk', and struck a deal with him."

The deal was for Eurotai to build machines destined for the Far East, particularly the large Japanese market, while the Brentford factory would continue to supply Europe and America. A licensing deal where the other party promises to build machines, market them, and pay you a healthy royalty sounds like a licence to print money, but these sort of arrangements can be expensive and potentially risky ventures. Brompton's confidence wasn't improved by a call from David Hon, the founder of Dahon, warning that Eurotai might not be a suitable partner. Dahon, of course, was Brompton's competitor, so hardly an unbiased source, but the warning set alarm bells ringing.

On the other hand, there were several strong arguments for going ahead: there was a real risk that Eurotai, if rebuffed, might start pirating the design anyway. Brompton also needed a breathing space to catch up with its overflowing order book, and the Taiwan link promised to provide a secondary source of components. It looked risky, but it was understandably a tempting deal at the time.

Training the Taiwanese engineers was a slow process, and involved a lot of effort and expense. First, the Eurotai engineers were brought over to Brentford for a week or two, before Andrew flew to the Far East to help design jigs, and train the engineers to build the complex and precisely-engineered frames. There followed a long period during which drawings and information were exchanged, at a time when Andrew was already in great demand improving and mass-producing the bike at home. The early Taiwanese prototypes were disastrous, as Ritchie later recalled:

"They were really taking short cuts. The wall thickness of the tube wasn't what it should be, and the material for the folding pedal was the wrong stuff. Everything was wrong and they'd just taken short cuts all over the place. Each bike - and they sent about six samples - was wrong. I wasted hours late into the evenings looking at these things, utterly pissed off with the way they were setting about it, cutting corners all over the place. Eventually I threw my hands up in despair and decided it was sort of near enough, but to this day I don't know how many of their bikes have broken. I gave them the go-ahead, and of course they then had the right to use the name Brompton. They did their best, but their best was crap. The jigging was appalling, the tooling was appalling, and it was all really badly made."

Eurotai had set up a new company, Neobike, to produce the Brompton. The promise was that Neobike would build and pay royalties on 50,000 bikes a year, but the actual figures were impossible to verify and Eurotai's irregular royalty payments left a lingering impression that it wasn't being entirely honest about the sales figures. Once the design had effectively been pirated, Neobike set about building as many bikes as it could and marketing them with mini-skirted models, playing vaguely on the bike's perceived value as a leisure machine. It was all too much for Andrew Ritchie, who had worked hard to convince the world that the Brompton was a serious commuting tool. To make matters worse, the Neobike bicycles carried large Union Jacks, whereas the British bikes made do with the tiny legend: 'Made in England. Patents Worldwide'.

Neobike played shamelessly on the Brompton's British associations, mixing images of London with sexy models (and bizarrely throwing in a New York icon in this example!).

58

Associating the bikes with a brand like Rolls-Royce was quite absurd when the Taiwanese machines were so poorly made.

One of Neobike's key targets was Japan, a wealthy country with a strong bicycle heritage, and no cultural problems with small wheeled bicycles! In 1996, Neobike approached Mac Nakane of Mitsubishi and demonstrated the Taiwanese Brompton. At this time, Mitsubishi was selling a number of bicycle brands, including Mizutani, a family-run Japanese business producing racing bikes and run by Toshi Mizutani. Faced with increasing competition from China and other low-wage economies, Toshi was in the process of winding down racing bike manufacture to concentrate on distributing other bikes, principally folders.

Early in 1996, he had signed a deal to distribute the Birdy, which was being made for Riese & Muller by Pacific of Taiwan. Unfortunately, the Birdy name had been registered by Suzuki, so the Mizutani Birdies were labelled B-D1. At about the same time, Toshi spotted the Brompton in a European catalogue but was unable to secure the brand. However, soon afterwards, while chatting with his friend Mac Nakane at Mitsubishi, Toshi couldn't believe his luck when Mac produced a Taiwanese Brompton, and said Neobike was willing to talk terms.

For a while, Mizutani had problems registering the Brompton brand name in Japan, but with hindsight the delay was a bonus, because in 1996 the build quality of the Neobike machines was still very poor. But by the following year the brand name was safely registered and the quality problems largely resolved. The Taiwanese Bromptons were cheap enough for sales to take off in quite a big way, and by the end of 1997, Mizutani had distributed around 1,000. Japanese sales continued to grow in the next few years, averaging 1,500 to 2,000 a year. Mizutani was selling twice as many B-D1's, but the Brompton soon became a good solid part of the company's range.

Very little of this had got back to London, of course. Neobike went on to cause problems by selling into Turkey (claiming that it was an Asian rather than a European country), and its bikes also began to turn up in the USA, which was potentially a much more serious issue. Andrew had had enough:

"The whole thing was a bloody waste of time, just a mess. I could have closed the agreement earlier than I did, because they were not honouring it, but was it worth litigating? We let it run for the ten years of the first stage until they had to renew, which they forgot to do anyway. But if they hadn't, I would have said 'sorry mate, this is the end of it'."

Unfortunately it wasn't the end of it. Neobike returned some nominal drawings and tooling, but kept a great deal, including the essential know-how. The company was subsequently sold on to a Taiwanese businessman, after which all prospects of controlling pirate manufacture were lost. In the years that followed Brompton clones continued to slip out of Taiwan destined for Europe, the USA and elsewhere. For Brompton, this would be an ongoing headache, necessitating legal action to impound the counterfeits. The most galling thing for Andrew Ritchie was that these poorly made copies were being produced using his own expertise and drawings, expensively shipped out to Taiwan in 1992.

With hindsight, it seems odd that Brompton didn't simply go with the flow, sort out the quality problems and buy the Taiwanese bikes themselves. After all, by the mid-1990s, British manufacturing companies had virtually abandoned metal-bashing in favour of cheap Chinese manufacture. Why could Brompton not simply do the same? According to Andrew Ritchie, this had certainly been investigated, and several prominent shareholders were keen on the concept of outsourcing, but there remained serious issues with quality, and the cost advantages weren't quite what they appeared:

"We did entertain the idea of getting Neobike to build bikes for us, but the marginal cost of buying from the Far East was a big problem, let alone the quality issues... Let us say it costs us a hundred quid to make one here in Chiswick. When we came round to it, the Neobike machine was going to cost £110 by the time it had landed. OK, we have overheads on top, so the true cost of building a bike here might be £140, making theirs slightly cheaper, but it wasn't miles cheaper. So for the hassle, for a sub-brand, it just wasn't worth it."

In the event, Brompton did source a few components from Neobike's suppliers in the 1990s, including, for a while, some rather unsatisfactory handlebars, but even this modest venture was later to turn sour, as we shall see.

The Asian approach to marketing was hardly subtle. A long way from the British Brompton's refined, often exclusive image - much to the dismay of Brompton UK!

And a Taiwanese Rival

With the Taiwanese adventure going horribly wrong, and customers and dealers crying out for bikes, a move to a bigger factory became essential, and in December 1993 Brompton moved two miles east, leasing what appeared at the time to be an enormous factory in Chiswick, opposite Chiswick Park tube station.

The move was a fairly fraught affair. Machinery movers were brought in to shift the lathes, brazing benches and flypresses, and in those simpler days before Health & Safety legislation went completely mad, the 15 or so staff simply downed tools and mucked in, dragging Dexion shelving, boxes of spare parts and other equipment to waiting removal vans.

The new factory (a 'cathedral' according to Andrew Ritchie) seemed big after the Arches, but with more staff arriving all the time, it soon filled up. After a pause, output began to ramp up and had soon reached 100 a week.

What had become of the competition? After Harry Bickerton's retirement in 1987, the Bickerton had begun to fade from the scene, a slow death that was hastened by the rebirth of the Brompton the following year. The Airframe had been designed back in 1978, but despite a great deal of promise, had never really entered into volume production and had disappeared by the late 1980s.

The Strida was an interesting machine. It had been designed by Mark Sanders, a young British industrial design student, as a means of overcoming his own walk to the railway station.

The Strida went into production in 1987, just before the reborn Brompton. Unlike most designs, it was a simple but elegant 'stick' folder - not the easiest thing to ride, but admirably fulfilling its design brief. The bike burst onto the market in a blaze of publicity, winning Best Bike at Cyclex in 1988, the year after Brompton. Sales at home were always disappointing, but the bike became a favourite in the Far East and by 1992 some 25,000 had been made. Unfortunately, the British manufacturer then went bust (after expanding into baby buggies, oddly enough), reportedly leaving some 15,000 unfulfilled Japanese orders. The Strida disappeared, but as with many folding bikes, this was not to be the end of the story...

British designer Mark Sanders produced the Strida in the late 1980s. It sold fitfully in Europe, but became a runaway success in the Far East, turning Mark into a delighted, if slightly bemused, folk hero.

© Mark Sanders

The only real threat to Brompton's dominance at this time was from the Dahon, which was still being sold by HGB Motorcycles of Ruislip, but since 1986 it had also been 'badge-engineered', selling through Bickerton-Rowlinson as the Bickerton Dahon. The arrangement between Mark Bickerton and David Hon seems to have been mutually beneficial, because it was set to continue with the Bickerton Californian in 1988, the Taiwanese bikes being listed in the Bickerton catalogue alongside the home-produced models.

Within a few years, Dahon would be a real force to be reckoned with, but these early 16-inch (305mm) bicycles were crude, heavy and rather laughable. The Bickerton Californian was considerably cheaper than the Brompton, costing £260 in late 1993 (£480 today), against £345.45-£477.05 for the Brompton (£635-£876 today), but it only really appealed to those who felt they couldn't justify the cost of the real thing, a point made by several road tests of the day. The Dahon might have been cheap, but in Britain's rather class-conscious society, there was something faintly oikish about the Stars and Stripes flag (they were actually made in Taiwan) and go-faster colours and finishes. The Dahon was to become an established favourite with the caravan towing classes, habitually dominating tests in that sort of magazine, but for more serious travellers, the Brompton was already in a class of its own. All these factors, plus HGB's rather half-hearted and downmarket advertising, meant the Dahon - for the time being - remained little more than a minor irritant.

With quality imports like the Birdy and Bike Friday still some way off, the Brompton had a near monopoly, a good product, a smart new factory and a dedicated management team. The only immediate obstacle was the company's inability to supply bikes fast enough.

Architect Graham Herbert with his Airframe folding bike.
The Airframe was a much cleverer design than the Bickerton and
would have sold in big numbers had it not been for the Brompton.

Competition Hots Up - the Mark 3s

The bike looked almost identical to its predecessor, but nearly every component was different beneath the skin.

Competition Hots Up - the Mark 3s
1994-2000

At Chiswick Park

For Andrew Ritchie, Julian Vereker, Nicola McGregor and the growing band of shop floor staff, the Chiswick Park days were probably their happiest. After the Stygian gloom of the Arches, the factory was light, airy and convenient. Although only a few short miles east of Brentford, Chiswick is London proper, and Chiswick High Street, just five minutes walk from the factory, included some of the best shops and eateries in the capital.

For staff and the increasing number of visitors from home and overseas, this was all very convenient. Encouraged by Julian, Andrew continued to take on employees, keeping the growth in bike output more or less steady at around 10% a year. Unusually for a manufacturing company, this steady growth was achieved from sales rather than borrowings, this meticulous financial husbandry being something in which Andrew Ritchie was to take special pride.

Julian Vereker was always keen to point out at shows that this was a genuinely British bike. After Raleigh stopped building its own frames in 1999, almost every bicycle frame sold in the UK would be produced in the Far East, and within a few years, complete bicycles would be arriving the same way, reducing once proud British companies like Raleigh and Dawes to mere marketing shells. By the late 1990s only two companies were building bikes by hand in any number: Pashley, which held the Post Office bike contract, and Brompton. Hand assembly meant exactly that. Brompton's increased buying power had made it possible for many mouldings and castings to be subcontracted out, but the bikes were put together in much the same way Andrew and Patrick had built the first 400. The frame parts and other steel components were cut and bent to shape, then inserted into complex jigs and brazed together. Once complete, the bare frames and other components were packed into special pallets and sent out to be painted.

Like many modern bicycles, the Brompton was actually 'powder-coated' rather than painted. In essence, the steel frames were cleaned, galvanized, and sprayed with a fine plastic powder, then placed in an oven, where the powder would melt and form a tough, seamless plastic coat. Clearly a rather complex process, the powder-coating was always done by outside sub-contractors, initially a few miles down the road, but later in South Wales, necessitating quite a trek out and back.

It was the complexity of the powder-coating supply chain that encouraged Andrew to stick with black for the extremities, and red or black for the frames, because with the small number of machines then being made, a range of colours would have added a disproportionate amount of complication and cost. The process was also a quality control nightmare, with a relatively high number of rejects, which had to be sent back to the sub-contractor, stripped back to bare metal and reprocessed.

The powder-coating shipments had to be built around another company's work schedule and holiday arrangements and timed to arrive back for final assembly to take place. Any mistakes in timing, or losses (one lorryload of frames - useless to anyone else - was stolen en route), and the factory could be in trouble.

Assembly was done at work stations equipped with all the small parts and accessories and a rotatable bike stand on which the bike would be built, each one taking anything up to 60 minutes or so, depending on the specification (the more complex 'T' type took a little longer). Once built, the bike would be sent to the quality control bench (as the years passed, more benches were added) for final inspection and rectification, and only then would the familiar 'Brompton' frame decals be added. Generally speaking, bikes were built to order, but common models could also be produced for stock, if orders were thin on the ground, and the parts available.

This sort of labour-intensive construction is time-consuming and expensive, each bike occupying around seven man-hours to build, but it was the only practical way to make such a complicated machine in relatively small numbers. Assembly staff were quite easy to train, and as in the early days, everyone from senior manager to the most junior clerk, was expected to learn the ropes by building a few bikes.

The real production bottleneck was the frame brazing, a specialist trade, and an area where poor workmanship could be expensive and potentially dangerous. Brompton faced a constant battle to find and keep enough brazers, and hold-ups often occurred in this area too, resulting in a shortage of finished frames for the assembly people, who would have to be found other roles at short notice.

In the early days these problems would all be dealt with by Andrew Ritchie. To the uninitiated he neither looked nor sounded like a natural personnel officer - he had a quick temper and didn't suffer fools, but he also had a ready smile and could communicate with anyone, from captains of industry to shop-floor trainees.

But managing these day-to-day purchasing, production and despatch problems inevitably took Andrew away from his core task of designing improvements into the bikes, so the management team began to grow, with new staff being brought in to specialize in particular fields - production, engineering, purchasing and so on. "I started taking on more brainy employees", says Andrew Ritchie, "all of whom wanted to be paid more than I was paying myself!" But there were to be no design staff at this stage, as it was an area he jealously guarded. For more than ten years he'd been working incredibly hard at it, sitting at his drawing board for long hours, often late into the evening after the last

The very skilled job of brazing continued to be a production bottleneck for Brompton. Each bike took around 7 man-hours to build.

of the staff had gone home, and the rest of the factory was in darkness. In later years, the design work was transferred to computer, but the iconic drawing board was to survive into the modern era, although seeing much less use than hitherto.

Once the dust had settled from the factory move, the incremental improvements came back on stream. Some were of a technical nature, like offset cranks, and a shorter crank axle, but in June 1994, the old Sturmey-Archer 2-lever 5-Star hub was replaced by the latest design, which utilized a single cable and rotary thumb shifter control. At the same time, the rear frame rollers were deliberately weakened. Bikes were usually packed in cardboard boxes and despatched by courier, and inevitably some of the boxes were dropped en route. If dropped the right way up, there was a risk that the extensions on the rear frame that carried the rollers would be bent, necessitating a return to the factory for a new rear frame. This was not only expensive and troublesome, but it was a particular menace when bikes were in short supply, as they often were, leaving the shopkeeper without profit and the customer without a bike. The new weaker rollers tended to break first, taking stress off the frame. They cost pennies to replace, and it was an easy job for the shops to do themselves.

Late in 1994, Brompton made an attempt to improve the brakes, which could be quite weak on early bikes, but the change from Sachs to Saccon calipers had little effect, and it was to be several more years before the braking performance reached a satisfactory level.

Meanwhile, Julian Vereker had been doing his stuff, generating publicity by nominating Brompton for a Queen's Award for Export Achievement. In early 1995, the award was confirmed, and although the subsequent publicity seems to have made little impact overseas, at home, the cachet of carrying the royal crest on company paperwork was a very tangible benefit, suggesting as it did that members of the royal family had somehow given the little bike a stamp of approval. Owners certainly included the great and the good of the day, but there is no evidence that members of the royal household were customers!

In the mid-1990s Brompton decided to introduce a new basic single-speed model, purchasing a batch of light and apparently serviceable rear hubs from Taiwan. Unfortunately, there were found to be problems with the freewheels during testing, and with demand for the 3- and 5-speed bikes rising all the time, the single-speed project was put on hold. It even appeared in the price lists in 1996 and 1997 as the C1 (Companion, single-speed) but was never actually made.

The gentle evolution continued in 1995, and again, some changes - like a lighter cartridge bottom bracket assembly, and lighter, stronger chrome-molybdenum front forks - were deliberate, while others were forced on the bike, as manufacturers and suppliers came and went.

The dynamo changed three or four times in this era, and continued to suffer from issues that were never really satisfactorily resolved. Dynamo seizures were relatively common, an issue eventually traced to the Brompton's folding action - in use, the dynamo bearing was shielded from rain and dust just as it would be on any other bike, but when the rear wheel was folded under the frame, water on the dynamo casing would run down into the bearing. Like most bicycle components, they were not designed to spend part of their lives upside down...

The handlebars were changed at this time too. For the first 18 months of production, Brompton had fitted bars produced by Chambers Churchill of Worcester. These had proved a bit frail and been replaced by larger diameter 15/16" bars made by GB Cycles.

Unusually in the folding bike world, Andrew was diligent about rig testing equipment to

British Standards, which laid down that components of this kind must withstand a certain number of flexures at a given loading, something that was easy to reproduce on a test rig running 24 hours a day to induce failure as rapidly as possible. The GB bars had passed the tests, but there had been a few failures since their introduction, so Andrew decided to test the Neobike bars. These were lighter, cheaper and stronger, and after passing British Standards, they were fitted to all bikes from mid-1995. It seemed to be a rare bonus from the collaboration with the Taiwanese, but history was to prove otherwise.

More Rivals Arrive

By late 1995, the price of the bikes had edged up to £378.35 - £534.63 (£656 - £927 in 2016), but the Brompton continued to sell well in an increasingly competitive market. This was a boom time for folding bikes, and the market was expanding rapidly, with nearly 60 individual machines on sale from 15 manufacturers. Some of these, like the Bickerton range, were the last stocks of time-expired designs, but there was much that was new. At the top end of the market, the Birdy from Germany and Bike Friday from the USA were making quite an impact. The Bike Friday, produced by GreenGear in Oregon, was designed for a rather different world. The company produced 20-inch wheel custom-made touring bikes (mostly fitted with 406mm wheels, but with a few 451mm) designed specifically for the

Whilst the Bike Friday was undoubtedly a quality machine, it was designed primarily for long distance air travellers, and could even be purchased with its own hardcase/trailer, into which it could be squeezed at the airport.

The Birdy appeared to be quite a threat to the Brompton, particularly the cheapest 'Red' variant shown here. However, cost was a big drawback, and although the bikes could be folded very fast in skilled hands, some people found them difficult to deal with on a daily basis.

© www.wiegold.de

US leisure market. Most Bike Fridays could, at a pinch, be 'quick folded' and carried by train, but they were really designed to be painstakingly dismantled and squeezed into a hardcase for carriage by air. These delightful racing bikes cost upwards of £1,000, and although Bike Friday also produced the 'budget' £695 Metro aimed more directly at rail and bus users, this didn't really hit the spot for European commuters. It was too cumbersome for regular folding, yet it lacked the custom fit and quality equipment that had become a Bike Friday trademark. In folding terms, the Birdy was a much more interesting prospect, and potentially a serious competitor. Developed in 1991 by Heiko Muller and Marcus Riese, two young German engineering students, the bikes had 18-inch (355mm) wheels, and folded in an asymmetrical manner. Rather than folding directly under the central frame tube, like the Brompton, the rear wheel came up alongside. The leading link front suspension then broke apart, allowing the front wheel to swing right around and pop up on the other side of the frame, rather like the early sketches for the Brompton.

This arrangement gave several advantages: with no mainframe hinge, the bike had a more rigid feel than the Brompton, it also had front and rear suspension, and most models came with derailleur gears, giving a wider gear range, and a slight efficiency advantage over the hub gears that were the norm on small wheelers.

When launched in 1995, the Birdy looked 'techy' and youthful, in contrast to the Brompton - which had not seen fundamental change for eight years and was beginning to look a bit middle-aged.

Unfortunately for Riese & Muller, there were problems. To keep the price down, the bike was built in Taiwan, but this Far Eastern manufacture meant compromises, particularly with weight, which emerged broadly similar to the Brompton, despite the use of aluminium alloy and some high-tech componentry.

In theory, 18-inch tyres were more efficient than the 16-inch (349mm) fitted to the Brompton, but the Brompton's tyres were nearer 17 inches in diameter in practice, and the range of tyres available in the (nominally larger) 18-inch size were pretty poor in the early days. Riese & Muller had designed the prototype around Dr. Moulton's excellent 17-inch tyre, which - rather confusingly - was a 369mm, so noticeably bigger than the 18-inch! They had only turned to the smaller 18-inch (355mm) tyres because the 369mm was made by just one manufacturer at the time, and was hard to find in Europe. With 369mm tyres it would have been a good bike, but it was to be some years before there were any really good tyres in the 355mm size and the Birdy was to be bugged by rapid tyre wear, poor handling and high rolling resistance. This was particularly unfortunate as it was a much sportier machine than the Brompton.

At this time, Brompton was still fitting the slothful (and historic) 55psi Raleigh Record tyre, inflated to 70psi to reduce rolling resistance to manageable levels! These too, occasionally failed, but by the mid-1990s lighter, freer-rolling tyres like the Primo Comet were being developed in the 349mm size, principally for the recumbent market, and these were just starting to arrive in the UK, giving the Brompton a real advantage for those willing to experiment.

The Birdy's derailleur gears gave problems too. If you didn't settle the bike into the right gear before folding it, the chain would come messily off as the rear wheel moved sideways. This didn't matter then or now to the dedicated enthusiasts, willing to take some care with folding, and often carrying a rubber glove for oily emergencies, but for everyday commuters, the finicky fold, reduced luggage options and lack of mudguards or fitted lights, made the Birdy less convenient.

Of course, for a younger, sportier market, such things as panniers, mudguards, hub gears and lights are positively negative attributes. The Birdy has always enjoyed a niche with this sort of user, but with prices ranging from £749 - £1,249 at the launch in 1995 (£1,299 - £2,170 at 2016 prices) it was never to gain widespread appeal.

At the cheaper end of the market, the Cresswell Micro and Fold-it looked quite a threat to Brompton for a brief period. These simple, straightforward machines were based on folding bikes designed by British engineer Peter Radnall in the 1970s. Both folded in half, the Micro around 16-inch wheels, and the Fold-it, which was originally designed to win the Post Office contract, around 20-inch wheels. Neither was successful in their original form, but in 1995, at the height of the folder boom, they were brought back into production by Richard Cresswell of Cresswell Cycles in Birmingham.

The Micro was a bit frail (shades of Bickerton here), but it was quite light, weighing only 9.5kg in basic single-speed trim. Both Cresswell bikes offered good value for money, the Micro being priced from £236 for the single-speed, to £299 for a 5-speed, while the larger Fold-it cost from £299 for a 3-speed to £378 for a SRAM 7-speed model - that's £409-£518 for the Micro and £518-£655 for the Fold-it at 2016 prices. This might not sound especially good value, but 'budget' folders in those days cost rather more than they do today.

Brompton, of course, had intended to respond to these cheaper bikes with the basic C1 model, which was to have been fitted with the single-speed hub and produced without mudguards as a cut-price leisure machine. Without the C-type, the cheapest Brompton was the L3, which now cost £378. For that price you could buy a Fold-it equipped with bigger wheels, a quality 7-speed hub gearbox, and drum brakes front and rear, but consumers weren't impressed.

The Micro sold in modest numbers to those looking for a cheap and cheerful occasional machine, but the Fold-it was a commercial failure. The bikes looked good on paper, and Richard Cresswell was an innovative hands-on engineer, but the Cresswell workshop was a chaotic place, and the bikes were relatively crude. Despite being a wobbly ride, and a bit frail, the Micro offered real advantages in certain markets, being much lighter than the Brompton, and folding almost as well. The Fold-it, on the other hand, was a big, clumsy beast. The ride was quite good, but the folded package was too cumbersome and heavy for regular commuting. It looked better value than the Brompton, but it was never a serious threat in practice.

Despite being given a thumbs down by the public, the Fold-it continued to be favourably reviewed, receiving the Gold Award for Best Cycle at the 1996 National Cycle Show. A few years later Cresswell Engineering was absorbed into the Pashley empire, and the Fold-it, and later the Micro, were dropped.

In 1996 the Fold-it won Best Bike at the National Cycle Show. Designer Richard Cresswell with the Fold-it (on lower stand) and Two's Company tandem (upper stand). The Fold-it offered value for money, but was never a great success.

The Micro sold in much bigger numbers. It was rather spindly and wobbly, but significantly cheaper and lighter than the Brompton.
This 3-speed model (right) is ridden by enthusiastic owner Dr. Graham Cooke.

Other manufacturers would try to tackle the Brompton's effortless dominance by going smaller - in some cases, much smaller. The MicroBike was a Swedish design, patented in 1986, with a clever hinge mechanism allowing it to fold into a narrow, if rather long package, the narrow width being helped by small 12½" (203mm) wheels. It was a light, intelligent design, but undergeared, and a bit unstable.

Twenty years later, in 2006, it was the turn of the French, with the Mobiky Genius. This used similar 12½" wheels, but folded concertina-style, with a double-reduction gear and 3-speed hub to give reasonably conventional gearing. It looked smart and effective, and it rode surprisingly well, but the figures just couldn't stack up against the Brompton: the Mobiky produced a bigger folded package, it was heavier, slower on the road, and more expensive.

Meanwhile, Sir Clive Sinclair had become obsessed with the folding bike problem, but his fixation with ultra-small wheels was to be his downfall. Working with Mark Sanders of Strida fame, Sir Clive produced a prototype X-bike in 1990, with 8-inch wheels and a simple frame that hinged like a pair of scissors from an 'X' shape to a long thin package. This machine failed to make it into production, but 16 years later Sir Clive did launch the A-bike - an 'A' shaped bicycle that concertinaed rather like the Mobiky. The A-bike was strikingly compact (less than half the volume of the Brompton) and light (more or less half the weight), but there were some fatal flaws. The 6-inch tyres, wobbly frame and single 41-inch gear made it almost unrideable on normal roads. The wheel size was later increased to 8-inches, which improved the rideability a little, but made the folded package bigger. A reasonable number seem to have been sold, but mainly to enthusiasts and collectors of folding ephemera.

Increasingly, the real challenge was coming from Dahon, now starting to find its feet in the UK under Mark Bickerton's guidance. Dahon bikes were still a bit cheap and cheerful, starting with some rather basic 16-inch (305mm) machines in the £200-£300 region. But Dr. Hon was beginning to realise that Brompton had this compact market pretty well sewn up, and Dahon gradually extended its range to include 20-inch and 26-inch bikes, the 20-inch models in particular selling well. One of the best from this era was the Dahon Tailwind. It wasn't particularly compact or light, but it rode well, undercut the Brompton by £20 and ticked most of the purchasing boxes for most people. Increasingly wily at marketing folding bikes, Dahon found that it could prolong the life of long-in-the-tooth models by 'badge-engineering' them. In 1996, Dahon was still only experimenting with this policy, but within a few years, half the folding bikes on sale in the world would be either Dahons, Dahon clones, or outdated variants badged as something else. When Dahon had finished with it, the Tailwind went on to bear a Ridgeback label, and was replaced in 2000 by a whole range of new Dahon 20-inch bikes, including the £299 Boardwalk, another serious Brompton competitor.

Change at the Top

But the 20-inch-wheeled Dahon revolution was still some years off. In 1996, most of the competition was heavy, difficult to ride or both, and even the bikes that undercut the Brompton didn't do so by very much. There was plenty of competition, but none of it was especially good, and for long periods at this time, Brompton's Chiswick Park factory was swamped under a torrent of orders. During these all too frequent production famines, when waiting lists grew too long, output of bikes was rationed. Output had recovered rapidly after

Sir Clive Sinclair had become obsessed with folding bikes, producing the A-bike in 2006. It was light and compact but almost unrideable, and thus little more than a curiosity as a transport machine.

the move to the Chiswick factory, climbing to 3,363 in 1995-96, and 5,196 in 1996-97, but for various reasons it then stalled. Brompton now had more than 80 dealers in the UK alone, and as panic grew about waiting lists and shortages, customers were ringing around looking for a bike - any bike - as long as it was a Brompton.

This panic buying caused a lot of trouble for Nicola McGregor's small sales team, still under instructions to look after the dealers which had shown faith when the Brompton was an unknown quantity, but under daily assault from bigger dealers and chainstores, a handful of whom could have taken the entire factory output, and they knew it.

The export market alone could have absorbed most of the factory's output at this time. In 1997, the ADFC (the Allgemeiner Deutscher Fahrrad-Club, similar to the British Cyclists Touring Club) gave the Brompton its Bike of the Year Award. It was, of course, a great honour, but the award put yet more upward pressure on sales at a difficult time.

Just five years earlier, Andrew Ritchie had likened the Chiswick factory to an empty cathedral. Now it was full and overflowing, and the only easy way to increase production was to move again, to bigger premises. In October 1998, Brompton moved back west, to an anonymous factory in Brentford beside the elevated section of the M4 motorway. With the Neobike affair still ongoing, the factory move finally brought an end to discussions about overseas assembly. In the short-term, the move caused considerable disruption, and annual production was to languish in the 6,000 to 7,000 region until the latter half of 2000, when output began to climb again, only to be knocked back by outside events.

Despite selling every bike it could produce, Brompton was starting to lose the technological race. In some ways the company had been the victim of its own success. The factory had been running to catch up for so many years that changes in the market had passed it by. In some ways the company had been the victim of its own success. The factory had been running to catch up for so many years that changes in the market seemed to have passed it by.

Enthusiasts had been fitting better quality brakes and tyres for several years, and the general feeling was that the factory neither knew nor cared about developing the product. This sort of talk was anathema to Julian Vereker, the instinctive marketing man, who had overseen the company's growth from the sidelines to a position of real strength, and was now pressing Andrew to pass at least some control to a younger management team.

Very gradually, the harmonious relationship between Ritchie and Vereker began to fracture, and Julian - who had always preferred fresh challenges to old arguments - began to spend more time developing his other businesses. He had supported Andrew Ritchie through all sorts of difficulties, and had backed him at crucial, and often lively, shareholder meetings. Now he was frustrated that the company was not developing as it might, and as a minority shareholder, he had no power to influence events, other than by persuasion.

During 1998 he was also becoming increasingly ill. When finally he was diagnosed with terminal cancer, Julian calmly decided to put his remaining energy into his core business, rearranging Naim Audio's affairs, to ensure that his widow would be secure, and the jobs of his employees safe, after his death.

With quite a large sum tied up in Brompton, and no further interest in playing a role, Julian asked Andrew to buy him out in May 1999, a request that would involve some complicated financial juggling. Under the circumstances, it's perhaps not surprising that the relationship between the two men was put under some strain, with Vereker refusing to return Andrew's calls at one stage.

As so often in the Brompton story, the answer lay in choosing the right person, and Andrew did exactly that, calling his old friend Tim Guinness. Since politely refusing the offer to invest in Brompton 23 years before, Guinness had gone on to do very well for himself in the financial world. In 18 years, his asset management business had grown from 20 employees to 350. Originally a subsidiary of a small merchant bank, the business had just been sold to Investec, a South African bank, and although he was still busy tidying up loose ends, Guinness was already looking for a new challenge. Initially, he had no intention of getting closely involved with Brompton, but he agreed to help out his friend by overseeing the delicate negotiations over Julian's departure. With a legal requirement for two directors, he also agreed to take Julian's place, but with no plans to make this a long-term commitment.

Tim Guinness was the perfect man for the job. He had a light, breezy manner that belied an incisive financial mind, and he quickly agreed terms on which Brompton would buy back Julian's 14,000 shares (an 18% shareholding) for £301,000. It was a considerable sum, reducing the company's assets by a quarter, but the company could now afford it, and it served to reduce the number of shares in circulation, to the benefit of the remaining shareholders.

By the turn of the millennium, everything was in place, and in November 1999, Andrew sent a memo to the shareholders:

"Following Julian's departure, I will be seeking the appointment of new directors, ideally with the skills needed to develop the business. Tim Guinness is assisting with this and he has agreed to join the board, with the main aim of assembling this team, and possibly remaining long-term himself. I will be able to outline progress in more detail at the AGM."

All went smoothly at the shareholder's meeting, the arrival of Tim Guinness clearly being seen as something of a coup for a small West London engineering works, and Tim Guinness duly joined Andrew Ritchie as a director. Andrew then asked Tim to become chairman. Initially, he refused, suggesting instead Christopher Stewart-Smith, a businessman involved in the computer software industry. In the event, Stewart-Smith joined the board, but in an unusual reverse coup, agreed with Andrew that Tim Guinness was the best man for the chairmanship! In January 2000, Julian Vereker died. He had not neglected his yacht business, and the computer-aided Wind-Express 48 was launched the same day. Vereker will be remembered by a great many people for a great many things, but his financial know-how and steady managerial hand had been essential elements in the Brompton story.

Brompton Mark 3

Despite pressure from Julian Vereker and a few shareholders, Ritchie had refused to relax his control of Brompton in the late 1990s, but this wasn't entirely a matter of stubbornness. As an engineer, he knew what needed to be done, and with the company settled in the bigger premises, and a competent management team keeping the lid on day-to-day decisions, he embarked on the biggest redesign of the Brompton since the launch of the Mark 2 in 1988.

The Mark 3, rolled out from March 2000, was a tremendous advance, and it effectively silenced the critics. Behind the scenes, the factory had looked closely at every element of the bike. The Mark 3 looked almost identical to its predecessor, but nearly every component was different beneath the skin (see the summary on page 77). With surplus capacity at last, the 'C' type was resurrected, partly as a way of using up stocks of Mark 2 components. For the time being at least, the C-type would only be sold as the C3, fitted with the 3-speed Sturmey-Archer hub gear, for £353, almost £100 less than the much improved L3.

The Mark 3 had its own Brompton-branded tyre, based on the Primo racing technology that owners had been fitting for several years. Andrew Ritchie had never designed a tyre, but with a mixture of engineering guile and dead reckoning, he seems to have done an excellent job. It rolled markedly better than the Raleigh Record, lasted for a considerable mileage, and it was lighter. The tyre was, however, criticised for a degree of waywardness on white lines and drain covers, particularly in the wet, although most owners were delighted with the easier pedalling, and it soon became one of the most popular retro-fit accessories, finding its way onto Moultons and Micros too. From being close to death, the 37-349mm tyre now seemed to be guaranteed a bright future, and in the years that followed, other manufacturers released tyres in this size, although to date none has quite matched the Brompton tyre's broad appeal.

Some of the changes, like a rear mudflap, might seem insignificant, but they were important. For years, owners had grumbled about the 'Brompton stripe' - a thin stain of mud thrown onto the rider's back by the rear tyre. Because of the way the bike folded, it wasn't possible to fit a conventional mudflap, but the Mark 3 had a small, tough flap that worked almost as well. Other changes were cosmetic, such as stainless steel spokes and fittings, but they were things the public had been requesting for years.

Like the tyres, braking had long been an issue, and again, the factory adapted the aftermarket accessories that had become popular with enthusiasts, settling on a much more powerful dual-pivot caliper design, again reworked especially for the bike, and matched with new shorter brake levers.

Elsewhere, the front end had been beefed up yet again, this time with stronger German-made handlebars, and the folding left-hand pedal - formerly an accessory - had become a standard fitting. The list of components went on and on. New suede-effect handlebar grips were lighter and more comfortable, and there was an improved pump that actually worked when you needed it. Lighting had been completely reworked, with halogen front lamp and Basta LED rear light on the 'T' type, and a similar battery-operated rear light on the 'L' allied to a rather dubious battery front lamp. Not perfect, but as there had previously been no battery lamp option, it was a huge advance.

Most of the changes added a little weight, but the Primo-style tyres were lighter, making the machines slightly lighter overall. The feeling was of a much stiffer, livelier bike, faster in a straight line, and - thanks to the lighter wheels - quicker to respond in fast turns as well. Just to demonstrate that Andrew Ritchie had finally relaxed his autocratic style and taken on board the desires of his customers, the gearing on the 5-speed had been reduced, keeping a practical top gear, but giving better hill climbing. And the colour range had finally been extended too. Green had been a popular option for some time, but it now became a standard colour, and the other recent options of yellow, ivory and blue had been extended to include aquamarine, and reduced in price. For an extra £30, you could have a rather flash silver.

In the greater scheme of things, the Mark 3 Brompton was a relatively insignificant engineering project, but it was big news in the folding bike world. Ritchie had demonstrated that his engineer-led management style could respond to customer demand in a positive and technology-led manner. In this respect, it was a considerable tour de force.

Brompton's bulging order book and relative lack of development had resulted in a flurry of investment by other folding bike companies. The Cambridge based Airnimal - a sporty long distance tourer designed to compete with the Bike Friday rather than the Brompton's

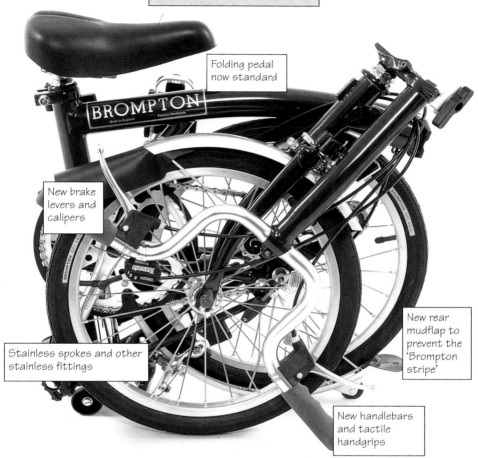

Folding pedal now standard

New brake levers and calipers

New rear mudflap to prevent the 'Brompton stripe'

Stainless spokes and other stainless fittings

New handlebars and tactile handgrips

Brompton own-brand tyres. Designed by Andrew Ritchie. A yellow band means 'normal' and a green band means kevlar puncture proofing.

The Mark 3 looked similar to the Mark 2, but was completely revised. A year later, Brompton was forced to drop the Sturmey-Archer 3- and 5- speed hub gears. This very typical green L3 is fitted with the post April 2001 SRAM 3-speed hub and gear shifter (left).

The bikes were also fitted with an improved pump, and at long last there was a battery lighting option for the 'L' type.

speedier, easier fold - had a low key launch in 1998, but by 2000 was gaining popularity with good reviews, especially from 'serious' road riders.

Also in 2000, the Airframe was back on the road to production, the Strida 2 had already been on sale for a year or so, Birdy and Bike Friday were making top-end inroads, and Dahon was expanding in all directions. If Brompton had not introduced the Mark 3 when it did, the bike would have drifted into a genteel middle-age, appealing to a diminishing pool of older enthusiasts. The unexpected revamp knocked the opposition right off its feet, and re-established the Brompton brand at the top of the pile.

By 2000 the Cambridge-based Airnimal was gaining popularity with good reviews. As a 'suitcase' folder it never competed head on with the Brompton.

Despite this success, there were boardroom battles over marketing. Sooner or later Andrew Ritchie was going to retire, and before this could happen a satisfactory succession would have to be arranged, both on the engineering and marketing side. Andrew Ritchie, with characteristic caution and thoroughness, wanted the right people in place, but this was proving difficult, especially on the marketing side. Tim Guinness had already concluded that the company needed a marketing manager, and an engineering / production manager, as a matter of urgency. One immediate change was the employment of Bubblegate, a design company based in Kent, to oversee Brompton's advertising and publicity material, its first rather thankless role being to produce a brochure for the Mark 3.

Ritchie had introduced a superior bike, agreed to compromise on colours, and even listened to his customers, but he continued to resist attempts to 'market' the bike with lifestyle images and trendy rather than truthful words and phrases. After a great deal of time, effort, and hair tearing by creatives, Bubblegate triumphantly unveiled a new brochure some months after the arrival of the bike. It contained a modest number of tasteful images of young, and young-at-heart users, plus a good meaty technical section. Once again, a compromise had been reached.

Another 21st century folder was the Skoot (left and below). Designed and built in Britain in 2001, it cost £1,000, weighed 15.8kg and had a single 55-inch gear. Folded volume was about the same as the Brompton, but in every other respect it was comprehensively outclassed. Within a year it had gone.

Against the Skoot, the Brompton Mark 3 looked pretty conservative, but where the Skoot failed, the Brompton continued to sell in even greater numbers.

It might have looked conservative, but the Mark 3 had incorporated lots of new technology, keeping it ahead in terms of ride quality and foldability.

The Modern Era The Mark 4 bikes were a triumph of lightweight engineering, and marketing too.

The Modern Era
2000-2011

"*So far we don't know whether the marketing is successful, because the bike's selling itself. We can't produce enough.*" TIM GUINNESS

"*The message is that we've taken a decision to grow and become a competitive global player. We're proud to be a British company, and determined to remain independent.*" WILL BUTLER-ADAMS

Bar Problems Sorted

The road to mass production can be long, hard and strewn with unexpected obstacles. In 2000, Brompton seemed to be safely established, with a new factory, big enough to accommodate foreseeable growth, a new chairman, and a highly respected and reasonably profitable product, recently revamped in Mark 3 form to good reviews. But during the following two years, Brompton was to be rocked by a couple of serious incidents. Neither put the company in jeopardy - it was now much too well established for that - but such incidents demonstrate the importance of double and quadruple checking the supply chain and reliability of third party components.

The first problem came out of the blue. We've already seen how Brompton had found it necessary to change handlebars several times. The handlebars - and particularly the point where the bars meet the stem - are a highly stressed and vulnerable area. And failure can have serious, and potentially fatal, consequences.

Most cycle manufacturers have had some sort of trouble with handlebars, and it's no surprise. If they're made of steel and clamped to the stem, there's not much that can go wrong, but steel is heavy, so handlebars are usually made of lighter, but more vulnerable, aluminium. Whatever the material, welds or brazing in this area will tend to weaken the bars (this was the weakness with the early steel Brompton handlebars), and if clamped to the stem, aluminium in particular has a tendency to scoring and scratching inside the clamp, especially if the bars are twisted. A scratch here is invisible but under constant stress, and if it fails, the bars can simply fall into two halves.

Even without stress gatherers like scratches and welds, all handlebars have a finite fatigue life, and the trick for a manufacturer is to use enough material to give a reasonable life without adding too much weight or price - a very tricky equation when there is so much at stake.

Andrew Ritchie had used steel bars on the prototypes, but these were replaced with aluminium for the production bikes. The first aluminium bars were replaced by a stronger design from GB Cycles after about 18 months, and these in turn had been replaced by the Neobike bars in mid-1995. There had been only a handful of failures with the earlier designs, but the upgrades had seemed worthwhile. In the late 1990s, a small number of Neobike bars began to fail, and it was decided to cure the problem once and for all by upgrading to a thicker, heavier and better quality handlebar produced by Humpert of Germany. This was introduced in September 1999 and brought an end to the problem. But what of the tens of thousands of older bikes in service?

On top of the low background failure rate of the older bars, it gradually became clear that an increasing number of the Neobike bars were failing, and the company started to watch the statistics with growing unease. It looked as though the handlebars - superficially well up to British Standards - were failing early through fatigue. But would this problem affect every single bar, or was it just a small batch? Were there geographical or chronological factors involved? There didn't seem to be, but the failures kept increasing.

In 2000, the rate of failures reached 0.4%, high enough to trigger action. Rather than recall every bike for the dealer to fit new bars (and possibly cause more damage in the process), it was decided to manufacture a brace and distribute these free to distributors and dealers and thus to owners worldwide. The brace clamped around the vertical parts of the handlebars, which had the effect of reducing the bending stress at the root of the bar, and in the event of a failure, keeping the two halves in place, enabling the bike to be brought to a stop safely.

It was a classically meticulously engineered little device, and once the bracing kits had been publicised and several thousand distributed and fitted, the rate of failures dropped dramatically, proving that the brace was a very effective remedy. It was also made available for £8.75 to owners of newer bikes who expected to ride hard.

The affair highlighted a growing problem for the Brompton. Designed as a commuting tool, the bike had proved able to perform all sorts of niche functions for which it wasn't intended, such as surveying, loaded touring and many other high-stress applications. Under the circumstances, Brompton seem to have got off quite lightly with the failure of a handful of frames and a larger number of handlebars. The crossbar braces have found all sorts of uses since, principally as a handhold when carrying children, another activity for which the Brompton really wasn't designed!

Photo by Paul Bader

The Brompton has been used for many expeditions including map surveying in the Himalayas, accompanying scientists to the South Pole (see inside back cover) and for trips through underdeveloped countries. Above left: Ishmahil Blagrove riding a Brompton through Cambodia in the mid-1990s. Above right: Adam Hart-Davis took his Brompton to various exotic locations in the 1990s, including the top of Mount Etna. Despite such varied and exacting use the handlebar issue has been the only significant concern over the bike's construction and safety. See page 162 for a photo of the brace issued to remedy the problem.

Dodgy Dealings

The other big problem started to develop at about the same time, and although it didn't involve safety issues, it very nearly stopped production of the Brompton altogether. Sturmey-Archer geared hubs had been manufactured in Nottingham for almost a hundred years and the hub was an integral component in the Brompton design. There were two other manufacturers of 3-speed hubs in the world - SRAM (formerly Sachs) in Germany, and Shimano in Japan - but neither was ideal for the Brompton. The SRAM was heavier and more expensive, while Shimano's Nexus hub was too wide, and fitted with a roller brake. This could be resolved, given time, but re-engineering the Brompton to accept either hub wasn't an easy option. And both involved the complication and expense of importing heavy components, whereas stock from Nottingham could be brought down the M1 in a few hours.

With the 5-speed hub, there really was no alternative source of supply. SRAM produced the only other 5-speed, but it was significantly wider and, like its 3-speed counterpart, heavier and more expensive than the Sturmey hub.

None of this seemed to matter in late 1999, because it was inconceivable that Sturmey would fail. The company wasn't very profitable, but it was part of the much larger Raleigh Group, which itself was backed by the giant Derby Cycle Corporation, a multinational based in the USA. Sturmey enjoyed a niche market, and after some uncertain decades as hub gears declined in popularity, sales had stabilized, and were now particularly strong in the large and reliable Netherlands market. The company had a full order book, and a healthy turnover in 1999 of some £12 million.

As late as September 1999 Sturmey had introduced a new variant of the 5-speed hub, the 'ball-locking' system, and Brompton, like many other end users, had no reason to imagine that supply problems were even on the horizon. But Derby Cycles was engaging in one of those periodic navel-gazing exercises which multinationals tend to perform once in a while, and a rather inexperienced US management team had reached the conclusion that Sturmey-Archer's eclectic output of hub gears, spokes, leather saddles (under the Brooks brand), and small components for the automotive industry didn't fit well with its global ambitions.

Consequently, the Sturmey-Archer and Raleigh factory sites were sold for a reported £4 million to the University of Nottingham, the aim being to relocate and downsize the bicycle business and sell Sturmey-Archer. Raleigh was primarily an assembly operation by this time, so relocation would be easy.

Sturmey-Archer was another matter. At first the Sturmey management was optimistic. The company would be sold, and a new owner would mean a new factory, new equipment, and hopefully the capital to invest in new products. It had several multi-speed designs on the drawing board at the time, and a considerable amount of engineering expertise, plus patents and drawings dating back over many decades. As a major customer, Brompton was kept informed, but had been assured that the change of ownership and subsequent factory move would have little or no effect on hub production.

On 30th June 2000 Sturmey-Archer was sold for a reported £3 million to a hitherto unknown investment group called Lenark, but the deal was not quite what it seemed. Quite how and why a respectable company like Derby - that relied on Sturmey-Archer's parts to support its other brands - had allowed one of its subsidiaries to be sold to an insalubrious, almost penniless outfit, then only two years old, is a great unanswered question.

It later transpired that one of Lenark's principals, one Simon Allso, was a recently discharged bankrupt with a criminal record for fraud. Derby had actually been paid the princely sum of £30 (about the price of a 3-speed hub!) for Sturmey-Archer after Lenark agreed to take responsibility for a redundancy bill of nearly £3 million.

In fact, Lenark was no more than a shell. Despite protestations to the contrary, the company had no intention of paying redundancies, building bicycle hubs, or anything else, other than getting its hands on Sturmey-Archer's assets, which amounted to some £300,000 in cash at the time of the transfer.

Matters came to a head on 11th September 2000 when the Sturmey MD Colin Bateman presented the Lenark directors with a £75,000 bill to cover the early stages of moving the factory and purchasing new machinery, and the Lenark people subsequently went to ground, Lenark director Clive Walton allegedly making a clandestine exit from the building via the fire escape.

In the next few days, the scale of the financial collapse became apparent - Sturmey-Archer was effectively bankrupt. On 15th September, Bateman brought together his 260 staff and told them that not only had their jobs evaporated overnight, but production was at an end, and there was no prospect of even paying the current wages bill, let alone redundancy payments. Lenark continued to drain the company's reserves until the bank accounts were frozen a few days later, but despite attempts to sell the factory, and an undertaking by Nottingham City Council to underwrite the cost of the move, no buyer was subsequently found for the business. Brompton actually gave serious thought to buying Sturmey-Archer itself, but for such a small company the financial and logistical nightmare of finding premises, and re-establishing a much bigger company some 200 miles north of its London base, proved just too big a risk.

While the receivers continued to search for a buyer, a skeleton staff of volunteers were winding down production at Sturmey-Archer. One morning, Andrew Ritchie received a call from Nick Sanders of Sturmey: if he could get up to Nottingham quickly with a van, he could 'liberate' stock before the whole operation collapsed. Brompton always kept a good stock of hubs to cover production irregularities, but an extra van load was a priceless offer. Ritchie headed north, and came away with 1,100 hubs, mostly 3-speed, and delivered them to Mike Hesson, Brompton's long-term wheel-builder in nearby Wolverhampton:

"It was a really helpful gesture on Nick's part. The van was well overloaded with all that weight, but we now had an extra six weeks supply, and enough hubs to keep production going for just over six months."

It wasn't much, but it gave a vital breathing space to negotiate a price for a slightly customized hub gear from SRAM and re-engineer the Brompton to accept the SRAM 3-speed. But there was no chance of replacing the 5-speed, and when stocks of hubs were exhausted, the model was deleted, never - as it transpired - to return.

In April 2001, the first consignment of SRAM hubs arrived, but it had been a damn close run thing: the factory had only two days' supply of Sturmey hubs left in stock. Any further delay would have meant redundancies at Brompton.

The only positive fall-out from the Sturmey-Archer affair was that Andrew had also 'liberated' Steve Rickels, Sturmey's chief designer, to help share the design workload at Brompton. Rickels' first role was to assist in the design of a very Bromptonesque replacement for the 5-speed.

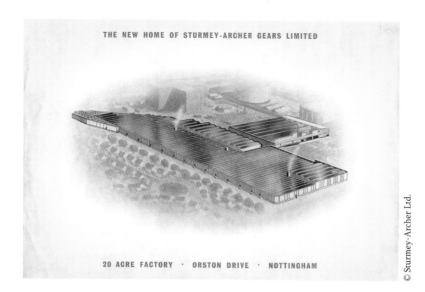

THE NEW HOME OF STURMEY-ARCHER GEARS LIMITED

20 ACRE FACTORY · ORSTON DRIVE · NOTTINGHAM

© Sturmey-Archer Ltd.

Raleigh's Nottingham factory and its Sturmey-Archer sister plant, pictured here when it opened in 1954, once employed thousands. All this came to an end in 2001, when a planned move to a new Nottingham site was fatally mishandled. Production subsequently moved to Taiwan, but the affair was very nearly disastrous for Brompton.

The shot below was taken in 2003 and shows all that was left of the once-mighty Raleigh works.

© Paul Lenton

85

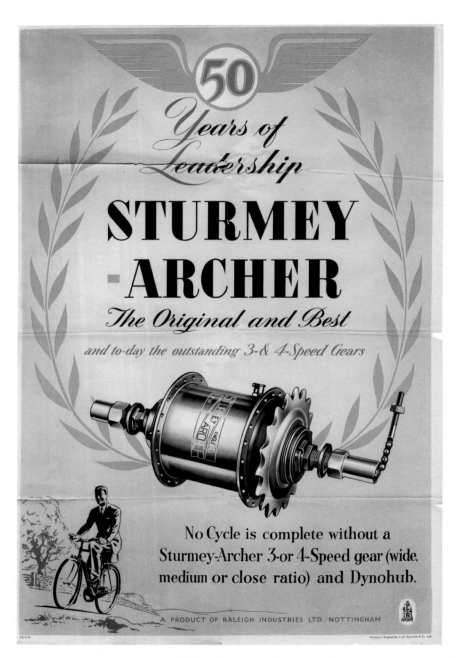

At the height of its success in the early 1950s Sturmey-Archer hub production reached over 2 million units a year. As this 50th anniversary poster from 1952 states, hubs came not only in 3- and 4-speed variants, but in a variety of gear ranges. More than half a century later, in 2009, Sturmey would collaborate with Brompton to produce an ultra-wide ratio hub, the Brompton Wide Ratio (BWR).

The Six-speed Emerges

Ritchie and his team had decided to put a 2-speed derailleur on the nose of a 3-speed hub, producing a 6-speed bike, and this was one reason SRAM had been asked to produce a custom hub.

This arrangement would have several advantages and several disadvantages. The gear range (the difference between the lowest and highest gears) would be a little narrower than the former 5-speed hub, but without the inherent inefficiency of the 5-speed's wide-ratio gears, this wouldn't be a great issue. Perhaps more of a problem was that there would now be two gear triggers, something that users had found so confusing on the original 5-speed. There would be a slight weight penalty too, but some intriguing prospects for saving weight on certain models, because the 2-speed derailleur could be fitted without a hub gear to a future lightweight version of the bike. This was uncharted territory for Brompton. The company would have to design a complex and unique derailleur assembly, plus a new derailleur trigger, again quite unlike anything else, and the systems would have to be prototyped, tested and put into production as soon as possible, because the lack of a multi-gear bike was losing customers and hitting the profitability of the bikes that were being sold. Design and testing of the 6-speed Brompton took exactly a year, and in April 2002, the new system was introduced. As always, it was carefully thought through and meticulously engineered. The Brompton had always been fitted with a chain tensioner to take up the slack in the chain when the bike was folded, effectively packing the chain away when out of use. In a bit of classic Andrew Ritchie ingenuity, the tensioner now performed a second role, keeping the chain correctly tensioned as the rider changed between the two derailleur gears. Technically, it was quite interesting. The derailleur idler wheels were allowed to 'float' on their mounting bolts to align with either of the two sprockets fixed to the input 'driver' of the hub gear. Derailleur changes were accomplished with a little shifter that pushed the chain one way or the other, and was controlled by a second lever on the handlebars.

With only two sprockets to worry about, the usual derailleur adjustment and indexing problems did not apply. The lever was cleverly spring-loaded in both directions, with enough spare movement to allow for cable stretch and wear. This two-way spring-loading meant that the shifter could be moved without damage when the bike was stationary, just like a hub gear shifter (important because the other lever still did control a hub gearbox) and once set up, the device was pretty tolerant to wear and tear, enabling it to keep working for some time before requiring adjustment.

The new 6-speed was technically clever - the chain tensioner, already fitted to the bike, doubled as a derailleur, the idler wheels floating on their mounting bolts, allowing the chain to move between two rear sprockets. Like all early 6-speeds, this example is fitted to a SRAM hub.

Testing and early production threw up a few technical issues. Situated low down next to the rear wheel, the shifter was rather vulnerable to mud and water, causing the tiny ball bearing inside to seize. It was soon replaced by a cruder and less delicate plain bearing, and in most other respects the system worked well. The gear range wasn't very wide, but it was adequate, and in marketing terms, it gave Brompton back its top end model.

When introduced in April 2002, the 6-speed sold for £524 in basic 'L' form, or £626 as a 'T' type; a premium of £65 over the 3-speed models, something of a bargain considering that two years before, the less sophisticated 5-speed had sold for a premium of £74 over the 3-speed. Despite some 6% inflation over those two years, the new bikes were only £10 or so more expensive than their 5-speed predecessors, a distinct cut in real terms that helped to get sales moving again after the long hiatus.

Sturmey-Archer had not actually died back in the autumn of 2000. The Brooks saddle business had been bought by its own management before being sold to Selle Royal of Italy, and in December 2000, just as the Sturmey assets were about to be liquidated, it was announced that the hub gear business had been bought for £750,000 by Sunrace of Taiwan. Consequently some twenty container-loads of equipment were shipped to Taiwan, together with three former employees. Alan Clarke, a Sturmey-Archer manager of 31 years standing, became general manager of the European arm, Sunrace Sturmey-Archer Europe BV, based in its core market, the Netherlands.

Production in Taiwan took much longer to build up than had been hoped, and it was not until June 2001 that the first 3-speed hubs reached Europe. Ironically enough the order was destined for Raleigh, arriving just as the Sturmey factory was finally being demolished!

By this time, Gary Matthews, the Derby chief executive who instigated the Sturmey-Archer debacle had gone, and within a few months, Derby itself had imploded, although most of the bicycle manufacturing businesses survived intact.

For Brompton, the resumption of Sturmey output from Taiwan brought a sigh of relief. At long last Brompton had two potential suppliers, and although the company did not immediately revert to using Sturmey hubs, the rear frames were adapted to enable either hub to be fitted.

Evolution and the Mark 4

The Sturmey affair had caused two years of uncertainty, and more or less stalled other engineering developments at Brompton. Almost unnoticed back in June 2000, the handlebar stem hinge had changed in shape. This change meant little to the average purchaser, but to Brompton it was a very big deal indeed. The change, from a forged to cast hinge assembly, was the first step in a scheme to automate some of the frame brazing. This programme had been held up during the Sturmey problems, but would soon be back on track.

Several minor changes were introduced during 2002 and 2003 - a new moulded nylon hook to 'catch' the front wheel when the bike was folded, a new seat pillar frame bush, and a thinner chainring to suit the two different widths of chain used on the derailleur and non-derailleur models. Later, the dynamo was replaced yet again, with a better Axa design, and a new handlebar catch introduced, finally laying to rest one of the longest-running grumbles from users that the bars would occasionally fly out from the folded package. A new, lighter front bag carrier frame was also introduced.

One of the technical difficulties unique to the Brompton was water ingress into the brake cables. Like the dynamos, these were affected by rain. Both brake cables pointed upwards when the bike was being ridden, and ingress of water was made worse because the small wheels put the brake calipers much closer to the ground than would normally be the case. The rear cable also had to contend with being flipped over and coiled when folded. Regular commuters rode home in the rain, folded their bikes, and left them in a warm hallway where the water would work its way down inside the cable, causing premature seizure, reducing the already weak brake performance. This was solved by fitting little rubber gaiters between the cable and caliper.

In 2002, Tim Guinness introduced two characters to the Brompton story who were to play key roles in the evolution of the bike in the modern era. First to arrive was a young engineer named Will Butler-Adams, who - for the time being - slotted quietly into the engineering team. The other was Edward Donald, a young marketing man who had worked for some of the big brands and seemed to offer a very clear vision of the way he wanted to carry Brompton forward. One of his first decisions was to put time and resources into the American market. Since 1995 sales in America had been handled in a gentlemanly and relaxed style by Channell Wasson, a laconic real estate agent, working out of Palo Alto, California.

Ed Donald decided to shift US sales up a gear by exhibiting the Brompton at the annual Interbike show in Las Vegas and building up a country-wide dealer network. At first, the US bike shop owners were bemused by the little European bike, but the policy gradually paid off, and sales began to build.

Meanwhile, Donald turned his attention to Japan. Japanese company Mizutani had been selling the Neobike Brompton for several years, but supplies had been cut off in 2001 when the agreement between Brompton and Neobike was wound up. From 2002 Mizutani had been forced to place orders for the British bikes, which travelled via Mitsubishi London and Mitsubishi Tokyo, a tortuous and expensive route. The price had rocketed overnight, causing sales to slump by 90% to 200 a year. This could all be sorted, of course, and Japan remained a territory ripe for exploitation, but with bikes in short supply there was little point in investing time and money in streamlining deliveries, cutting costs and increasing sales, in Japan or anywhere else.

For Edward Donald, marketing the Brompton was proving a frustrating process. He could see numerous opportunities, but limitations on the production side made them impossible to exploit. When he had arrived, in July 2002, the company had been selling 8,000 bikes a year, but with the clearing of the Sturmey log-jam, and launch of the 6-speed, demand began to outstrip supply, despite record growth in output.

The following year (2004) saw a small change that heralded a major revision that would culminate in the Mark 4 Brompton the following year. As part of the ongoing project to automate some of the frame brazing, the mainframe hinge had received the same treatment as the handlebar stem two years before. But this time, some subtle juggling of the geometry had resulted in a 3cm longer mainframe. An increase in the wheelbase from 102cm to 105cm sounded pretty minor stuff, but it resulted in a surprising amount of extra room for taller riders, and gave the bike a noticeably more 'grown-up' look, all for no penalty in terms of folded size.

When it arrived in early 2005, the Mark 4 effectively brought the bike into the modern era, and although there were many innovations, the revamp was also interesting for the increased emphasis on marketing, suggesting that Andrew Ritchie was at last loosening the reins and passing control to his younger team. The new brochure was relatively short on technical information, but full of big, colourful lifestyle shots of pretty young things fooling about on a Mediterranean photoshoot. The overall feel was slick and smart, and once again in tune with the times. Rather than the take-it-or-leave-it Stalinist output of the early factory, the customer was now in charge, and free to order from an impressive range of accessories, specs and colours, including a vaguely grungy 'raw lacquer' finish - basically a coating of clear powder rather than pigment, that exposed the underlying brazes and cosmetic tube imperfections. The list of options was now so large that Brompton was able to boast that each bike was effectively custom-built, something that could never be emulated by the likes of Dahon, building millions of identical bikes 5,000 miles away.

From 2005, the long-standing model designations - T, L or C, followed by the number of gears - changed to a more complex system. The first letter now denoted the type of handlebars, of which there were three designs: 'M' for the traditional 'violin case' bars, 'S' for a new lower straight bar, and 'P' for an extraordinary touring bar, designed to give a choice of riding positions. The only exception to the handlebar nomenclature was the 'C' type, which had become the C3E.

As before, the number related to the number of gears, but the last letter now denoted the model type: 'E' (Excluding mudguards) being the basically equipped 'C' type, 'L' still meant Lightweight, and the former 'T' had become a more logical 'R', denoting a machine with a rack.

For older and more conservative customers looking for basic models, little had changed apart from the model numbers, and a few pounds here or there on or off the price. The C3 had become the C3E at £380, the L3 the M3L at £480 and the T6 the M6R-PLUS at £635. But thereafter, the range of bikes, options and accessories was almost unrecognizable.

New parts were relatively few. New reach-adjustable brake levers, a lightweight fi'zi:k saddle, and a clever Pentaclip saddle adjuster designed by Steve Rickels and Andrew Ritchie. All these parts were introduced on the more expensive models, but the Pentaclip was later to migrate across the range. The most obvious change was that the Sturmey-Archer 3-speed hub was back, and with Steve Rickels on board, and the bigger buying power that comes from increased sales, Brompton was able to work with Sturmey to produce a Brompton-specific 3-speed hub - the BSR, or Brompton Standard Ratio. For the time being, the SRAM hub continued to be fitted to the 6-speed models, but the new rear frame meant that either hub could be used.

After the false start in 1996, Brompton had finally designed its own single-speed hub, and this could also be fitted with the derailleur from the 6-speed to give a 2-speed option, both these derivatives being light and cheap for the yachting and leisure markets.

But the real changes were reserved for the top end, where a number of titanium parts had been introduced. Having learnt a hard lesson with the Sturmey debacle, this time Brompton took care to source the titanium from two completely different factories - one in Russia and the other in China!

A titanium frame had been suggested many years before by shareholder Richard Goode, who had links to the Russian aeronautical industry, but for various reasons the project hadn't progressed at the time. Producing the hinges in titanium raised all sorts of engineering challenges, so when titanium was finally introduced, its use was restricted to the seat pillar, the rear frame and the front forks, plus mudguard stays and the folding pedal centre bolt.

The Mark 4s are available in three broad ranges (above), classified by handlebar type - S, M and P from left to right above.

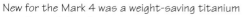

New for the Mark 4 was a weight-saving titanium rear frame (above). Smaller weight saving measures included a new lightweight fi'zi:k saddle (right),

Also new were the Pentaclip (above, right), for stepless seat angle adjustment, and Eazy-Roll rack wheels (above, left) for those taking the folded bike over rougher ground. To the left of the wheels is a seat pillar bung, allowing storage of small items in the seat pillar.

Rather than run out of steam at £600-£700, the Brompton range was now finally able to confront its upmarket rivals. The purchaser could specify virtually any combination of parts, but in as much as standard models existed, the S2L-X at £965 and P6R-XDL (£1,225) stand out. The S2L-X was a real delight, becoming an overnight classic. It was light, yet even with two gears, it was fast enough in a flat city like London to undertake serious daily commuting. The P6R-XDL was completely the opposite: seemingly bigger, it actually occupied the same folded volume as the 'S' type, but it was heavier, despite the full titanium kit. However, fitted with the rear rack, dual-position bars and a special narrow SON hub dynamo, it was the package serious leisure riders had been asking for.

These machines were introduced to satisfy the perceived needs of Brompton owners, but they also helped Brompton to do battle with the 'go faster' folders, the Birdy, Bike Friday and Airnimal.

Although edging up into four-figure price territory, the titanium Brompton variants were still far and away the cheapest of the 'super-folders', and much more compact, although limited gear range remained an issue, even with the 6-speed hub/derailleur system.

One option, taken up by enthusiastic owners over the years, was to fit an aftermarket chainwheel gear known as the Mountain (or Speed) Drive. This Swiss-made device doubled the number of gear ratios, giving a mountain bike gear range, but it was expensive, heavy and

inefficient. Another alternative was to fit wider range sprockets to the 2-speed derailleur, and a kit was produced by Highpath Engineering for a while. This gave Mountain Drive results, without the upfront cost, inefficiency and weight, but the sprockets had quite a short life. Most users found these options too complicated and expensive, but it would be some time before Brompton finally cracked the gear issue in-house.

The P6R-XDL offered full touring features at a little over 12kg - rack, dynamo lights and mudguards included! This was largely due to the extensive use of titanium parts extending from the rear frame through to many smaller parts such as mudguard stays and pedal axle bolts.

The new Mark 4 bikes of 2005 were built to customers' specification, but of the many spec packages two became instant classics - the S2L-X (above) has become unbeatable as a fast, lightweight commuter (9.7kg) with two gears and many titanium parts - for example forks as inset. The P6R-XDL (12.1kg) was designed for longer leisure or touring rides, its bars ideal for altering hand position to stop wrist fatigue and its beautifully engineered and ultra-reliable SON hub dynamo giving superb lighting.

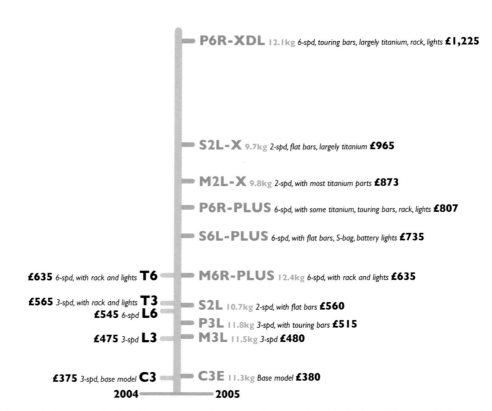

P6R-XDL 12.1kg 6-spd, touring bars, largely titanium, rack, lights **£1,225**

S2L-X 9.7kg 2-spd, flat bars, largely titanium **£965**

M2L-X 9.8kg 2-spd, with most titanium parts **£873**

P6R-PLUS 6-spd, with some titanium, touring bars, rack, lights **£807**

S6L-PLUS 6-spd, with flat bars, S-bag, battery lights **£735**

£635 6-spd, with rack and lights **T6**   **M6R-PLUS** 12.4kg 6-spd, with rack and lights **£635**

£565 3-spd, with rack and lights **T3**   **S2L** 10.7kg 2-spd, with flat bars **£560**
£545 6-spd **L6**   **P3L** 11.8kg 3-spd, with touring bars **£515**
£475 3-spd **L3**   **M3L** 11.5kg 3-spd **£480**

£375 3-spd, base model **C3**   **C3E** 11.3kg Base model **£380**
2004   **2005**

The Mark 4s spanned a bewildering range of specs and prices - but the budget C3 was still there as the C3E (below). The C-type has since been deleted, but using Brompton's 'B-Spoke' ordering system, the customer can order an M3E with very similar spec.

Available in a previously unthinkable range of styles and colours, the Mark 4 Bromptons have become style icons with young and old alike.

© Andrew Stevenson

The Opposition Regroups

The launch of the Mark 4 had resulted in a big increase in demand for the Brompton, while production continued to rise at a relatively steady 10% a year. Edward Donald had arrived too late to influence events, but he felt that under the circumstances the engineering effort put into the lightweight bikes and other upgrades would have been better spent on increasing production.

Factory output had been hit by the Sturmey debacle, hovering just below 8,000 in 2001-02, and the arrival of the 6-speed had created demand that the factory just couldn't satisfy, output rising to 9,563 in 2002-03, but stalling at 9,888 in 2003-04. By the time the Mark 4 was launched, the waiting list had reached six weeks, with the number of pre-orders from desperate dealers allegedly reaching 19,000 bikes for a while. Demoralized by the company's inability to supply this growing demand, Donald left in October 2005. Ironically, production was just starting to pick up, which was fortunate because his early marketing work was bearing fruit. Output rose 15.6% to 11,432 in 2004-05 and a further 19.1% to 13,620 in 2005-06. Brompton was back on track with a vengeance.

In March 2004, Tim Guinness had flown out to Japan and arranged for the paperwork trail to be streamlined. After prolonged negotiations, Mitsubishi agreed to bow out and a direct sales line was established with Mizutani, where former Mitsubishi manager Mac Nakane had now become the International Manager. Gradually Japanese Brompton sales improved, until by 2008 they had reached 1,800 a year. America too, was starting to see increased activity.

The waiting list for Bromptons had not gone unnoticed by its competitors, and 2005 was to see an explosion of relaunched and newly designed folding bikes. The most interesting, and in many ways the first serious competitor to the Brompton, was the Mezzo. Designed by Jon Whyte of ATB Sales, this was an interesting attempt to capitalize on Brompton's failure to engage with the more fashion-conscious end of the market.

The Mezzo got off to a flying start with younger males, as Whyte had done design work in Formula One, as well as producing high-end MTBs. Like the Brompton, it featured 349mm 16-inch tyres, but with its gunmetal grey colour scheme, and chunky, techy looks, it was a world apart.

By rights, the Mezzo should have done a roaring trade, but there were a couple of self-imposed weaknesses. The first i4 bikes were fitted with Shimano's rather uninspiring 4-speed Nexus hub gear and the later i9 with the much better Shimano Capreo derailleur. But the gear ratios were laughably low, top gear in both cases being much lower than top on the Brompton 3-speed, and lower even than the 2-speed. This was all compounded by sluggish and outdated tyres that made pedalling hard work.

The Mezzo was a reasonable, if rather heavy, folder, but despite its youthful, sporty good looks, it was (literally) streets behind the Brompton in terms of rideability, because of this poor choice of componentry. It's hard to image a designer of the calibre of Jon Whyte designing a mountain bike around dubious tyres and gears, and one is left with the distinct impression that he simply hadn't taken the folding bike format as seriously as he should. Mezzo insisted for a while that market research indicated a desire for low gearing in the folding bike sector. It might have been true in the sub-£200 sector, but left the £600 Mezzo looking a bit sad. Three years later, the tyres were improved and the gearing quietly sorted, but by then it was much too late. The Mezzo was something of a wasted opportunity.

Increasingly, the real competition was coming from Dahon. UK importation and distribution had long been in the hands of Mark Bickerton's Cyclemotion, but in early 2004 Fisher Outdoor Leisure was appointed UK distributor, and this bigger, more aggressive company soon became the importer too.

The Mezzo looked sporty and had an ingeniously designed and compact fold - one of the few attempts to really try and rival the folded package of the Brompton.
Unfortunately it was let down by unsuitable components, out of keeping with its fast and futuristic appearance.

© Peter Eland / Velo Vision Magazine
www.velovision.com

Within a short space of time, the size of the dealer network, and UK sales, had exploded, many dealers taking Dahon because of Brompton's hub problems and continuing difficulty in meeting demand, even for 3-speed bikes.

In 2004 Dahon was selling 28 different own-brand machines (not all available in the UK), of which 20 were core 20-inch bikes of various kinds. Two years later, the company was producing 33 distinct models, most of the growth being in larger conventional machines, but with a continued presence at the compact end of the market. Dahon prices had gradually crept up too, until by 2006 the mean price of £745 was slightly higher than the £741 mean of the Brompton range.

Considering that ten years before Dahon had been regarded as a purveyor of cheap and cheerful Chinese tat, this was a remarkable turnaround. The Dahon bikes covered a huge price range (£350-£1,730), and at the bottom end - where Dahon no longer bothered to look for sales - Dahon badge-engineered bikes filled the gaps down to £100 or even less. Sitting in the middle of this vast range of folding bicycles, Brompton looked vulnerable, and in truth, it had only really survived through the sheer quality and originality of its design, helped by the regular, well-timed upgrades.

But Brompton had survived and it was looking stronger and more self-assured than ever. As the Mark 4 settled down, the company entered a period of relative stability, concentrating on increasing output and quality. Some dealers covered themselves by selling both brands, but most - a fickle lot bike dealers - simply swapped back to Brompton, citing Dahon's poor spares back up, and a range that was too big to handle.

Meanwhile, two bikes from the past were making a comeback. The Airframe had been

brought back to life in 2002 by Silkmead, an engineering company based in Dunstable. Despite a lack of torsional stiffness, it was a decent bike, but set against the titanic Brompton/Dahon battle, it struggled to make serious inroads into the market. In 2004 an improved 'Super 8' version was launched equipped with the Sturmey-Archer 8-speed hub, which had originally been conceived by Brompton's Steve Rickels whilst an employee of Sturmey-Archer. But despite a competitive weight, price and gear range, it failed to make any serious headway, and production of the Airframe was later quietly wound down, although the bikes continued to be produced in small batches. Mark Sanders' Strida had never sold well in the UK, but it had a big following in the Far East, particularly

Dahon were behind a huge range of 'badge-engineered' folders - in this case a Kalkhoff.

in Japan and Korea. It was relaunched in Mark 2 form by British company Roland Plastics in the late 1990s, but when this operation ran out of steam, it was passed to Steedman Bass, whose Midlands factory saw it through a Mark 2.5 version to a Mark 3. In 2005, the Strida was sold to Ming Cycles of Taiwan, which made a lot more sense, as the primary markets for the bike were in the Far East. The number 4 is considered unlucky in China, so under Ming Cycles control the series jumped to a Mark 5. The new machines are greatly improved: easier and safer to ride, making the Strida a cheap and practical leisure bike for those who can live with one, two, or more recently three gears. The Strida went on to become established as the top-selling folding bike in South Korea, spawning a whole family of models in two wheel sizes. Rather inexplicably, sales in the UK remain small, but it is recognised today as one of the most interesting and innovative folding bikes around.

In 2007, Bike Friday unexpectedly broke away from its traditional 20-inch sports market, launching the 16-inch Tikit. This was a really interesting design: comfortable and fast to ride, reasonably light, and with an extremely fast 'Hyperfold' folding mechanism, helped along by Bowden cables which allowed the stem to fold down automatically when the rear wheel was folded under the bike. It didn't fold very small, but was compact enough for regular rail or occasional bus use.

At £870, the Tikit was competitively priced for a quality American product, and right in the middle of the Brompton range. Interestingly the Bowden cables suffered from the same problems as the cables on the Brompton prototype, and were later made an option.

The Bike Friday Tikit was an innovative US design that rode well, was well-priced and folded very quickly. However, it failed to fold as small as the Brompton and didn't make serious inroads into the UK market.

© Peter Eland / Velo Vision Magazine: www.velovision.com

For thirty years the accepted wisdom had been to outsource engineering production to the Far East, but in 2007-2009, this policy would be called into question. The global 'credit crunch' brought turmoil to world markets, with a period of volatile raw material and fuel prices, plus a collapse in the value of sterling. For home manufacturers, high fuel costs and a weak pound were less serious, the weak currency actually helping exports, but for importers, it was another matter. Brompton was, of course, still a British manufacturer, but in the decades the company had been building bikes in Britain, many of its home component suppliers had disappeared. By 2009, most of the components on the bike (including big items like hub gears) were imported, mainly from the Far East.

In both 2008 and 2009, Brompton managed to keep annual price increases down to 5%, markedly below those of its competitors, but the reliance on imports was taking its toll, and for 2010 the company was forced to increase prices by an average of 12.5%. Surprisingly, in such straitened economic circumstances, the biggest increases were aimed at the cheaper bikes, the humble M1E rising by 20%, and the mass-market M3L by 18%, while the pricey titanium machines rose by only 10%.

Its competitors - without exception importing complete bikes - did even worse. During the summer of 2009, Birdy prices fluctuated wildly, falling by 11% in August, and rising by 29% later in the year. Dahon prices had been similarly chaotic in 2009. In November, new distributor Zyro revealed that the number of models reaching the UK would almost double in 2010, from 16 to 28. Not all the bikes were comparable, but those that were had risen in price by an eye-watering 35% year-on-year. And with a general move upmarket, the average price of a Dahon had risen even more, from £582 at the end of 2009 to £955 in 2010. Even five years before, it would have been hard to imagine a typical Dahon costing almost as much as the most expensive Brompton variant. In the end it all proved to be too much, and in June 2011 Zyro dropped the brand, citing poor spares availability and an over-large and over-priced range. Back in Taiwan, Dahon also seemed to have over-extended itself, and it was announced that the parent company would split, with David Hon's wife Florence, and son Joshua leaving to set up a new folding bike company called Tern, and taking much of the management and overseas sales teams with them, including Mark Bickerton in the UK. In late 2011, with Joshua's father David threatening legal action, Dahon's UK distributorship in disarray, and the Tern range yet to be launched, the Hons were - temporarily at least - on the ropes. Tern went on to do more or less everything right, with subtle more youthful advertising, and a carefully chosen bike range. In the UK, Mark Bickerton's links with Tern were to result in a reborn Bickerton brand, albeit using badged Tern machines.

Dahon fell on its feet in the UK by landing a distributorship deal with Raleigh in 2012. By 2016, the two rival Hon companies had begun to occupy surprisingly similar territory, but with Tern at the slightly classier end of the market. Within a few years of the credit squeeze of 2008/09 prices had stabilised, and a measure of order had returned to global trading. All the major folding bike manufacturers had survived, but the ensuing 'Great Recession' had depressed output and sent a chill wind through the industry. Not at Brompton, where sales just rose and rose, far outstripping the modest 10% annual growth of the early years.

With precious little UK manufacturing available, and Brompton conveniently situated in west London, government ministers were tripping over each other to fly the manufacturing flag in Brentford. Just a decade after Sturmey-Archer had effectively been left to rot, British manufacturing was very much back on the agenda. For companies like Brompton, now heavily dependent on imports, a resurgence of British component manufacturing would be very welcome.

A New Generation

In 2007, after some thirty years in the driving seat, Andrew Ritchie was preparing to hand over control of Brompton to a new younger team. The changeover was overseen by Brompton chairman Tim Guinness, who would later regard the smooth transfer of power as his most important contribution to the company.

Emerson Roberts had joined Brompton in January 2006 with a brief to lead a growing marketing department, but management of the company was to go to Will Butler-Adams, the young engineer who had arrived in 2002. Tim Guinness had met Butler-Adams - then maintenance manager of a petro-chemical factory on Teeside - back in 2001. Still in his '20s at the time, Butler-Adams had been raised in Yorkshire, leaving Newcastle University with a 1st class Honours degree in Mechanical Engineering. He was, in his own words, "madly passionate about all things mechanical. And mesmerised by Andrew Ritchie's invention."

Butler-Adams seemed ideal. He had already demonstrated leadership skills on expeditions to the Amazon and Argentinian Andes, and he had five solid years industrial experience behind him in Middlesbrough, but crucially he was an engineer. The various players in the Brompton story have denied that this was a prerequisite for leadership, and Butler-Adams himself makes it clear that he is a very different sort of engineer to Ritchie, "I'm not a designer, and I'm not good on the detailed stuff!" But there's no doubt that Andrew Ritchie was only persuaded to hand over because he knew the company would continue to be engineer-led.

Joining the engineering team early in 2002, Will Butler-Adams initially expected to stay for about five years, improve the operational efficiency of the factory, and move on, but he gradually worked his way up, becoming a director in 2006.

As he saw it, Brompton could follow one of two roads: it could remain as a small specialist manufacturer, rather like the Morgan car company, building perhaps 15,000 bikes a year, and generating modest profits for its group of long-standing shareholders. Brompton was growing at around 8% a year at the time, but the market was growing at 25%, so the company's market share was effectively slipping year on year. The other option was to rise to the challenges and grow with the market, with the aim of developing into a serious global player. If the company chose the first course, he would move on to face fresh challenges elsewhere, but if there was backing for growth, he was prepared to invest his own future by leading the company.

It was a convincing argument, and the young engineer found backing from chairman Tim Guinness, the majority of the shareholders, and finally and reluctantly, from Andrew Ritchie. After all the years of talk about the 'succession', Andrew was finally satisfied that he had found a potential leader who had empathy with the Brompton philosophy, and understood the bike. Will Butler-Adams was made of the right stuff, and he wasn't just a manager - he knew every component, and every stress and strain in the Brompton design.

The Butler-Adams deal, completed in 2008, was quite a complex affair. Just as Andrew Ritchie and Julian Vereker had done in 1988, Will Butler-Adams and a group of family and friends bought shares in Brompton, although this time they were buying existing shares from existing shareholders. Some of the original shareholders sold all their shares, but most - including Andrew Ritchie - sold half. For the first time, Andrew's personal holding fell below 51% - he had lost overall control.

The first stage of the plan was to invest in the Brentford factory, then three years into a 15-year lease. A total of £1 million was spent on enhancements, principally moving the offices to a new mezzanine floor above the engineering shop, giving vital extra production space below. The second stage involved increasing the manufacturing efficiency, with a significant investment in further auto-brazing equipment and other modern machines.

The luxury of success - a totally refurbished modern factory.

In November 2008, Brompton unveiled an intelligent solution to the gear ratio problem. The 2 x 3 derailleur/hub system introduced in 2002 had always been seen as a stop-gap measure, because although it was light and efficient, the gear range was simply too low. Several options presented themselves, but none quite fitted the bill. A pure derailleur system was out of the question for all sorts of reasons, leaving a multi-gear hub; an option that had its adherents. A hub like the Shimano Nexus 8-speed could be squeezed in without too much re-engineering, and a kit had been produced in Germany by Juliane Neuß for several years.

But it was a relatively expensive hub, and it weighed at least half a kilo more than the Sturmey 3-speed which Brompton was already using. Worse still, like most multi-speed hub gears, it worked through compound gears, so that the rider's leg power wound its way up and down through a series of cogwheels before it reached the rear wheel. This arrangement was relatively inefficient, and put together with the cost and weight of the hub, ruled out this option. Other hubs existed, some better than the Shimano Nexus, but all were big and heavy.

The answer, first discussed some years before, was to design a special wide-ratio version of the archetypal Sturmey-Archer AW 3-speed hub, the BWR (Brompton Wide Ratio), which would be made, like the BSR, in Sturmey's new Taiwanese factory. The BWR kept the light weight, low cost and reasonable efficiency of the hub, but extended the range, giving three very widely spaced gears. The new hub would work in tandem with the 2-speed derailleur already in production, but with revised sprockets, to give a total of six evenly spaced gears.

In late 2008 Brompton went into the hub design business, introducing the BWR, or Brompton Wide Ratio hub - basically a 7-speed gear range in a 3-speed package.

This cutaway shows the simple, rugged construction and Shimano-pattern multi-spline output shaft, enabling the hub to work reliably with sprockets as small as 12-tooth. The BWR is manufactured for Brompton by Sturmey-Archer, now part of the Taiwanese Sunrace group.

In earlier days, such a task would have been beyond Brompton's capabilities, but it was now a bigger, more self-assured company, with enough engineering expertise to handle day-to-day problem solving, leaving former Sturmey-Archer engineer Steve Rickels to concentrate on the new designs.

The weakness of the new arrangement was the need to continue with dual changers, but otherwise it was all positives. Using modern design techniques, the BWR actually weighed some 60 grams less than the standard 3-speed, but increased the existing 177% gear range to a generous 245%. With the 2-speed derailleur mounted on the hub driver, the overall range increased to 302%, which was only a shade less than the heavier, less efficient 7- and 8-speed hubs produced by SRAM and Shimano. It was a typically clever Brompton solution, and it was the first major development engineered by a team, rather than Ritchie alone. Finally he had demonstrated enough confidence in the group to take a back seat, albeit remaining (in Andrew's words) "very closely involved"! He was not to know that it would be the last significant development for some years.

The new hub really was the final piece in the jigsaw, answering the last of the long-standing criticisms that had held it back. Gears had always been a weakness, and the Brompton now had a bigger gear range than most of its competitors.

How was the new regime bedding in? Speaking in the summer of 2009, Tim Guinness remained cautiously optimistic: "So far we don't know whether the marketing is successful, because the bike's selling itself. We can't produce enough..."

Brompton as Icon

By 2009, Brompton had become something of a national icon. For overseas visitors, the little bikes were now as much a part of the London scene as the red double-deckers and policemen's helmets. As if to confirm the bike's new status, a Brompton was used to represent London in the closing stages of the Beijing Olympic Games.

Down in Brentford, Andrew Ritchie would still sit at his drawing board once in a while, the relic taking pride of place amongst the smoked-glass, the PCs and modern engineering tools. He now worked part-time, still commuting to the factory from his flat in Brompton two or three days a week. For a while, it looked as though married life and semi-retirement in Oxford would take him away from the factory on a more permanent basis, but this turned out to be a step too far, and neither the marriage nor the retirement was to last very long. Although technically he was no longer in charge at Brompton, whenever there was a flurry of activity at the drawing board, the engineers got nervous. Either Andrew had had a new idea, or was looking again at something they had hoped to sign off. Part-time perhaps, but very much a guiding role.

Ritchie's real achievement had been to develop a 1970s design for three decades to the point where this young management team (few of whom were over 40) could take over and hopefully move the design on. Such longevity is not unique in the transport world, but it's extremely unusual, and testament to the clarity of vision behind the machine all those years ago and Ritchie's dogged persistence in honing and perfecting the design, often in the face of considerable opposition. And despite his rather donnish appearance and sometimes unconventional business methods, Andrew Ritchie had demonstrated an instinct for the realities of the commercial world, without which his company could never have survived. Throughout the long evolution of the Brompton, Andrew Ritchie - and indeed the Brompton itself - had received surprisingly little official recognition, but in October 2009, against a formidable shortlist of the Great & the Good, he won the 2009 Prince Philip Designer's Prize 'for outstanding achievement in design'. For the engineer behind an intensely practical and 'non design' creation, it was a long overdue honour.

Cycle historian Tony Hadland is an authority on folding bikes, and he has no doubts about how and why the Brompton succeeded where so many others have failed: "The key to its success is that the bike rides reasonably well, is relatively light, well engineered, soundly constructed, and folds and unfolds quickly and easily. Any folding bike should do all these things but in practice, very few do. Most are deficient in at least one of these parameters, and some are deficient in all of them. With the Brompton, however, the original design compromises were exceptionally well balanced and over the years the detailing has become increasingly refined."

Andrew Ritchie with bike-builder Terence Franklin, one of several members of the Franklin family employed at the London factory.

Brompton's iconic status became associated with business success in times of difficulties, and the factory saw several high profile visits from Conservative and Liberal politicians in 2011. Here former London mayor Boris Johnson, himself synonymous with cycling in the capital, tries out an electric Nano-conversion whilst on a factory visit.

Brompton and the Future Could the Brompton Dock herald a revolution in personal transport? This internal shot of Brompton's public bike hire concept gives an idea of how space efficient the Docks are. In fact it can fit forty folded Bromptons into a single car space.

Recent Developments and the Future
Beyond 2017

"Describing our bike takes 30,000 to 40,000 drawings, but in describing the machines to make our bike there are maybe 300,000 - 400,000 drawings. So the cleverness is in the bike, yes, but there's far more cleverness in how to make the bike."
WILL BUTLER-ADAMS

The severe winter weather of 2010/11 should have been an opportunity for Brompton. Following a number of productivity improvements, the company had eliminated its long-standing waiting list, and was planning to use the slack winter season to initiate the long-awaited 'big bang': reconfiguration of the bike assembly area, from batch (i.e. one man building one bike at a static work station) to production-line manufacture. In the event, the hardware wasn't ready for the planned November 2010 changeover, and the company hit December with the old system still in place. The severe snow storms and prolonged freezing weather of that most unusual winter resulted in shortages of key components and a collapse in sales. Suddenly, Brompton was unable to build or sell bikes, something the company hadn't experienced for a very long time. Sales faltered badly, but true to recent form, turnover and profitability showed barely a ripple.

By June 2011 the production line system was finally on stream. Unlike the process that revolutionised car manufacture in the early 20th century, the Brompton bike builders were free to move up and down the line to help out where needed. There was also something of a high-tech efficiency drive at this time, with the introduction of computerised quality control of frames, new technology for testing hinge plates and further automation of the simpler brazing procedures.

Sales were soon back on track and Brompton was looking to the future again, but December 2010 had sent a chill wind through the company. Profitability had been more or less steady at 10% of turnover for nearly 20 years, but it dipped badly, and would remain depressed for a couple of years. Sales, however, resumed their meteoric rise, turnover doubling to £12 million in 2010-11, and almost doubling again to £21.3 million two years later. At long last the production log-jam had been cleared, allowing sales to bounce up to find their own level. It sounded just the medicine the company needed, but the drive to increase output inevitably came at the expense of engineering developments.

Titanium from Sheffield

The dash for sales would result in some engineering *faux pas* that one suspects would not have happened with Andrew Ritchie at the helm. The most serious involved the October 2010 change to a nickel-plated aluminium seat pillar to replace the titanium pillar on Superlight bikes. This was 40 grams heavier than titanium, but it was much cheaper, and was expected to replace steel on all Bromptons from 2012, but within weeks incidents began to arise of the nickel plating flaking and failing, resulting in a panic withdrawal in June 2011. As stocks of titanium pillars had been used up by this time, and the contractual arrangements with the manufacturers discontinued, Superlight bikes were quietly fitted with the everyday steel pillars thereafter, and this unsatisfactory state of affairs has continued to the present day. Embarrassingly, Brompfication, an aftermarket manufacturer in Hong

Kong, stepped in with a neat titanium pillar with a stated weight of 300g, although the company later ceased trading. In late 2016 New York's NYCeWheels began selling an H&H branded titanium pillar with a claimed 237g weight.

In mid-2012, Brompton also quietly withdrew the lightweight front hubs fitted to 1- and 2-speed bikes after a few failures, and replaced the Superlight's titanium folding pedal axle bolt with a lightweight steel item. It looked mean, and the impression was of a company chasing the bottom line rather than developing the best components for the job. The flagship Superlight bikes were more expensive than their predecessors, with fewer titanium components. By 2016, a typical Superlight bike would cost around £1,600 and weigh the better part of 11kg.

Another rather regrettable incident was the neat in-frame toolkit, developed by fashionable consultant Goodwin Hartshorn, but made in Taiwan. It was introduced in 2012, but rapidly withdrawn after breakages, and grumbles about the impracticality of some of the tools. The issues were eventually sorted, but the affair left the smell of a company losing its engineering focus.

This was all to change with a remarkable project launched in 2013, not in Brentford but in South Yorkshire.

Importing titanium components from Russia and China had worked reasonably well for eight years, but it involved long distance relationships with countries that - to be frank - might not always have the UK's best interests at heart. There was a very real prospect that trade sanctions or something more serious could cut off the supply of components overnight.

Brompton had always prided itself on building frames in the UK, primarily from brazed steel tubing, but fabricating the remaining titanium parts - the rear frames and front forks - was just too specialist for the Brentford factory. The answer was to find a partner in the UK with the necessary skills, and Brompton's Specialist Products Design Manager, Paul Williams found just the company in C W Fletcher of Sheffield. Fletchers was a long established Sheffield steel maker, best known for its high quality 'flatware', primarily cutlery and kitchen utensils. This part of the business had been sold to US company James Robinson Inc in 2002, leaving C W Fletcher to concentrate on specialist materials including titanium, much of its output being jet engine parts for Rolls Royce and others. But aerospace is a rather cyclical business, and in 1999, after settling into a big new factory on a former coking works outside Sheffield, C W Fletcher was looking to diversify. Brompton was looking for expertise, and C W Fletcher was looking to build a consumer product in titanium. It was a near perfect match.

The two companies set up Brompton-Fletcher Ltd with the aim of going where British manufacturing hadn't really gone before, producing consumer-level titanium components at a price level to compete with the Russians and the Chinese.

C W Fletcher provided a small self-contained working area in the heart of the Sheffield factory, and began recruiting and training staff. South Yorkshire - not unlike Brentford - had seen its industrial base decimated in 30 years, so there were grants for training and recruitment, and plenty of willing volunteers. Seven started the training - drawn from such unlikely employers as Sports Direct and Thorntons - and four saw the course through to join the payroll, with a fifth arriving in 2016. Bizarrely, one of the potential recruits picked by C W Fletcher had previously done time in the Brentford factory as a brazer before moving north to assemble frames for Mercian. Applicants were not told they would be making components for Brompton, and Fletchers didn't know about his background until he started work in October 2015.

By the summer of 2016 Brompton-Fletcher was turning out 200 rear frames a month, or around ten each working day. These were very small numbers for Brompton, which was building some 3,500 bikes a month at the time but, with the Russian rear frame contract cancelled, there was plenty of incentive to gradually increase output. The medium-term aim is to meet current demand of around 400-500 lightweight rear frames a month, which will need a total staff of eight or nine.

When brazing steel components, the speed of manufacture is only really limited by the skill of the operative, but titanium oxidises very readily when heated, and it absorbs oil like a sponge. Oxygen and oil are the front runners for ruining welds, and there are plenty of other potential contaminants. No parts can be touched with an ungloved hand without constant cleaning, and welding has to take place in booths screened with thick red plastic curtains. This is partly to shield passers-by from the arc glare, but also to minimise draughts around the welding jig. To prevent contamination, the jig is bathed in inert argon gas, but if the gas is blown clear of the weld before it has cooled, the weld will be ruined. After each operation, the welder has to sit completely still in the red booth, waiting for the heat to dissipate out of the weld.

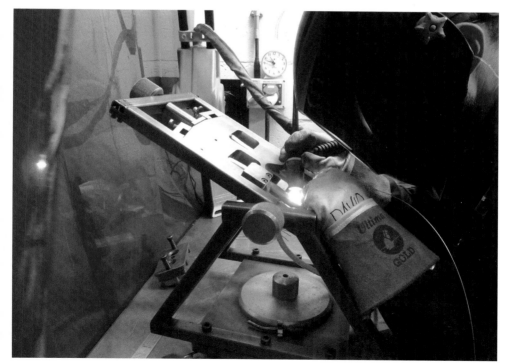

Titanium welding is a painstaking process. Here you see the eerie pink glow of the welding itself and also the thick orange screen - partly to protect the eyes of passers-by but also to prevent draughts diluting that essential pool of argon.

Like so much else in the strange world of titanium mass-production, the exact length of the pause (a few seconds) has been found by trial and error. With each raw tube costing around £4.60, scrapping even a sub-assembly can be annoying, and a momentary lack of concentration with a complete rear frame can ruin your day.

Argon is mighty expensive, and currently costs around £6-£7 per frame, so it isn't practical to swamp the work area in the stuff. The flow has to be carefully metered through the jig at each work station, bathing the exterior and interior of the tubes to keep the dreaded oxygen at bay. Once the argon is flowing and welding has commenced, the operative needs total concentration, sitting absolutely still for the required time, spinning the jig to do the next weld, and so on, until the rear frame is finished. After quality control, frames are checked for alignment and shot-blasted, then oiled to prevent finger marks marring the finish (the principle being that if it's absorbed oil, it can't absorb any more) and another frame is carefully placed in a plastic pouch in the despatch boxes. At the end of the week a large van leaves Brompton and makes the long journey up the M1, bringing back 18 to 20 of the filled boxes to the Brompton production line.

The intention was to mark each frame with the date and batch number, but the staff wanted the parts to be given an individual number and welder's code, something Paul Williams was happy to accede to.

Lightweight Bromptons sold from late 2016 carry this code on the plate that bears against the rubber suspension unit. The first number is a week code, the second identifies the year, the third letter is the welder's personal code, and the fourth shows how many he had completed that week.

If the rear frame fits precisely in the quality control jig (above left) it's time for the welders to relax before their concentration moves onto the next frame.

Individual numbers and welder's codes (left) show the pride the welders take in the finished product.

This frame was made in week 22 of 2016 and is the fourth one produced by operator F.

With a plant still getting into its stride, the future seems a very long way away. Writing in early 2017, the little Brompton-Fletcher assembly line is still a tiny venture to both companies. Richard Phillips, Business Development Manager at C W Fletcher, accepts that it's a small venture, but it's one element in the process of diversification: 'If it turns over £300,000 a year, it will only be one-point-something percent of Fletcher's turnover, but it's helping the company diversify away from Rolls-Royce and the aerospace industry.' Once the initial target of 400-500 rear frames has been reached, the company may look at the seat pillar too - a large, but much more straightforward component. And after that? A whole bike? 'I can't say, says Paul with a smile.

One of the longer-term aims is to redesign the components one by one to suit the strengths and weaknesses of titanium, which is as tough as steel, but relatively elastic. Initially, the Chinese and Russian factories were just given the drawings for the steel components and told to remake them in lighter stuff. To achieve the full weight-savings - allied to long life at reasonable cost - will mean some fine-tuning, but this process will take time. The eventual ambition - although you won't get anyone to admit it - is to build a folding bike of lightweight materials. A 6kg bike seems perfectly feasible, but the factory doesn't intend to run before it has mastered walking.

The Electric Bike

Another 'post Ritchie' project that was destined to be an astonishing eight years in development, was the power-assisted bike. Ritchie had hinted at power-assist in his original patent application, but for the next twenty years the Brompton remained a pedal-only machine, until small-scale after-market conversions began to appear in the 2010s. The power-assisted 'Nano' is mentioned in the 'Brompton Specials' chapter, and the Electric Transport Shop in Cambridge , Freedom eBike of Israel, and NYCeWheels in New York, have produced similar machines.

When introduced in 2007, the Nano-Brompton was fitted with a 100mm wide Tongxin motor in the front wheel - the smallest and lightest unit around at the time - later reduced to 80mm in width. The company went on to reduce weight even further by the option of small 36-volt battery packs designed for powering garden equipment. In terms of weight, the Nano-Brompton would be a hard act to follow.

Brompton rightly concentrated on reducing the size and weight of the motor at first, aiming to produce a 2-speed power-assisted bike that was lighter than most non-assisted variants, but the design gradually became bogged down in unsuitable technology from unsuitable Far Eastern partners. The electric variant was to be shown for the first time at the Eurobike show in Friedrichshafen, Germany in September 2011. With other folding bike companies busy developing power-assisted machines, the Brompton package needed to be as practical, light and user-friendly as the original Brompton. It was a very tall order.

The final product was expected to go on limited sale in Germany and the UK in early 2012, with a more general roll out later in the year, but the project foundered and the whole concept was quietly put to one side. It was, however, still simmering on a back burner, and in the early summer of 2015, Brompton surprised everyone by announcing that it was working with a new partner - Williams Advanced Engineering, the commercial arm of the Williams Formula One team. The project smacked rather of public relations, as it didn't look likely that the Formula One company's Kinetic Energy Recovery System would be of much practical use on a folding bike, but Williams had plenty of expertise in developing race-hardened electronics, and their input proved invaluable.

With the launch set (still provisionally) for 2017, the Brompton design is beginning to crystallise. The motor is in the front wheel, with the battery bag mounted on an especially-adapted front carrier block. Luggage capacity is still available, using a special pannier bag that fits round the battery, so the bag can be removed with the battery or on its own.

It's a clever and very neat system, but does have the disadvantage that the pannier and carrier block are unique and not interchangeable with other Brompton equipment (the Nano bag can be used on any Brompton, and any pannier can be fitted to the Nano, other than early models with a steel pannier frame!).

In keeping with European law (this may not always apply of course), the Brompton electric bike has a bottom bracket torque sensor instead of a twistgrip throttle, so that power-assistance is dependent on the rider pedalling, and proportional to the pedal effort. To avoid folding issues with switches and cables, the machine will not have any handlebar controls, the assistance level, light switch and battery meter being easily accessible from the top of the battery. This is expected to have a capacity of about 300Wh, a reasonable weight/range compromise.

The electronics are well shielded in the special pannier block and inside the motor, which also has a unique gearing arrangement, and produces an impressive amount of torque. The only obvious potential weakness is weatherproofing of the multi-way connector on the pannier block, although again everything is well shielded. Testing will no doubt be thorough, and it will need to be, because the public can misunderstand, force, misuse, and ultimately break just about anything.

The aim of the project is to widen the scope of the bicycle, and increase its appeal to those who might not consider themselves regular or commuter cyclists. This market is huge. Despite rising fuel prices and chronic traffic congestion, more than 60% of regular commuters still travel by car in the UK. Of the remainder, modest numbers walk or use public transport, but less than 3% cycle. Even encouraging a tiny percentage of car drivers to shift to a Brompton or car-Brompton commute would result in hundreds of thousands of sales, and a big increase in market share. One way to do this is to make the prospect of cycling less physically daunting.

As well as commuters, the Nano after-market kit has proved popular with old and infirm cyclists, parents pulling child trailers (or carrying children on the bike), and leisure cyclists in hilly areas. Interestingly, Brompton is adamant there will not be a power-assist upgrade kit, although there are no technical issues to fitting the bits to existing bikes.

Predicting future electric-assist sales is tricky, but it's worth noting that in the cycle-friendly Netherlands, electric-assist bikes accounted for 57% of bike sales in 2015 by price and 28% of bike sales by volume, or 276,000 units. In the slightly less enthusiastic German market, electric bikes accounted for 15% of sales by volume, some half a million bikes. The difficult price-weight-performance equation has kept folder sales very limited, but there will be rich pickings for the manufacturer who cracks the problem.

Has the failure of so many other folding electric bikes (see following chapter) caused any nervousness? No, Will Butler-Adams is confident that power-assisted bikes will continue to take a large share of a growing cycle market, and the Brompton will take its place as the premier power-assisted folder: "The average distance to work is nine miles. The folding electric bike isn't the whole solution, but it has to be part of the solution."

Other Projects

With the titanium offshoot and the electric project at last starting to bear fruit, Brompton turned its attention to the rather confused mishmash of rider controls. The gear and brakes levers had fallen into place at different times between 2002 and 2005, and a long-held ambition was finally realised to design new matching 2- and 3-speed shifters, and integrate the shifters and bell with improved brake levers. After a prolonged period of testing, the changeover to the new controls came in November 2016, together with new lockable handlebar grips.

© Alexander Henshaw

Integrated shifters, brake levers and bell became available in late 2016.

Brompton had begun to look like a marketing, rather than engineering-led company, and there certainly was a period when the roster of marketing managers overtook the engineers, with the main thrust of developments in such things as colour schemes, designer bags, option packages and even a range of clothing.

But with the success of the complex titanium venture, the redesign of the handlebar controls and progress with the electric bike, Brompton does seem to have turned a corner, and the momentum is back with the engineering team. "We've got to innovate", says Will Butler-Adams. "A company that isn't willing to innovate isn't going to be here in ten years."

Meanwhile, the marketing operation has been inspired. The Brompton World Championship series, which evolved from some lighthearted entertainment arranged by the Spanish distributor, was adopted by Brompton itself in 2005, and turned into a world series, with a final in the UK each year, initially at Blenheim Palace in Oxfordshire, then rather less successfully at the Goodwood Motor Circuit in West Sussex before settling on central London in 2015. In 2016 the series attracted a slightly reduced nine regional heats (there were 12 in 2013), from Europe and the USA to Japan and Korea, with heat winners travelling to London to join 500 British competitors for the final on the Mall in front of Buckingham Palace. For Brompton, the publicity works on several levels. The concept of racing folding bikes may have started as a bit of a joke, but it rapidly began to attract a top international field, and the races are now taken very seriously. The public impression is that the bikes are race-proven, yet the requirement for competitors to wear everyday clothing has helped to widen the appeal of cycling - and more specifically, cycling by Brompton. If top athletes can win races on this little bike, Mr (and more particularly, Mrs) Joe Bloggs should be able to cycle to work on it. The car manufacturers use exactly the same techniques to associate their everyday products with achievement and success.

Brompton has engaged in numerous cycle promotion activities too, especially in London, where it has been a lead sponsor to the 'Love London, Go Dutch' campaign. It's hard to imagine a better placement for Brompton. Go Dutch is about moving the image of cycling from reflective clothing, helmets and Lycra, and empowering ordinary people to cycle in the capital. The campaign has been hugely successful, persuading a rather half-hearted London Assembly to increase cycle funding. The city still has a long way to go, but Brompton has played a unique role in the campaign, both as a local manufacturer, and - in terms of commuter volumes - providing the raison d'être for better facilities. Legislators have belatedly realised that cycle facilities are not only a potent vote winner, but a simple and cost-effective means of improving the transport environment in London. Sponsorship deals of this kind work both ways, of course. Many of the ordinary folk tentatively trying the new cycling experience will purchase the non-threatening, but subtly race-proven locally-built bike. So getting more ordinary Londoners cycling means increased sales for Brompton, and increased employment for what is now one of London's biggest manufacturing companies. Not surprisingly, Mayor Johnson (with Mayor Khan presumably soon following in his footsteps) and other local and national politicians have become regular visitors to the West London factory, and every political visit brings the media in tow.

Rather than spend money on glossy advertising Brompton has chosen to rely on looking after existing customers and supporting the annual Brompton World Championships - illustrated by this classic poster image by Diana Powell (far left). The championships have also spawned their own sartorial style too! (near left)

Image www.dianapowell.co.uk

Brompton Dock

Perhaps the most daring project in recent years has been the Brompton Dock. This had nothing to do with the technology of the bike itself, but it promised a revolution in the way it was used.

The idea came to Will Butler-Adams after Brompton launched a bike hire project at Waterloo station. This early trial worked well, but only because South West Trains had agreed to store and hire the bikes from the fully staffed Lost Property Office at the station. To roll-out a network of hire centres nationally, and indeed internationally, the process would need to be automated - a Brompton dispenser in effect. To do this, Butler-Adams teamed up with a company called Street Associates that had developed an automatic storage system for bicycles called CycleDock: effectively a cycle shed accessible by text from a mobile phone. CycleDock was not a commercial success, primarily because it required a great deal of bulky hardware to store a handful of bicycles, but Butler-Adams had concluded that if the system could be reconfigured to suit the ultra-compact folded

Brompton it stood a chance of being made commercially viable.

Brompton Dock was set up as a sister company to Brompton in April 2011, claiming to be the only bicycle hire scheme in the world to operate without grants or subsidies from government or transport authorities. The idea was that local government, transport operators, colleges and hospitals could buy the Dock and the bikes, and either join the national 'public' hire network, or establish their own 'Exclusive Network'. Either way, Brompton Dock would manage every aspect of the scheme, including bike repair (usually sub-contracted to a local Brompton dealer) and maintenance of the hardware and software of the Dock itself.

Specifically designed around the Brompton, the Docks are cost-effective, and economical on space, even the largest 40-bike model taking up only a single car parking space. Manufacture had been kept in the UK, the Docks currently being made by Birmingham electronic engineering manufacturers CHH CoNeX.

The first fully automated 'B-Dock' opened at Guildford railway station in July 2011, after which there was a pause of almost a year while teething issues were settled, before the next two opened at Manchester Piccadilly and Stoke-on-Trent railway stations in partnership with Virgin Trains. These initial Docks were rapidly followed by another for Ealing Borough Council, close to Ealing Broadway rail and tube station, and two for First Great Western at Exeter St David's and Bristol Temple Meads railway stations in October 2012. Three Docks were also installed at the University of Greenwich.

An ambitious programme of openings was planned for early 2013, with the aim of getting the brand established in 25 towns by the spring of that year, but in practice things went rather slower than had been hoped. In March 2013, new public Docks opened at Peterborough and Oxford, bringing the total to ten, but growth thereafter was fitful, and concentrated on the southeast of England. Two years later there were still fewer than 40 Docks. In truth, the complex wireless technology and computer software had been so plagued by technical problems ('Every problem under the sun', says Will Butler-Adams), that Brompton had stopped seeking new sites, at least for the time being.

In June 2013, the Docks were rebranded by design consultancy Form, and in May 2015, the company was renamed Brompton Bike Hire Ltd. The reason for this ostensibly suicidal change was a very modern one - potential customers were using the search terms 'Brompton' and 'Hire'. The new name gave a clearer indication of its raison d'être, but was clumsier and less dynamic than the 'Dock' concept, although the actual hardware has kept the smart new Dock branding.

With partner organisations paying upfront for both the bikes and the Dock, it's difficult to see how the concept could lose money, but the losses continued to mount, and Brompton found itself supporting the bike hire arm for rather longer - and to a greater extent - than had been hoped. An initial capital injection of £200,000 in 2011-12 was followed by smaller sums in the next two years, and a massive £745,000 in 2014-15, when the operation should have been well into profit.

By June 2016, Brompton held shares with a nominal value of nearly £920,000, but the network remained stalled at 45 sites and around 1,000 hire bikes. Inevitably, the Docks have tended to be placed where the Brompton is already well known and well used - seven in London and five in Birmingham - but they remain thinly spread elsewhere, and completely missing in Scotland, Wales, and England north of Manchester.

The 'Catch 22' for Brompton Bicycle Hire is that take-up depends on a comprehensive network, and growth of the network depends on seed corn funding by willing partners or demand from an existing core of users. Hundreds more Docks, and tens of thousands of new members will be needed to create a viable international network, but despite all the technical issues, growth in usage continues to be strong, averaging 40% a year.

With this relatively small network, users generally hire and return bikes at the same place, but the much grander long-term aim is to integrate the scattered units, including any private schemes that wish to come on board, allowing full interchangeability of both users and bikes. If the scheme does eventually take off - and further expansion is very much in the balance - the impact will be huge. For occasional Brompton users, actually owning a bike might no longer be necessary. Registered users have their own pin-code, and with a comprehensive network, they would be able to access a folding bike wherever and whenever they need it. After a period of hire that might be anything from a few hours to several months, they would return the bike to the original Dock, or to any other worldwide. In the event of a failure - right down to a simple puncture - the user simply swaps bikes at a convenient Dock. The system automatically reports the failure to the local service agent, and prevents it being hired until the repair has been completed. This concept of 'leasing' rather than buying a bicycle brings several advantages. The user has the freedom to pick up a bike when it will be most useful, and - more importantly - to get rid of it again when it would be a hindrance, as on a crowded train, and that's what interests the train operating companies.

Initially Brompton Dock offered two tariffs: frequent users paying £50 a year, plus £4 a day, and occasional 'leisure' users paying £10 a year, plus £8 a day. The tipping point between the two options was at 10 days a year, or just under one hire a month. This was rather more than the company had hoped to charge, and the high annual fees proved a stumbling block with such a new and innovative scheme. It was found necessary to cut the regular user charge to £20, with the leisure charge being reduced to just £1. With the 2016 Brompton M3L costing almost £1,000 to buy, leasing a bike on easy terms is certainly a cost-effective option for occasional users, particularly as the cost includes all maintenance and repair.

In London, of course, there is stiff competition from the Santander 'Boris' bike scheme, which charges in a slightly different way. There's no pre-registration, and users can simply turn up and go using a credit card, booking access for £2 per 24 hour period, plus £2 for each riding period in excess of 30 minutes.

For public transport operators, concerned about the increasing number of folding bikes on busy train, plane and bus services, the concept of commuters picking up a bike from a dispenser at journey's end is a seductive one, and this project promised to help defuse the thorny issue of bikes cluttering up valuable passenger space. Environmentally and financially, there's little sense in carrying a 12kg bike for perhaps thousands of miles as luggage, particularly on a plane, when an identical machine could be made available at the traveller's destination.

The original Guildford Dock worked with smartcard technology, the user simply turning up and running a personal smartcard through a reader on the Dock. This made booking in advance difficult to arrange, but a guaranteed advance booking was essential to attract business users. Someone arriving at (for example) Manchester Piccadilly station for a business meeting in the city needs to be quite confident that a bike will be waiting, or

Initially Docks were intended to be made to the same basic forty locker template (below). At less than 1.6m tall there is no requirement for planning permission in the UK and they can be relatively easily delivered and even moved around on site if required.

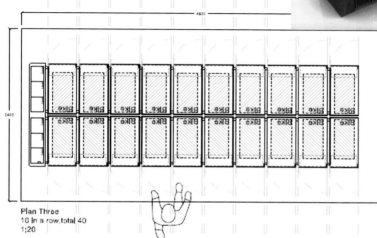

Plan Three
10 in a row, total 40
1:20

Docks could be produced in a variety of colour schemes to suit the organisation running the scheme (above).

A Brompton Dock takes shape at Street Associates' factory. Not only do the Docks have to be storm, vandal and user proof, but the high-tech electronics required mean each locker has to be wired up as part of the construction process.

The contract for manufacture has since been awarded to CHH CoNeX and docks are made at their sizeable Birmingham plant.

they'll opt for the reliable old-tech taxi-rank instead. The Docks are now controlled by text messaging from mobile phones, enabling a bike to be booked the night before, giving guaranteed availability. And the technology has gained a much friendlier face. In case of problems, users can speak to one of a small team of home working mums with the fingertip technology to remotely inspect a Dock anywhere in the world in real time, and sort out bike retrieval and return issues.

The current Dock design is much sleeker than the original slightly industrial appearance (see previous page), with some having the option of solar power providing the electricity for their running. This obviates the need for connecting to the mains supply, itself a process that can be problem fraught.

The Brompton Dock concept could yet fulfil its potential. Transport operators, local authorities and others are as keen as ever (desperate in some cases) to reduce their reliance on cars and car parking. And just as the Brompton itself has become a fashion icon, a Dock pin number may yet become the norm for busy urbanites.

For Brompton itself, the advantages are less sharply defined. The thousand-odd hire bikes to date represent a mere pinprick on the annual sales of around 40,000. If the scheme takes off as hoped, sales of bikes to individuals may actually reduce slightly, but the hope is that long- or short-term bike hire will draw in new users who might not have been tempted to risk buying a Brompton of their own. And the assumption is that many of these new users will choose to buy one after hiring for a few months. Even if they don't, the high profile of the Docks at railway stations and other transport nodes, should increase demand one way or another. In some ways, the development of the Dock is an admission that the Brompton cannot realistically be made much smaller or lighter. The neat lateral thinking behind this scheme has been to change the way the existing bike is made accessible to users: if it doesn't need to be heaved into a car boot, or carried by train, the bulk and weight of the machine becomes less of an issue.

Moving House Again

In 2013-14, bike sales amounted to 44,755, of which 77% were exported, and turnover once again broke all records at £27.2 million, yielding record profits of £3.5 million. The following year, the seemingly inexorable growth stuttered for the first time since the Sturmey-Archer collapse of 2000. This was partly down to running-in a new Benelux distributor and issues in Japan, but the primary cause seems to have been overstocking by dealers and distributors in 2013-14, when output finally exceeded demand after another of the periodic famines. Sales fell to 42,941 bikes, turnover almost levelled off at £27.5 million, and profits plummeted to £2.2 million, and then £0.2 million the following year. Staff costs were on the rise too, and another big expense was starting to make itself felt, as the company began the move from the Brentford factory to bigger premises. Brompton had looked closely at Wales, Northern Ireland, and even Eastern Europe, but eventually concluded that the theoretical cost advantages were far outweighed by the loss of that iconic 'Made in London' tag, so the search was refocussed on west London.

In truth, the company had outgrown the Brentford factory some years before. Stock storage space had long been overwhelmed, and the company had leased a satellite site just off the Great West Road in April 2013. This was primarily used for storage, but had increasingly become a sub-assembly area too. Running back and forth between two factories, and sending more and more frames to Wales for painting was clearly expensive, inefficient and unsustainable. To achieve further growth - and Brompton was aiming to more than double output to 100,000 units a year - it was essential to bring everything back under one roof.

After a few fruitless leads, the company found a warehouse in Greenford, a few miles to the north. In logistical terms it was ideal, sandwiched between Greenford's tube and railway station, and the Paddington arm of the Grand Union canal, giving easy cycle access to central London, and - in the longer term - the proposed Old Oak Common HS2 station. In the more immediate future, the factory would be a couple of cycling miles from Ealing's Crossrail station.

Formerly used by the H&M fashion chain, the warehouse offered some 84,000 square feet of factory and office space - four times as much as the Brentford factory. Tellingly, the new unit looked quite well filled almost immediately, but there was now room for expansion.

Back in the 1990s, with a handful of staff and a few manually-operated machines, moving from the Arches to Chiswick had been no more than a temporary inconvenience, but with over 200 staff building 100 bikes a day, it was a much bigger deal. The move alone cost over £2 million, with the extra rent and rates of the new factory expected to add around £1 million to the annual outgoings. On the other hand, a great deal is already being saved in reduced transport costs and tighter control over logistics through bringing everything in-house (except of course the Yorkshire titanium operation). Even in a worst-case scenario of zero growth the new factory is expected to pay for itself.

The factory move was announced in August 2015, with the move and build-up of production at the new site being carefully phased to minimise disruption to production schedules. The new plant was substantially up to speed by early 2016, and officially opened by His Royal Highness the Duke of Edinburgh in November 2016.

Core of the new plant is the much bigger factory floor, including brazing stations, and two production lines. As the Brentford factory reached capacity, the single line had gone to a seven day week, operated by two teams - one working four days, and the other a three day weekend (at a time and a half rate - an expensive solution). The two lines now work conventional hours simultaneously, but of course the capacity is there to introduce two or even more shifts per line.

Workers conditions and pay have changed almost out of recognition. The days of piece work - when workers were encouraged to churn out as much as possible - are long gone, and Brompton now pays employees by their skill level, a change that has staff positively queueing up to pass out with new skills. The multi-skilled are especially prized for their ability to move on and off the various assembly jobs as required. Generally speaking, each line runs with 19 staff at full speed, or eight or nine at half speed.

The bigger shop floor (above) could now accommodate two production lines like that below.

© London Cyclist

Frame brazing underway at the new Greenford factory. The aim is to increase quality and production in this critical area with the introduction of these bespoke built brazing bays, complete with gas piped directly to the station.

The brazing stations are essentially unchanged, but gas is now piped in rather than stored in bottles at each station. This eliminates the time-consuming, and sometimes back-breaking task of swapping bottles.

In place of that 'break' from work, brazers are encouraged to rest and exercise at intervals. Again, without the piece work, brazers are paid a set skilled rate, with build and quality-control targets. The accent is on a steady pace rather than periods of frenetic time-is-money activity. Efficiency is slightly up, and there are currently 35 brazing stations, slightly fewer than at Brentford.

Writing in late 2016, two areas of production are still outsourced: wheel-building and painting (actually powder-coating, as it has been since Brompton's earliest days). The Greenford paint shop cost half a million pounds, and is gradually taking over the painting operations from the long-established subcontractor in South Wales, which has been given two years notice, to allow a carefully phased transition.

The paint shop - a convoluted miracle of tightly coiled hanging conveyors - carries components through a dense spray of oxsilan primer/bonding agent, followed by a low-temperature drying oven, a visit to the main robotic spray booth, followed by a high temperature oven bake, which melts the powder to produce a tough, durable finish. Early Bromptons were primed with gold-coloured zinc phosphate, which was later outlawed for its toxicity and replaced with less effective iron phosphate, recognisable by its black colour. Oxsilan is nearly as effective as zinc, non-toxic, and its application uses less energy and water.

When the plant is up to speed, it will have more than enough capacity to undertake subcontract work for other companies, and - although no-one will even hint at this openly - make it much easier for Brompton to introduce variants such as child-carriers in the future. Wheel-building is a specialist craft, still carried out at two small factories in the West Midlands, but again, both suppliers have been put on notice that this operation will gradually be brought in-house. One is the very long-established Mike Hesson, by now

The paint shop will bring the operation in house and allow for extra capacity to take on work from other firms.

© Alexander Henshaw

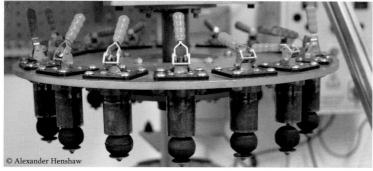

© Alexander Henshaw

Having painted frames more readily to hand (above) will increase efficiency at the new factory. Indeed, the large new Greenford premises are a blend of the innovatively practical, such as the new 'rumbling machine' (left - for more on this see page 128) and a new management culture that encourages relaxation as one element in producing an efficient workforce (below left).

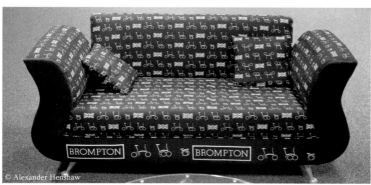

© Alexander Henshaw

123

somewhat past retirement age, who has built wheels for Brompton from the earliest days. The new factory is an airy, relaxed place. Fig trees grow from old handlebar boxes (an Andrew Ritchie-esque touch, but actually post Andrew), and staff are encouraged to relax in a Google-style mezzanine play area, complete with elderly, but serviceable piano, a pool table and a bar area, brazed, as you might expect, from reject rear frame tubes.

In the early days, Brompton was too small to develop an 'us and them' management-worker culture. Today it is big enough, but enlightened enough to avoid such industrial pitfalls. There are no remote 'suits' upstairs, and no awkward union reps on the shop floor.

Quality is the key word. For 15 minutes every morning workers from every area, both upstairs and downstairs come together for a Quality Team meeting, Brompton's answer to the Japanese Kaizen (or continuous improvement) concept.

The Future

Where is Brompton heading in 2017, and what technology are we likely to see on new bikes in the future? One thing looks fairly certain - after a decade which saw the bikes getting lighter by around 100 grams a year, the era of easy weight loss is over, at least for the time being. The only practical way to reduce weight further would be a complete titanium frame, but despite the success of the Brompton-Fletcher subsidiary, it will be some time before the Sheffield factory is able to produce titanium front forks and seat pillars, so the early introduction of a main frame is extremely unlikely.

Other technologies might be worth experimenting with, if only to rule them firmly out. The 1/2-inch pitch bicycle chain has been around for more than a century, albeit narrower and lighter than in the past. A smaller pitch - and chains down to a 6mm pitch and 7.4mm width are widely available - weighs around half as much. More importantly, with more teeth, smaller sprockets and chainrings can be fitted, saving yet more weight.

Toothed polymer belts offer a clean(er!) drive, a big bonus on a folding bike. They have tended to be a heavy, cumbersome option in the past, but again, the strength, weight and efficiency of micro-pitch belts has improved a lot in recent years.

Tyres are another area where weight can be saved and ride and handling improved. Back in 1999, Andrew Ritchie designed the Brompton tyre around the lightweight Primo, which offered a step-change by reducing weight and rolling resistance. Lightest and freest rolling of the two Brompton tyres was the non-Kevlar 'Yellow Flash', but its alleged skittishness on some surfaces led to its being withdrawn in 2008, leaving only the 'Green Flash' - a good tyre, but it wasn't all that light and it didn't roll as well.

Sixteen years after the introduction of the Brompton tyre, research into its replacement seems long overdue. Tyre compounds and tread patterns are better understood today than they were at the turn of the century.

Another area where modern tyre compounds are worth investigating is so called 'solid' tyres. These bring the enormous benefit of total puncture resistance - something that many users would be keen to see as an option. In the past, solid tyres have tended to be heavy, and hard work on the road, but the best available today are broadly comparable with a typical pneumatic tyre. With access to state-of-the-art materials expertise, and the purchasing muscle that comes with an annual output of 40,000 bikes, Brompton could realistically specify and market its own solid tyre.

A number of other projects have been discussed, but are unlikely to progress for now. The

6-speed (or more accurately, 2x3-speed) bikes are very efficient, but some customers dislike the twin gear levers. The factory hoped to combine both into a single lever linked to a control-box near the back wheel, operating both the derailleur and hub gear systems, but this highly complex project has been put on hold, although the detailed design of the existing triggers has been improved.

It's really no surprise that the complex combined shifter failed to pass the 'Brompton' test. The bike has succeeded in part because the surplus fat has long been hewn from the design. All mobility machines - from pushchairs to jet aircraft - tend to become flabby and over-complex in middle age, as new ideas are bolted on. It's a trap the Brompton designers are determined not to fall into. Replacing the 6-speed with Sturmey-Archer's new S50(w) wide-ratio 5-speed hub gear has been rejected too. Returning to a 5-speed hub would tick a number of boxes: a single shifter, and a wide gear range, but experience with the previous 5-speed in the 1990s showed that efficiency was relatively low and reliability a bit unpredictable. To improve resilience, Sturmey has made the new hub quite a bit wider, making fitting to the Brompton impractical. Brompton's own 6-speed solution is light and effective, with a wider gear range, and in-built redundancy! If one of the two gear systems fails, the user still has two or three gears to get home with. And with well-established 1-, 2-, 3- and 6-speed options, the company is wary of confusing the public further by adding to the range.

But for now, says MD Will Butler-Adams, the factory needs to concentrate on making production more efficient and improving quality. Fine-tuning build quality has become something of a Holy Grail at Brompton. Obviously a better bike yields happier customers, but an improvement in quality can improve productivity too:

"...If you're not up to speed with quality, you have a lot of rejects, a lot of rework and a lot of wasted time, energy and effort. If you find a mainframe problem after you've built a complete bike, think of the amount of work needed to take that out and replace it. Or if someone has reamed a hinge wrongly and there's play in it, the time it takes to get the entire bike back and replace it! Get it right first time. So actually, by improving quality you improve efficiency and you increase output..."

And in these tougher times, Brompton has fought hard to control prices. In 2013, a typical M3L cost 6.3% more than it had the previous year. The annual price increase was brought down to 2.7% in 2014, 0.5% in 2015, 1.6% in 2016, and -1.5% in 2017 - a real fall of 3% over the four years, allowing for inflation.

Backing Britain

Brompton has rarely advertised in the past, and sees little place for advertising in its ambitious future growth plans. The marketing budget, says Will Butler-Adams, is best spent on looking after existing customers. Experience has shown that happy customers are ambassadors for Brompton, enthusiastically demonstrating and selling the bike. The company will continue supporting events like the annual Brompton World Championships, helping it fulfill its aim of continued growth without advertorial, along with continuing dealer support, all in the best tradition of the Ritchie marketing philosophy that has worked so well for so long. Is the future an exciting place?

"The message is that we've taken a decision to grow and become a global player. We're proud to be a British company, and determined to remain independent. Hopefully, we'll still be here in another 25 years!"

For Will Butler-Adams, the future holds many challenges. In 2011/12, annual output reached 30,000 bikes, and in 2016-17, it's hovering around the 40,000 region, with the new factory giving plenty of room for expansion. If the company can build 40,000 bikes profitably in Greenford, one might assume it could build 300,000 a year even more profitably in China. Is Brompton still committed to manufacturing in the UK? Fifteen years ago building bikes overseas might have been an option, but in post-Brexit Britain, manufacturing is very much back on the political agenda, and with the pound at a historic low, the balance sheet has moved decisively towards the UK. Brexit is something of a mixed blessing for Brompton. The low pound is good news for the 80% of output that's exported, but bad news for imports, and - as we've seen - Brompton imports a lot of parts. Nevertheless, the company was able to reduce net prices by 7% globally in September 2016, which can only be good news for sales. Leaving Europe might also result in favourable trade deals with the Far East and the USA, but in the short term at least, the company's very important European sales look likely to suffer.

Brompton's issues are broadly those of UK PLC. The company has always been dependent on links to Europe, but Europe now takes only 30% of output, and that proportion is shrinking. There's growth just about everywhere else, from the USA to China, which already accounts for 3% of output from a standing start. Favourable trade deals with the Americas and the Far East could be of huge benefit to Brompton, as indeed, to other British manufacturers. A new generation of Government ministers and opposition spokesmen are already queueing up to deliver soundbites from the Greenford factory floor, and who can blame them?

For all sorts of entirely practical reasons, Will Butler-Adams is adamant that Brompton will continue to build bikes in the UK:

"Ours is an intellectual property business. There are some 1,200 parts in a bike, and a lot are unique. Describing our bike takes 30,000 to 40,000 drawings, but in describing the machines to make our bike there are maybe 300,000 - 400,000 drawings. So the cleverness is in the bike, yes, but there's far more cleverness in how to make the bike. As soon as you take that out to China, you teach people how to do it and they will leave, perhaps to work for Cannondale, who are out there already. So we haven't patented anything, but we keep our knowledge in-house in our staff. If you go out to China you make more money for a couple of years, then suddenly the copy from Dahon really is good because all your cleverness has gone into the Dahon. Suddenly you have to cut your margins, so you don't have enough money to do R & D, you don't have enough money to develop new ideas and it just stagnates and sits there. Game over."

Asia won't be ignored though. In Japan, where the Brompton costs ten times as much as some cheaper brands, consumers have demonstrated a willingness to pay a premium for a quality European product, and sales remain strong.

In March 2011, Japan became the test-bed for a new Brompton innovation when 'Brompton Junction', a Brompton-specific store, opened in Kobe. The policy was an instant success, and stores followed in Hamburg, Amsterdam and, signalling the company's Far-Eastern aspirations, Shanghai. By 2016, these pathfinder stores had been joined by London (naturally), Milan, Beijing, Chengdu, Munich, Tokyo, Barcelona and Suzhou. The branded stores present the bike in a uniform and carefully manicured form, with expert staff willing and able to demonstrate the numerous options. Even if they weren't profitable in themselves (and they are), the Brompton Junction outlets are marketing gold - a priceless shop-window.

As with the Docks, the risk is usually shared with local partners. Most Junction shops are based on existing bike shops that had found the majority of their sales were of Bromptons and Brompton spares. There are exceptions though, notably in China, where independent bicycle dealers simply didn't exist. The Chinese outlets had to be set up and paid for from scratch, a somewhat riskier business, and one shop has subsequently closed.

The Chinese market is different in almost every respect from the others. Folding bike commuting is unknown there, and as in much of Asia, the bike is seen as an expensive European toy ("Not just a premium product", says Will Butler-Adam, "It's a super-premium product!").

But China is a breathtakingly vast market and its giant cities are beset by pollution issues. The Brompton needs to become mainstream in China, and no doubt it will.

In China, as elsewhere, Butler-Adams believes that the continuing concern over global warming may see cars eliminated from some cities and a great increase in cycle infrastructure. Brompton starts with a unique product and expertise in dealing with transport planners and public transport providers, expertise that could be exported anywhere in the world.

What of the competition? "Forget the small-fry like Dahon. The real competition is going to come from the likes of Giant and Trek. They don't have serious folding bikes now, but they haven't really been trying. They're not stupid."

The opening of the Shanghai Brompton Junction store in July 2016 reinforced Brompton's commitment to becoming a global player.

Throughout most of this story, Brompton has been one of a handful of small British cycle manufacturers, fighting for the market scraps left behind by three or four really big companies, such as Raleigh and Dawes. Today, only Brompton and Pashley manufacture bikes here in any number. Of the two, Pashley held top spot until it lost the Post Office bicycle contract. Since then, Brompton has found itself at the top of the tree - an almost unimaginable scenario, even ten years ago.

Previous printings of this book ended with the bike's designer still very much involved, but sadly, on 3rd March 2016, Andrew Ritchie resigned as a director, citing differences with the Brompton management team. The company kept this resignation quiet, and it was not until September that the story broke in the conventional media and as a series of outlandish conspiracy theories on social media. In fact, Ritchie remained the biggest shareholder, with an 18% stake, although now a very long way from controlling the company.

Why did he feel the need to go? He had been frustrated by the occasional engineering own goals, but the engineering expertise was reawakening by 2016. The truth seems to be nothing more than a difference in management style. Andrew had always controlled and overseen every single aspect of his small, then medium-sized company, from floor cleaning products through the purchase of nuts and bolts to the design of jigs and work-stations.

Will Butler-Adams' style is about *enabling* the much bigger workforce to do their creative best. Perhaps the engineering hiccups had been exacerbated by Andrew's continuing presence. With such a strong and multi-talented character looking over their shoulders, the new team had never really felt willing to take responsibility, always expecting Andrew to fine-tune projects and sign them off. They really were on their own now.

Besides the bike itself, Andrew Ritchie designs are everywhere in the new factory. One of the last projects to carry the hallmarks of the Ritchie genius was the wonderfully Emett-esque 'rumbling machine'.

Grit blasting brazed components had always been a messy, dangerous and polluting process, with stray grit causing all sorts of issues at the painting stage. The rumblers are built around a ring of squash balls that expand to grasp the inside of frame tubes, allowing them to be lowered into a frothing, boiling mass of ceramic beads floating in lime juice. As the beads circulate, they cause the ring of components to float slowly round without outside assistance. The machines are supremely elegant, practical, and world-class in their effectiveness. Also hypnotically watchable.

Feeling the need to strengthen the boardroom with Andrew's departure. Butler-Adams brought in several new faces, including Dan Cobley former MD of Google UK, but the one that caused a minor media storm was 'serial entrepreneur' Luke Johnson. As Johnson is known in part as a successful venture capitalist, there was a great deal of suspicion at first about his intentions. Was he there to asset strip the company and flog the intellectual property to the Far East?

The reality is that Johnson's venture capital firm was not involved, and - apparently a bit of a Brompton nut - he had bought a small 3% personal shareholding to bring his considerable expertise to the board.

Johnson is a long way from the typical venture capitalist, and indeed, something of a philanthropist - chairman of the Institute of Cancer Research and a former Chairman of Action on Addiction. He has also involved himself with the arts, as chairman of Channel 4 from 2004 to 2010, and chairman of the Royal Society of Arts from 2009 to 2012.

He's a very big financial beast, and an extremely tough and able businessman. "Luke has made board meetings rather less comfortable… he holds us to account," says Will Butler-Adams. Crucially, his appointment has also met with the quiet approval of Andrew Ritchie. And so, as the Brompton enters its third decade of production, the company looks secure, both financially and intellectually. But what of Andrew Ritchie, the brilliant engineer who started it all? In 2016, free at last, Andrew decided to start all over again, leasing a small workshop hidden away in a garden off the Goldhawk Road. It's The Arches all over again, but with a few quid in his pocket, Andrew has been able to buy slightly newer machinery. What is he going to design? He won't say, but then perhaps he doesn't know. There's a whole world of industrial adventure out there waiting to be discovered. At some point - perhaps mulling over a pint in a favourite Chiswick watering hole - Andrew will hear a chance remark or spot the blindingly obvious thing that no-one else has spotted, and the spark of an idea will take root. We wait with trepidation.

2016 saw Andrew Ritchie return to his own workshop where he has a blank slate to turn his attention to any new engineering conundrums he might choose...

The World of Brompton Specials This Juliane Neuß designed 'Brecki' recumbent is a superb example of the way the Brompton has inspired other cycle designers and engineers to come up with their own take on the machine.

The World of Brompton Specials

Steve Parry and the SP Specials

Inevitably, the neat fold and quality ride of the Brompton has attracted inventors of various kinds over the years. Perhaps the most prolific Brompton-adaptor was West Country gas fitter Steve Parry, who has produced a number of sporty SP derivatives over a couple of decades.

Parry had emigrated to Australia but returned to the UK in 1997 and began experimenting with the Moulton, Birdy and Brompton. He soon found that there was particular interest in customized versions of the Brompton and by 1998 the bike had become the core of the SP product range.

The SP bikes built up quite a following amongst enthusiasts. Like the Brompton itself, machines were specified on an individual basis for customers. The more radical machines were completely reworked, with different seat pillars, handlebar stems, and even frame tubes, but customers could also buy a basic Brompton upgraded with a selection of 'go-faster' accessories. The first SP bikes were fitted with the 7-speed Shimano Nexus hub, but later machines used derailleur gears, offering a wider range and closer ratios than Brompton's own hubs. These conversions took on a special significance in 2001, when the supply of 5-speed Sturmey-Archer geared hubs dried up, and the factory output was limited to 3-speeds. Derailleurs can cause chain alignment problems when folding, so like the Birdy, the SP bikes needed to be folded with a little more care, but they certainly filled a gap in the market between the standard machines and the much more expensive Birdy and Bike Friday.

Other derivatives included a superb single-speed, a 6-speed (3-speed hub with dual-chainring), a Shimano Nexus 8-speed, and eventually the Rohloff 14-speed, which proved to be the most popular variant, with more than 50 sold by 2009.

Steve Parry's superb single speed.

The front of the SP trike is built from two mainframe tubes and two rearward-facing Brompton forks, but as trikes go, Steve Parry's Brompton tricycle is relatively compact when folded. Only one has been made to date.

Early SP bikes were often fitted with V-brakes, but when the Brompton brakes improved, these became largely redundant. Parry also fitted disc brakes to a few Brompton SPs.

Perhaps the most intriguing SP was the hingeless Brompton, which kept the standard rear triangle hinge, allowing the rear wheel to fold under the bike, but featured a long, custom-made frame tube of aluminium, with detachable handlebars. The basic fold was only in one plane, resulting in a long, tall, and very thin package, but the bicycle also came apart Bike Friday-style, and could be carried in a hard case.

Once Steve Parry's fertile imagination had settled on the Brompton, there was no stopping him, and the SP family were soon joined by a tricycle and a tandem. The extraordinary SP Trike was made for a friend with balance problems in 2004. The spider-like machine was effectively a normal Brompton aft of the steering tube, where the conventional frame tube met two other mainframe tubes mounted at right angles, each carrying a front wheel at its outer end. Folding amounted to tucking the rear wheel under, dropping the seat pillar, and folding down the handlebars. This produced an unwieldy package measuring 92cm wide and 92cm long, but by trike standards it was pretty compact, and small enough to be manoeuvred through a wide door, or fit into an estate car.

The tandem was, in some ways, the most conventional SP design, being a standard Brompton and a half, with some additional cross-bracing to strengthen the, by now, very long mainframe. Folding wasn't quite to Brompton standards, because although the machine retained a rear hinge, this no longer served any purpose, but it wasn't bad. The rear wheel folded under, the stoker handlebar stem folded down to the left, and the captain's frame tube and handlebar stem folded to the right. Quite a large package, but like the trike, very small by the standards of its contemporaries, and surprisingly rigid and pleasant to ride. The prototype was equipped with a Rohloff hub (the extra width making no difference in this case), front hub dynamo and V-brakes.

The first SP trailer bike, produced as far back as 2001, was a superb machine - basically a standard Brompton with a double-length frame tube, terminating in a universal joint, cleverly produced from a Brompton head-set and rear frame bearings. The trailer bike clamped around the seat pillar using the front part of a frame tube and seat pillar clamp. This worked very well, and could even carry a small adult over moderate distances (one took part in the London-Brighton ride in 2007) but the cost of manufacture was prohibitive and it was destined to be a critical success, but a commercial failure. The SP child seat filled a major gap in the market, left when the Spanish distributor temporarily stopped producing the IT Chair (see following chapter).

The SP business relied on a steady stream of wealthy cycle enthusiasts, and was badly affected when Brompton began to produce up-market derivatives in-house in 2005, when the sportier part-titanium bikes were introduced. Business was further hit with the credit crunch of 2008 and arrival of the Brompton Wide Ratio hub, which made it possible to buy a wider gear range 'off the shelf'. Steve Parry produced a few more machines with exotic gear conversions, such as the 14-speed Rohloff and 9-speed SRAM, but the core business had gone and in the summer of 2009 he ceased trading. Other firms have followed where Steve lead, (though undoubtedly lacking his true flair for innovation), with Kinetics of Glasgow currently still finding there is a market for such Brompton modifications as disc brakes and hub gears.

Steve Parry   tel:01934 516158

Steve Parry demonstrates his folding tandem at the 2008 Brompton World Championships. Although the rear frame clamp is visible, it is only for show, as the frame tube aft of the front hinge and associated braces are brazed into one rigid unit. When folded, the rear wheel folds under, and the front wheel folds round, with a rigid frame in between! Total length is a little longer than two Bromptons, but it's still more or less unique in tandem terms.

The SP Rohloff special with disc brakes.

135

Juliane Neuß

Juliane Neuß is one of a handful of female cycle engineers who have had a disproportionately large effect on the trade. Juliane, now based in Clausthal-Zellerfield in Germany's Harz mountains, was a recumbent enthusiast, who discovered the Brompton in 1993. As so often the case, her Brompton recumbent was born of necessity: local trains in Germany provide space for bicycles, but fast, long distance services usually do not.

Unable to take her recumbent to a rally in Hamburg in May 1996, Juliane travelled with her Brompton. During the journey she began to ponder whether the Brompton itself could be turned into a recumbent, and later in the day, she pushed the saddle right down, thrust her feet forward to engage imaginary pedals, and coasted off. It worked!

Four weeks after this first trial, the prototype 'Brecki' recumbent was born. The Brecki was a clever adaptation utilizing a toothed rubber drive belt from a replacement chainring on the normal bottom bracket to a boom ahead of the front wheel. The saddle was replaced with a recumbent seat sat on top of the main frame tube, with the handlebars staying pretty much as Brompton intended. Luggage was either a backpack hanging from the back of the seat, or small panniers on the rear rack. The beauty of the conversion was that it came as a bolt-on kit, so the bike could be reconfigured in an hour or two, and indeed, the kit could be sold and transferred to another Brompton.

The Brecki worked quite well, and what's more, it folded into a package little bigger than a standard Brompton (L75cm x H67cm x W34cm), which in recumbent terms was (and still is) nothing short of miraculous.

As Andrew Ritchie had found, producing the prototype was the easy bit. After the first trials in June 1996, and an enthusiastic reception from recumbent enthusiasts, Juliane spent more than a year searching for a manufacturer, before deciding to go it alone. After a draftsman friend had risked his job producing CNC-compatible drawings at work early one morning, Juliane and her boyfriend, Ingo Kollibay, were able to start home manufacture, and the first production machine was tested in August 1998.

By 2004, nearly 90 had been produced, but Juliane lost a lot of money making the kits, and seems to have been relieved when Brompton altered the frame making the kit impossible to fit, thus bringing manufacture to an end!

Like Steve Parry, Juliane Neuß has adapted as the market for Bromptons and Brompton accessories has changed. Since 2004, her main business has been fitting the 8-speed Shimano Nexus hub to give a wider gear range (albeit on a wider bike!). But although the Brecki is long gone, she continues to receive regular enquiries, and doesn't rule out relaunching an improved kit: "During all those years, several people tried to make a folding recumbent, but none folded as small as the Brecki!" In 2017, she became Brompton's mechanic-in-chief in Germany, training other bicycle mechanics.

Juliane Neuß   email: info@junik-hpv.de   tel: +49 0173 930 1111
web: www.junik-hpv.de/html/brompton_tuning.htm

Juliane Neuß's Brompton recumbent, the Brecki, was a great feat of engineering, folding to little larger than a standard Brompton package. As Juliane demonstrates with the prototype below, it rode pretty well too. When Brompton introduced the long wheelbase frame in 2004 the kit could no longer be fitted and production ceased.

Weight Watchers

Weight is a far more serious problem with folding bikes than conventional machines, and numerous engineers, both amateur and professional, have turned their attention to the Brompton. A typical Brompton today weighs about 11.5kg, with the S2L-X - the lightest factory variant - listed at 10.5kg, although Brompton does produce a few single-speed versions of this bike that are lighter.

In the early days, it was possible to trim weight from the bike fairly easily, but as the factory has sourced lighter components, this became increasingly difficult, although the recent retreat from lightweight technology, has made the DIY options more numerous! With some effort and expense, a 1990s-vintage Mark 2 L3 can be lightened from 12kg to about 10.4kg, but going beyond this can be expensive expensive. With a fair amount of expensive technology, it's possible to produce a fully-equipped bike (ie, with mudguards, a front carrier block and at least two gears) weighing about 9.2kg. To go further requires a titanium mainframe, and the expert in this field is Len Rubin...

Len, a native of Trenton, New Jersey, now working as a computer consultant in Portland, Oregon, was the undoubted champion of the lightweight Brompton. Rubin has had a long involvement with the bike trade, having owned several bike shops over the years. Although, in his own words, he has, "no formal training or natural aptitude for engineering or construction," Len has devoted much of his spare time to developing a better folding bike. Like Steve Parry, he quickly became captivated by the Brompton, but he caught the bug much earlier, writing to Andrew Ritchie in 1986, before the bike was even in mainstream production.

The first Rubin 'SuperBrompton', produced in 1996, was more an exercise in improving the braking and gear range of the bike, than removing weight. But gradually Len Rubin's machines became more sophisticated, utilizing the latest and lightest hydraulic V-brakes, derailleur gears, wheel rims and tyres, together with a number of custom-made parts such as double-butted spokes, lightweight hubs, and much else in titanium.

The 27-speed SuperBrompton weighed 9.7kg, and went on to be shown all over the world. Priced at US$6,000, Rubin sold about twenty in the next few years, before moving on to other projects. But as so many people close to the Brompton story have found, the possibilities kept nagging him, and in 2009 he unveiled a prototype of a full titanium version. What drives him to keep developing these superlative machines? "Anybody in their right mind would quit", says Len Rubin, "but I believe America really needs a bike that can tempt people out of their cars." The Brompton has this disturbing ability to fire up ordinary people with 'la vision grande'.

Only on the west coast of America would a designer have the sheer nerve to call a machine the UFB, or 'Ultimate Folding Bike', but Rubin was probably right. The entire frame of the SuperBrompton was made from beautifully-crafted titanium, broadly similar in appearance to the factory-made steel frame, but with thin-walled oversize tubes. The prototype was fitted with a 27-speed derailleur, and even in this form, Rubin claimed a weight of around 7.3kg (16lbs), making it almost certainly the lightest multi-speed folding bike ever made. Rubin also calculated that a single speed version would come in with a projected weight of 6.75kg. The UFB was expected to sell for "somewhere in the region of US$10,000", but even in California there's a limit, and the bike failed to attract customers, although Len may yet build more. Like Steve Parry in England, Len Rubin also intended to market high quality accessories, including a lightweight trailer.

Len Rubin e-mail: lenrubin@mac.com   tel: +1 503 287 2453
web: https://ufbusa.ishopserver.com/

Len Rubin and an enthusiastic customer with two early 'SuperBromptons' (above) and his latest ultralightweight 'UFB' or Ultimate Folding Bike (below).

Power Assistance

Although considered a purist, Andrew Ritchie made it clear in his original Brompton patent that the machine might at some stage be fitted 'with an electrical or internal combustion engine', his personal view was that the technology was some way off. How right he was! It was to be another 15 years before electrically-assisted bicycles became commonplace, and practical folding versions have taken much longer to arrive. The problem is weight, the old enemy of the folding bike. It's difficult enough to make a pedal-powered bike that can be carried with ease, but bringing batteries and motors into the equation takes another whole layer of cutting edge technology.

Several appalling power-assisted Chinese folders were produced in the first years of the new millennium, none being light enough, or compact enough to be regarded as practical machines. The breakthrough came in 2000 with the SRAM Sparc, a 5-speed hub incorporating an electric motor, which was adopted by Dahon and fitted to the 20-inch Roo in 2002. This Roo EL variant was powered by a tiny battery on the rear rack, feeding power to the motorized rear hub.

This original Sparc system had limited range, and offered weak assistance, but it was redesigned in 2005, making the Roo EL quite an effective machine. At 18kg, the bike was a touch heavy to lift, and the cost of the Sparc system had pushed the UK price up to £1,200, which in 2005 was pretty expensive. Despite a reasonable power-assisted range of about 20 miles, it failed to sell well, although it had demonstrated what could be achieved. The Roo EL remained in production until 2009, by which time it cost £1,400 and was selling in very small numbers.

After this promising start, Dahon's electric adventure seems to have involved a succession of duds, at least in terms of sales. The Boost utilised a Sunstar crank-drive motor in 2010, but it weighed 19.6kg, cost £2,000, and also appears to have sold in very small numbers, if at all. In 2013, the company teamed up with Currie Technologies to produce the single-speed IZIP E3 Compact, a conventional machine with a front hub motor and rear rack-mounted battery. The following year, the company experimented with the BionX EPS system, producing the 17kg Formula S18, which seems to have sold for a while in the USA for around $3,000. For certain other markets, Dahon introduced the Ikon, a rather cruder design, similar to the IZIP, with a TransX front hub motor and rear rack battery. At 21kg, this was not a very practical machine, although it still appears to be in production.

Other early 21st century attempts at popularising a folding electric bike included the Japanese produced Panasonic Will and the largely British Airnimal Joey Move. The former was a well-designed high quality folding pedelec (in other words an unusual beast indeed) but suffered from being underpowered compared to full size pedelecs (that is bikes where the power is switched on by pedalling rather than by throttle) and had a rather small battery.

The Joey used the high quality Canadian BionX EPS system, which boasted regenerative braking and a sophisticated computer console allowing the rider to adjust the power and regeneration (electric braking via the motor) settings. This was undoubtedly a nice ride, but the 24" Airnimal folder was never intended to have a quick, compact fold like the Brompton and you had to carry the front wheel separately. Like the Panasonic Will, it weighed around 17kg, which was fairly light, but still something of a problem for many potential users. You could remove the hefty 4.5kg battery from the Airnimal's frame, but you would then still be faced with the challenge of moving three separate components around - bike, front wheel and battery.

Above: The Nano hub motor generates great torque and so is good for heavy loads. But have plenty of towing experience before you take on a dinghy!

Below: Tony Castles engineered the Tongxin hub motor kit for the Brompton. Features included a protected cable run inside the front wheel catch and a luggage mounting block adapted to act as a battery connector. Unfortunately the kit was a victim of its own success and the project was overwhelmed by demand.

Despite this relatively cumbersome folding performance, Airnimal's offering seems to have found a niche and sold fitfully for a few years before being quietly withdrawn.

Cautiously eyeing these rather disappointing developments, Brompton did nothing officially, but in June 2007 an independent conversion was introduced by electronics engineer Tony Castles. The Nano-Brompton made use of the Tongxin, the lightest, most effective motor technology then available. This little motor went in the front wheel, with the brilliant lateral thinking of electrical contacts on the front carrier block, so that a battery could be fitted in the removable front pannier bag. This meant that the only extra weight on the bike was the motor and control electronics - around 3kg. A typical Nano-Brompton might weigh 14.4kg, but fitting the kit to an S2L-X could reduce the weight could be reduced to less than 13kg. The battery and pannier weighed another 4.4kg, but this could be carried in the other hand. It was still a relatively heavy package, but much more practical than anything that had come before.

With low motor gearing, the Nano-Brompton wasn't very fast, with a top assisted speed of only 12mph, but it was a very impressive hill-climber, and it could go great distances, with a range of up to 50 miles. Unfortunately, Tony Castle's small company was not prepared for the deluge of orders it received throughout 2007 and 2008, and problems with motor supply and battery reliability soon brought the project to a premature close. But the Nano had demonstrated the viability of an electric folding bike, and that there was plenty of demand for the right machine.

In 2008 Tongxin introduced a narrower, lighter motor (the original 100mm Nano motor needed custom forks to fit the Brompton) and updated kits to suit the Brompton (and other bikes) were introduced by the Electric Wheel Company. Sadly the reliability issues with motors and batteries soon resurfaced, and by 2010 production of the kits had been brought to a stand by outstanding warranty claims, principally over batteries. In February 2012, Tony Castles relaunched the machine as Nano 2.0, with numerous improvements, and the Nano Electric Bike company has sold conversions ever since. An increasingly popular option is a smaller Bosch 144Wh power-tool battery. This reduces range to 8-16 miles, but weighs only a kilogram, reducing the weight of the front pannier to around 2.5kg. A key advantage is that the Bosch battery is small enough to circumvent the ban on carrying lithium-ion batteries by air, and is accepted by most airlines as hold or carry-on luggage.

For a while the Nano had no real competition, but its success didn't go unnoticed, and the Electric Transport Shop chain launched the Brompton Sparticle, with a similar front motor layout, but a rather clumsy saddle stem battery pack. The battery was later moved to the front pannier, but the system still lacks the finesse and light weight of the Nano. It is, however, considerably more powerful.

Frustrated with Brompton's inability to supply an electric option, NYCeWheels of New York introduced a power-assist kit broadly similar to the Sparticle, but with a quieter (but weaker and heavier) direct drive motor. The battery goes in the front pannier, but like the Sparticle, this design lacks automatic contacts on the pannier block, so the battery must be clumsily disconnected before taking the pannier off the bike. NYCEWheels gets round the airline regulations with a twin 72Wh battery option, the two smaller batteries going in the pannier rear pockets.

Back in the UK Cambridge-based ARCC Innovations produced a neat looking front hub motor in 2015, initially only for demountable Moultons and the non-folding Cinelli. By 2016 they had extended their offering to Bromptons but the retro-fit kit prices, starting at £1795, may price them out of many potential sales. The ARCC system borrowed heavily from the Nano design in that it utilised Bosch powertool batteries with the option of carrying this in the front bag which features an electrical connection.

At a cursory glance it isn't at all obvious the Nano-Brompton is electrically-assisted. The battery powering the front hub motor is hidden in the front pannier whilst the controller is fixed to the handlebars.

143

Despite Brompton's plans to launch an electric version, there may well still be a market for a retro-fittable electric Brompton. Two contenders are Velospeed's friction drive (left) and the Pendix crank drive (below), both from Germany.

© Faltrad XXS

© Faltrad XXS

The latest power-assist kit for the Brompton utilises some neat lateral thinking. Velological of Germany makes a neat and extremely efficient rim-driven bottle dynamo recognised as one of the best lighting options around if you can afford it. In 2015, the company developed the technology to *provide* rather than generate power, with the Velospeed. This utilises two tiny motors sprung inwards against the rims of the front or rear wheel, and can be fitted to a wide range of bicycles. Junik-HPV, run by Brompton specialist Juliane Neuß has produced a mounting kit to fit the Velospeed motors onto an adapted Brompton rear rack. The entire kit is claimed to weigh less than 2kg, and give assisted range of up to 25 miles. When not in use, the motors can be sprung away from the rim, leaving a completely normal drive system. The Brompton Velospeed kit is expected to cost from €1,400 in 2017.

Another attempt to hit the magic compromise between weight, foldability and cleaness of electric integration comes from German firm Pendix. This system cleverly fits a gearless motor onto the non-chain side of the bottom bracket. The idea has clearly struck a chord in the electric bike design hotbed of continental Europe as it has also been taken up by Swiss-Italian collaboration Bimoz who have conceived a similar system. The world of electric folding bikes still clearly awaits a step change in technology before they become as popular as their non-folding electric cousins but designs like this look as though they might just point the way forward.

Meanwhile, the race is on amongst other manufacturers to introduce a practical, and reasonably priced electric folding bike before Brompton gets the market sewn up. Some of the better folding electric bike designs have brought together a Dahon-style folding bike with the excellent Panasonic crank drive motor. These include the E-motion Volt (rather tellingly reduced to £1,600 in 2016), and now with sensible and modifiable hub gearing as opposed to the original undergeared derailleur version, and the Swiss Flyer (superbly equipped, with a good gear range but costing over £3,000 in the UK in 2016).

In 2016 Tern announced that the Vektron electric folder, powered by the market leading crank drive motor system from Bosch, would be on sale in 2017 in both Europe and the US. No doubt this will be a very solid performer, but at over 22kg it's hardly in the highly portable category that a true folding electric bike should be.

Nano Electric Bikes
e-mail: lynda@nanoelectricbikes.co.uk
tel: 0845 094 2735
web: www.nanoelectricbikes.co.uk

Junik-HPV
e-mail: info@junik-hpv.de
tel: +49 0173 930 1111
web: www.junik-hpv.de

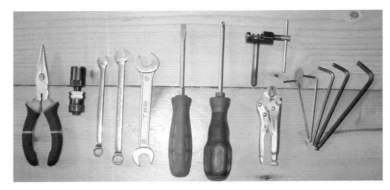

Using and Maintaining a Brompton The Brompton can be serviced in a small space and with a surprisingly basic list of tools. The exact make-up of the Brompton toolbox will vary according to the age of the bike, with a general move from spanners and screwdrivers to Allen keys, but this is a typical list (from left to right): pliers, crank extractor tool, 8mm and 10mm combination spanners, 13 x 15mm open-ended spanner (older front axle and saddle securing nuts may be different), 6mm x 100mm slotted screwdriver, Phillips #2 x 100mm screwdriver, chainlink extractor, 110mm Mole wrench (optional), 6mm, 5mm, 4mm, 3mm and 2.5mm Allen keys. Other items that might get infrequent use are a 10mm Allen key or 24mm AF socket to release the left-hand folding pedal, Sturmey-Archer cone spanner for hub adjustment, and a thin 32mm or 34mm open-ended spanner for adjusting the headset.

Using and Maintaining a Brompton

Note: The following maintenance and usage tips are not intended as comprehensive. For more detail on maintenance see PDF Owners Manuals at www.atob.org.uk Folding Bike Zone pages

Versatility and Handling

Over the years, the Brompton has found all sorts of roles way beyond the original brief of a car boot or rail commuter machine. Not only is the bike used to get to work, but increasingly it has *become* the office for many people. The Brompton quickly found a niche amongst surveyors, map-makers and other transport professionals who need to get around a small area quickly, with the convenience of being able to pack the bike away quickly and easily into a car, bus or train. A Brompton has even found its way to the Australian observatory at the South Pole. Other bikes are used for serious touring, the machine being quite capable of 60 to 70 miles in a day, or even more if set up carefully.

The Brompton is easy to ride, but for those who have never tried small wheels, the almost total lack of gyroscopic action from the front wheel can be unnerving at first. Some people never really acclimatize to this twitchy steering behaviour but most soon adapt, after which the cumbersome response of a big-wheeled bike will seem strange! A little more care is needed on pot-holes and rough surfaces, but in general, a Brompton can go anywhere and do anything a big-wheeled bike can do, even in surprisingly rough (but not muddy) off-road conditions. In city traffic, the short length of the machine, hub gears, and quick steering give a real advantage in nipping through traffic.

The bikes are easy and cheap to maintain and the factory's ability to provide spares for older models means a healthy resale value. However, there are a few points to watch, especially on older machines...

Buying Secondhand

Except for the most expensive Birdy and Bike Friday variants, folding bikes don't keep their value, but the Brompton is an exception. As a rule of thumb, an older Brompton can be expected to sell for its original price, so a Mark 1 might make £150 to £200, and a Mark 2, £300 to £350. This rule falls down slightly with newer bikes, but writing in 2016, Mark 3s and 4s generally fetch in excess of £400, and sometimes more, particularly when production hiccups result in a feeding frenzy for secondhand bikes. Rare colours and variants tend to attract higher prices, as do lightweight titanium bikes. These come up only rarely, but seem to sell for more than their original price, which isn't surprising, as they are lighter than the latest models. With new SL bikes only really being available to order, and sometimes with a waiting list, good secondhand examples are changing hands for close to the new price.

Brompton prices have stayed so buoyant because of the refreshing lack of inbuilt obsolescence that tends to plague other folding bikes, particularly the Dahon, which has a reputation for being impossible to mend. By contrast, Brompton can usually supply original parts, or better newer parts which will bolt straight on to the older machine, effectively upgrading it.

There are a few exceptions though. Mark 1 bikes have many hand made parts that have been out of stock for years, such as the chain tensioner and hinge assemblies. But the factory is generally keen to help and will always make efforts to keep older bikes on the road, with each case being taken on its merits.

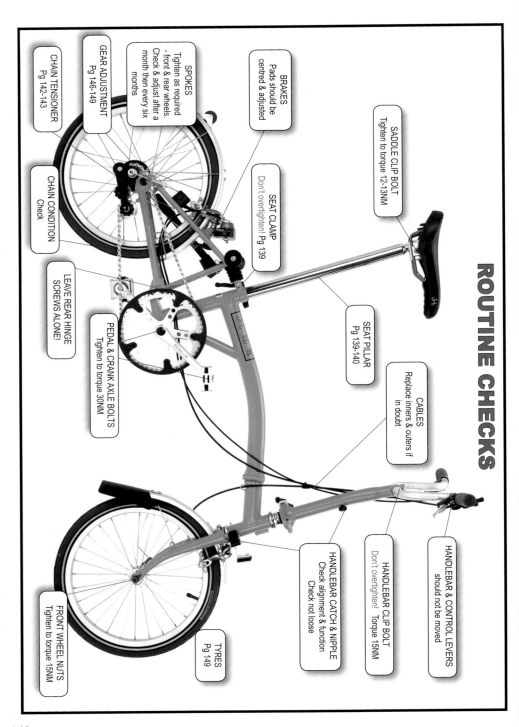

ROUTINE CHECKS

CHAIN TENSIONER
Pg 142-143

GEAR ADJUSTMENT
Pg 146-149

SPOKES
Tighten as required
- front & rear wheels.
Check & adjust after a
month then every six
months

BRAKES
Pads should be
centred & adjusted

SADDLE CLIP BOLT
Tighten to torque 12-13NM

CHAIN CONDITION
Check

SEAT CLAMP
Don't overtighten! Pg 139

**LEAVE REAR HINGE
SCREWS ALONE!**

PEDAL & CRANK AXLE BOLTS
Tighten to torque 30NM

SEAT PILLAR
Pg 139-140

CABLES
Replace inners & outers if
in doubt

HANDLEBAR CATCH & NIPPLE
Check alignment & function
Check not loose

HANDLEBAR CLIP BOLT
Don't overtighten! Torque 15NM

HANDLEBAR & CONTROL LEVERS
should not be moved

FRONT WHEEL NUTS
Tighten to torque 15NM

TYRES
Pg 149

LUBRICATION

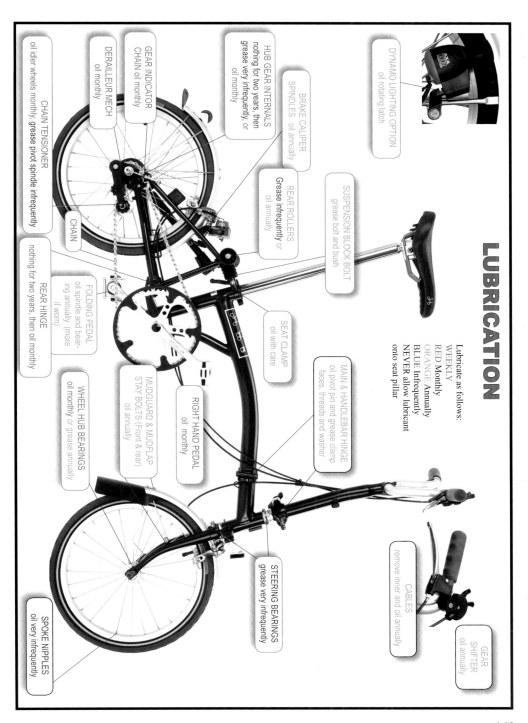

Lubricate as follows:
WEEKLY
RED Monthly
ORANGE Annually
BLUE Infrequently
NEVER allow lubricant
onto seat pillar

DYNAMO LIGHTING OPTION
oil rotating latch

HUB GEAR INTERNALS
nothing for two years, then
grease very infrequently, or
oil monthly

DERAILLEUR MECH
oil monthly

GEAR INDICATOR
CHAIN oil monthly

BRAKE CALIPER
SPINDLES oil annually

CHAIN TENSIONER
oil idler wheels monthly, grease pivot spindle infrequently

CHAIN

REAR ROLLERS
Grease infrequently or
oil annually

SUSPENSION BLOCK BOLT
grease bolt and bush

REAR HINGE
nothing for two years, then oil monthly

FOLDING PEDAL
oil spindle and bear-
ing annually (more
if worn)

SEAT CLAMP
oil with care

MAIN & HANDLEBAR HINGE
oil pivot pin and grease clamp
faces, threads and washer

WHEEL HUB BEARINGS
oil monthly or grease annually

MUDGUARD & MUDFLAP
STAY BOLTS (Front & rear)
oil annually

RIGHT HAND PEDAL
oil monthly

STEERING BEARINGS
grease very infrequently

CABLES
remove inner and oil annually

GEAR
SHIFTER
oil annually

SPOKE NIPPLES
oil very infrequently

149

Upgrades

With post-1988 bikes, almost anything can be fixed, although the failure of Sturmey-Archer caused some complications for a while, and there has been continued fallout in terms of spares. Mark 2 and early Mark 3 rear frames will only accept 3- or 5-speed Sturmey hubs, while later Mark 3 frames will only accept the SRAM 3-speed hub (or 6-speed variant), although they can be adapted to accept Sturmey hubs too. More recent Mark 4 bikes (post January 2005) have a universal rear frame, so any of these hubs can be fitted.

There were problems for the years that Sturmey hubs were not available, especially for owners of Mark 2 5-speed bikes, for whom hub failure (not uncommon) could mean replacing the entire rear frame. This is no longer the case, now that the 5-speed is back in production, but the short axle version unique to the Brompton is no longer made.

The derailleur changer braze-on (needed to convert 3-speeds into 6-speeds) is arrowed here. It was introduced as standard in spring 2001. Without it the rear frame will have to be replaced for one with the braze-on.

Fortunately, the longer axle fits perfectly well, albeit with a slight protrusion from the folded package. This can be ground off without causing harm to the hub.

Any rear frame fitted with the derailleur changer braze-on can be upgraded to 6-speed or the latest 6-speed BWR spec, but later Mark 3 frames will require a little modification to accept the BWR hub. With older bikes, the rear frame will have to be changed. As these bikes fetch good prices secondhand, an upgrade of this kind is unlikely to be cost-effective - you might just as well sell the bike and purchase a new one.

Generally speaking, newer bikes are more rigid, freer running, lighter and roomier, so although an early Mark 1 will in theory do everything a modern bike can do for less than half the price, it will never be quite as good. Upgrading to modern spec can more than double the cost of an early bike, so do think carefully before buying secondhand.

Common Problems

There are a number of ailments common to all Bromptons, many of which can be cured with a drop of oil or a minor adjustment. Starting with the most frequent issues:

Suspension Block Bolt

After a certain mileage, the bolt in the centre of the suspension block will begin to squeak rhythmically as the rider pedals, a sound that can be extremely hard to trace. This is caused by the factory-applied grease being washed out, so it will occur relatively rapidly on a commuter machine used daily in wet conditions, and may never occur on a leisure bike ridden only on sunny days.

With the rear suspension assembly removed from the bike, the bolt shaft and bush (arrowed) can be greased. If the bush or bolt shaft are badly worn, they will need to be replaced. These examples are marginal!

An immediate cure is to simply grab the suspension block and turn it around, presenting a new face to the bearing, which should instantly stop the noise. As soon as possible, the assembly should be stripped down and the bolt thoroughly greased before reassembly. In bad cases, the bolt and/or bearing may be badly worn and need renewing.

Lighter riders may prefer a softer suspension block. Standard blocks post-2008 are supposed to be softer than the older block. If this still feels hard, suitable polymer or rubber blocks, or even steel springs, can be found in a variety of strengths, and a bit of experimentation should yield something that works well for you. Since 2009, Brompton has produced an optional harder block, ideal for heavier riders or anyone riding hard who doesn't want to waste energy bouncing the suspension.

Seat Pillar

The seat pillar and bush can be affected by two contrasting conditions: slippage when fully tightened, and seizure when loose. If you're really unlucky, your bike may suffer from both conditions at the same time!

Slippage

This is usually caused by oil or grease contamination of the pillar and bush - even a tiny drop of hand cream or sun tan lotion is enough to make the pillar slip, but problems are much less common on bikes built after July 2007, which are fitted with a new clamp design. Before dismantling anything, check the condition of the clamp assembly. If the action is stiff, or the parts look dry or rusty, apply a drop or two of oil very sparingly to the eccentric, making sure oil is kept well away from the seat pillar. With the action working smoothly, check the tightness of the adjusting nut in the clamp. On older pre-2007 bikes this is a big self-locking nut, leading heavy-handed owners to overtighten it, which can distort or damage the frame. Adjustment may be required after the first few months of service, but extremely rarely thereafter. Movement of the nut must be made in very small increments, no more than one face ($1/6$ turn) at a time before rechecking the tightness of the clamp, and the sliding action of the pillar both clamped and unclamped. As a very rough guide, the early clamp - once properly lubricated - should close with the pressure of two fingers, and the later one - which clamps more efficiently - should close with one finger.

If the seat pillar slips, or the clamp is stiff to operate, a few drops of oil in the clamp eccentric will help it to move freely and increase clamping pressure. But oil MUST NOT be allowed to get near the seat pillar! The bush is inside the top of the frame, and on an elderly bike like this, may well need replacing.

If the pillar continues to slip after lubrication and adjustment of the clamp, remove the saddle, slide the pillar out from under the bike, and degrease both the pillar and the bush inside the frame with an old toothbrush and dilute detergent or an industrial solvent such as ketone (also useful for binding pillars - see following section). If this fails to work, it may be worth trying a different pillar, as the metallurgy can vary, and in extreme cases fitting a new frame bush, but cleaning and adjustment should work in 90% of cases.

Binding

A binding seat pillar can be caused by a number of factors. The most common is a worn or partially collapsed frame bush, or a bush distorted by underlying rust inside the frame, but other less common causes include a bent or badly scored seat pillar, or a distorted frame, usually caused by overzealous tightening of the clamp, as above. If a new bush is required, it will have to be 'superglued' into place, after all traces of old glue and rust have been removed. When the bushes are factory fitted, they are reamed to precisely the correct size, but this can also be done by hand. Insert the pillar as far as possible, tighten the clamp a couple of times, turning the pillar if you can, remove the pillar, and using a torch, look for shiny high spots. When these have been filed down, repeat the operation until the pillar runs freely when unclamped and locks firmly when clamped. As with other major frame operations, the Brompton factory can replace the seat pillar bush.

Frame and Stem Hinges

The alloy hinge clamp plates have tapered faces, so they tend to bend outwards as they are tightened, this regular flexing giving the plates a finite life. Look closely for signs of cracking on the corners, and replace the plates immediately if even a tiny crack appears, or the plates are sufficiently worn to 'bottom out' when fully tightened. When reassembling, put a smear of grease on both faces of the washer, on the screw threads and the mating faces of the plate.

Over time, the hinge pin will wear, particularly if the grease has been washed out after extended use in wet conditions. As with all moving parts, a regular drop of oil will greatly extend the pin life. Some wear is not a serious issue, but the increased flexing in use will tend to wear out the hinge clamp plates at a faster rate. Brompton can supply oversize pins, eliminating the wear (up to a point), but the frame needs to be reamed to suit, making this a job for the factory.

Rear Hinge

The hinge linking the main frame to the rear frame will gradually wear over time, at a rate of around 1mm (measured at the extreme rear of the bike) every 2,000 miles. The bearings are grease packed from new, but once they have become a little worn, the remaining grease will soon be washed out, and regular lubrication with a few drops of heavy oil will greatly extend the life of the bearings. Modest play in the bearing has little effect on handling, so replacement can wait until sideways movement at the rear of the bike exceeds 6mm. But do check carefully if you find a sudden increase in movement. The shaft inside the hinge is secured by two countersunk screws locked into place at the factory. If one or both of these screws come loose, movement in the bearing will rapidly increase and the screw head may begin to stand visibly proud of the frame. Under these circumstances, the screw must be removed, and the screw and shaft thoroughly degreased before the screw is locked back in place with a drop of thread-locking fluid, provided it is not badly worn. Failure to thread-lock the bolt back into place can result in the suspension collapsing.

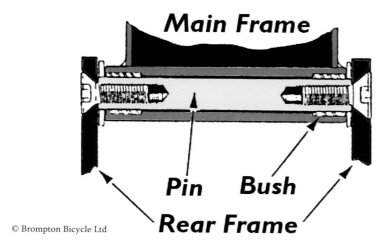

Main Frame

Pin Bush

Rear Frame

Once play becomes apparent in the rear pivot, the bushes can be sparingly oiled as below. The Allen head screw in the foreground must not be touched, and should be flush with the paintwork as here. Note the low frame number of 7110, traceable to 1992 (see appendix III).

153

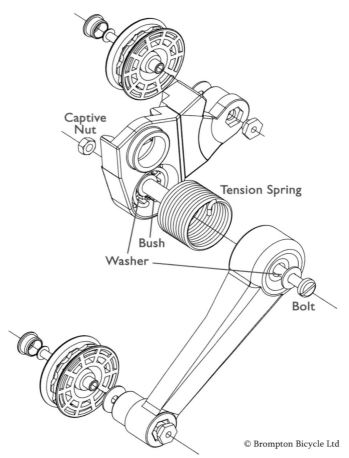

Captive Nut

Tension Spring

Bush

Washer

Bolt

© Brompton Bicycle Ltd

This exploded view is of the latest 6-speed chain tensioner. Earlier tensioners do not have the floating idler pulleys, and very early examples have threads cut into the plastic, rather than replaceable captive nuts, but the basic design is the same. The spring must be assembled with the ends engaged in the slots, and the bolt partly tightened. The arm can then be flipped over the raised boss, and the bolt fully tightened. The jockey pulleys can also be dismantled for cleaning and lubrication.

Chain Tensioner

The tensioner has a hard life on the Brompton, particularly in wet and muddy conditions, but it will continue to work for a considerable mileage, with very limited maintenance. All the same, an hour or two every six months dismantling and cleaning the tensioner will extend its life and improve its action. If the chain falls off when folding and/or unfolding the bike, suspect tensioner problems - the Brompton chain should never fall off.

With the bike part-folded and standing on its rear rollers, remove the chain from the long tensioner arm and check the action of the tensioner. It should have a strong spring action and flick back instantly when released. If the spring is weak, or the action sluggish, the tensioner will have to be stripped and checked.

A common mistake is to loosen the centre screw of the tensioner while removing the rear wheel. This bolt supports the tensioner bearing, which is clamped between two washers. If the bolt is taken out too far, one of these washers may slip out, causing the tensioner to seize when the bolt is retightened. An inexperienced mechanic will then leave the bolt loose, which can result in the tensioner flying apart or breaking after a few weeks. On older tensioners, the threads were cut into the plastic, resulting in stripped threads if overtightened - another cause of the assembly falling apart. This older design can be replaced with the newer type which has a steel captive nut and other improvements. If there is wear in several parts this might be the best course of action.

A common, but easily cured, problem with older bikes is seizure or partial seizure of the pivot bush. Carefully strip the assembly down, taking note of the order and condition of the parts. The bush is in the centre of the long arm, and should be easy to push out by hand. If seized, knock the bush out, clean it and - provided it is in reasonable condition - regrease and reassemble.

Reassembly looks extremely difficult, but it's easy once you know the procedure. Assemble the spring (taking care that the spring ends have located in their respective housings), the two washers and the bush, then partly tighten the centre bolt. With the assembly part tightened, the long arm can be turned against the spring, past the raised centre boss on the short arm, after which the screw can be fully tightened. The tensioner should now have a strong spring action and instant response when released.

Tensioner idler wheels on early Mark 2 bikes are fitted with 6mm centre bolts. There are no spares available for these, so the whole tensioner assembly will have to be replaced if problems occur. The same is true for slightly more recent tensioners with 5mm bolts, which can suffer from stripped threads, and again the only practical answer is to replace the assembly.

Tensioner idler wheels can become partially clogged with road dirt and muck, although this doesn't usually cause problems, other than rough running. Dismantle each wheel, checking the position of all washers, and check the steel bearing bushes. If these are badly worn or corroded, the idler wheel will need to be replaced. If satisfactory (some play is fine) thoroughly remove all traces of road dirt and grit - a small saw blade will help remove trapped debris in bad cases. Oil the bearings, reassemble the idler wheels, and with the tensioner back on the bike (but the chain off) check that the wheels, rear sprocket and chainring line up with each other with the tensioner in the folded and unfolded position. Small alignment problems can be dealt with by fitting or removing washers, but in a bad case the tensioner arm may be bent, and possibly cracked, and will have to be replaced. All the above also applies to the 'floating' idler wheels fitted to the 6-speed, but in this case the wheels also need to float freely along their shaft as well as revolving smoothly.

Worn chains, chainrings and sprockets can also cause problems. The Brompton chainring will last for years, but chains and smaller 12- or 13-tooth sprockets need regular replacement, and must be replaced together. In an emergency a worn sprocket can be turned around and put on backwards. A build up of dirt, grass or mud around the sprocket can cause the chain to jump mysteriously and intermittently, but this is easily solved by careful cleaning. Again, the smaller sprockets are particularly vulnerable to this.

Lighting

The Brompton has always suffered from lighting problems. Wiring looms have a tough life as the bike folds and unfolds, rear lamp bulbs can fail if the rear frame is folded under carelessly, and dynamos suffer from vibration and water ingress. Later parts were much better: the loom was improved, LED rear lights are more shock-resistant, and the dynamo - once considered an annual purchase by many commuters - became tolerably reliable. From 2010, Brompton eradicated the bottle dynamos and troublesome old-fashioned bulbs, offering instead a special narrow version of Shimano's hub dynamo, allied to a halogen front lamp and LED rear standlight and for those with £338.50 to spare, a SON hub dynamo, powering a light-sensing Busch & Muller front LED lamp and rear standlight.

The hub dynamos are heavy and expensive, so for all but the most battle-hardened daily commuters, battery-powered LED lights probably make more sense. Brompton introduced a battery lighting set with the Mark 4, but the two versions of the Spaninga LED rear light and diminutive S-sun LED front light were never more than adequately powerful, and reliability left much to be desired. The front light has now been replaced by a much better Cateye Volt 300, which fits in place of the reflector above the mudguard... a much better position on a bike that needs to fold regularly and rapidly. The Volt 300 is compact but powerful, and the internal lithium-ion 18650 battery can be recharged via a USB port. These batteries will only survive for a year or two of hard use, but the battery cartridge is replaceable, and you can buy spares, and keep one in the pannier for emergencies or longer journeys. The Volt 300 is not cheap at £50, but don't be tempted to save a few pounds elsewhere, as the Brompton version comes with a model-specific bracket.

The Spaninga LED rear light is a first-generation LED device and well past its sell-by date. The light output is limited, and reliability far from satisfactory, so at £15 it's a rotten purchase. Brompton also sell the rather better Cateye Rapid Mini for £20. Like the Volt 300, this is rechargeable via a USB port, but it has the big disadvantage of fitting under the saddle. If you wear a long jacket, or loose clothing that might sag down over the back of the saddle, don't even consider it. Replacing the Spaninga isn't easy because there are few

LED rear lights designed to fit a 50mm bracket. Probably the best is the Oxford Ultra Torch OF287 carrier light. This light costs £7-£10, it's 30 grams lighter than the Spaninga, and much brighter. It fits neatly in the same position above the rear mudguard, and has a similar integral reflector, a legal requirement on a rear light in the UK and many other places. The only disadvantage is that the smaller AAA batteries will need changing more frequently than the Spaninga's AA batteries.

The SON XS hub dynamo is the lighting solution most likely to prove trouble free in the long-term, especially if coupled with an upgraded front light such as the Busch & Muller IQ.

Brake Problems

The brakes on the Brompton have gradually improved over the years, but by modern commuter bike standards, Mark 1 and 2 brakes are positively dangerous. If you can afford it, upgrade to the latest caliper and brake blocks, which will have a near miraculous effect. If not, just fit the latest brake blocks (currently the Brompton specific Fibrax ASH410-BR), a much cheaper solution, offering a worthwhile improvement in efficiency.

Older cables operate poorly unless well lubricated. Even on newer bikes, water ingress can be a problem, and if the cable isn't well oiled, it will quickly corrode. The only answer is to remove and clean the inner cable and feed it back with lashings of oil. If in doubt, replace the inner - again with plenty of oil - it isn't expensive, and failure can be serious.. There isn't usually any need to replace the outer cable unless it's clearly damaged. Precise cable routing is essential and must exactly follow the original. The new cable must also be exactly the right length - watch out, newer long-wheelbase bikes have a different cable. But in most cases removing, oiling and refitting the inner cable will cure any problems.

Alloy wheel rims have been fitted to Bromptons from early Mark 2 days. These offer much improved wet weather braking over steel, but have a tendency to wear. The alloy rims on the Brompton and other small-wheeled bikes are particularly vulnerable, due to their reduced surface area, and they may need replacing every couple of years, on a well-used commuter bike. Making sure that brake blocks are cleaned and/or replaced regularly may help reduce rim wear, but in the end, it's just something users have to put up with.

Keep an eye on rim wear and aim to replace the rims long before they fail. On pre-Mark 4 bikes, judging the degree of wear is a matter of experience. Any obvious wear lip either side of the rubbing surfaces, early signs of rim distortion, or a rhythmic knock under braking, particularly after inflating the tyres, can mean imminent rim failure. This is a job for a dealer, unless you are experienced at wheel building. On later bikes, a telltale indicator groove is machined into the rim, the idea being that the rim should be replaced when the groove is no longer visible, but there are reports that this might not be a 100% accurate system, so regular inspection is still important.

The early design of side-pull brake (above left) was inefficient when compared to the modern dual-pivot brake (above right).

Overheating of rims can be a potential problem after severe and prolonged braking. Most commuters will be doing well to get their rims lukewarm, but ride down a twisty mountain pass on a 16-inch wheel bike with alloy rims and after descending several thousand feet, tyre failure becomes a real possibility through the build-up of heat from the brakes. Quite simply, there's less rim to absorb the heat, so it can build up to dangerous levels more quickly than it would on a big-wheeled bike. The answer is to take it easy, or adopt one of the alternative solutions...

Failure of alloy rims is probably the Brompton's primary weakness today, and there are two permanent solutions for bikes that get very hard use. In dry conditions, steel rims offer a complete cure, but be prepared for braking efficiency to plummet in the wet. Modern high-efficiency brake blocks may well improve matters, but little research has been done into this. For all-weather use, the best solution - on the front of the bike at least - is to fit a Sturmey-Archer drum brake. The standard drum is too wide for the Brompton, but Greenspeed, once the Australian Brompton importer, produces a narrow drum kit, which can be fitted by a competent mechanic.

Greenspeed Recumbent Trikes e-mail: ian@greenspeed.com.au

Hub Gears
Hub gears are more reliable than derailleurs, and as long as the sprocket is replaced at the same time as the chain, the hub itself should last for a considerable mileage - in the tens or even hundreds of thousands of miles. Sturmey-Archer hubs made before July 1987 were fitted with an oiling point, so Mark 1 Bromptons and very early Mark 2s can be topped up with oil as required. More recent hubs are pre-greased at the factory, the manufacturers claiming that routine lubrication is not required between major services, when the hub should be stripped and reassembled with fresh grease. True enough, a hub that has seen gentle leisure use will last for years or even decades without fresh lubricant, but hard-ridden commuter bikes need better lubrication than old grease can provide.

The most important element of servicing is to replace the grease once it has gone hard or been washed out. Quite when this might be is a matter for judgement. A very noisy hub can mean a lack of grease, but partially seized pawls and ratchets can also become relatively quiet, suggesting hardened grease. If a well-used hub develops a problem, such as a sticky unreliable change or a missing gear, lack of lubrication may well be the cause, so don't replace the hub without investigating. In any event, oiling will do no harm, but once you start, you have to continue. Neither Sturmey nor SRAM hub gears are sealed, so with oil lubrication they effectively operate on the 'total loss' principle, as car engines and gearboxes once did. As there is no oiling point, the bicycle must be laid on its side, the indicator chain removed, and a few drops of light oil run into the hole. It makes sense to do this whenever the wheel is off for other purposes, such as mending a puncture. Don't overdo it, because the oil that runs out of the hub will be as black as ink, but make sure to oil the hub at least every six months, and immediately after riding through heavy rain or floods.

Adjustment is not too critical with any of the 3-speed hubs. As a general rule, if the cable is *just* tight in first gear, and *just* slack in third gear, adjustment is about right. The 5-speed Sturmey hubs are much more critical and need to be carefully adjusted using a coloured band on the indicator chain, which should be flush with, or up to 1.5mm proud of the axle,

With the bike lying on its side and the indicator unscrewed and removed, oil can be dripped into the hole. This is an early 3-speed, but the technique is much the same for newer bikes. A few drops will last quite a while in dry weather.

in second gear. The indicator chain should be just slack in gear five.

Another common problem with the 5-speed is failure to align the guide roller with the cable pulley assembly after replacing the rear wheel. Poor alignment will result in an inconsistent change, and possible damage to the hub.

The Brompton has used three gear shifters over the years. From the very start of production until April 2001, all 3-speed Sturmey bikes were fitted with Sturmey-Archer's 'Classic' 3-speed trigger. Developed in the late 1930s, the Classic is arguably the most successful hub gear trigger ever devised, and still in production, after more than 70 years. If treated to a drop of oil every few months, these triggers rarely go wrong, and if they do, replacements and basic spares are cheap and easy to find almost anywhere in the world. Early 5-speeds were fitted with a pair of 3-speed triggers, which was a less than ideal solution - difficult to understand, and difficult to adjust for the less mechanically minded, but at least the triggers were reliable.

From June 1994, the single-cable 5-speed was introduced, and Brompton had to choose between a twistgrip or the 'Nimbus' thumb shifter. To ease the cable run, and keep weight to a minimum, the company opted for the Nimbus, but it was a rather crude thing, the gears being locked in position largely by friction rather than positive stops. With age, the action of these triggers can become quite sloppy, but more friction can be applied by removing the large red centre cap, and tightening the crosshead screw beneath. If the controller still won't hold onto first or second gear reliably, it's best replaced, as inaccurate gear selection can destroy the hub.

With the demise of the 5-speed in early 2001, it was back to the archetypal 3-speed trigger until April 2001, after which all bikes were fitted with the SRAM 3-speed hub and SRAM 'Torpedo' shifter. This was broadly similar to the Sturmey-Archer trigger, but less precise, and certainly less robust.

From April 2002, the '2x3' 6-speed model was introduced, the 2-speed derailleur element being controlled by a new shifter designed by Brompton. This has been generally quite successful but it's made largely of plastic and open to the elements at the top, so it needs a drop of light oil every few months, or whenever the action becomes heavy.

Above: Gear triggers, from left to right, 'Classic' Sturmey-Archer 3-speed (up to April 2001), Sturmey-Archer 5-speed (1994-early 2001), SRAM 3-speed (April 2001- January 2005), Brompton 3-speed (from January 2005), Brompton 2-speed (from April 2002).
Below: Brompton has used both SRAM (left) and Sturmey-Archer (right) 3-speed hubs but bikes from January 2005 have universal rear frames that will accept either make.

From January 2005, Brompton introduced the 'universal' rear frame, suitable for either SRAM or Sturmey hubs, and matched it with a new universal 'Y' shifter, compatible with either hub. This met with a less enthusiastic response than the 2-speed shifter, mainly because it followed on from the supremely ergonomic and effective Sturmey Classic shifter, which was bound to be a hard act to follow. As with the 2-speed, a drop of oil will keep the mechanism running smoothly but note that Brompton says lubrication is not recommended, and may cause the shifter to jump past gear 2 when changing up.

Even the humble 3-speed hub is a complex piece of precision machinery, and stripping and reassembly is only practical for those with some engineering knowledge. Sturmey-Archer keep .pdf files covering maintenance of all new and recent hub gears. The 5-speed is even more delicate, and servicing really is a matter for an engineer familiar with hub gears, an endangered species these days. Fortunately, internal failures are rare, and apart from lubrication and cable adjustment, the only regular servicing necessary is adjustment of the hub bearings, which can be done by a home mechanic with care. A very small amount of 'play' or looseness at the rim is normal, but adjustment will be necessary when this play becomes excessive.

Ideally, the hub should be mounted in a vice, but adjustment can also be made on the bicycle. In both cases, the right-hand bearing (the one under the sprocket) should be left alone, and adjustment carried out at the other end. If making the adjustment on the bike, loosen the left-hand axle nut sufficiently for the rear frame to spring away from the hub slightly - it may need to be gently knocked to accomplish this. With the hub secured on the right side - either in the Brompton frame or a vice - but the left side loose, the amount of play will probably have increased, but it will reduce as the wheel is refitted and/or the axle nuts are fully tightened, so it must be adjusted slightly loose at this stage.

To adjust the bearings, you will need a Sturmey-Archer cone spanner, or similar very thin 5/8"AF or 16mm metric spanner. Carefully loosen the outer locknut, and make the adjustment with the underlying bearing cone. This should be carefully tightened (preferably by hand) until resistance is felt, then backed off a little and the lock nut retightened. If correctly adjusted, the sprocket should spin easily, with noticeable side-to-side play, the wheel should rotate freely, and there should be a little play at the wheel rim. Finally, either refit the hub to the bike, or tighten the left-hand axle nut and recheck for freedom of rotation and play. The hub should be completely free running, and there should now be just discernible play at the rim. Final adjustment may take a few attempts. If in doubt, err towards loose bearings, as tight bearings will damage the hub. If you're not sure of your abilities, and feel the same about your local mountain bike specialist, Bicycle Workshop in West London is extremely knowledgable about hub gears and Bromptons, but there's often a waiting list for servicing.

Bicycle Workshop, London W11   tel: 020 72294850   web:www.bicycleworkshop.co.uk

Tyres

A subject of endless debate, and changing quite fast at the time of writing. The lightest and best rolling tyres are the Primo (now hard to find), the standard 'yellow flash' Brompton tyre (earlier tyres with black shoulders discontinued in 2008), the Schwalbe Stelvio (discontinued in 2009) and the Schwalbe Kojak, an excellent tyre, and - fortunately - still very much available.

Tyres that roll less well, but probably last longer, and arguably provide better grip and/or puncture-resistance (user surveys don't necessarily bear this out) include Brompton's 'Green Flash' tyre (with either black or grey shoulders), the 'Yellow Flash' tyre with grey shoulders (discontinued in 2010), and the Schwalbe Marathon. For ultimate puncture resistance, albeit with a considerable weight and rolling penalty, the Schwalbe Marathon Plus is the best option.

Older tyres, such as the Raleigh Record, and some new ones, such as the Panaracer Crosstown, have no redeeming features and are best replaced.

Whatever tyre you use, tyre pressures are far more critical than they would be on a big-wheeled conventional bike, particularly with heavier, less free-running tyres.

As a guide, the rear tyre should be inflated some 15psi more than the front, but more air is useful in the front tyre if carrying a heavy pannier. The Raleigh Record is rated at 55psi, but Brompton has always recommended a pressure of 60-75psi. The more modern tyres have a much higher rating. The rear tyres should be inflated to at least 70psi, the actual pressure depending on your weight, and the road conditions. A harsh ride suggests overinflation, while a 'soggy' bouncy ride and increased pedal effort suggests underinflation.

Handlebars

Slight fore and aft adjustment of the handlebars is permissible, but this must be done very sparingly, and the cable runs and handlebar catch adjustment carefully checked with the bike folded. There is no vertical adjustment, but this is less important today, with four handlebar options now available, from the low flat 'S' bars, through the standard 'M', multi-position 'P' to tall 'H' bars, introduced in late 2011 (see page 157 for more detail).

If buying an older bike second-hand, check carefully against the chart. Older bars - whether braced or not - should ideally be replaced with the latest design, as aluminium handlebars have a finite fatigue life, and with a second-hand bike, you have no way to judge how the bike has been (mis)used. At the very least, examine the handlebars carefully – if there are any cuts, cracks or other damage, they must be replaced straight away. If upgrading to alternative bars, bear in mind that the inner and outer cables will probably also have to be changed, as they are a different length. Older short wheelbase bikes have different rear cables too, and on bikes with Saccon brakes, the cables are different again. Cable length and routing MUST be exactly right, or there may be problems folding.

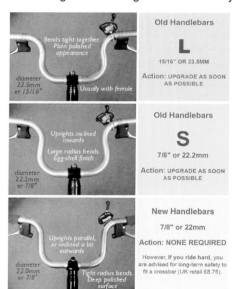

When handlebar failures became a problem in 2000, Brompton produced a chart to assist users and dealers identify whether they needed to be concerned. The 'L' bars are the early GB Cycles bars, few of which will remain in use today, the 'S' bars are the Neobike bars used from 1995-1999, and the modern Humpert bars are at the bottom. 'L' or 'S' bars are still eligible for the free crossbar upgrade, but after all this time, new bars would be strongly recommended anyway. The age of a bike can be confirmed by checking the date stamped on the Sturmey hub shell, and comparing the frame number with the dates listed in appendix III, but neither of these methods provide a guarantee. The latest bars are extremely strong, but Brompton does still offer the crossbar (part number QXBARS-D, £10.00 at 2011 prices) for those who ride hard and want extra security.

The crossbar (right) is being fitted between the two vertical parts of the handlebars, and will now be clamped in position. This 1998 bike has Neobike bars (and some telltale scoring on the surface) and should certainly be braced or replaced as soon as possible.

Folding Pedal

After a high mileage (or quite a low mileage if you ride hard), the bearing in the folding pedal will require replacement. Once play becomes evident, the life of the bearing can be extended by running a few drops of oil into it once in a while, with the bike lying on its side. Once a replacement is required, the pedal can be returned to Brompton for reconditioning. Removal requires a 24mm AF socket, and when replacing the pedal, make sure to fit the washer first. If you find yourself getting through Brompton folding pedals, a cheaper folding, demountable or conventional pedal can be fitted instead, but at the expense of a wider folded package.

Front Mudguard Stay Hook

On older bikes these were made from a bent section of mudguard stay. These are easily bent out of shape, but just as easily straightened. A loose hook can cause the bike to fall apart when folded, and a tight one will fit too snugly around the chainstay, making the bike difficult to unfold. It's worth noting that two slightly different stays were produced for 3- and 5-speed, bikes, the 5-speed example being longer, to accommodate the wider 5-speed gear shifter mechanism. Since early 2000, a moulded nylon block has been fitted instead and these are retrofittable to all older bikes, except the 5-speed.

Handlebar Catch

This small catch performs a vital role, keeping the handlebars clamped against the folded package. For many years, the catches caused problems, giving insufficient clamping pressure after prolonged use. This can be solved in several ways - a 'U'-shaped metal bar dropped down through the holes in the catch will strengthen the action, as will a small cable-tie looped through the holes. Modern catches are more durable, but may still need a cable-tie if the bike is folded very frequently. The catch must enter the nipple completely square for best results. The nipple can be screwed in and out to allow for slight variations in package width caused by altered handlebar or brake lever position. Note too that the handlebar catch securing screw has a tendency to work loose, or even fall off. If it doesn't work, check that it's still there!

Lower Stop Disc

The other key adjustment with respect to folding is the lower stop disc that traps the lowered seat pillar, thus holding the folded bike together. Early eccentric discs have a tendency to work loose and must be offset to the left, so that pressure from the seat pillar tightens the screw. Clearance between the pillar and stop when fully folded should be 3mm. If problems persist, a later-style concentric disc is a worthwhile upgrade. Clearance on these can be reduced to 1-2mm.

Rear Mudguard Stays

The rear mudguard stays on the 'L' type are very vulnerable to clumsy folding, and can become quite badly bent. In mild cases, the stays can simply be pushed back in, lifting the mudguard clear of the tyre, but if the stays are seriously buckled, they will have to be removed, straightened in a vice and refitted. Note that the three stays are different lengths (shortest at the front) and must be refitted exactly as they came off the bike. If the stays are badly bent or corroded, treat yourself to a set of titanium stays, which don't cost much more, are less likely to bend, and will never corrode.

Other Weak Spots

Brompton has been lucky, or perhaps it's down to Andrew Ritchie's dogged attention to detail, but major failures have been rare. Apart from the handlebar issue, breakages have been mercifully few. A handful of frames failed just forward of the hinge, a metallurgy issue that seems to have been resolved, and older rear frames may fail through invisible internal corrosion if used regularly on salted winter roads. A recent failure has been the short-lived nickel-plated alloy seatpost that replaced the titanium post in late 2010. Much cheaper than the titanium post, and only a few grams heavier, these proved to be vulnerable to pitting in use and were rapidly withdrawn. There are no safety issues, but a badly pitted seatpost will damage the frame bush and should be replaced. Until a permanent cure has been found, lightweight bikes will be sold with steel pillars. Other cycle parts, like cranks and chains, may break once a while, just as they do on conventional bicycles, but there are no specific problem areas.

Old & New Compared

This book covers Bromptons made between 1981 and 2017. In those 36 years, the bike has seen tremendous changes. Although to outward appearances, they all look very similar, riding one of the earliest Mark 1 bikes against the latest Mark 4 can be pretty instructive.

First impressions are that the Mark 1 Brompton is astonishingly heavy compared to the P6R-X. In fact, at 15kg, the older bike is not as heavy as it feels, the weight being in part an illusion brought about by its compact size. We've chosen a P6R-X to represent the modern bike, because it has a rack and lights like the Mark 1. But despite a full titanium kit, it weighs a relatively chunky 12kg, a faintly disappointing 20% less than the original Brompton.

Weight reduction is a tough engineering task, and the process has not been entirely one way, with some modifications over the years putting weight on. As a result, the modern bike is much stronger and more rigid. Sit astride the Mark 1, and you have a feeling that a gentle touch might be needed, but the Mark 4 gives a lot more confidence. From that perspective, the 20% weight reduction seems much more impressive. On the other hand, when we published the second edition of this book in 2011, the advantage over the 1981 model was 25%.

Unfolding the older bike is a slow process, but immeasurably quicker and easier than typical compacts of the era, such as the Bickerton. The Brompton's hinges engage quickly enough, but the knob must be screwed down to lock the hinge in place, which adds a few seconds. Finally, a few seconds are needed to double check that everything has been done correctly. The folding pedal is a wonderful device - you simply push a lever and the pedal engages, but as you do it you can't help thinking about the weeks Andrew Ritchie spent cutting the parts from the solid. It was clever, but much too heavy and expensive for mass production.

The Mark 4 has a quicker, more foolproof fold. The lighter rear frame folds under more quicker and smoothly, and although the screw-up clamps look crude and fiddly, they release in a few seconds. The whole operation is balanced and balletic.

Unfolding the Mark 4 is also a more predictable operation. It's a process that really can be done in complete darkness, with confidence that clamps cannot be fastened in the wrong position, or mis-fastened. There's no need for that telltale look round of the older bike - you just ride straight off.

On the road, the real surprise is how similar the bikes feel. The Mark 1 has a softer, more relaxed gait, but our new bike has the post-2008 soft suspension block - the difference would have been more marked with the optional hard suspension. But riding gently, the bikes do feel astonishingly similar - the gearing is about the same, and the rolling resistance is little different. Even the plastic headset bearings of the Mark 1 have little effect when riding on the flat.

Reach a hill, and the differences become more marked. On the Mark 4 you can stand out of the pedals and pull on the bars just as you would with a conventional bike, but care is needed with the Mark 1. Pull on the bars and the plastic headset and spindly steel handlebar stem begin to flex.

After riding the bike, it's easy to see how much of a milestone the early Brompton was in the age of the wobbly Bickerton and heavy, cumbersome Raleigh RSW. You begin to understand why a handful of journalists wrote those rave reviews that got the project off the ground. And why Julian Vereker took the advice of the pretty girl on the yacht and phoned Andrew Ritchie, effectively kick-starting the project.

Is the modern bike as good against its peers as its predecessor? Rather depressingly, it is. Many folding bike designs have been produced in that quarter of a century, and new machines come along every year, but for all the advances in materials and computer-aided design, none has yet come close to matching the Brompton's effortless combination of rideability and convenience. Some bikes are lighter, some are more suitable for long rides, some fold a little quicker, and some fold smaller, but these attributes all belong to different folding bikes. None of the Brompton's many competitors achieve all four of these attributes at once, and that's the continuing magic of the Brompton.

Using the Brompton

Rail Commuting

This is the classic reason for owning a Brompton, and in most people's eyes, the raison d'être of the bike, although as we have seen, Andrew Ritchie also perceived the bike as a tool for motorists hemmed in by parking restrictions. Some motorists certainly do park on the edge of town and ride in by Brompton, but the big market turned out to be amongst rail commuters. When the Brompton was being developed, most trains had spacious luggage areas in at least one carriage. These areas had been designed to carry parcels, but were being used almost exclusively for bicycles by the early 1990s. However, on newer trains luggage space largely evaporated, and commuters began to look for practical alternatives. Today, most trains have space for two or three non-folding bicycles, but there are complex peak hour restrictions, and at other times the number of bikes is usually strictly limited. There are no restrictions on the carriage of folding bikes, but for all sorts of practical reasons, if travelling at peak times, it makes sense to use the most compact design, and this is where the Brompton excels.

The front pannier system is essential for commuting, so there is very little point in purchasing an 'R' type, because the rack serves little purpose. The classic 'M' type bars are ideal for urban use, and there is little advantage in buying a 6-speed unless you are commuting some distance, or in a very hilly area, so a basic M3L is ideal for rail commuting. If you can afford the extra £400 or so, the M3L-X is lighter, and thus easier to carry. Some railway companies have placed peak hour restrictions on wheeling bikes within the station, so weight has become increasingly important. The Brompton offers a bonus over most other folding bikes in that it can be wheeled like a small suitcase, and this can be useful when crossing large railway or airport concourses.

A little known Brompton characteristic is that it can be used as a seat on a busy commuter train or platform, thus liberating a seat for someone else, much to the delight of the railway companies. The seat should be lowered right down, so that your weight passes to the floor via the seat pillar and not the rear rollers, which can be easily broken. The seat should be locked in this low position on a skew of about 45° to enable the rider to sit on the mainframe. Folding bikes no longer need to be covered on trains in the UK, but it might make sense to use a cover on very busy services.

One of the Brompton's better known trademarks is the little trolley wheels - four on variants with a rear rack, and three on lightweight models, as here. The wheels are unsuitable for rough surfaces, but cope well with airport concourses and similar smooth surfaces. Brompton can supply larger 'Eazy Wheels' for bikes that are frequently used on rougher surfaces. Waiting for a train? Many owners aren't aware that the bike can be turned into a practical seat while waiting at a railway station, or even on the train itself. The saddle needs to be pushed right down, tilted towards the handlebars at about 45°, and locked with the pillar touching the ground (in contrast to pulling the bike along, when it should be raised a centimetre or so). The stem then carries most of the weight, and locks against the floor, preventing the bike from rolling away. Not enormously comfortable, but better than standing on a long train journey.

Donald Wilson, station master at Marylebone, gives the Brompton his seal of approval on Bike to Work Day during the late 1990s.

Buses and Aircraft

Bus and coach companies generally expect folding bikes to be covered, and as the door is usually beside the driver, it makes sense to cover the bike well in advance, and keep a low profile. Never use the word bicycle, and try to avoid conflict. Unlike a railway guard, a bus driver has complete autonomy when away from base, and can turn anyone away for any reason, so argument is pointless. With these provisos, the Brompton can easily and conveniently be carried by bus, particularly the newer low-floor models.

Air transport causes many headaches. US manufacturer Bike Friday knows this market well, and that's why their bikes mostly dismantle and pack into a hard case, which will stand the rigours of automated and manual baggage handling.

Brompton finally gave in to consumer demand and announced its own 'Brompton Pod' hardcase in 2010, but like so many projects in the modern era, it didn't see the light of day as promised, although case manufacturer Polaris went it alone, launching the case as the EVA Brompton folding bike pod. The pod weighs less than 5kg, so complete with bike and a few clothes it should come in under the 20kg weight limit and 158cm length+height+width restriction imposed by most airlines. Travelling by air is easier with a 'naked' bike, but damage is always a possibility. Putting the seat pillar right down will help, because this will help channel the weight of stacked luggage safely down the pillar. As Brompton discovered, weakened 'sacrificial' rear rollers can be helpful where the bike is likely to see rough handling. It can make sense to remove lights and reflectors too, as these are easily damaged. Beyond that, you are in the lap of the gods. Perhaps one in three air trips will see minor damage, but one in ten will result in serious problems, and very occasionally the frame will be distorted badly enough to make the bike unrideable. Rather unfairly, many airlines - principally the cheaper carriers - will impose an extra charge for a folding bike, even when it's within the size and weight limit of the free luggage allowance. Like many such rules, it's discriminatory, but there's nothing you can do. In some cases, if the check-in person is either sympathetic or stupid, it may help to describe the contents of the bag as 'sports goods'...

All airlines will expect the bike to be covered. The Brompton Pod will give the greatest protection, but adds weight, and makes riding away from the airport almost impossible. A more practical alternative is the Brompton 'B' bag, a soft bag with 5mm of padding, but this will only really protect the machine against scratches. Some regular travellers argue that an ultra-thin membranous cover is the best option: cheap, light to transport and leaving the machine looking vulnerable, which might just prevent the baggage handlers from throwing it too hard. Most airlines will provide stickers to verify that the luggage is delicate, and there's not much else you can do but pray.

Riding

To anyone used to a conventional bike, small wheels might seem odd at first, but don't be misled - this isn't instability as such, but a reduced gyroscopic action from the smaller, lighter wheels. After getting acclimatized, most people learn to appreciate the faster steering and more rapid acceleration, but there's no escaping the fact that riding one-handed - as when indicating - requires more care. More vigilance is needed too, because smaller wheels are more likely to be affected by potholes and kerbs. On the other hand, the faster steering makes holes easier to avoid, and the smaller, lighter front wheel is more easily lifted up small kerbs. Riding a Brompton isn't more difficult, but you may find the techniques a little *different*.

Some cyclists criticize the Brompton for being hard work to ride, but this usually means they haven't actually ridden one, or have ridden it wrongly. Tyre pressures are of enormous importance, and as on page 161, it's worth making a few experiments to find the perfect pressures for your weight, tyres and regular commute. Never let the pressure drop too low. Saddle height is also very important, and arguably more important than it would be on a big-wheeled bike. The complication is that the saddle has to be brought up to the correct height every time it is unfolded, and finding that height can be difficult. There is quite a bit of adjustment available at the saddle end of the seat pillar, so with luck you can tweak the height by a centimetre or two until full extension of either the standard or extended pillar suits your build. This will make unfolding the bike a much quicker operation, and do your knees a real favour. Most people should be able to achieve this, if necessary by adding the Brompton saddle adapter pin, which gives even greater adjustability.

For shorter people, the base of the standard seat pillar can be cut off, and a new flare produced at the right height, but if you go too far, the bike will fail to lock together. This is a job for a skilled engineer, and it makes the bike unrideable for taller people, but will bring the saddle up to the correct height every time.

It sounds obvious, but taller people using the telescopic seat pillar can put the main pillar at full extension, make the final adjustment using the telescopic section, then fold the bike using the main adjuster. This will leave a section sticking out from the folded bike, but the height will always be correct. In September 2011 Brompton announced the new H-type bar configuration for taller riders or those who want a more upright riding position. On the H-type the height of the grips from the ground was raised by 60mm compared to the classic M-type and forward reach to the grips from the saddle increased by around 13mm. This has been achieved by raising the handlebar hinge by 30mm. While this means that the hinge protrudes further from the bike than on other models, the highest point on the folded bike remains the saddle, so the H-type fits into all existing transportation bags and covers.The weight increase over an M-type is approximately 100g.

Riding style is important. Since 2008, Brompton has produced two different grades of rear suspension, with soft being the default on a new bike. Accepted wisdom is that the hard block suits hard riding, and the soft block suits gentler pottering, but this isn't necessarily the case. The hard block is only necessary with a rather aggressive riding style, which can otherwise make the rear of the bike bob wastefully up and down. With practice, smooth, steady pedal pressure works best, and without the need for firm suspension.

Tyres we've mentioned already. The rolling resistance of the tyre can have a huge effect on the enjoyment of riding a small-wheeled bike, and if you don't enjoy it you will avoid using it, making the effort seem all the greater when you do, creating a negative spiral. Set a Brompton up correctly, and you can expect to ride at least 75% as far and as fast as you would with a good conventional bike.

Gearing has caused numerous queries and complaints in the past, but with the BWR wide-ratio hub these have been largely answered. The ordinary 3-speed hub is surprisingly effective for most purposes, and if you can live with a low top gear, the overall gearing can be reduced by fitting a larger rear sprocket, smaller chainring or both. The 6-speed now offers a sufficient range of gears for touring and commuting in hillier country, and again, the overall gearing can be reduced quite easily at the expense of a lower top gear. If none of these options is suitable, and you need to reduce gearing down to walking pace or even lower, a Mountain Drive internally-geared chainring will double the number of gears to six or twelve, and provide some extremely low ratios without compromising the high gears. But it's an expensive and heavy option.

Luggage & Touring

Brompton and a few aftermarket manufacturers produce a vast and ever growing range of panniers and bags for the front of the Brompton, and Steve Parry (see previous chapter) has made a few luggage block carriers designed to be fitted on the rear of the seat pillar to put another bag behind. An alternative is Brompton's own 'R' model with a rear rack and dynamo lights. The rack can either be fitted with twin miniature panniers or Brompton's own Rack Sack bag.

The growth in long distance loaded touring has been one of the surprises of the Brompton story. From the pioneering rides of a few adventurous souls in the 1980s and '90s, the concept of touring on a folding bike with 16-inch wheels has become quite common today. The ability to combine cycling with other forms of transport - train, bus, taxi, ferry (even a foot ferry), hydrofoil and air - can greatly enhance the touring experience, and eliminate the uncertainty of booking cycle spaces ahead. It can also save a surprising amount of money, as folding bikes nearly always travel free.

The Folding Society has long excelled at demonstrating complex multimodal day trips and short tours, including some unusual transport, such as narrow gauge trains, electric trams, horse-drawn trams and a mountain railway, as well as the more obvious ferries and aircraft. The Brompton obviously excels at this sort of thing, but a bike cover (not necessarily a bag) makes a lot of sense in places where big luggage might cause problems.

Attaching various kinds of box is an extremely practical way for carrying everything from the small but valued to very sizeable loads indeed. The space over both front and rear wheels will carry loads of about equal size.

© Phil O'Connor

© Dave Holladay

Above: The P6RX with touring pannier on the front and Rack Sack on the rear - ideal for extended touring, especially where you want to combine cycling and other forms of transport. The Rack Pack is specifically designed for the Brompton rear rack, with tall, stiffened sides. Sleeker options for lighter loads include the C-bag (above centre right) and the S-bag (above top right), the only bag that will fit the S-bars.

Below: Axelle Presse and Vincent Burgeon crossed Switzerland's Furka Pass with standard Brompton 6-speed gearing, the first time they had ridden such high mountains. It was 'very hard' according to Vincent.

© Vincent Burgeon

Touring Emergency Kit

In the early days, Brompton recommended touring with a pile of spares because so much on the Brompton was unusual or unique. If something went wrong, there were few dealers in the UK, let alone overseas, where some countries had to make do with a single outlet, and others had no Brompton dealer at all. Today, Brompton spares are available right around the world, and can be ordered from a number of internet mail-order specialists. Inevitably, of course, if you do have a problem it will be somewhere remote. Whether you're stuck in the Outer Hebrides or crossing Afghanistan, a few basic spares can save a great deal of legwork and delay. Top of the list must come tyres and inner tubes, both of which fail relatively frequently. You can get away with fitting a smaller tube, but the tyres must be right, and the Brompton's 349mm tyre is almost unknown in many countries. 16-inch tyres are quite common, but they all have different 'bead seat' diameters and will not fit the Brompton rims. Nominally 16-inch tyres can be anything from 305mm (very common), through 317mm, 335mm, 337mm (all quite rare) and 340mm (a French 400A) to 349mm, which is closer to 17-inch.

A spare tube folds up very small and weighs just over 100 grams. Whatever tyres you have fitted to the bike, consider carrying at least one Schwalbe Kojak with kevlar bead as a spare (Brompton part number: QTYRKOJAK). These weigh 175 grams and cost £34 each, but they roll up quite small. You might never need it, but if you shred the sidewall on a Brompton tyre, a spare will provide excellent insurance. After tyres, spokes are probably the most common failure, and half a dozen spare spokes should see your bike through the most gruelling tour. In theory there are several different lengths, but most failures occur in the rear wheel, and the 150mm rear spokes fitted to hub-geared bikes (QSPOKR3SS) will fit most front wheels at a pinch. For the rear wheel of 1- or 2-speed bikes, the slightly longer 155mm spokes are part number QSPOKR2SS. Worn sprockets can be reversed, but a chain is worth carrying, because 1/2" x 1/8" chain is much less common than it used to be, and if the sprocket is worn, the chain certainly will be too. Choose your chain with care, because Brompton now sells 1/8" chain in four lengths, and 3/32" chain in another two! A smaller and lighter part that's very vulnerable is the Sturmey or SRAM hub gear indicator chain. If this breaks, or falls down a roadside drain during a puncture repair, you will be stuck in top gear, and hub gear parts are rare in most countries. There are five varieties, so make sure to carry the right one. In an emergency, the chain itself can be repaired with a bent nail or similar.

In terms of frequency, wheel rim failures probably come next, but if you depart with new or as-new rims, you should be able to travel many thousands of miles without a failure (serious accidents excepted of course). If a rim begins to fail, it usually bulges outwards long before catastrophic failure occurs. The bulge makes itself known as a rhythmic judder when the brakes are applied. If you're somewhere remote, and the failure has been caught at this early stage, it should be possible to carry on very cautiously with reduced tyre pressure, even for hundreds of miles.

Another occasional failure point is the chain tensioner. This can get smashed in an accident, and bits sometimes drop off or seize up, especially in wet and/or freezing weather, so a complete spare tensioner (plus the vulnerable securing nut on the Sturmey-Archer 3-speed) will, once again, provide good insurance. The 2- and 6-speed derailleur tensioner is part number QCTADR, while all others are QCTA. Gear and brake cables are pretty standard, but it makes sense to carry at least one of each inner cable because they're light and take up little space. Front and rear mudflaps fail quite often, and the handlebar catch and bolt can drop off or break, but a failure won't leave you stranded. The same can't be said for the 'L' type rear mudguard, which might appear to be in good condition, but can shatter into pieces the first time you fold the bike clumsily. If undertaking a long tour, a spare mudguard (QMGRLA) might be worth considering.

Finally, prevention is always the best repair tip. Check the bike over carefully before undertaking a major expedition. If the spokes are loose, tighten them before departure, and if items like wheel rims, brake blocks or tyres look worn, replace them before you go! Once on the road, keep the tyres well inflated, and carry a small oil can and a tiny pot of grease. With well-inflated tyres, and occasional lubrication (frequent in wet weather) a Brompton can run for thousands of miles without a single reliability issue developing.

© Andy & Sue Black

This example emergency repair kit (above) weighs about 1kg and comprises adjustable spanner, multitool, gear and brake cables, mini high pressure pump, spoke key, spokes and nipples, chain, hub gear indicator chain, inner tube and Schwalbe Kojak foldable tyre.

With the right kit a surprising range of repairs can be made roadside (right).

Flatbed trailers - above and below - are useful for unusually shaped and sized loads, whilst the rear rack can also be pressed into service as passenger space!

Riding with Children

This is another growth area that Brompton simply hadn't expected, but child carriers are one of the most frequently requested accessories. Rear-mounted child seats will fit on the Brompton, just as they do on most other bikes, and being well clear of the rear wheel, they're also much safer. The only point to watch is that the clamp will need to adapt to fit the Brompton's 32mm seat pillar.

The Spanish Brompton distributor Bike Tech SL produces the ITChair, a clever tube that fits between the seat pillar and main frame tube, complete with saddle and folding foot rests (the latest aluminium version has fixed foot rests). Suitable for slightly older children (up to seven), the ITChair is a fantastically useful accessory and children absolutely love travelling this way. It is not a Brompton-approved accessory, but puts little additional strain on the bike. The only current stockist in the UK is BikeFix of Lambs Conduit Street, London. Many users have fitted Brompton's handlebar strengthening crossbar (Brompton part number QXBARS-D) to give the child a safe handhold, but this is not essential. The Brompton itself can be adapted quite easily for older children. With shorter cranks, smaller pedals, lowered suspension (this puts the pedals closer to the ground) and straight 'S' type bars on a normal stem, the Brompton can be converted into an excellent folding child's bike, and all the elements are reversible as the child grows.

When the child grows too old to carry as a passenger a Brompton can be converted to produce a superb folding child's bike. The short handlebar stem shown on this early conversion can now be replaced with flat bars on a standard stem, but everything else is obligatory to produce a safe and reliable conversion.

Short-reach Brake levers

Saddle Adaptor Pin

Short Stem

Short Seat Pillar

Short-travel Suspension

145mm Cranks

If you really want a front-mounted seat, choose one that can clamp around the handlebar stem. In this design, the seat quick-releases, and the mounting block stays in place when the bike is folded. A front seat is sociable, but it's difficult to avoid bumps, and impossible to lift the wheel over small kerbs.

What not to do. This child seat has been fitted to the Brompton front carrier block. It looks convenient, but this is a dangerous place to carry a child, and the block (rated at 10kg) is really not strong enough to cope.

The IT Chair, introduced by Spanish Brompton distributor Bike Tech, is a centrally-mounted child seat, ideal for carrying older children (below and right).

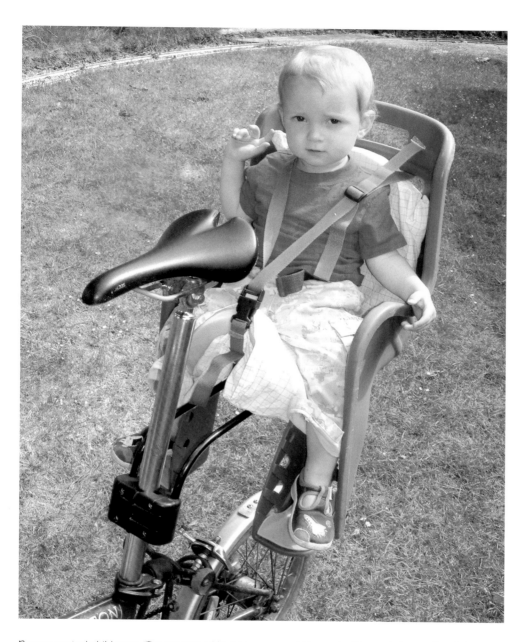

Rear-mounted child seat. The mounting block is now round the seat pillar, so it has to be slid to the top or removed when the bike is folded, but this is by far the best way to carry a child. The bike responds as normal, and the child sits in the empty space where a big rear wheel would normally be, so their hands and feet are well clear of danger. The clamp can be fitted lower to accommodate bigger children - up to four years old.

Brompton People & Places

The Early UK Brompton Scene

In the late 90s the Folding Society ran a series of three 'Folder Forum' shows - two at Weymouth, and the last at Ventnor on the Isle of Wight. The Folder Forums were open to all folding bikes, but had a strong Brompton influence, attracting an international crowd of enthusiasts.

(Left) Taking part in an agility test at Weymouth in 1996 is the late Channell Wasson, at that time the exclusive distributor for Brompton Bicycle in the United States.

Although billed as entertainment, the Folder Forum shows had a serious practical purpose, demonstrating that folding bikes (and perhaps the Brompton in particular) could change the way we travelled. In 1997, more than 100 cyclists departed from Weymouth by train for Wareham, where the party cycled to Norden to catch another train to Swanage on the Swanage Railway. Fitting that number of conventional bicycles on a normal service train would have been impossible, and the resulting television and magazine coverage put folding bikes firmly on the map.

The 1997 Folder Forum ride put folding bikes firmly on the map in the UK.

In 1997, with folding bikes still a relatively new and outlandish concept, the Natural Theatre Company's 'Cone Heads' were chosen to promote the second Weymouth show (below). The publicity stunts might have caught the attention of the media, but for the participants, the enduring image is of the visitors from outer space inspecting and photographing the Brompton (right).

The Folder (the Folding Society magazine) was relaunched as A to B in 1997, and is still regarded as the best source of information on folding bikes, including news and reviews of Bromptons.

A to B Magazine   email: atob@atob.org.uk   web: www.atob.org.uk   tel: 01305 259998

Making a Brompton

Making a Brompton consists of several stages:

* Organising the supply of components - for example wheels were still being handbuilt for the company in Wolverhampton in early 2017, but this will soon be brought in-house (below left).
* Frame brazing (below right) is a critical and highly skilled stage. In the time-honoured Brompton method steel frame tubes are secured in a jig and high temperature liquid copper alloy is run around the joints to 'glue' the tubes together. Unlike welding, the alloy in the brazing rods melts and flows at a lower temperature than the steel tubes, so the steel does not melt.
* After brazing, the finished frames and other parts are sent out of the factory for painting.

© Olivier Pascaud

* After the frames and other major assemblies have been powder-coated, everything arrives at the assembly stations where the bikes are built on rotatable bike stands. The photo on the left shows the old 'batch' method, where one builder built one bike at a time.

Left: Brompton has continued the tradition of training key personnel to build bikes, the assembly practice giving a priceless insight into the way the bicycle is built and why. Here, in summer 2009, the company's new US agent Ed Rae, takes his turn at one of the assembly stations. Avid Brompton watchers may have worked out that Ed is building one of the most expensive variants, an S6L-X.

© Alexander Henshaw

* Assembly lines at the Greenford factory have been designed from the ground up. Here 'production line' manufacture - ironically the process that revolutionised car manufacturing in the early 20th century and helped the car become an economic choice for the masses - sees one worker specialise in becoming as efficient as possible at one aspect on bike building. In contrast to car production lines however, the Brompton bike builders are free to move up and down the line to clear log-jams. This doesn't mean Brompton has gone entirely high-tech - there is still a place for the Victorian hand presses bought cheaply by Andrew Ritchie in the 1980s!

One of the new auto-brazing machines in action; cameras are used to detect the optimum temperature for the braze metal that flows into the joints, creating the strongest bond possible.

Computerised quality control; here a CMM (Co-ordinate Measuring Machine) checks the dimensions of a manufactured part against a computer image of the ideal dimensions. Previously the process involved clamping the piece in a jig and measuring by hand.

Appendix I - Chronology

1975 Andrew Ritchie first comes up with the folding bike idea.

1976 Brompton company formed, with friends as shareholders. **Prototypes P1 and P2 produced.** P1 has Bowden cables linking the folding sections, both have 18-inch wheels.

1977 **Prototypes P3 and P4 produced**, both with 16-inch wheels.

The P3 prototype from 1977

1978 Andrew decides to raise cash and produce the bike himself.

1979 Efforts to raise cash fail.

1981 First batch of 30 **pre-production bikes** pre-sold to shareholders to raise capital. Another 20 pre-production bikes were also sold.

1982 Mark 1 production begins in batches of 100.

1983 Cessation of hinge manufacture brings production of Mark 1 to an end after 450 have been made.

1984 Brompton approached by potential licensee which falls through. Attempts to raise capital fail.

1985 **Julian Vereker** joins Brompton.

1986 Finance package is pulled together, and tooling produced for production.

1987 In March the Mark 2 Brompton wins the Cyclex award. In November, **the first factory** is established in the Arches, Brentford.

1988 In March **the first Mark 2** bikes are sold. The bike is now in two forms: 'L', without a rear rack, and 'T', with a rack. Attempts are made to build a dealer network.

1991 Brompton takes over second arch, and **Nicola McGregor** arrives. Steel wheels replaced by polished aluminium. GB Cycles handlebars introduced.

1992 Chain tensioner assembly improved and in September handlebar stem diameter increased from 30mm to 35mm.

1993 In April the headset was increased in size from 1" to 1⅛". In December, Brompton moved to a **bigger factory in Chiswick Park**.

1994 From June, the 5-speed Brompton changed from the dual-cable Sturmey-Archer 5-Star hub to the new single-cable Sprinter. In October, the Sachs brakes were replaced with Saccon.

1995 Brompton wins the **Queen's Award for Export Achievement.** The forged bottom bracket assembly was replaced by a FAG cartridge, and the Soubitez dynamo replaced by a Union. Neobike handlebars introduced.

1996 Introduction of a basic 'C' type is investigated, but the idea is quietly shelved. Steel front hub replaced by KEYIN alloy hub. In August, the dynamo changes from Union to Jos, then in December, from Jos to Axa. In December, polished alloy rims replaced by anodised alloy.

1997 In June a new concave alloy hub replaces the KEYIN, and in November the mudguards were temporarily replaced with a round profile. Brompton wins **ADFC Bike of the Year Award** in Germany.

1998 In February, the anodised rims were replaced with milled-finish alloy. In October, Brompton moves to the **bigger Brentford factory**.

1999 Julian Vereker falls ill and withdraws from Brompton. Tim Guinness joins the board, then becomes Chairman. Stronger Humpert handlebars introduced in September.

2000 In March the **Mark 3** is introduced. New Brompton tyres, dual-pivot brakes, rear mudflap, battery light option, wider standard and optional colour range. Basic 'C' type finally introduced. Handlebar brace issued to owners of older bikes. In May, the 'ball-locking' version of the Sprinter hub is introduced. In June, the handlebar hinge was changed from a forging to a casting for auto-brazing. In September, **Sturmey-Archer ceases trading.** The 5-speed is withdrawn when stocks of hubs are exhausted.

2001 In April the 3-speed changes over to SRAM hubs.

2002 In April the Brompton 2 x 3-speed is introduced. Will Butler-Adams arrives.

2003 New Axa dynamo in May, new handlebar catch in June, new lightweight front carrier frame in July.

2004 Main frame hinge changed from forging to casting for auto-brazing, producing a longer wheelbase.

2005 **Mark 4 introduced**. C-type remains, but L and T types replaced by M, S and P variants, according to handlebar style. Many detail changes, including reach-adjustable brakes, a single-speed hub, a return to Sturmey-Archer hubs on 3-speed models, new saddle, Pentaclip saddle clamp, XL lightweight titanium variants, new battery lights, SON dynohub option.
Brompton adopts the World Championship series of public-entry Brompton races, held around the world.

2007 New seat clamp quick-release, and optional rear frame clip.

2008 **Will Butler-Adams** becomes Managing Director. In May, the Brompton tyres are reconfigured with softer rubber on the shoulders, giving improved grip, but slightly inferior rolling resistance. Double-butted lightweight spokes introduced on the 1- and 2-speed rear wheel. New softer foamed polyurethane suspension block introduced.

The global credit crunch sees an ensuing period of significant folding bike price rises for Brompton and its competitors.

£1 million invested in the Brentford factory to increase efficiency and productivity.

2009 In January the BWR 3-speed wide ratio hub replaces the SRAM 3-speed on all 6-speed models. An optional hard suspension block is introduced, and all paint finishes are changed from gloss to satin. In May, Brompton introduced a new 'handgrip' saddle, non-folding right-hand pedal to match the folding left-hand pedal, and a lightweight front wheel on selected models, featuring cartridge bearings and double-butted spokes.

In October Andrew Ritchie wins the Prince Philip Designer's Prize 'for outstanding achievement in design'.

2010 In October the titanium seat pillar fitted to XL models is discontinued and replaced with a **nickel-plated aluminium pillar**. The intention is to fit the pillar to all models later on.

2011 March sees the launching of the first Brompton Junction store in Kobe Japan. Many others follow. In May, Brompton releases a limited edition of **150 'Royal Wedding' bikes** for Korea, Japan, Singapore and Taiwan. The bikes sell out very quickly.

In June, the **alloy seat pillar is withdrawn** following flaking and surface pitting of the nickel plating. For the time being, all bikes are fitted with the standard steel seat pillar, with XL purchasers receiving a £35 rebate, but the alloy pillar is never sorted satisfactorily, and the steel pillar becomes a permanent fitting. In July, Brompton launches the **'Oratory' jacket**, the first in a proposed line of Brompton-branded cycle clothing. The company also launches the first public hire **Brompton Dock** at Guildford railway station. September sees the first new handlebar configuration for seven years, the **H type**. It caters for 'taller riders and for those wanting a markedly more upright riding position'. The height of the grips from the ground has been raised by 60mm compared to the classic M Type.

2012 In March, after two years of development, Brompton's neat frame-mounted Toolkit wins a Design & Innovation Award at the Taipei Cycle Show. Introduction is promised for early summer, then December, then April 2013. 2012 also sees a further **eight Brompton Dock openings**. In the summer of 2012, Brompton quietly withdraws the titanium folding pedal bolt from XL models, replacing it with an improved, but slightly heavier, steel bolt.

2013 Manufacture of titanium rear frames begins at joint venture **Brompton-Fletcher Ltd**.

2015 Brompton announces it is working with Williams Advanced Engineering (part of Williams Formula One team) with the aim of developing an electric assist Brompton.

In May Brompton Dock rebranded as **Brompton Bike Hire**.

Entrepeneur Luke Johnson appointed a Brompton director in September.

2016 Brompton-Fletcher now producing 200 titanium rear frames a month.

Andrew Ritchie resigns as a director of Brompton in March.

New 84,000 square foot factory officially opened by the Duke of Edinburgh in November in **Greenford**.

From November, new integrated gear and brake levers fitted to all bikes, together with colour co-ordinated lock-on handlebar grips. Double-butted spokes now only fitted on lightweight variants of 1- and 2-speed bikes.

RIDE AWAY...

"On the road the Brompton is a revelation... Overall a definite winner."
BICYCLE ACTION

...STOW AWAY

A Brompton is the most versatile bike you can own: take or stow it anywhere and enjoy the freedom of a bicycle wherever you wish.

These original posters were produced by Philippa Steward in the late 1980s when Brompton was still struggling to find its niche, and amounted to pretty much the sole thrust of the company's marketing at the time. But the 'Go Anywhere... Take Anywhere' slogan was spot on, summing up the adaptability that would later become the cornerstone of the company's phenomenal success. Like the bike, the posters have become a design classic.

GO ANYWHERE...

"... creates a new range of situations in which bicycling becomes attractive"
FINANCIAL TIMES

...TAKE ANYWHERE

The Brompton folds smaller than any other bike: yet in use it is a fast, lightweight and versatile machine which offers countless new ways of travelling about.

Appendix II - Gearing Options

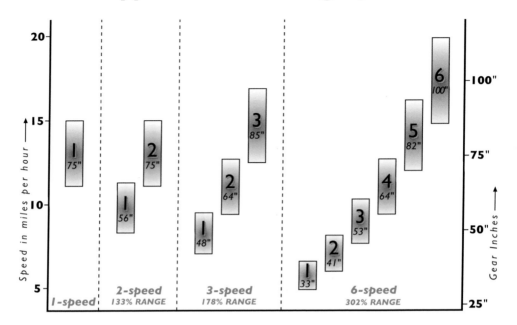

The chart shows optimal road speed for each gear with the four current Brompton variants (note that 3-speed gear ratios have been the same for many years). The 6-speed not only provides a much wider gear range than the 2- or 3-speed, but more overlap between the gears too, making changes smoother and progress more efficient. But don't write off the 1- and 2-speed bikes because a chart can never tell the whole story! In practice their lighter weight, improved efficiency and faster gear changes give excellent acceleration and hill-climbing. The gear ratios shown can be fine-tuned up (3- or 6-speed only) or down (all variants) to suit local riding conditions.

Note on Gear Inches: This British measurement (shown on the right hand side of the graph and elsewhere), dates back to mid-Victorian times, and indicates the diameter a 'Penny-Farthing' wheel would have to be to achieve the same gearing. An 85" gear, for example, would require a wheel 7' 1" (2 metres 16cm) in diameter. This comparison means little today, but the concept of gear-inches has remained popular in many countries as a guide to how 'easy' or 'difficult' it is to pedal in each gear. High gears are needed for speed and low gears for climbing hills and carrying loads. Gear-inches make a useful measurement because they can be applied to any bicycle, whatever the actual wheel size or gearing setup, allowing for easy comparison. But once again the size of the gear cannot tell the full story as it gives no indication of gear efficiency.

Special Brompton factory-fitted gearing options :

1-speed with 19% reduction = 61"   1-speed with 7% reduction = 69"
2-speed with 19% reduction = 46"-61"   2-speed with 7% reduction = 52"-69"
3-speed with 18% reduction = 39"-69"   3-speed with 12% reduction = 42"- 75"
3-speed with 8% increase = 52"-92"   6-speed with 8% increase = 36"-108"
6-speed with 12% reduction = 29"-88"

(Mathematical note: The 19% reduction on 1- and 2-speed bikes is actually 18.52%. For simplicity it is described by Brompton as an 18% reduction, but marginally closer to 19% in reality).

Gear 'range' is the difference between the lowest and highest gear, generally expressed as a percentage. On the graph below, Brompton's 'standard' gear ranges (shown in blue), are contrasted with non-standard options. For example, the 2-speed and 6-speed bikes have 12- and 16-tooth sprockets as standard. Replace the 16-tooth with a 19-tooth (the largest that can easily be squeezed on) and you get a 158% range on a 2-speed bike, and an impressive 388% range on the 6-speed. At the expense of some some rather odd gaps between gears, this conversion makes the bike suitable for loaded touring, even in very hilly areas.

However, some Brompton riders either want a wider range or don't feel comfortable with the twin-lever system. Alternative gear options fitted by such riders are shown here in pink, but all involve a loss of efficiency vis-a-vis the 6-speed bike, particularly in very high or low gears, and in most cases, extra weight. Also note if you fit a non-standard conversion yourself the manufacturer's warranty may be invalid, so the cost of professional fitting could well be worthwhile.

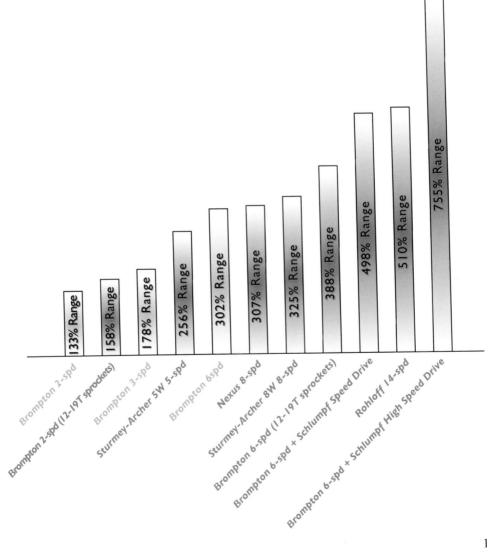

Appendix III - Frame & Serial Numbers

The frame number can be found stamped on the main frame just above the rear frame pivot bearings. Rather confusingly, frames seem to have been stamped in batches of 500 within a set period, typically one or two months, but very often (especially in the early days) the batch would not be entirely used up before the next began, and in other months (particularly later) several batches might be running at once. In any event, the date might have been stamped some weeks or even months before the bike was actually shipped out of the factory, so the frame number can be no more than a guide to the date of sale. Appendix II should be used with other evidence, such as the Sturmey-Archer hub date, stamped on the steel shell, and chronology in Appendix 1.

From October 2001, bikes were also given a unique serial number as well as a frame number, but serial number stickers were not added to the bike immediately. The sticker can be found on the top back of the seat tube, or the bottom of the tube from 2013. The first four digits of this unique identifying number indicate the date of manufacture: the first pair the year, and the second pair the month. From late 2015, the sticker changed to a laser-etched plate.

Important Note: Frame numbers are only a rough guide to a bike's age. Neither Brompton, nor Excellent Books, nor the author is suggesting that a particular serial number guarantees a bike of a particular age.

Frame No.	Range	Approx build date		Frame No.	Range	Approx build date	
600	1103	Jan 88	Dec 88	36500	36999	Mar-97	Apr-97
1104	1674	Jan 89	Aug 89	37000	37499	Apr-97	Jun-97
1675	2234	Sept 89	Feb 90	37500	37999	Jun-97	Aug-97
2235	2760	Mar 90	June 90	38000	38499	Aug-97	Sep-97
2761	3290	July 90	Oct 90	38500	38999	May-97	Sep-97
3291	3814	Nov 90	Feb 91	39000	39499	Jun-97	Jul-97
3815	4837	March 91	Aug 91	39500	39999	Sep-97	Oct-97
4838	6086	Sept 91	April 92	140000	140499	Oct-97	Nov-97
6087	7249	May 92	Oct 92	140500	140999	Aug-97	Jan-98
7250	8316	Nov 92	Mar 93	141000	141499	Dec-97	Jan-98
8000	8499	May 93	Jul 93 *	141500	141999	Dec-97	Jan-98
8500	8999	Sep 93	Oct 93	142000	142499	Feb-98	
9000	9499	Aug-93	Nov-93	144000	144499	Jan-98	Feb-98
9500	9999	Oct-93	Jan-94	144500	144999	Feb-98	Jun-98
11000	11499	Jan-94	Mar-94	145000	145499	Mar-98	Jun-98
11500	11999	Mar-94	Apr-94	145500	145999	Mar-98	Aug-98
12000	12499	Apr-94	Jun-94	146000	146499	Apr-98	Aug-98
12500	12999	Jun-94	Jul-94	146500	146999	May-98	Oct-98
13000	13499	Jul-94	Aug-94	147000	147499	Aug-98	Nov-98
13500	13999	Aug-94	Sep-94	147500	147999	Sep-98	Dec-98
14000	14499	Sep-94	Oct-94	148000	148499	Oct-98	Jan-99
14500	14999	Nov-94	Dec-94	148500	148999	Oct-98	Mar-99
15000	15499	Nov-94	Feb-95	148000	148499	Oct-98	Jan-99
15500	15999	Feb-95	May-95	148500	148999	Oct-98	Mar-99
16000	16499	Mar-95	Jun-95	149000	149499	Jan-99	Apr-99
16500	16999	Jun-95	Sep-95	149500	149999	Feb-99	Apr-99
17000	17499	Jun-95	Sep-95	150000	150499	Mar-99	Jun-99
17500	17999	Jul-95	Sep-95	150500	150999	Nov-99	Jun-99
18000	18499	Aug-95	Sep-95	151000	151499	Oct-98	Jan-99
18500	18999	Sep-95	Oct-95	151500	151999	Nov-98	May-99
19000	19499	Oct-95	Jan-96	152000	152499	Feb-99	Jun-99
19500	19999	Nov-95	Dec-95	152500	152999	Jun-99	Sep-99
20000	20499	Jan-96	Mar-96	153000	153499	Jun-99	Sep-99
20500	20999	Feb-96	Jun-96	153500	153999	Jul-99	Sep-99
21000	21499	Mar-96	Jul-96	154000	154499	Aug-99	Oct-99
21500	21999	Mar-96	Jun-96	154500	154999	Aug-99	Nov-99
22000	22499	May-96	Jun-96	155000	155499	Sep-99	Dec-99
22500	22999	Jun-96	Aug-96	155500	155999	Oct-99	Dec-99
23000	23499	Aug-96	Sep-96	156000	156499	Oct-99	May-00
23500	23999	Aug-96	Oct-96	156500	156999	Nov-99	May-00
34000	34499	Sep-96	Nov-96	157000	157499	Dec-99	May-00
34500	34999	Oct-96	Dec-96	157500	157999	Dec-99	May-00
35000	35499	Nov-96	Jan-97	158000	158499	Apr-00	Jul-00
35500	35999	Dec-96	Jan-97	158500	158999	Apr-00	Jul-00
36000	36499	Feb-97	Mar-97	159000	159499	Apr-00	Aug-00

159500	159999	Apr-00	Aug-00
160000	160499	May-00	Sep-00
160500	160999	Jun-00	Sep-00
161000	161499	Jul-00	Sep-00
161500	161999	Jul-00	Sep-00
162000	162499	Aug-00	Oct-00
162500	162999	Aug-00	Nov-00
163000	163499	Sep-00	Oct-00
163500	163999	Oct-00	Dec-00
164000	164499	Nov-00	Dec-00
164500	164999	Nov-00	Jan-01
165000	165499	Dec-00	Jan-01
165500	165999	Dec-00	Feb-01
166000	166499	Feb-01	Mar-01

166500	166999	Feb-01	Apr-01
167000	167499	Mar-01	May-01
167500	167999	Apr-01	Jun-01
168000	168499	May-01	Jul-01
168500	168999	Jun-01	Aug-01
169000	169499	Jul-01	Aug-01
169500	169999	Aug-01	Sep-01
170000	170499	Aug-01	Sep-01
170500	170999	Aug-01	Sep-01
171000	171499	Sep-01	Nov-01

* **Note** There are discrepancies in the records regarding the precise manufacturing dates of these early frame numbers - certainly up until around July 1993.

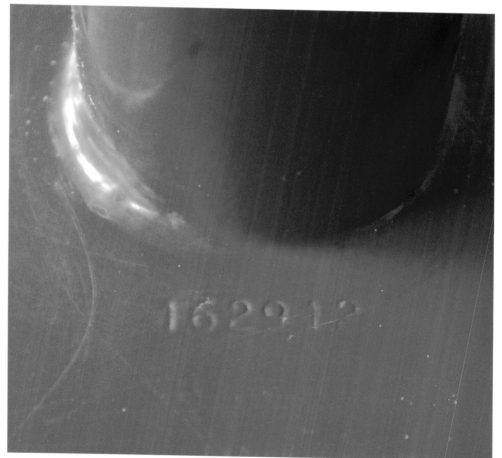

Frame numbers aren't always easy to make out. This example, 162912, gives an approximate date for the bike's manufacture; between August and November 2000.

Appendix IV -
Profit & Sales Figures

Brompton's success has been helped by Andrew Ritchie's meticulous financial husbandry ("Call it meanness!", says Andrew). Growth has been remarkably steady, despite mixed trading conditions, and since the start-up years, achieved without borrowing. The company has been profitable since 1990, even during the Sturmey-Archer crisis of 2001-2002. A very notable achievement.

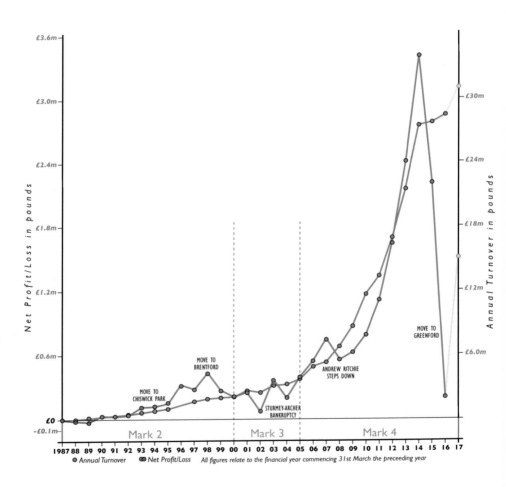

Note: 2016-17 figures are based on estimates.

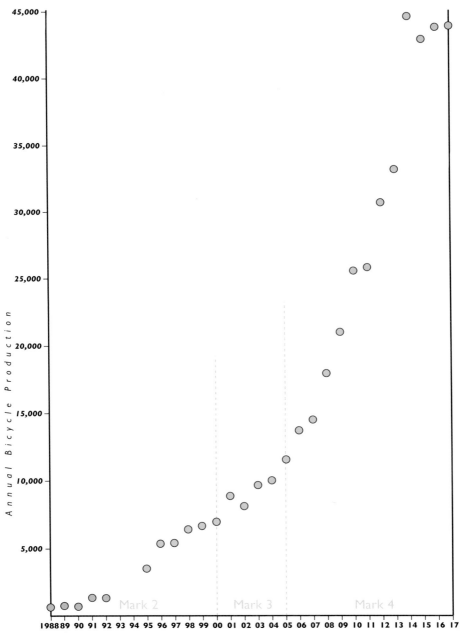

Annual Bicycle Production

Mark 2   Mark 3   Mark 4

1988 89 90 91 92 93 94 95 96 97 98 99 00 01 02 03 04 05 06 07 08 09 10 11 12 13 14 15 16 17

Figures for model year shown relate to the financial year commencing 31st March the preceding year
Figures are based on weekly output for the calendar year

191

Appendix V - Useful Contacts

A to B
'Alternative' transport magazine run by Brompton Bicycle book author David Henshaw.
40 Manor Road
Dorchester DT1 2AX
01305 259998
www.atob.org.uk

Brompton Bicycle Ltd.
Unit 1, Ockham Drive,
Greenford
London UB6 0FD
020 8232 8484
www.brompton.com

Brompton Dock
Managers of the Brompton Dock project.
www.bromptonbikehire.com
Helpline: 0203 474 0700

Brompton Junction
Concept store details at
www.bromptonjunction.com

Diana Powell
Cover from an illustration by Diana Powell. Various Brompton inspired prints available from
www.dianapowell.co.uk
07821101667
0117 3297188
diana@dianapowell.co.uk

Excellent Books
Brompton Bicycle book publishers and specialists in cycle publishing and journalism
5 Viking Avenue
Emley HD8 9SE
07762 545543
richardpeacecycling.com

Also see the chapter The World of Brompton Specials for details of 'specials' makers

NYCeWheels
US Brompton dealer stocking titanium seat pillars and racks
353 East 58th Street,
New York, NY 10022
(212) 737 3078
www.nycewheels.com

Text Note: Victorian Prices Compared to Modern-Day Equivalent Prices

Throughout this story we have tried to show modern-day equivalent prices wherever possible. These take account of the increase (usually) in the Retail Price Index since the product or service was first advertised. However, they can seem unrealistically cheap today, because the RPI takes no account of the increase in Gross Domestic Product per capita in the intervening years. In other words, we're all much wealthier now, making discretionary purchases like bicycles less painful. This disparity is particularly striking with prices from the Victorian era, when the majority of working people would consider a bicycle a very major purchase.

Index

ʻForeword

by Councillor Ian Ellis

Chairman of Boughton Monchelsea Parish Council

It gives me great pleasure to write a foreword to Dr. Paul Hastings' book. The book is the result of a great deal of painstaking research and provides the first comprehensive history of Boughton Monchelsea. The text is illustrated by some seventy photographs which have been brought together by David Millar. Each has a story to tell and many will recall familiar situations. Thanks must go to those residents who so willingly allowed the inclusion of their photographs within the book. The maps and other illustrations are the work of Denis Coggins. The graphs were made by Gordon Morris. A survey of Boughton's buildings was undertaken by Sarah Pearson. Again thanks are due to all those householders whose properties were visited.

The book was made possible by the decision of Boughton Monchelsea Parish Council to commission a historical study as a part of its new millennium celebrations. The generosity of Maidstone Borough Council and Kent County Council must also be acknowledged for their valuable contributions towards publication costs.

I congratulate Paul Hastings on his book which will give immense pleasure to all lovers of Boughton Monchelsea. Paul has taken endless trouble to recapture the story of the parish throughout its long history. This is not only a very worthwhile historical record but also an invaluable portrait for present and future generations to enjoy.

Ian Ellis.

Boughton Monchelsea, 1999.

Contents

Maps

Graphs & Plans

Acknowledgements

I have received help from many people in the preparation and writing of this book. I should like to express my warmest thanks to Chairman Ian Ellis and the members of Boughton Monchelsea Parish Council whose concept it originally was and whose financial support ultimately brought the idea to fruition. The Archivist and Staff of the Centre for Kentish Studies, Maidstone and the Staff of Maidstone Library were unfailingly courteous and helpful in providing access to the historical documents within their care. In the parish itself Councillor Beryl Bush was of great assistance and generously placed her notes at my disposal. Councillor Ian Ellis, always helpful, furnished me with details about the activities of Boughton Monchelsea Parish Council post-1980 and Boughton Monchelsea Amenity Trust since 1994. The incumbent, the Reverend R. Geoffrey Davis, and Norman Manning, Secretary to the Parish Council, kindly gave access to those parish records which they still hold and were invariably supportive. Charles Gooch, former owner of Boughton Monchelsea Place, loaned me the manor court books while John Allen, landlord of the *Albion,* lent me the records of the Boughton branch of the Ancient Order of Foresters.

The professional expertise of Sarah Pearson, formerly of the Royal Commission on the Historical Monuments of England, was invaluable in conducting a buildings survey of the parish which she accomplished while the remainder of us watched speechless with admiration. Her reports largely constitute the basis of the last section of the book. This would have been impossible, however, without the co-operation and generosity of the owners and occupiers who invariably welcomed us to their homes and provided both help and hospitality. Brian Philp, Director of the Kent Archaeological Rescue Unit, gave information upon Boughton's archaeology and John Butcher volunteered assistance over ragstone quarrying.

My former colleagues and friends in the History Department at Middleton St. George College of Education and in the History Inspectorate and Advisory Service in Kent also gave unstintingly of their time and skill. Denis Coggins was my cartographer and illustrator; Gordon Morris drew the computerised graphs while Dr. Ken Fairless translated those documents which were in medieval latin. The photography is the work of David Millar, former history advisory teacher in Kent. Photographs were kindly provided by the Kent History Centre and by Ian Coulson, my successor as Kent County History Inspector; by Councillor Steve Munford and Bob Taylor, Headteacher of Boughton Monchelsea Primary School; by Mrs. Kendrick of Boughton Monchelsea Place and by the people of Boughton Monchelsea itself. The help of Elizabeth Hirons as a peripatetic research assistant was invaluable. I must also pay tribute to the work of the late Denis Tye, Headteacher at the School from 1955-1981. His consuming interest in village schools and their history resulted in his trilogy *Boughton Monchelsea School Log Book Extracts 1863-1963, A Village Remembered, Boughton Monchelsea 1850-1970* and *A Village School; Boughton Monchelsea 1850-1970* in addition to a collection of oral history tapes now deposited in the library of the University of Kent. All have been consulted and have proved most valuable.

Finally, I would like to express my thanks to Victor Skipp, who first introduced me to the techniques of local history in the late 1950s, and to my long-suffering wife who has borne with me stoically throughout. She has, of necessity, been researcher, secretary, chauffeuse and carer and literally acted as my right hand. We should both like to dedicate this book to the past, present and future villagers of Boughton Monchelsea where during our fifteen-year stay we made so many good friends.

Paul Hastings – *Norfolk, 1999*

The author and publishers are indebted to the undermentioned householders of Boughton Monchelsea who so kindly made their houses available for the buildings survey in September 1998 and May 1999.

Mr. & Mrs. G. Anderson	Mr. C. Foreman	Mrs. P. Murray
Mr. & Mrs. C. Anscombe	Mr. & Mrs. D. Goulden	Mr. C. Norfolk
Mr. & Mrs. M. Butcher	Mr. & Mrs. D. Hayman	Mr. & Mrs. D. Powell
Mr. & Mrs. S. Casswell	Mr. & Mrs. R. Hitch	Mr. N. Poulter
Mr. & Mrs. G. Clarke	Mr. & Mrs. N. Hughes	Dr. & Mrs. I. Roberts
Mr. & Mrs. R. Dawkins	Mr. & Mrs. J. Kenward	Capn. & Mrs. D. Roome
Mr. K. Davis	Mr. & Mrs. R. S. Lankester	Mr. & Mrs. G. Rose
Mrs. J. Davies	Dr. P. & Dr. C. Lewis	Mr. & Mrs. W. Skinner
Mr. & Mrs. A. Ellis	Mr. & Mrs. R. Lewis	Mr. & Mrs. W. Wilson
Mr. & Mrs. I. Ellis	Mr. & Mrs. J. Luckhurst	
Mr. & Mrs. W. Evans	Mr. & Mrs. S. Macbean	
Mr. & Mrs. Y. Ezra	Mr. D. Murdoch	

The author and publishers also wish to record their gratitude to the undermentioned photographic archives and individuals who so kindly allowed publication of their photographs. Since some photographs were originally published in the form of postcard collections possession is often duplicated in a number of different hands. The same applies to some individual photographs. It has not, therefore, always been possible to establish either the original photographer or the original owner. We apologise for any failure on our part to inadvertently make the correct acknowledgement.

Kent County Council Centre for Kentish Studies Educational Resources Centre. Formerly the David Millar Collection in the Kent History Centre.
Mr. Bob Taylor and the Boughton Monchelsea School Photographic Archive
Mrs. Kendrick and the Boughton Monchelsea Place Photographic Archive
Maidstone Museum
South-Eastern Newspapers Ltd.
Mr. I. Coulson
Mr. G. G. Dearing
Mrs. E. Greenaway
Mrs. J. Johnson
Mr. D. Clyne
Mr. D. Millar
Mr. S. Munford
Mrs. D. Ralph

Upon the Quarry Hills

A History of Boughton Monchelsea

Fig. 1 *Boughton Monchelsea – Salient facts*

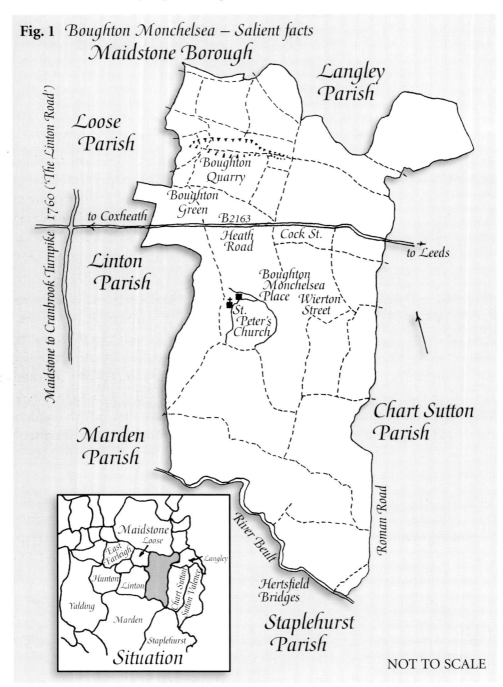

Maidstone Borough

Langley Parish

Loose Parish

Maidstone to Cranbrook Turnpike 1760 ('The Linton Road')

Boughton Quarry

Boughton Green

to Coxheath

B2163

Heath Road

Cock St.

to Leeds

Linton Parish

Boughton Monchelsea Place

Wierton Street

St. Peter's Church

Chart Sutton Parish

Marden Parish

River Beult

Roman Road

Hertsfield Bridges

Staplehurst Parish

Situation

Maidstone

Loose

East Farleigh

Langley

Hunton

Linton

Chart Sutton

Sutton Valence

Yalding

Marden

Staplehurst

NOT TO SCALE

Boughton Monchelsea – Salient facts

Boughton Monchelsea in 1842 was a parish of some 2,200 acres lying on the southern ragstone ridge overlooking the Weald commonly called the Quarry Hills. Situated three and a half miles south-east of Maidstone and 34 miles from London it was in the diocese of Canterbury within the county of Kent. A Local Government Board Order of 1888, which transferred Lockham to Langley parish and a detached portion of Langley to Boughton, increased Boughton's overall area to 2,374 acres. When a further part of Langley was added in 1934 Boughton expanded to 2,820 acres despite some loss of land to Maidstone.[1]

The parish is bounded to the north by the parishes of Maidstone and Langley; on the east by Chart Sutton; to the south by Staplehurst and Marden; and on the west by Linton and Loose. It is bisected east-west by the B2163 which gave access to the military camp established during the French Wars of the eighteenth and early nineteenth centuries upon the 'large, unenclosed commonland called Coxheath'. The B2163 joins the A229 at Linton crossroads. The latter follows the approximate line of the Maidstone and Cranbrook Turnpike established in 1760. The railway station at Maidstone opened after the building of the Paddock Wood to Maidstone line which linked with the South-Eastern Railway's main line to London in 1844. A second station lay at Marden 4 miles to the south.[2]

The parish population did not exceed 700 before 1801. After 1801 it grew steadily to 1,106 in 1841 and then remained much the same for the rest of the century. Slow but steady growth resumed in 1911 but only after 1961 was there any major increase following housing development which took a population of 1,189 in 1951 to 1,525 two decades later. By 1991 residents numbered 1,704.[3]

As in many Kent parishes there was no single nucleated mediaeval village at Boughton Monchelsea. Instead settlement was concentrated in the four scattered hamlets of Boughton Green, Boughton Quarry, Wierton Street and Cock Street. By 1786 Wierton Street consisted of 'six or seven dwellings and some dispersed farm houses'. In 1834 the greatest number of houses was still at Boughton Quarry whose extensive sources of Kentish ragstone had been extracted and exported to London and other parts of Kent since Roman times. In the twentieth century, however, it was Boughton Green, extending down Church Street, which became the modern centre of village activity following the growth of pre-war and post-war housing along Heath Road, Green Lane and at Lewis Court and Haste Hill.[4]

The Parish Bounds

By the tenth or eleventh centuries some twenty new parishes or chapelries, including Boughton Monchelsea, had been created from the Minsterlands of Maidstone and Hollingbourne in the wooded belt of the Quarry Hills between Maidstone and Ashford. Among the other new parishes were Loose, Linton, Leeds, Langley and Chart Sutton as the Church streamlined its organisation after the conversion. Boughton's parish and manorial boundaries appear to have been the same.[5]

Parish boundaries were jealously guarded to prevent encroachment by the farmers of neighbouring parishes. Where natural or irremovable man-made boundaries existed these were used. Thus to the south and south-east Boughton was bounded by the River Beult and the old Roman road (Forge Lane). Since the remainder of the parish lacked natural boundaries boundary points were handed down by word-of-mouth and re-inforced by an annual perambulation. At Rogationtide each year the villagers, led by the parish priest, proceeded from one boundary mark to the next praying for God's blessing on the growing crops and ceremonially beating the children of the community to impress upon them the whereabouts of boundary markers and the need for their preservation. In the Middle Ages perambulations were enrolled at the manor court. Later written descriptions were produced.

Only part of a Boughton perambulation has survived. On Friday 27 May 1720 a party of parishioners led by the vicar, the Rev. Samuel Pratt, met at nine in the morning at 'the Cock in Cockes Heath'. In order to complete their task within the day they divided into two 'companies'. One 'going the Upper (southern) boundary' the other the Lower (northern) boundary. The route of the former has survived.

Proceeding along the hedgerows the vicar and sixteen others including William Martin, Churchwarden, and John Baker, Overseer of the Poor, checked the existence of nineteen boundary marks before reaching the stone at 'Hersfield Bridge' and a further twenty-one on their homeward journey. Most marks were made upon trees which were pollarded for longevity and to limit them to a suitable height. Pollard oaks were preferred plus ash, maple and a sprinkling of other woods. 'An Appletre between 2 willows' and 'a whitethorne in John Triggs hedge' also carried boundary markers together with 'a Crab Stock' in John Potter's field and 'an olden stub' at John Trigg's corner. There were only five boundary stones including one 'at Thos. Brownes forge' and a second 'at Wid.Martin's gate'. The sole boundary post was `in Spice's ground against ye River'(Beult).

Hertsfield Bridges.
One of the southernmost boundary points of the parish. Built of ragstone in the 14th and 15th century the bridge crosses several streams of the River Beult. It is partly in Staplehurst parish.

Only in the nineteenth century when the parish began to decline as a unit of local government did parish boundaries become less important. Even so as late as 1907 Boughton Monchelsea Parish Council annually beat the bounds on Easter Monday while the 6″ Ordnance Survey Map 1909 still indicates the parish boundaries by some 59 boundary stones and markers.[6]

Fig. 2 *Quarry Wood Camp*

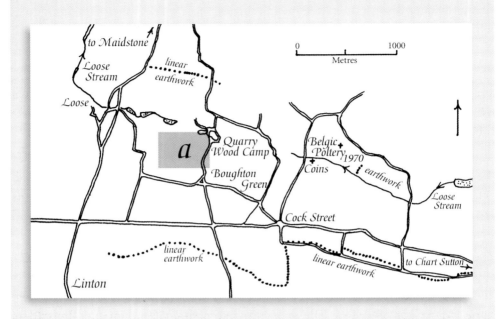

NOT TO SCALE

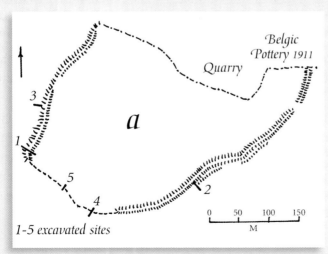

1-5 excavated sites

Based upon the plans of D.B. Kelly in Arch. Cant. Vol. 86. 1971

The Natural Landscape and Pre-Roman Settlement

The soil of the parish varies. It consists generally of a shallow, fertile loam covering a ragstone subsoil. To the east of the hamlet of Cock Street, however, it changes to a red earth intermixed with flints which is much less fertile. Only Wierton has a heavy subsoil of Wealden clay hindering drainage and causing seasonal surface wetness.[7]

In the period before man settled permanently in the district and began to modify the landscape the relatively poor, hill country of the Chartland was largely wooded. While man remained a hunter and food gatherer it continued unchanged. As late as 1842 562 acres, approximately one quarter of the parish, were still wood and wasteland.[8]

There is little evidence of human activity at Boughton before the Iron Age. (700B.C.-43 A.D.) Two Neolithic (3500 B.C.-2000 B.C.) axe heads have been discovered on its northern boundary at Park Wood and a third Neolithic polished stone axe has been found near Charlton Farm. The area stayed comparatively untouched by settlers during the Bronze Age. (2000 B.C.-700 B.C.) The only small find dating from that period is a bronze brooch uncovered opposite Brishing Court in 1841.[9]

Towards the close of the second and at the beginning of the first century B.C. the Belgae from Gaul began crossing the Channel. They came at first to plunder but later to invade and colonise. Led by a warrior aristocracy they established themselves in East Kent as far as the Medway and made Durovernon (Canterbury) their local capital. They maintained contact with the Belgae of Gaul exporting to the continent corn, cattle, iron, gold, slaves and hunting dogs. Belgic Kent was a relatively prosperous region. Caesar, who made brief military expeditions into Kent in 55 and 54 B.C., described the area he called Cantium as the most civilised part of Britain and a populous farming district. Its economic development was limited, however, by inter-tribal warfare and the fierce hostility of the Kentish tribes towards Rome which led ultimately to the Roman invasion of 43 A.D.

Before the coming of the Romans, Boughton had undergone its first major settlement with the creation of Quarry Wood Camp, a fortified Belgic oppidum (township), covering much of the northern half of the parish and beyond. The Camp, two and a half miles south of Maidstone, lay partly in Loose parish and partly in Boughton Monchelsea. Only the western and eastern banks of the earthwork remain and part of the ditch on the eastern side. The western bank is 300 yards long and ranges from 21 feet to 8 feet in height. The eastern bank is 8-9 feet high and 380 yards in length. The southern side of the Camp was levelled by the landowner, Mr Charlton, in the early nineteenth century to make the land more usable during the Napoleonic Wars. The north side has been destroyed by ragstone quarrying. If the Camp earthworks included the disused quarry to the north plus any defences south of the Loose stream then some 30 acres were enclosed by a single bank and ditch. No gateways have survived although there may have been one at the south-west corner of the enclosure. [10]

This strong central fortification was given extra protection by outworks on three sides. While the Camp was protected to the west by the Loose valley there are traces of linear earthworks on the north, east and south which lack natural protective features. Few traces of the northern and eastern earthworks remain but a bank and ditch runs $2^3/_4$ miles from Linton Park to Chart Sutton. The ditches enclose a huge area of land and represent together with the Camp a massive human effort in which large numbers of people have been organised and occupied for a number of years.[11]

Alec Detsicas believes that Quarry Wood was one of several settlements created at strategic points along the Belgic trade routes dating from the early first century B.C. While the hill fort at Bigbury, forerunner of Belgic Canterbury, dominated the crossing of the Stour, Quarry Wood, anticipating Belgic Rochester, controlled the Medway crossing. Further west Oldbury hill-fort commanded the Darent valley.[12] D.B. Kelly, excavator of Quarry Wood between 1963-67, dates the earthwork from pottery found on the site to the end of the Belgic period in the second quarter of the first century A.D. The reason for its construction was, like the contemporary strengthening of the hill fort at Oldbury, fear of a Roman invasion. Since it was built in an emergency the site was not well-protected by natural features, compared with similar oppida elsewhere, nor sufficiently near the Medway to control the important river crossing. Nevertheless, if the Romans had crossed the Medway near Aylesford, Quarry Wood would have provided a refuge for the Belgic population in the Maidstone district and a suitable stronghold for a final stand. Its wide, shallow ditches were intended to counter the Roman siege method of filling them with brushwood and earth. The limited excavation provided no evidence of Roman attack. The Roman reduction of Oldbury shows, however, that such strongpoints were rarely by-passed.[13]

The extent to which oppida were permanently occupied is still a matter for debate. A large part of the Belgic population, it is believed, continued to live in peacetime in open settlements. Only when danger threatened did they retire to the protection of their fortifications.[14] Nonetheless it should be noted that the immense area covered by Quarry Wood and its outworks embraced the later settlement sites of both Boughton Green and Cock Street. Much of the labour force was undoubtedly brought from outside to build such an oppidum for Maidstone district. The size of Boughton's Iron Age population is unknown but it is likely that it only reached this size again in modern times.

The Roman Conquest and Occupation 43-410 A.D.

The importance of Quarry Wood was short-lived. In 43 A.D. the Roman Emperor Claudius despatched Aulus Plautius with 40,000 legionaries to conquer Britain. Landing unopposed at Richborough he overcame Belgic opposition at Canterbury, crossed the Medway after a two-day battle and pursued the retreating tribesmen across the Thames at London. There was no further fighting in Kent. Within a few years the Romans had subjugated lowland Britain and for nearly four centuries the province of the Cantiaci, with the rest of southern Britain, became part of the Roman Empire. Most Belgic oppida were succeeded in the Roman period by important towns. Quarry Wood was too remote. Instead Rochester became the pre-eminent Roman town on the Medway.[15]

Peace was quickly established behind the advancing army. Roman roads linked the Channel ports and the Wealden hinterland first with Canterbury and Rochester and ultimately with London and beyond. The Roman conquerors were eager to exploit their new province. Corn for the Roman army became the most sought-after south-eastern crop. As the Roman armies moved through Kent new settlers seized the opportunity to get rich and the defeated Iron Age farmers were displaced by incoming Romans and Gauls. By the second century, however, many of these small farms had been replaced by the villa estates of wealthy agrarian capitalists with large houses, mosaic floors and luxurious baths. Boughton seems to have become part of a large Romano-British estate centred upon Maidstone which also included Boxley, Thurnham, Detling, Bearsted, Otham, Loose, Marden, Linton and Goudhurst.[16] Despite the discovery of a Roman bath house on the south bank of Brishing stream in 1841 no villa site at Boughton has been found. Romanisation for most inhabitants of this stony, wooded chartland can have meant little more than some improvement in living standards created by better trade and communication. Few could have abandoned the Iron Age way of life with its round huts and ditched enclosures or native farms with timber-framed cottages.[17]

In the absence of agrarian expansion most wealth at Boughton in Romano-British times seems to have come from exploitation of the ragstone quarries running from Brishing towards Loose. As a building material ragstone was used extensively in Roman Kent. It was also exported by barge via the Medway and Thames to construct the city walls, great private houses and public buildings of Roman London. Most Romano-British remains in Boughton are presumed to be connected with the quarrying of ragstone.[18]

The detached Romano-British bath house, excavated in 1841 in a field opposite Brishing Court called the Slade, was an oblong building 60 feet long and 30 feet wide. The external walls were 2 feet thick and built of Kentish ragstone. The bath house had a classic layout. At the centre of the building was a large, hypocausted room with two apsidal plunge baths served by a furnace to the south. A partition wall probably divided this room into a *caldarium* (hot room) and *tepidarium* (warm room). To the north lay the *sudatorium* (sweating room) supplied with hot air from the *caldarium*. A *frigidarium* (cold room) and apsidal cold plunge bath led from the *caldarium*. The bather followed a medically-designed circuit as in a Turkish bath today passing through a series of rooms with progressively increasing temperatures which sweated the impurities from his body. He then took a cold plunge bath to close his pores. The bath house is likely to have been constructed close to the waters of Brishing Stream in the second century and continued in use until the fourth century. Unless a villa remains undiscovered nearby, the bath house either served the local farming community as a rural public baths or acted as a 'pit head' bath for quarry workers.[19]

The following year C.T. Smythe, excavator of the bath house, uncovered the remains of a Romano-British cemetery between Pested Bars and Lockham Farm. The cemetery, which lay 11 yards west of the Roman road from Maidstone towards Sutton Valence and the Weald, (A274), was a rectangular enclosure 85 feet long and 77 feet wide. It was bounded by strongly-built walls of Kentish ragstone and contained 2 tombs, 2 cists and 5 urn burials. Pottery, glass and bronze vessels, iron lamps and 2 amphorae were found leading to the conclusion that the inhabitants of the neighbourhood were few but wealthy. Local farmworkers had long suspected the presence of a further building a short distance north-east of the Brishing bath-house. In 1933 a more systematic investigation revealed a large concentration of ragstone fragments interspersed with Roman brick and tile. There was also a scatter of potsherds which were mostly Romano-British but contained some Iron Age remnants. The site was again thought to be associated with the ragstone quarries which as the chief source of Kentish ragstone, may have been under Imperial control like the iron industry of the Weald.[20]

The Boughton bath house appears to have been first wrecked and then burnt towards the end of the fourth century as Roman rule began to collapse throughout the province under the attacks of foreign barbarians – principally Saxon sea-raiders. The countryside became increasingly at the mercy of these marauding bands and when in 410 the Roman legionaries were withdrawn to meet a barbarian threat to Rome itself the *Pax Romana* was over and the Dark Ages had begun. The public life and buildings of the towns disappeared. The villas were abandoned and left to decay or destroyed by the Saxon invaders who did not understand or value the Roman way of life. At Boughton the only permanent trace of four hundred years of Roman occupation was the line of the Roman road running from Rochester to the iron-working area of the Weald which, although falling into disuse, later became part of the eastern boundary of the parish.[21]

The Anglo-Saxon Settlement

By about 450 A.D. Roman control was over. The Germanic tribes of Angles, Saxons and Jutes, who had been raiding Britain's coasts for over a century, began to settle permanently. Traditionally Vortigern, post-Roman King of Kent, attempted to hire 'Jutish' mercenaries to protect his kingdom against other invaders. He offered their leaders, Hengist and Horsa, land in Kent in return for military assistance. When the Jutes saw the weakness of the Romano-British and the richness of the land they sent home for re-inforcements and seized Kent for themselves. From about this time the Saxon settlement of Kent and England began. We say 'Saxon' because the Jutes, who came from Frisia and the Rhine valley, soon merged with the Angles and Saxons.[22]

The settlement in Kent was long and complex. It was hardly complete by the Norman conquest. The first settlers, travelling in family groups and small war bands, penetrated inland via the rivers occupying the most fertile districts and those which were easiest to clear. The impenetrable forest of the Weald, the swamps of Romney Marsh and the sandy, acid soils of north-west Kent were avoided. Sometimes the Jutes took over existing communities. On other occasions they cleared new land for themselves. In any event, as population increased, it was necessary to colonise the previously uninhabited parts of Kent. The general movement of settlement was from north and north-east to the south and south-west. The original Jutish settlements were established on the foothills and in river valleys. From there settlement moved into the Downland and then southwards into the wooded Quarry Hills. From all three groups the herdsmen moved in summer to the drovedens of the Weald. From the 10th century onwards these summer pastures became independent settlements themselves but the process remained incomplete until the 13th or 14th centuries.[23]

Some forest pastures of primary settlements in Holmesdale had developed into permanent settlements in the vicinity of Sutton Valence and Great Chart by the 7th and 8th centuries. By the 11th century much of central Kent was relatively well-settled. The date of the creation of the Jutish settlement at Boughton Monchelsea is unknown. Place names, sometimes helpful in this respect, are of little value. *Boc tun*, from which the names of all the Kentish 'Boughtons' has originated, meant in Old English 'a farmstead or settlement situated in a beech wood clearing' or 'a farmstead or settlement granted by charter'. The Old English *tun* originally meant 'an enclosure' and subsequently 'an enclosure with a farmstead'. Later it came to mean 'the village which developed around the farmstead'. It is thus not always possible to determine the precise meaning of the word when found as a place name. Moreover, use of the place name element extends throughout the whole of the Old English period until at least the 13th century. We do not know if there was any continuity of settlement at *Boc tun* from Romano-British times. Probably there was. The first written mention of the name is *Boltone* in the Domesday Book 1086. By c.1100 it has become *Boctune*. *Wierton* (Wighere's farmstead) receives no written mention until 1225 although certainly established earlier.[24]

Domesday Boughton

Kent, although it suffered during the Danish attacks of the 9th century, underwent no permanent Danish settlement and therefore, like the rest of southern England, had no Danish admixture of population. The final wave of invaders to come to Boughton were the Normans when William the Conqueror secured his new Kingdom as a result of his victory at Hastings in 1066. The rule of the Norman military minority was neither popular nor secure. After 1066 William, confronted with the task of ruling a hostile Anglo-Saxon population of about a million with only, perhaps, 100,000 Normans, including women and children, crystallized the feudal system of government which had been evolving in England since the 9th century, into a rigid social structure which was to dominate the medieval period.

With few exceptions the Anglo-Saxon landowners were stripped of their lands. The King, to whom all land belonged, retained some royal estates for himself and distributed the remainder among the land-hungry barons (tenants-in-chief), who had fought for him at Hastings, in return for fealty (loyalty) and military service. Each baron promised not only to serve the King personally but also to provide a number of knights, depending upon the size of his landholding. In order to provide the requisite number of knights the tenants-in-chief, after keeping some manors for themselves, granted the rest to knights upon similar terms to those which they had been granted by the King. Since oaths of fealty were not always kept William scattered some of his own royal manors among those of his tenants-in-chief lest any baron should become too powerful in a specific area. No baron also had all his land in one block thus trying to avoid the dangerous growth of local autonomy.

The Anglo-Saxon peasantry (villeins) were tied to the manor upon which they lived at the time of the Conquest whether it was allotted to King, baron or knight. They were required to work unpaid upon the lord's demesne (home farm) for a certain amount of time. A proportion of their produce was paid to their lord; their corn was ground at the lord's mill and their bread baked in the lord's oven – privileges for which they had to pay. When a villein died, a heriot or death duty was levied before his holding could be taken up by his heir. Fines were exacted if his son or daughter left the manor. These services were enforced in the lord's manor court. In return the villein was also granted land and could be virtually self-supporting. In the early middle ages, however, the villein's lot was not an attractive one.

The Domesday Book was compiled in 1086 to provide a basis for future taxation. It originated from the outcry caused by royal taxes levied to meet the threat of Danish invasion in 1084. Little is known of *Boltone* or its inhabitants until immediately prior to the Conquest when it was held by a Saxon landowner named Aluuin from Godwin, Earl of Wessex, and father of Harold, the Saxon claimant to the throne who was defeated and killed at Hastings in 1066. By 1086 it was in the hands of Odo, Bishop of Bayeux and William's half-brother, one of the most powerful men in England. The King had conferred on him the earldom of Kent and nearly 200 manors in the county plus 250 in other parts of the land. Kent needed to be in loyal hands because of its value as a bulwark against invasion. Odo, who was ambitious, wealthy and warlike, made Rochester his power base until his scheming to advance his temporal and ecclesiastical power forced William to arrest and return him to Normandy.[25]

Odo had granted *Boltone* to Hugh, a Norman knight. While the dispossessed Saxon lord, Aluuin, may have lived in his hall among his people in the village of *Boltone*, the manor house of Hugh and his successors was undoubtedly on the site of Boughton Monchelsea Place overlooking the Weald and the deer park, where they enjoyed the privileges of the chase. The manor house was also a safer distance from the dual dangers of disease and rebellion among the Saxon subject population at Boughton Green and was where the Norman lord held his manor court.

In 1086 the manor is described as follows:-

> *Hugh, grandson of Herbert, holds of the bishop of Baieux Boltone. It was taxed at one sulung. In demesne there is nothing. But five villeins have five carucates there and two acres of meadow. Wood for the pannage of twenty hogs. There is a church. In the time of Edward the Confessor and afterwards it was worth eight pounds, now six pounds. Aluuin held it of earl Godwine.*[26]

The sulung was a unit of taxation, like rateable value, peculiar to Kent. The carucate was the amount of land that could be worked by a plough team of eight oxen and is thought to have been about 120 acres. The demesne was, as yet, undeveloped. Land was still plentiful having only recently been reclaimed from the waste. A servile population of five villein families cultivated roughly 600 acres of arable land between them. They had additional meadowland for hay and grazing rights in the woodland for their pigs for which they paid a rental of 20 hogs per year. The value of the manor had declined since the Conquest but Boughton already possessed a church.

Kent was the first of the Saxon kingdoms to be converted to Christianity after the arrival of St. Augustine at Canterbury in 597. A second diocese was created at Rochester in 604. Foundation of the parishes pre-dated that of the parish churches and central minsters serving the outlying congregations until daughter churches could be built. Most Kentish minsters were deliberately established in former Romano-British communities in the 7th century. Boughton, together with Loose, Otham, Linton, Loddington, Bearsted and Marden, was in the Minsterland of Maidstone comprising seventeen parishes and stretching as far as Goudhurst.[27] We do not know when the pre-Conquest church at Boughton was built nor whether it stood in Boughton Green among its Saxon parishioners. The majority of Saxon churches were small, timber structures. The present St. Peter's church has traces of Norman work in its tower but a stone church would have been built after 1086. If five is taken as a multiplier for the average Domesday family, Boughton had an approximate Domesday population of 30 including the household of its new Norman lord.

The Descent of the Manor

When Bishop Odo was disgraced his lands returned to the Crown passing in the 12th century to the Norman family of Montchensie from Mont Canisi in Calvados. By 1278 the manor and parish were both called *Bocton Monchansy* and a year later *Boulton Munchensey* to distinguish it from the other Kent villages named 'Boughton'. By 1610 it had become *Bocton Munchelsey*. The Montchensies were notable barons in medieval England and large landowners in Norfolk, Suffolk and Kent who played a leading role in the Barons' War against Henry III. As tenants at Boughton they had the Hughams from Hougham, near Dover, whose rental included a payment for castle guard at Rochester. The Montchensies died out when the last of their male line, William de Montchensie, was killed at the siege of Dryslwyn Castle, near Carmarthen, in 1287.

Boughton Monchelsea Place.
Site of Boughton's medieval manor house the Place was largely the work of Robert Rudston between 1567 and 1590. Pardoned after Wyatt's Rebellion he spent his later years quietly rebuilding his manor house. It is built of ragstone from the Quarries with a plain tiled roof. Later alterations and additions were made in the 17th-19th centuries.

After the Montchensies the manor passed by inheritance or sale through the hands of various Kent families until in 1551 it was purchased by Sir Thomas Wyatt of Allington Castle. He sold it in the same year for £1,730 to Robert Rudston whose descendants occupied it until 1887. Rudston was the son of a Lord Mayor of London who had made his fortune as a London draper and in Kent's textile trade. Three years later in January

1554 he was persuaded to join the rebellion of the 'Men of Kent', led by his friend Wyatt, against the Catholic Queen Mary. The rebellion failed, Wyatt was executed and Rudston was fortunate to be pardoned. In 1555 he was allowed to re-purchase the manor from the Crown for two-thirds the sum that he had paid for it four years earlier and wisely devoted the remainder of his life to quietly rebuilding his manor house in the Elizabethan style. He was described by his grandson, Sir Francis Barnham, as 'a brave gentleman... of a very loving disposition but so furiously cholericke as required a great deal of discretion to avoid the incounter of that humour'. Rudston was basically responsible for creating the house in its present form by extending an essentially medieval hall house and adding further wings. He left Boughton to his younger son upon whose death in 1613 the male line of the Rudstons ended and the manor passed to Sir Francis Barnham, son of Robert Rudston's daughter.

Barnham was a man of some culture. Among his friends were Camden, the historian, and Twysden, the antiquary. He was also politically active representing Grampound in Parliament from 1603-14 and serving as a member for Maidstone from 1621 until his death in 1645. At the beginning of the English Civil War he was a moderate Parliamentarian and sat on the County Committee which administered Kent on behalf of Parliament. Later his Parliamentary sympathies diminished. He was a stockholder in the Virginia Company and one of his sons appears to have settled in Virginia. His eldest son and successor, Sir Robert Barnham, was also M.P. for Maidstone 1660-1679. He was more of a Royalist than his father. Before his election he was briefly imprisoned in Leeds Castle by the County Committee and took part in the abortive plot against the Protectorate known as the Kentish Rising of 1648. After the return of Charles II he was made a Baronet in 1663. In the absence of a son Boughton passed in 1685 to his daughter, Philadelphia, who had married Thomas Rider of Essex three years earlier.

The Riders had made their fortune in Tudor London. The dynasty held Boughton for over two centuries. Little is known of the first two Riders – Thomas (d.1698) or Sir Barnham (d.1728) – except that they were hard drinkers. Philadelphia bequeathed £400 to her grandson, another Thomas, 'to educate him... so that he might be sensible how fatal intemperance had been to his father and grandfather'. Her money seems to have been well-spent. His reign of nearly sixty years saw the start of sweeping alterations to the house which were completed by Ingram Rider and his son, a third Thomas, in the early nineteenth century.[28] While the function of the aristocracy in the eighteenth and early nineteenth centuries was to assist the monarch in national affairs the daily business of ruling the local communities was left to the landed gentry. From their ranks came the Justices of the Peace responsible for the maintenance of law and order at Quarter Sessions. Through Quarter Sessions they were also responsible for county administration including the poor law, roads and bridges, licensing, fixing wages and prices, and regulating apprenticeship and popular entertainment. Many justices were more concerned in protecting their own interests and property than their other duties. This was not the case with the third Thomas Rider, who despite his many interests including gardens, estate management, travel and religion, worked conscientiously at his time-consuming responsibilities until his death in 1847 aged eighty-two.

Another man of culture he had a real sympathy for the poor and played a grass roots part in the administration of poor relief in Boughton which was unusual for a member of the gentry. He was an overseer of the poor in 1810 and 1811 – an office usually left to the more prominent farmers in the community. When a Select Vestry Committee was established in 1821 he chaired it most effectively as he did the Coxheath Union, the Gilbert Union of which Boughton was a member before the 1834 Poor Law Amendment Act. When the Coxheath Union was visited in 1832 by Commissioner Majendie he found 'a very well-regulated workhouse' whose 'good management is... due to the superintendence of a principal proprietor of the neighbourhood who acts as chairman at the meetings of the guardians'.[29] When the incorporated workhouse at Coxheath was replaced by a union workhouse under the New Poor Law in 1835 Rider became an ex-officio guardian of the new institution. He was also a staunch advocate of Parliamentary reform in an essentially Tory county where most members of the circle in which he moved considered reformers to be 'traitors'. As early as 1817 he was advocating at county meetings reduction of the standing army, the termination of sinecures and unmerited pensions and the need for constitutional reform. He also petitioned for the return of the *Habeas Corpus* which had been suspended in the same year.[30]

Returned with his friend T. Law Hodges as Liberal M.P. for West Kent at the time of the Reform Bill of 1832 he helped to carry parliamentary reform to a successful conclusion. He lost his seat at the next election but a memorial commemorating the 1832 Act was placed in the hall of Boughton Monchelsea Place. His Parliamentary career, albeit fairly short, saw his support given to measures intended to destroy class legislation and benefit the people at large. He voted for the ballot and shorter Parliaments; for abolition of impressment; admission of dissenters to the universities;

Church of England reform; and the removal of bishops from the House of Lords. A man who never carried political differences into private life he was respected by all parties and, unlike so many of his contemporaries, his personal life was irreproachable. At his death he was commended both for his liberal principles, which were in advance of his age, and for his moral courage in advocating the people's cause. His funeral service, conducted by Rev. J.D. Haslewood vicar of Boughton, at St. Peter's Church, although private was crowded with local inhabitants 'anxious to pay this last tribute... to one who had been so deservedly respected'.[31]

Badslade's View of Boughton Court in 1719.

The 'Court' at this time was the seat of Sir Barnham Rider who held it from 1698-1728. Note the Deer Park, described in 1669 as 'stocked with deere and conyes' (rabbits), and the view of the Weald. The main entrance through the stable yard was replaced in 1818-19 by Thomas Rider III who took advantage of the Enclosure of Coxheath 1817 to create the present drive which was intended to make a 'romantic' approach to the house. He also swept away the formal gardens and planted a chestnut copse and a stand of beeches. The south wing, the oldest part of the house, was re-built to make more bedrooms and the Place given a uniform roofline.

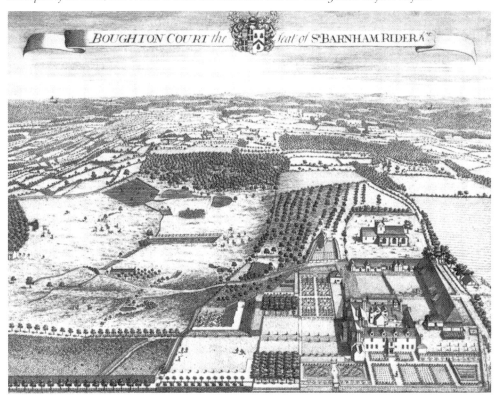

BOUGHTON COURT the Seat of Sᵗ BARNHAM RIDER Aᵗ

Holbrook
A 17th century farmhouse
with 19th century
additions and facade now
marks the site of the
'reputed manor' of
Holbrook.

Rider was hailed by the *Maidstone Gazette* as 'one of the oldest ... most honest and consistent reformers in Kent'.[32] Certainly he was among the best remembered of Boughton's lords of the manor. His successors were less memorable. The fourth Thomas left Boughton in 1868 for his wife's village in Wales. When he died he bequeathed the property to his cousin in America; he failed to return to England and the Place stood empty again for some years. In 1902 Lt. Colonel G.B. Winch came to Boughton. His son having died in World War I and a later adopted son having been killed in World War II it passed to his nephew Mr. Michael Winch, diplomat and journalist, in 1954.[33]

In addition to the manor of Boughton Monchelsea there were two lesser manors within the parish. The 'reputed' manor of Holbrook belonged in the later Middle Ages to the Halbrook family and still existed, according to Edward Hasted, in the late 18th century. It survives today as a small farm. The manor of Brishing is first mentioned in the reign of Edward I when it was held by Thomas de Brissing and continued to exist in the parishes of Boughton and Langley into the eighteenth century.[34] Two further great houses were never manors. Nonetheless their owners, at various times, threatened to overshadow the occupants of Boughton Monchelsea Place. In the east of the parish Adam de Wierton and his descendants owned Wierton House (later Place) from the thirteenth until the late fourteenth century. In Stuart times it passed to the St. Legers who were influential in Ireland. By the eighteenth century it belonged to Sir Christopher Powell, who in 1734 became a County MP. Following his death it was bought by John Briscoe, a London gentleman, who rebuilt the mansion on the brow of the hill a short distance south of the former house.[35] In the 19th century its owners included Thomas Best, William Moore and the banker, Herman Kleinwort.

The second house was Boughton Mount, originally named Wychden, which lay 'on the northern side of Cocksheath near the parish of Loose'. In the reign of Elizabeth it belonged to John Alchorne passing in the seventeenth century to John Savage, gent. His son, also named John, inherited the estate in 1726 and was made sheriff of Kent but died in the same year. It was bought in 1824 by John Braddick who had made a fortune in the West Indies partly, it was rumoured, from the slave trade. The original mansion which stood on the opposite side of the road, was a 'clock house... of... Mary or Elizabeth'. It probably stood on the site of the present Rock House with some twenty rooms downstairs and thirteen upstairs. In 1726 seven of these rooms were situated in a 'new wing'. Nevertheless a year before his death in 1828 Braddick, 'a generous promoter of all scientific pursuits', rebuilt Boughton Mount on the present site nearby where he could conduct his agricultural experiments. Rock House was erected as a Dower House for his widow. The ownership of the estate by his son, John Wilbraham Braddick, coincided with the long absence of the last of the Riders. Braddick filled the vacuum and almost assumed the role of lord of the manor entertaining the Foresters at their Anniversary, chairing the School Board and becoming the first chairman of the Parish Council. When he died in 1896 the estate, 'a charming residential and sporting property' consisted of 430 acres in Boughton, Loose, East Farleigh and Maidstone and included Rock House, Swiss Cottage, the Boughton Malthouses and 30 cottages in Boughton alone.[36]

Fig. 3 *Boughton Monchelsea –*
Conjectural Landscape: Thirteenth to Seventeenth centuries

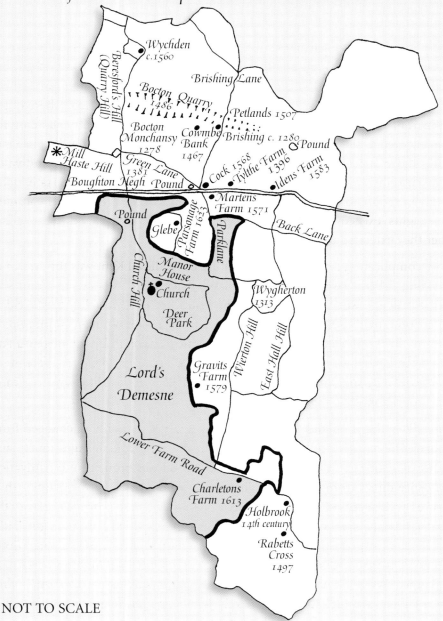

NOT TO SCALE

The Medieval Landscape

Virtually nothing is known of the topography of the parish in the early Middle Ages. Only after the mid-fourteenth century do we get a collection of 54 ancient deeds dating from 1354-1585. Even in these many topographical features are impossible to identify.[37] The Midland medieval open field system, whereby the arable land of the community was divided into three or more fields extending for several hundred acres unenclosed by fences or hedgerows, never prevailed in Kent. Nor does there appear to have been common ploughing. Instead most cultivated land was held in severalty. 'There are no common fields in this county', stated John Boys in his report to the Board of Agriculture in 1794. At Boughton common pasture rights existed on the extensive wasteland of Cokkyshoth (1489) but whether they extended to all villagers is unclear.

Another complicating factor in the agriculture of medieval Kent was the system of landholding called Gavelkind. When a landowner died intestate his land was divided equally between his surviving sons instead of passing solely to the eldest son. Partition by Gavelkind produced numerous smallholdings. It intensified during the thirteenth century growth of population although by the fifteenth and sixteenth centuries it was growing less common. Nevertheless it helps to account for the existence of 61 smallholders at Boughton in 1842 as opposed to 9 much greater landed proprietors.[38]

It seems likely that Boughton's field patterns remained basically unchanged from the fourteenth century and perhaps earlier. In the early Middle Ages much land being heavily wooded and having generally poor soil was brought into cultivation by enclosure direct from the waste. There is no evidence of anything other than enclosures in the deeds surviving since 1354. Certainly by the sixteenth century the modern landscape seems well-established. The farms, which appear in the Tithe Award 1842, mostly take their names from the surnames of their early owners. John Tylthe (Tilts Farm) appears as a witness to a land grant in Boughton as early as 1396. John Cowmbe (Coombe Bank) is witness to a similar deed in 1467 while Willyam Rabett (Rabbit's Cross) provided for his wife and daughter in his will of 1497.[39]

The Parish Registers do not commence until 1560. While they continue to record events appertaining to the Tilts, Coombes and Rabbits the family surnames given to other parish farms also make their appearance in the form of the Martens (Martins Farm) 1571, Gravitts (Gravitts Farm) 1579, Idens (Iden Farm) 1583 and Charletons (Charlton Farm) 1612. Even earlier in 1557 Edward Marten and John Combe gave evidence to Archdeacon Harpsfield's Visitation as churchwardens, an office usually reserved for substantial farmers in the community, while John Iden was one of only seven parishioners to do the same. A survey for an enclosed Parsonage Farm survives for 1623. It seems likely, therefore, that most parish farms date as enclosed units from at least the sixteenth century, when their owners coincide in the parish. The strong likelihood is that they existed as such long before.[40] Even though fields were fenced or hedged stray animals could still be a menace to crops in a subsistence economy subject to local famines. There were therefore at least three pounds, where strays could be impounded, until reclaimed by their owners. One is represented by Penfold Pond in the north-east of the parish. A second, stone-built pound was situated down Church Hill between the school and the modern vicarage, while a third Pinfold is marked west of the Cock Inn on the Enclosure Award Map for Coxheath 1817. This unenclosed, 'long common' extending into Linton, Loose and East Farleigh and stretching as far eastward as the Boughton Cock would have allowed strays to wander unrestrained towards the fields of the enclosed farms.

The medieval landscape would have been completed by the lord's manor house, demesne and deer park together with his windmill at Haste Hill and St. Peter's Church. We know little of the unfree peasantry, the medieval villeins and their families, who populated this landscape except that by the fourteenth century many hated their servile tenure and were anxious to shake off the restrictive bonds of villeinage and be personally free. This would allow them to compete with free tenants in the struggle for subsistence. The lords, on the other hand, suffering an acute labour shortage after the heavy mortality of the Black Death 1348-49, were equally anxious to maintain both social control and the enforcement of the hated labour services upon their demesnes. The Great Peasants' Revolt which took place from June-July 1381 engulfed much of Kent besides other parts of the kingdom. Maidstone and the Weald were major centres of disturbance but Boughton seems to have been untouched. When, however, the promises made to the rebels by Richard II at Mile End were revoked there was a movement in the district to enforce their re-establishment.[41]

On 30 September 1381 Thomas Hardyng, a Linton mason, met a number of other conspirators by night on 'Boughton Hegh'. They planned to kill the King, Sir Thomas Cobham, Sir William Septuans and others, and replace Richard II by his uncle, the Duke of Lancaster. They also aimed to burn Maidstone and force others to join them. John Startout, later testified that he was ploughing when compelled to follow them. A second witness complained that he was taken from his bed while asleep. Among the conspirators were five from Lynton, four each from 'Marden, Maydestone and Loose' and two from Hunton. They were betrayed by John Cote, another mason from Loose, who turned King's evidence. Hardyng and ten others 'having risen in insurrection' were sent to the Tower until their trial at Westminster on 15 October. Only one was reprieved. The rest paid the penalty for treason. Hardyng was disembowelled before he was hanged and his head placed upon Palace Gate in barbaric medieval fashion. The men executed were from villages throughout the area – Hunton, Loose, Farleigh, Frittenden, Staplehurst, Marden, Linton, Benenden and two from Cranbrook. 'Many other malefactors in like manner congregated... of whose number and names John Cote was utterly ignorant'. It is difficult to believe that some were not from Boughton particularly in view of the fact that a sizeable contingent from the village joined Jack Cade in another Kentish peasant uprising in 1450. Like Wat Tyler in 1381 Cade also marched on London. After the rebellion was suppressed between eleven and fourteen Boughton peasants were pardoned.[42]

Religion

The Church played a central role in medieval life. The earliest stone church dedicated to St. Peter stood on its present site overlooking the Weald. It was first built early in the 12th century with stone from the local ragstone quarries and consisted of nave, tower and chancel. The latter contained only the altar and was in the form of an apse. Ragstone rubble can still be seen in the chancel and the lower section of the tower. The tower is the oldest surviving part of the church and parts of the original Norman tower arch are still visible.

St. Peter's Church, Boughton Monchelsea. The earliest stone church was built in the 12th century with ragstone from the local quarries. It was probably an 'estate church' built by a Norman lord-of-the manor and replaced a pre-Conquest timber church.

By the early 14th century the population and wealth of the parish had increased as a result of the thirteenth century expansion and there was a substantial re-building. The chancel was rebuilt and enlarged and a north aisle and chapel (now the organ loft) added. The east window has 14th century tracery but Victorian glass. The four perpendicular windows of the north aisle were added to admit more light in the 15th century when the magnificent Lychgate was built. Between 1530-1540 the tower and north aisle were partially re-built and the tower slightly heightened.

Of the pre-Reformation furnishings an aumbry (cupboard), in which religious books and sacred vessels were kept, is recessed into the east wall of the chancel. A piscina and sedilia seats are on the south wall. The former was used by the priest for washing his hands together with the chalice and paten (plate) after Mass. A drain from the piscina allowed the water to run directly into the churchyard and thus into consecrated ground. The sedilia seats were occupied by the priest's acolytes. A blocked-up reliquary for holy relics is visible on the east wall of the tower while the blocked door to the rood loft is also visible above the lectern from the body of the church. A part of the old rood screen divides the choir stalls from the organ loft. It seems probable that the tower, above the chancel arch, held a room with fireplace which was lived in by the priest.[43] Until the close of the Middle Ages the nave would have been almost without seats except for the most wealthy worshippers. Most villagers sat upon the floor. Only the aged and infirm went to the stone seats around the walls of the nave. Since the bible and the church service were in Latin the interior of the church was covered with wall paintings to educate a largely illiterate population in the teachings of Christianity.

The church was undoubtedly built by an early lord of the manor. In 1285 another lord, Henry de Bocton, presented the living to the Prior and Convent of 'Ledes' which kept the income until the Dissolution. It then went to the Dean and Chapter of Rochester before passing in 1914 to the Archbishop of Canterbury. At the dissolution a monk, who was vicar of 'Bocton Monchensie', was granted a royal pension of £2.0.0. per year.[44] Alexander, priest of 'Bocton', signed the grant to Leeds Priory in 1285. At the 1295 Visitation Robert Muffliard, a priest of Boughton, was accused of 'fornicating with diversity', a sad commentary upon the low moral condition which the medieval church had reached. There is no official record of Boughton's other priests before 1311 since Robert Kilwardy, Archbishop of Canterbury, after quarrelling with the King, left the country with the official registers.[45]

During the religious upheavals of the Reformation and Commonwealth the Rood Screen was dismantled and the images destroyed much to the annoyance of a Mr Goldsmith whose father had recently left 4d. 'for the painting of St. Stephen and St. James'. The stained glass in the windows was smashed but one or more parishioners, faithful to Catholicism, salvaged some of the fragments which were later incorporated into three windows on the staircase of Boughton Monchelsea Place.[46] This vandalism was the work of extreme Protestants who gained the ascendancy during the reign of Edward VI (1547-1553) after his father, Henry VIII, had broken with the Pope and become Supreme Head of the Church of England. The extreme Protestant aim was to bring religion nearer to the people in a form which did not smack of 'superstition and idolatry'. To this end the interiors of churches were 'whitelimed' and the wall paintings replaced by the Ten Commandments while the altar was exchanged for a plain wooden table. The religious confusion was intensified when Mary (1553-1558) returned the country to Catholicism and its old rituals.

In 1557 Archdeacon Harpsfield visited Boughton to see what progress had been made. He was disappointed. The Church was in disarray. The vicar, William Hall, like many clergy had taken advantage of the Edwardian Reformation to break his vow of celibacy and marry. Four years after the Marian Counter Reformation he was still `married' and Edward VI's arms were still above the altar. The vicar and his churchwardens were ordered to set up a side altar and to provide silken hangings with 'the image of Christ for halliedaies' and 'paynted clothes with the image of Christ for woorking daies'. They were also ordered 'to set uppe the sacramente decentilie' and to restore the altar stone, cast aside in the church yard, to its rightful place. Other instructions were:

> To provide a challice of silver with a patten (plate) before Christmas and the vicar not to minister withoute after the same daye
>
> To provide a paxe of latten (brass) with the image of the crucifixe before Christmas
>
> To provide two towelles for the priestes handes before the feast of Allsaintes and also a fine corporas cloth and to kepe the crismatorie (holy oil) under lock and key
>
> To provide a crosse of non latten with the image of Christe before Palme Sonndaie
>
> To provide a paier of latten candelstickes before the feast of Allsaintes
>
> To provide a cope (vestment) before Easter and also an albe (surplice) with other thinges belonginge therto for the best vestmente before Christmas
>
> To provide a vele (veil) and coveringes for the imagies before Lente
>
> The Marie & John and the patrone of the church be not carved but painted
>
> To provide a convenient lighte before the roode at this side the feaste of Sainte Michaell tharchaunngell
>
> To provide a lock and keye for the fonnte before Allsaintes and also a lampe
>
> To provide two convenient banners before Rogacion weeke.

The rector and vicar were also instructed to repair the windows of the nave and chancel and provide a cover for the desk before All Saints and a handbell, basin and ewer before Christmas.[47]

The vicar and his wardens, however, had no need for concern since next year Mary was succeeded by her half-sister Elizabeth. Elizabeth was more interested in political unity than religious doctrine. She adopted a 'middle way' over religious matters and returned to her father's Church of England of which she became supreme governor. The clergy had to adopt a uniform service based upon the English prayer books of Edward VI. Those that refused were dismissed. Most accepted this moderate settlement but neither Catholics nor extreme Protestants were happy. There appear to have been few Catholic recusants in Boughton but the extreme Protestants or Puritans were more influential. The tardiness to comply with the Marian Counter-Reformation was perhaps not without significance although it may also have arisen from poverty, general lack of religious zeal and low morale. Anthony Carriar survived as vicar from 1560-1580 and so was presumably acceptable to the Elizabethan authorities although the Church was criticised in Archbishop Parker's Visitation of 1573 for;

> ...*Absence of a Book of Common Prayer; a byble in the largest volume (and)*
> *a carpete for the Communion Table. Their font lacketh a good covering; the*
> *chancel windows are at some reparacions; their Church yard is not kept*
> *very well according to thartick icle; Minister doth use to say common prayer*
> *in main body of Church... There Church is to be repayred and they lacke*
> *the Table of the 10 Commandments....*

By 1582, however, Leven Wood, a Presbyterian had become vicar. He delivered one of the first sermons in Kent against the evils of dancing and was dismissed in 1584 for his 'Geneva' tendencies. His parishioners petitioned in vain for his re-instatement since 'they were now utterly destitute of the ministry of the Word'.[48] Henry Disborough and Francis Cacott, his successors, remained in office until 1648 when after Parliamentary victory in the Civil War the latter was ejected under the Commonwealth in favour of Mathias Rutton, Boughton's 'Vicar of Bray'. Rutton would almost certainly have been dismissed at the Restoration in 1660 but Cacott had died and at the petition of the parishioners Rutton was again appointed until his death in 1685. That Puritanism was still alive in the parish during the early seventeenth century can be seen from some of the Puritan Christian names given to children. Richard Joyce, for example, married 'Godly' Iden in 1631. During the Civil War some Boughton Puritans were prepared to risk death for their beliefs. In 1645 Richard Usmer, a Boughton Monchelsea butcher, received a grant of £5 for wounds in the arm and side while fighting the Royalists at Yalding.[49]

In the Compton Census of 1676 Mathias Rutton reported the presence in the parish of only one papist and thirteen Nonconformists. The latter consisted of Anabaptists, Quakers and Fifth Monachy Men – sects which had come to the fore during the Civil War. A Quaker conventicle, or place of irregular religious worship, was recorded in 1669. [50] By 1720 nonconformity had almost totally vanished. 'We have... two dissenters only who are called Presbyterians. We have no meeting houses in our parish...', reported Samuel Pratt, who had become vicar in 1719. 'There are no papists that I know of nor any place where such assemble for divine worship. There are no Presbyterians, Independents or any other dissenters whatsoever... except one ancient woman near eighty years of age who is an 'Anna Baptist' and goes sometimes to a meeting of that denomination in Maidstone', re-iterated Rev. Peter Wade in 1758. Other visitations tell the same story.

Lack of competition engendered complacency in the secular age of the eighteenth century. Some Boughton vicars were pluralist and non-resident. Others lived in the parish but not in the discomfort of the ancient vicarage. John Crompe, vicar 1686-1719, 'resided personally upon his cure though not in the vicarage house' but in 'a convenient house three quarters of a mile from the Church'. His successor, Samuel Pratt, also found the vicarage, 'situate in a very low, damp and unwholesome bottom', not to his liking living instead in the house of William Wilkins. He was followed by George Pratt, (1722-47) who 'resided pretty much but not constantly' in Boughton 'by reason of my being obliged to attend another living'. Peter Wade (1755-83) was a minor canon of Rochester Cathedral. He lived at Rochester but went to Boughton 'as often as my business at Rochester will permit'. James Andrew (1783-1823) held office at Loose as well as the living at Boughton. He also lived at Loose. George Pratt's curate was at least resident in the parish and was allowed sufficient salary to perform public service twice every Lord's Day. Joseph Hardy, Wade's curate, also officiated at Boughton for which he was given a salary of £35 per year. To make ends meet he was also a schoolmaster living at 'town Sutton' three miles distant. Andrew's curate, William Fell, was unlicensed and also dwelt in Loose parish. While public services were maintained twice every Sunday throughout the century there was no evangelical tradition. Samuel Pratt noted in 1720 that it was 'the custom of this parish to have a sermon in the afternoon only except on sacrament days'. This custom still existed seventy years later.[51]

A century of neglect had its effect. Rev. Peter Wade M.A. felt in 1758 that Boughton parishioners were 'remarkable in their attendance at the public worship of God'. 'There are none that treat religion with contempt', stated Joseph Andrew in 1786. 'The few absentees, led away by insolence and intemperance, cover... the right cause... by frivolous excuses'. They did not know their flock. The parish population was rapidly increasing but Church attendance was falling. Samuel Pratt reported communicants to be 'about 80' in 1720. In 1786 Andrew stated that 'about sometimes 50 attend'. Poverty and famine were beginning to take their toll. Neglect of souls and lack of pastoral work brought in turn disregard of the Church fabric. In 1728 George Pratt wrote that 'The Church and chancel is *most of it* in very good repair'. Amid the distress created by the Napoleonic Wars, however, a much-changed James Andrew was obliged to embark upon a major refurbishment. By 1806 he was no longer non-resident but living in the vicarage at Boughton upon which he had spent over £200 'in rebuilding one part and repairing the remainder'. He had no other benefice and no curate as he had done twenty years before. The pulpit and pews on one side of the Church had been 'lately rebuilt' and orders given 'for re-building or repairing... those that are not yet in good order'.[52] His efforts seemed ruined, however, twenty-six years later by the disastrous fire of 1832.

The fire took place on 30 December. Much of southern England was still in a state of tension as a result of the rick burning, machine breaking and rioting which had spread from Kent in 1830-32, known as the Swing Riots. The parish had already recently witnessed the Battle of Boughton Quarries as a part of this disorder and at first arson was suspected. The conflagration originated, however, in a flue from the stove providing heat for the congregation. This became a slow-burning fire which smouldered among the vestry roof timbers and finally burst forth after dark when the Church was deserted. When the correspondent of the *Maidstone Gazette* arrived on the scene at 11.00 p.m.

> *The interior of the Church presented the appearance of a vast furnace... The flames, bursting through the beautiful tracery of Gothic windows, produced an effect not to be described... The fire raged most furiously in consequence of the scarcity of water, the engines never having more than ten minutes supply. The only well in the vicinity was soon pumped dry. At about 1 o'clock, the roof having fallen in, the fire abated and by the great exertions of the Kent and Norwich office firemen the chancel and tower, which had ignited, were saved.*[53]

The fire was in danger of spreading to Boughton Monchelsea Place via a range of timber stables a few feet away. Fortunately a recent downpour had saturated the loose straw in the yards. It said much for the local popularity of Thomas Rider that many labourers toiled hard and long to save his mansion from the flames when farmworkers elsewhere in Kent were prepared to stand by and watch the handiwork of incendiaries take its course. In some ways the fire was beneficial. The nave, which was completely destroyed, was re-built by May 1834 at a cost of £1,250. Forty years later a further enlargement and re-building was carried out by the Victorian architect, Habershon. The cost was met by William Moore of Wierton. The West end was extended, the north aisle was re-built and a south aisle constructed with a vestry at the eastern end. Thus by 1874-75 the parish had gained almost a new Church as a result of the fire and Victorian restoration. There was no further re-building until the twentieth century when a car park was constructed, the West end re-ordered, toilets added and improvements made to the north porch and entrance doors.[54]

Population – from the Eleventh to the Eighteenth Century

If we translate the number of Domesday households into a crude population total the best factor to use is five giving Boughton an estimated population of 30 in 1086. There is little further chance to estimate numbers before the sixteenth century. In some counties the fourteenth century Lay Subsidy Rolls enable a calculation to be made but in the Kent Lay Subsidy of 1334-35 the taxpayers are not listed under their manors and so cannot be identified. We, therefore, have to content ourselves with general county trends.

Kent's medieval population reached its peak in the late 13th and early 14th centuries. At Boughton this economic prosperity and demographic expansion was marked by the re-building of the chancel, north aisle and chapel of St. Peter's Church. Population growth was then checked by the Black Death 1348-49 which brought a dramatic reduction in numbers. There is no record of the epidemic's depredations in the parish except that the priest, Robert de Trueley, was replaced in 1350. Priests were very vulnerable because of the need to administer the last rites to the dying. Two further priests were replaced between September 1361 and

April 1362 which marked a second outbreak of bubonic plague. The first half of the 15th century was another period of recession with economic and climatic difficulty intermixed with further epidemics. Four more Boughton priests came and went between January 1440 and December 1441 suggesting that the parish did not escape lightly in this period of prolonged difficulty. Nevertheless it is likely that by the 16th century, or even earlier, population figures had returned to 14th century levels.[55]

The parish registers commence effectively in 1561. Henceforth it is possible to calculate an approximate population figure for each decade until the first census of 1801. The totals shown on the graph have been reached by using the Cox Estimate method. The resulting figures are no more than a crude indication but the trends are more accurate. Even if the overall validity of the method is accepted certain limiting factors must be borne in mind. One of these is defective registration. In 1594 Boughton's churchwardens reported at the Archdeacon's Visitation that:-

> *Our book of register hath been duly and orderly kept since this our minister*
> *came to us but before it was mangled and many things cut out, we know*
> *not by whom.*

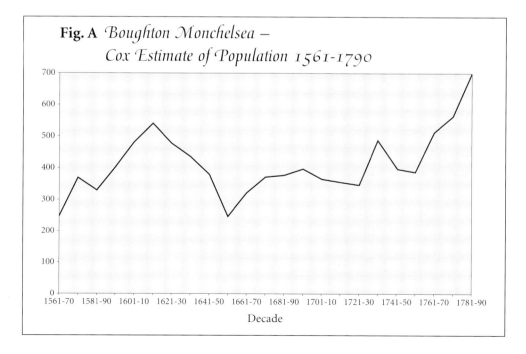

Fig. A *Boughton Monchelsea – Cox Estimate of Population 1561-1790*

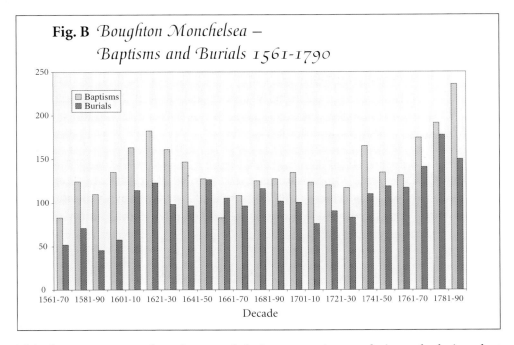

Fig. B *Boughton Monchelsea –*
Baptisms and Burials 1561-1790

Baptisms
Burials

Decade

This does not seem to have been unduly important in population calculations but during the Commonwealth period when 'John Philips was made Parish Registrar in accordance with the Act of 1653' registration was chaotic and undoubtedly defective. Another factor sometimes influencing registration was that not all parishioners were baptised at the parish church. In particular papist and nonconformist recusants tended to avoid this. Roman Catholicism, however, was never strong in Boughton after the Reformation with only one papist reported present in the Compton Census 1676. Protestant nonconformity was more influential in Tudor times but the early Boughton Protestants seem to have operated within the Church. A Quaker conventicle or place of irregular worship existed in the parish in 1669 but there were only 13 nonconformists listed in 1676 and by 1720 nonconformity had almost completely vanished. In these circumstances we must conclude that religious dissenters did not greatly influence population estimates.

The factors controlling population fluctuations are fourfold. An excess of births over deaths tends to increase numbers. So, too, does immigration. Conversely, an excess of deaths and emigration will tend to decrease them. If we turn to the graph the estimate for the decade 1561-1570 is 246 which, in view of the comments to the Archdeacon's Visitation in 1594, may appear to be somewhat low. Archdeacon

Harpsfield's Visitation to Boughton in 1557, however, records the number of communicants as 180. If we increase this total by 40% to allow for children below communion age the estimate of 252 for 1557 is remarkably close to 246. Thereafter population grew steadily peaking at 540 in the decade 1611-20. Thus it had more than doubled in half a century. During these decades baptisms regularly exceeded burials and like many isolated rural parishes Boughton avoided the recurrent population crises of the towns.

If we define an annual number of burials which was one and a half times greater than the moving average over a twenty year period as a minor crisis mortality year and classify a year with double the moving average as a major crisis mortality year then Boughton underwent only 7 minor crisis mortality years and no major ones during this time. In the same fifty years urban Maidstone underwent no fewer than 21 plague outbreaks alone including that of 1603 when there were 184 burials within the year. Even when Chart Sutton suffered a severe outbreak in 1612 Boughton appears to have escaped. That is not to say that the parish was free from all threat. Poor harvests brought frequent subsistence crises often followed by famine, by typhus or famine fever, or simply lowered resistance to winter respiratory complaints such as influenza. 66% of Boughton's deaths in 1580 occurred between 19-26 December. In 1608 44% took place in January. The fact that 1595 was a minor crisis mortality year is not unconnected with widespread harvest failure in 1594-95.

After 1620 Boughton's population growth was effectively checked for the next 140 years. In 1621-30 the population dropped below five hundred. By 1641-50 it had fallen to 378 and in 1651-60 there were more burials than baptisms for the only decade in the entire period 1561-1800 although this was partly a result of defective registration. 1628, 1635, 1636 and 1649 were minor crisis mortality years. In the county as a whole a sample of registers in 48 parishes suggests that there were more burials than baptisms in the years 1651-90 and again in 1711-20 and 1741-50.[56] In Boughton the number of baptisms remained marginally ahead and the population stayed relatively static for about a century never falling below 300 but only once exceeding 400. There were 13 minor crisis mortality years between 1660 and 1760 but no major one. Again problems were of subsistence as much as epidemic disease. 1679 and 1680 were years of high mortality nationally. Similarly 1693 and 1694 were also 'barren years' of famine. Thirty deaths in 1730 followed hard on the heels of the 'great dearth' of 1728-29 while the minor crisis mortality years of 1740 and

1742 were the aftermath of the national subsistence crisis of 1739-41. 1757 was another famine year nationally. The minor crisis mortality years of 1705, 1719-20 and 1722 are less easy to explain.

There was a brief recovery in 1731-40 when population again rose to 489 but the recovery was short-lived and checked again by the subsistence crisis of 1740-43. In five of the ten years 1741-50 more Boughton residents were buried than were born. A population of some 390 occupied 'near 100 houses' in 1758 but after 1760 births were inexorably rising while at the same time the death rate began to fall. There were still problems. Bad harvests brought another minor crisis mortality year in 1782 while the 'great dearths' of 1795-96 and 1799-1801 were yet to come. 1778-79 was the only year of major crisis mortality to be recorded in over two centuries. 50 burials took place during the year. But this is deceptive. 600 troops at Coxheath Camp succumbed to an outbreak of bilious fever and 42 of them died.[57] 30 were buried in the churchyard at Boughton between August and November 1779 together with 4 of their 'wives' and 3 children. In 1761-70 the Boughton population passed the five hundred mark for the first time since 1620. By 1790 it had reached 699. A decade later at the first census of 1801 it was 712.

Livestock and Crops in the Seventeenth and Eighteenth Centuries

It is impossible to discover any detailed information about agricultural practices until the seventeenth century. From the late seventeenth century some of the inventories survive of the 'goods, cattels and chattels' of Boughton inhabitants taken at their deaths for probate purposes. Here are listed the crops, growing and garnered, and the livestock kept by the deceased. Twenty-six such inventories (1686-1748) have been studied and from these much can be learned about farming methods in late-Stuart and early-Georgian times. The inventories cover 9 craftsmen/ tradesmen, 8 yeomen/husbandmen, 7 widows and 2 gentlemen. The value of the personal estates concerned varied greatly ranging from £14 in the case of Alexander Meriam, thatcher (1748) and £18 in the case Joanna Carr, widow (1702), to the £1,068 of William Wilkins, tanner (1723) and the £3,892 of John Savage, proprietor of Boughton Mount (1726). The craftsmen/tradesmen were the most wealthy occupational grouping, excluding the gentry. They included in their number 3 freemasons, 2 tanners, a blacksmith, butcher, carpenter and thatcher. Their average estate was £209 although this owed something to the large personal wealth of William Wilkins. John Dicken, the second tanner, had an estate valued at £353 (1700) as compared with Robert Towker, butcher, £148 (1694) and Thomas Joy, blacksmith, £94 (1693). The estates of the 3 freemasons ranged from £84 to £23. The widows were not all penurious like Joanna Carr. Mary Wilkins, possibly the widow of William Wilkins, who died in 1735, had possessions worth £636 while the estate of Mary Gipps (1705) was valued at £212. The average value of the widows' possessions was £151. In contrast the yeomen/husbandmen, often considered to be among the more solid of Kent residents, averaged only £86. William Tame, who died in 1694, had property worth £207. The remaining 7 farmers averaged only £69 between them.[58]

Although only 8 (32%) of the deceased were farmers only 5 inventories (20%) show a complete absence of crops or stock and 2 of these – both the inventories of widows – indicate the presence of hop poles showing that they or their husbands had sometime speculated in the growing of hops. Katherine Martin (1687) had 'one old ladder and hoppoles upon one acre of Ground next the house' valued at £7.4.0. Even most craftsmen/ tradesmen were involved in agriculture part-time. The majority farmed largely for subsistence in an era when local famines were frequent. Of the 2 wealthy tanners John Dicken (1700) had a hog together with '2 acres of oates on ye ground, 2 acres of Barley and a small parcell of Beanes'. William Wilkins (1723) possessed a cow, 3 hogs, wheat on the ground, hay and straw. Alexander Martin, freemason, (1687) had no stock but three and a half acres of wheat worth £12. His fellow mason, Thomas Joy (1691), had 2 cows, 6 hogs and 2 young hogs plus 'wheat on the ground' and 'hay in the barn'. His namesake, Thomas Joy, blacksmith, (1693), however, may have been providing partly for a local market since he owned not only a cow but '1 barrowe hogg, 1 Sow and Six weaning piggs' together with five and three quarter acres of 'wheate in the blade' and nine and a half acres of oates 'lately sowen'.

During this period the ragstone ridge became pre-dominantly the region of 'balanced' agriculture within the county where attention was devoted more equally to mixed farming than elsewhere. The area around Maidstone also became one of the earliest and most important fruit and hop growing areas in Kent.[59] Boughton fitted well into this category. Sixty-four per cent of deceased inhabitants combined both corn growing and grazing. The total values of crops and stock was approximately equal. A slightly higher percentage of Boughton farmers (68%) kept cattle than hogs (64%). While Kent was a major wool-producing county only 7 Boughton farmers (28%) kept sheep. Moreover, with the exception of the 8lbs. of yarne and 2 spinning wheels mentioned in the 'Kitchin Chamber' of Widow Banks (1717) and the spinning wheel of another widow, Mary Gipps, (1705) there is no reference to wool or to spinning. This may be because wool, like fruit, was regarded as a commodity created by God and therefore not included in inventories or else it had been sold before the inventory was made. The most likely explanation, however, is that the majority of sheep were kept for personal consumption although some of the larger Boughton `flocks' may have been partly kept for breeding and the market. William Tame, yeoman, with 40 sheep almost certainly had this in mind. Richard Iden, gent. (1699) (15 ewes and 12 lambs), William Martin (1698) (8 sheep and 2 sheats or sheep sheared but once) and Nicholas Jeffrey, husbandman (1697) may also have had the same idea. The statistics are complicated by the fact that a 'hogg' can be a term for a yearling sheep as well as a pig although in most inventories the meaning is self-evident.

Most cattle, like sheep, were kept for personal consumption too or else for dairying although milk, butter and cheese were not produced as yet in any quantity for sale. Exceptions to this rule may have been the yeomen farmers James Board (1686) (6 cows and heifers, 2 yearlings), William Tame (5 cows, 3 yearlings) and Francis Bunger (6 cows, 2 calves, 2 heifers) together with Elizabeth Meriam (1690) (6 cows, 2 heifers, 2 calves) who appear to have placed more emphasis on breeding and the fattening of young cattle for sale. Oxen were said to be widely used on the ridge for ploughing, harrowing and draught. Yet only 2 steers are mentioned in Boughton inventories at this time. Both were the property of Nicholas Jeffrey, husbandman (1697). On the other hand 64% of this sample of Boughton agriculturalists owned horses, a statistic very close to the estimated two thirds of all ridge farmers who were said to possess them.[60] Most Boughton cultivators had only the one or two animals but William Tame had 7 and William Wilkins 4. Horses were largely used for pulling carts or for riding. The mounting steps placed at strategic places throughout the parish testify to the latter. One is left, however, with the inescapable conclusion that either there was a great pooling of oxen between parishes during the autumn and spring ploughing seasons, which is unlikely, or else horsepower was more widely used in seventeenth century agriculture on the ridge than has previously been believed.

The information given by inventories about crops depends on the time of year when they were taken. When Nicholas Jeffrey's inventory was made in November 1697 'all was safely gathered in'. He had an unspecified amount of wheat and oats and 6 loads of hay in his barn which was so full that a further 12 bushels of wheat were stored in the garrett. Between October and December the winter corn was sown and by the following Lent the spring corn was also planted. Richard Iden, who died in May 1699, had three and a half seams (a seam = 8 bushels) of wheat in the barn and 9 acres of oats and 3 acres of barley 'on the ground'. Thomas Joy had only recently completed sowing his spring corn when he died in April 1691 since he had 'five acres three quarters of wheate in the Blade and Nyne Acres and a halfe of Oates lately sowen'. That there was a strong bias towards spring corn is shown by the tithe payments made in 1775 to Parsonage Farm. Forty-eight farmers paid tithe on a total of 797 acres of land yielding winter corn, Lent or spring corn and grass. While the acreage of Lent Corn was 41.9% that supporting winter corn was only 22% doubtless because the yield was more reliable.[61] The principal winter corns were wheat and rye. The spring sown crops included wheat, oats, barley and peas. Fourteen (56%) of all cultivators grew wheat as opposed to 11 (44%) who grew oats. Only 6 (24%) grew barley. Two farmers only grew peas and one, Richard Iden, grew rye. Beans do not occur in any inventory until 1700 and do not reappear until 1717. Oats, in addition to being fed to horses and cattle in winter, served for making oatmeal and were sometimes used in the brewing of beer. All grains could be used to make bread the proportions varying in accordance with availability. Whereas in the Midlands and the North barley and rye were used extensively in bread making, in the south wheat was principally used. Barley was also the main 'drink corn' providing the basis for the ale which our ancestors consumed.

In the early seventeenth century Kent held the leading place as a fruit-growing county. Cherries and apples were first introduced in the 1530s. Defoe claimed in 1724 that Kentish cherries grown on the ridge in the vicinity of Maidstone supplied 'the whole city of London'. Yet none are mentioned in the Boughton inventories of the late seventeenth and early eighteenth centuries. These have only one reference to 'apples and pears' (1704) and another to 'fruit' (1717). In fact most fruit, apart from cherries, grown by farmers at this time on the orchards adjacent to their farms which was not consumed domestically, went no further than the immediate locality. Only later did the London market become especially dependent on Kentish fruit.

Even in the seventeenth century, however, a considerable quantity of apples were grown. Many were local varieties, which have long since disappeared such as the East Farleigh pippin mentioned in an early seventeenth century document relating to Parsonage Farm. Apples, which were windfalls or were bruised, were often used for making cider which was an important beverage in seventeenth and eighteenth century Kent. William Owlett, yeoman (1695), had a cider press in his brewhouse. So, too, did Richard Iden, gent in his oasthouse together with 3 empty pipes and 2 hogsheads. A pipe was a cask holding 2 hogsheads. A hogshead was 54 gallons. John Dicken, tanner (1700) and Thomas Davis, carpenter (1719) both had cider mills and Widow Banks (1717) a designated 'Sider Room'. These made cider for personal consumption but Thomas Joy, blacksmith (1693) had a profitable sideline. In the cellar of his house he had '5 hogsheads of syder, One barrell of beare, 6 syder pipes, 4 hogsheads… eight dosen of Glass Bottles and 6 Mugg Potts'. His 'Syder house' and Cellar in the Quarries contained another '5 hogsheads of Syder, One syder press and Mill… and a parcell of Syder Casks and Tubbs'.

Hops were introduced into Kent about 1520. At first they were grown only upon a small scale. When it was found that sweet, spiced English ale lasted only a fortnight while beer, made with hops, lasted a month hop growing rapidly increased. By the early seventeenth century small hop gardens, influenced by the demands of the London market, were springing up rapidly along the ridge. Hop growing could be extremely profitable. It was also highly speculative and could easily fail. The cost of dressing the hop garden, buying the poles, of which two or three were placed around each plant, picking and drying and the risk of almost total loss of a crop from bad weather or disease, made most cultivators initially grow in plots of not more than two acres.

In the Boughton inventories 9 persons (36%) were involved in hop growing. When he died in 1687 Alexander Martin, freemason, had a pocket of hops worth £14 – over 16% of his total wealth. Robert Towker, butcher, (1694) had 'a small parcell of Hopps' in his parlour. William Wilkins, tanner (1723) – possibly the largest grower in the sample – had 'three bags and one end of hops' valued at £45 plus a parcel of hops worth £4. His stock of hoppoles on the ground was valued at £14. He probably possessed an oasthouse, too, since 'charcoale' is listed among his possessions. The only 2 oasthouses to receive specific mention belonged to William Owlett, yeoman (1695). Within them were 'oasthaires', charcoal and ladders. There were also 'hoppoles in the Hoppgarden there'. The remaining 5 possessed 'hoppoles', 'hoppes' or both. In 1726 Brishing Court Farm was cultivating 1,900 hills of hops with poles worth £19.

Compost and manure were universal fertilisers. William Owlett and Richard Iden, among others, were the owners of 'dung carts'. The value of manure is emphasised by the fact that Richard Wemborn, when he took the lease of Brishing Court Farm in 1726, agreed to leave 'all dung' on the premises when the lease ended. Over 100 loads of manure was worth 1s.0d. per load.[62] It was no accident that 'Muck in the Stables' was valued in the inventory of Robert Towker, butcher (1694). Lime and marl were also used on the ridge. The former was brought from the Downs and often burnt on the spot. Marl was dug wherever it was found. The name of the area Marlpit probably dates from this time. Widow Spice, who died in 1692, had 'clover on the ground' while Richard Wemborn was granted the seed clover on Brishing Court Farm during his tenancy. The use of clover became more widespread for improving the fertility of the soil in the second half of the seventeenth century.

Farm tools and equipment were basic and fairly similar throughout. Most farmers owned, like Nicholas Jeffrey, 'one plough and an old cart, one harrow and some other small husbandry implements'. Richard Iden had 'One cart and wheels, one dung court (small cart), 2 harrows and one barley roller'. Even farmers' widows still possessed farm equipment. Katherine Martin died in 1687 in possession of 'One old harrow'. Elizabeth Meriam (1690) left in her yard 'One old court and cart and an old plow'. At the bottom end of the scale Alexander Meriam (1748) had only 'one spard (spade), one spud (a small, narrow spade with a short handle), one iron maddock (mattock), one hoe and two handbills'.

It seems doubtful whether at this time most Boughton farmers did more than serve their own subsistence needs and supply some commodities to local markets. John Savage Esq, fell into a different category. His Boughton Mount estate had a total value of £3,892. To cultivate the farm he had 'a waggon, two courts, a plough, five harrows, one Rake, one court and wheels, one Hoppole Tugg, one Stone Roll and other small utensils.' There was also a Cyder press and Mill. 25 quarters of wheat, 20 quarters of oats and 20lbs. of hops remained from the previous harvest. At the time of his death in late April 1725 he also had 55 acres of wheat and Lent corn valued at £64.11.05 together with 6 acres of clover. Moreover he was speculating in hops for the London market. Ten and a quarter acres of ground were planted with hops which were being cultivated on 3,400 hop poles. Eleven bins and eight oast hairs awaited the picking and drying process in September. There is no mention of an oasthouse but there must have been one since 'Six loads of charcoal' worth £20 were there to heat the drying floors.[63]

Houses and Furnishing in the Seventeenth and Eighteenth Centuries

Social historians of the 1950s and 1960s suggested that the period 1570-1640 was the time of a 'Great Rebuilding' or 'Housing Revolution' when increased prosperity, especially during the reign of Elizabeth, enabled many houses of all classes to be extended or re-built except in the northernmost counties. More recent study suggests that there was a great deal of regional diversity in the process. Nevertheless Kent and the other prosperous south-eastern counties were in advance of the rest of England. The county had building materials readily available in the form of timber from the Weald which remained abundant until the close of the sixteenth century. Later, Wealden clay provided material for bricks and tiles which became increasingly used in the building of new houses and the repair of old ones. Lime from the Downs was a basic ingredient in mortar and plaster. Population was increasing and more houses were needed. The money and materials were available to provide them. By the mid-fifteenth century new or partially re-built timber-framed dwellings with exposed oak timbers and an infilling of lath, horsehair, cowdung and 'daub' were beginning to appear.

These timber-framed houses, built mostly for Kentish yeomen farmers, were known as hall houses or Wealden-type houses. Presumably some houses remained basically two-roomed with a principal living room called the hall, open to the roof and a second room known either as the parlour or chamber, which was used as a bedroom, although very few have been identified as yet in Kent. Other dwellings were basically three-roomed with the central hall still the main room of the house and a parlour at one end and a buttery or milkhouse or both at the other. The latter were separated from the remaining rooms by means of a cross passage running from front to back of the house. At Boughton most of the early surviving buildings date from the mid-to-late 15th century. A second phase of building or rebuilding took place during the 16th century in response to changing demand and increasing population although buildings constructed during the earlier phase were so high status and substantial that they were not wholly replaced. Finally there was a third phase in the 17th century. What type of dwelling was occupied by the very poor is still not really known.

Of the 36 surviving timber-framed houses listed in 1987 by the Department of the Environment as buildings of special architectural or historical interest 12 or one third were erected in the fifteenth century. Brishing Court, Charlton Farmhouse, Lewis Court and Rabbit's Cross were Wealden Houses. Martin's Farm and the Swallows were Hall Houses.[64] As housing improvement quickened a further 17 houses (47%) show evidence of building work in the 16th century including 11 houses which were newly-built. The latter included Rock Cottage; Hart's House; White Cottage and Iden Farmhouse. Improvement took a number of forms. Originally there was a central open hearth in the hall and outlets for smoke were provided, in the absence of chimneys, by smoke vents in the roof. Not only was life rendered uncomfortable by swirling smoke in the Hall but the risk of fire was considerable. More sophisticated smoke management was aided by the insertion of smoke bays containing the hearth and conducting the smoke to the roof by means of plaster partitions although this, too, had its dangers. Finally the insertion of internal chimney stacks made life not only more comfortable but also much safer. A brick stack not only meant wood, and later coal, could be burnt more safely but the inglenook could also serve a second fireplace at its back in a service room or even in the parlour. Hitherto much cooking had tended to take place in the hall itself or in a detached kitchen. The way was now clear for a purpose-built kitchen within the house. The end of the use of an open hearth meant also that a floor could be inserted to create an upper storey which became continuous across the whole house. At first access was by ladder. Eventually this was replaced by a staircase. While some houses were converted to the new features in the sixteenth century new houses were built with the innovations as part of their original plan.

The original 15th century Kent farmhouse was constructed with a limited roof span. This meant that the house could be of only one main or two subsidiary rooms in width. Any enlargement took the form of an extension in length or at right angles, or else the creation of an outshot at the rear or at one end of the house. Rooms were normally reached by passing through one room to another. Some houses were enlarged by an additional upper storey of garrets, by the partition of larger, ground floor rooms or the use of outhouses for domestic purposes. A bakehouse, a brewhouse, a boulting house where flour was sifted and a milkhouse or dairy were often outhouses. Unique to Kent among the counties of the south-east was the wash-house, which unlike other rooms, often possessed a water supply. The upper storey was usually divided into chambers corresponding to the rooms below. Thus there was 'the Chamber over the Hall', 'the Chamber over the Buttery and Milkhouse', 'the Chamber over the Wash-house'. One or two upper chambers were sometimes reserved for storage of produce such as the 'Wheat Chamber'. In larger houses rooms were set aside for annual farm servants of both sexes who were bound each year to their master until the system ended in the nineteenth century. William Wilkins in 1723 had a 'Servants Chamber' in which there were three beds. The process of enlargement culminated in the seventeenth century. Sixteen (44%) of Boughton's surviving timber-framed houses show evidence of building work at this time. In contrast the corresponding figure for 18th century dwellings is five. These dwellings, such as Tilts Farm, were largely built of brick.

By the time our twenty-six inventories (1686-1748) had come into being the process of transformation was well-underway. Rooms are specified in 13 houses between 1686-1699 and a further 8 between 1700-1748. Houses in the former period yielded an average of 8.6 rooms. No house had fewer than 6 rooms. All had upper storeys. In the eight-roomed house of Widow Kathleen Martin (1687) the change was fairly recent. On the ground floor an 'Old Buttery' existed alongside a 'Buttery' as evidence of a recent addition. The presence of 'one small table and chest, three chayres and three stooles' on 'ye topp of the stayres' is an indication that the staircase had only recently been built replacing the ladder by which access had been gained to the upper storey. Ten houses had kitchens. In 6 cases these appear to have replaced the Hall. In all two houses had 6 rooms, 2 had seven, 4 had eight, 1 had ten and 4 had eleven. In the period 1700-1748 there was an average of 8.25 rooms per house – slightly more than in the first period. One house had 5 rooms, 1 had six, 3 had eight, 1 had nine, 1 had 10 and 1 had 11. Unfortunately no rooms are specifically mentioned in two houses. Nine inventories 1686-1748 belong to tradesmen or craftsmen. Four of these had specialist premises. Robert Towker, who died in 1694, included in his eleven-roomed house a 'Butcher's Shop and Slaughterhouse'. Similarly, Thomas Davis, carpenter, who died in 1719, had 'a small ware Shopp' and a 'Workshopp'. In the latter and 'without Doors' he possessed 'timber, sawed planks, Boored Materrialls and Stuffe cutt out for husbandry use, poles, poste Railes, Laths, Ladders and all the working tools...' worth 44% of his total wealth. Both tanners had tanyards and leather. John Dicken (1700) had 'One hundred and thirty Backs of Leather, One hundred and tenn upper leather Hydes, Sixteen dozen of Calve skinns, Some other small skins, a Parcell of Hornes and Haire, Twenty-five loades of Taw (leather dressing) and a parcell of working tooles' valued at £220 or 62% of the value of his 'goods and chattels'. William Wilkins (1723) had 'lether in the yard' and 'in the two barnes bark' jointly worth £640 or 61% of his total wealth. Bark of oak and other trees was used in tanning. In contrast Alexander Meriam, (1748), thatcher, had goods valued at only £14.11.6d and was the owner of only 'his theetching tools' and two ladders.

Henry Iden, yeoman, who died in 1722 with goods worth £35.15.0d, and Alexander Meriam were among the poorest parishioners to have inventories made. Iden's five-roomed house was only 'two up and two down' with 'Fire Room (Hall), Brewhouse and Milkhouse' on its ground floor and 'Best Chamber and Next Chamber' above. Meriam similarly had 'Kitchen, Brewhouse and Buttery' below and 'Kitchen Chamber, Farther Chamber and Garret' above. The majority of persons whose goods, chattells and cattell' were itemised were, however, from a fairly well-to-do rural middle class. The 1664 Hearth Tax lists 'Boughton Munchelsey' as having a total of 97 houses. Sir Robert Barnham, Baronet, of Boughton Monchelsea Place topped the social pyramid paying tax on 24 hearths. One landowner, John Alchorne of Boughton Mount, paid tax upon 12 hearths, another upon 11 and a third (Robert Rabett) upon 6 hearths. Three paid tax on 5 hearths, eight, including vicar Mathias Rutton, on 4 hearths and eleven on 3 hearths. Twenty paid tax upon 2 hearths and twenty-six upon a single hearth cottage. A further 25 householders, eight possessing two hearths and seventeen with 1 hearth, were too impoverished to be charged the Hearth Tax at all. Roughly a quarter of the parishioners therefore constituted a rural proletariat who had fallen below the poverty line. Another 46 taxpayers upon 1 or 2 hearths were just above it. Most of these were too poor to have inventories made at their deaths. The Hearth Tax was chargeable upon hearths not rooms but there is no doubt that most persons who fell into this category would still be living in houses of the older type with a smaller number of rooms.

If we turn to the two 'great houses' in the parish we encounter a totally different world. At Boughton Monchelsea Place Robert Rudston had, by 1575, converted an essentially medieval hall-house into an Elizabethan mansion. The inventory of his son, Belnapp Rudston, taken at his death in 1613, reveals that the house contained a hall, gallery, 2 dining rooms, and 14 bedchambers in addition to 3 other living rooms and 13 service rooms. The latter included kitchen, cellar, buttery, larder, scullery, 'stillinghouse', 'backhouse', milkhouse, wheatloft, brewhouse, fishhouse, and a 'wet larder'. The first description that we get of Boughton Mount is in the inventory of John Savage, Esq., made over a century later in 1726. There were no fewer than 21 rooms on the ground floor or beneath. The service rooms consisted of kitchen, scullery, pantry, bakehouse, brewhouse, buttery and laundry. Beneath were a meal cellar, small beer cellar, milk cellar, a cross cellar and a wine and ale cellar. There were also a parlour, hall, 2 studies and a gesture to eighteenth century fashion in the form of a Blue Room (with closet) and a Yellow Room. Additionally a New Wing had been added containing another hall, parlour and cellar. Upstairs the Old Wing held 5 bedrooms including the 'Best Chamber', a Dressing Room, the Nursery and a Staircase Gallery and Closet. The New Wing contained a Maids' Chamber, a Little Chamber and a second gallery. Another servant obviously slept in the 'Bell Garret' upon a 'pallate bedsted'. 'On the Terress' stood the 'Great Clock and Bell' which gave the estate workers the signal to begin and finish work. In the grounds was a Summer House.

The so-called 'Great Rebuilding' was accompanied by a 'Great Refurnishing' as homes increased their furniture thus enabling many to live in greater comfort. When our inventories begin this second transformation was also well underway. Furnishings in all houses were simple and sparse by modern standards but joinery – the making of morticed and tenoned furniture – had already arrived in Boughton. Made by a joiner 'joynt' furniture was more elaborate and better made than the crude furnishings knocked together by a carpenter. Thomas Joy in 1691 had in his hall or main living room 'one table and ffoorme... and one ffolding

Board' (table) but his 'fforer stooles' were 'joyned'. John Cheesman (1693) and Richard Iden (1699) also possessed joined stools. William Owlett (1695) had a 'joynt bedstedd' in his Best Chamber and a joined chest. Cupboards were mostly side tables on which articles were placed unenclosed. Richard Iden, however, owned a 'press cubboard', a large, usually shelved cupboard for clothing which could be placed in a wall recess. So, too, did Elizabeth Banks in 1717. Francis Brunger, yeoman (1704) was the only owner of a court cupboard, a movable cupboard or dresser with open shelves.

The fireplace provided heat for warmth and for cooking. James Board, yeoman, who died in 1686, still lived and cooked in his hall. His hearth furniture consisted of '2 pair of pothangers, fire shovel and tongs, 2 pair of andirons, 1 Jack, 3 spitts, 1 warming pann, 2 tin dripping panns, 2 gridirons with other small things'. Andirons or fire dogs were used for supporting burning logs in lieu of a grate. Gridirons were used for broiling flesh or fish over a fire. The warming pan, whose ownership in Boughton was widespread, provided welcome heat in bed at night and by the eighteenth century was made increasingly of copper or brass. By 1691 the volume of cooking and hearth furniture had increased but its basic usage was still the same. Thomas Joy, blacksmith, had that year in his Kitchen 'One paire of Andirons, firepan and tongs, One paire of pottingers (small basins), Two Spitts, One Tinn dripping pann, Two gridirons, Two Toasting Forrks, One paire of Bellowes... One paire pewter candlesticks, 3 Brass Kettles, One Brass Pann, One Brass pott and Skillett, (three-legged saucepan with a long handle which stood in the embers of an open fire), 2 Iron potts, 3 Iron Kettles, 1 Ffry pan, 2 Warming pans, Three pewter salts (salt boxes)... 4 wire candlesticks'. The last are a reminder that firelight gave insufficient illumination for most tasks after dark. By the eighteenth century candlesticks were made increasingly of brass. From 1690 lanthorns appear increasingly, too, in Boughton inventories. The insufficiency of artificial light for close work caused many to retire early besides the rigours and length of the working day.

The best bed and its 'furnishings' that is the 'valans' or curtains, the feather or less luxurious 'flock' mattress, the blankets, coverlets, bolsters, pillows and other bedding was often among the most valuable items in the house. There were also less elaborate beds including the low truckle beds which could be pushed beneath larger beds to save space. Other concessions to comfort took the form of 'cushens'. Richard Iden possessed the only carpet in his 'Parlor' although whether it was on the wall or the floor we do not know. After 1693 clocks began to appear among personal possessions and there are a handful of looking glasses. In the eighteenth century a new piece of furniture began to feature increasingly, namely the chest of drawers. Examples of indoor sanitation, however, remained few. Richard Iden had two pewter 'Chamber potts' in 1699 – very properly in the home of a gentleman. He also had 'One bedpan' although it is doubtful if it was in use since it was situated in his Brewhouse! Mary Gipps, a widow of some substance, had 'a bedpan and close stool' in 1705. Three houses, however, had built-in, internal garderobes – Charlton Farm, Tanyard and the Cock. Other rare items were books and firearms. Richard Iden possessed 'a birding piece' in his hall and 'One bible, one dictionary and several old Lattin Books' in his Parlour Chamber. Nicholas Jeffrey, husbandman, had 2 birding pieces but no books. Ironically the only other man to have 'Sume old books in the Garrett' and 'One Gunn' (for poaching?) was the poor thatcher, Richard Meriam. His neighbours assessed his goods as worth only £14.11.6. His possessions were pitifully few but they included a clock, a looking glass and the only 'large picture' in the inventories.

Today when a man's fortunes take a turn for the better he tends to invest in consumer goods such as a new television, refrigerator or washing machine. In the late-seventeenth and early eighteenth centuries surplus cash tended to be invested in brass, in pewter, the poor man's silver, and in linen. The latter was normally stored in a chest. James Board in 1686 had '10 payer of sheets, 2 dozen napkins, 4 table cloths, 1 dozen of towels, 4 pillow cases and other small linnen'. Eight years later Robert Towker, butcher, had 'in linnen' '14 paire of sheetes, 6 dozen of Napkins, 1 ffine sheete, 6 paire of pillow coates, 14 table cloathes, 1 dozen and a halfe of Towells, a paire of pillow coates and 1 odd one, 4 Napkins, 4 Baggs'. John Dicken, tanner, had in his kitchen in 1700 nineteen pewter dishes and two pewter candlesticks. Nicholas Jeffrey in 1697 had 2 brass skilletts, 2 brass kettles, 1 brass warming pan and 1 brass chaffing dish (a small portable grate filled with burning charcoal to keep food warm). Yet he and his family were obviously content to eat from 'one dozen of trenchers' (wooden plates). The table fork does not seem to have arrived in many households by the time the inventories end in 1748. Instead food continued to be eaten with a general purpose knife, a pewter, brass or wooden spoon and the fingers!

Moreover from the sixteenth to the eighteenth centuries the same domestic round must have persisted. Bread was made in the home. Kneading troughs, bread kivvers (tubs) and moulding (kneading) boards are present in most inventories throughout the period. So, too, was beer and cider. The churn for butter-making in the Dairy or Milkhouse also appears frequently. Most butter was made for home consumption. The '12 casks of butter' which appear in an inventory of 1697 are unusual. Cheese making in Boughton was rarer still. Several cheese presses occur but its manufacture seems to have been less popular. Food in the house is only mentioned once. Alexander Meriam left Pork worth £2.0.0 which must have been salted or smoked for the winter since he died in December. Little information is given upon 'wearing apparel'. Only the value is given. Certainly overmuch care was not exercised upon it since, despite the number of dwellings with wash-houses, only two irons – a smoothing iron (1697) and a box iron (1748) – appear in inventories throughout.

Again a comparison between Boughton Monchelsea Place and Boughton Mount, and the other Boughton residents illustrates the great gulf in wealth and diet which existed in the seventeenth and eighteenth centuries between those that headed the local social pyramid and the rest. Both great houses had to feed and maintain large households. In many ways the difference in time between the two is reflected in their inventories. While the Place reflects the material standards of 1613 Boughton Mount has the more numerous and luxurious equipment of the 'Age of Elegance' a century later. The kitchen at the Place, as befitted the kitchen of a large household, contained all the standard cooking utensils of the day. These included a jack, 4 'spitts', 3 dripping pans, 4 mortars for mixing food, 2 brass pots and a skillet, a cullender, 2 chafing dishes, 3 pairs of pot hangs, a gridiron, 2 frying pans and a flesh hook. In the Boughton Mount kitchen the equipment was not only more plentiful but also more sophisticated. It included an iron oven, 2 spit racks, 2 pair of pothangers, 2 cranes, chain line pulleys, a multiplying wheel and weights, 6 spits, dish covers, a basting ladle, a frying housewife, edge slices and steak tongs, a brass plate warmer, 2 apple roasters, a 'sallat strainor', pewter cullender, pudding plates and tobacco tongs. Moreover in the kitchen alone were '7 dozen plates, 18 knives and forks and 12 desert knives and forks'. Heat was provided by coal since there was a pair of 'coal racks'. There were 3 box irons and heaters. The adjacent scullery held a fish kettle and fish plate, a copper kettle and brass kettle, 5 skillets, 3 saucepans, 1 iron kettle, 2 skimmers (for removing cream)... some trenchers, 2 tea kettles and a plate rack. The other service rooms were similarly equipped on a grand scale. The Meat Cellar, for example, had 6 brine tubs, 1 keeler (cooling vessel), 2 chopping blocks, 1 stalder (cask stand), 1 salting trough and a cleaver – equipment used in the preservation of meat for a large household.

Domestic fittings and furnishings at Boughton Mount were also luxurious. Each room was equipped with its window curtains, hangings and valances. Even the Staircase Gallery, lit at night by 4 pairs of brass candlesticks, was curtained. The Blue Room was decorated with blue 'paper hangings' and curtained in white. The Yellow Room was appropriately fitted with 'Yellow cambelet furniture and two paires of Yellow Cambelet window curtains'. Among the room furniture was a set of china, a stone teapot and a sugar dish. Throughout the house there were a total of 6 flock and 6 feather beds. The Hall Chamber contained 'a mohair bed lined with white sarsenet' while the Best Chamber held 'one striped camblet bed lined with Green Satten (satin). There were 4 looking glasses and 2 swing dressing glasses spread throughout the various rooms. Three wigs and a wig stand were in the staircase closet. John Savage, Esq., was evidently a man of some education. The 'Study in the Hall' contained not only a 'large collection of medals' but also 'a large parcel of books'. A second 'large parcel of books' shared pride of place in his personal study with his writing desk and 'a large collection of Italian prints'. Nor was the appreciation of art limited to Mr Savage's study. There were a further 80 prints in the Hall Chamber and 22 in the Best Chamber while 60 lined the staircase gallery. 59 were displayed in the Old Hall and 50 in the Yellow Room. As if this was not enough there were 10 pictures in the Parlour, 30 pictures in the Kitchen Chamber together with a Coffee Mill and 6 pictures and half a dozen 'mappes and prints' in the New Hall. The Dressing Room held 2 pictures 'one sett in Silver Gilt'.

China and glassware again convey the impression of gracious living. The Old Hall contained a China Punch Bowl, 8 China dishes, 10 Jelly glasses, 6 Water glasses, 6 Wine glasses, 2 Glass candlesticks, 3 Cruets and 4 Glass salts. In the Buttery were 1 dozen China plates, 8 China basins, 18 Delft plates, 2 Delft dishes, 6 Wine glasses, 1 dozen Pattey pans and 6 Coffee cups. The Parlour contained a glass bell for summoning the servants together with a card table and a tea table. The House had a clock and case in the Old Hall and another clock in the Laundry Chamber. There was 'one weather glass' (barometer) in the Hall and another in Savage's study. While weaponry was scarce among the peasantry Savage had two guns and six 'old swords' in the kitchen and three more swords in the staircase gallery together with a sword belt. There was a carbine and a pair of pistols in the Chamber over the Laundry and a second brace of pistols in the Chamber above the Scullery. Savage left linen worth £45 and plate, gold and diamond rings valued at £117. Indoor sanitation, however, was still scarce with only a close stool pan on the Staircase Gallery and two closets possibly situated adjacent to bedrooms.

The fittings and furnishings of Boughton Monchelsea Place were typical of the early seventeenth century country gentry. The 'Dyninge Room' was furnished with table, court cupboard and 'syde cupborde' of 'wallnuttree' and had 3 'grene Brode Cloth Carpetts' and a 'little grene fringed carpett' (on its walls). Its 'joyned chayres, formes and stooles' were also of 'wallnuttree'. Added comfort was provided by 6 'turkey worke cushions'. The further chamber was also very comfortably furnished with '2 Turkey Worke Carpetts' (soft, thick carpeting) and a third in the adjacent 'closett' with 2 Turkey Work cushions. The furniture was 'joyned' as was the 'bedstedd' which had 'wainscott tester' (canopy) and '5 Curteines of stryped linsey wolsey' and 'vallence of the same with curteine rods'. There was additionally 'a chayre of black figered satten' and '2 low stooles of grene chamlett' (camel hair). Mrs Rudstone's chamber was also well-furnished with another Turkey Work carpet, 'seaven Turkey work stooles and one turkey work chayre' among its other furniture. The 'little Dyning Roome' had a Turkey Work carpet too but in other living rooms and many of the service rooms furnishings were old and relatively sparse. The Hall, for example, contained only '2 longe tables, 6 formes, 1 syde table, 2 stooles, 1 payer of tables and 3 cushions'.

Conversely, while furnishings in some parts of the Place were lacking, there was ample evidence that its occupants were persons of culture and religion. Books and maps were scattered throughout the house. The Little Dining Room contained 'one parte of the booke of Martyrs, sixtene small Bookes and eightene small Statute Books' along with other volumes. The gallery held a further 'tenn small Bookes' and 'seaventene Mapps'. There was 'one great byble and one little byble' in the Wardrobe Chamber and another bible in the Hall. Mrs Rudstone had in her chamber 'A Paraphrase of Erasmus' and 'a Book of Common Prayer' plus 'three little pictures' while the closet within the Further Chamber housed the works of Chaucer and a second part of the 'Booke of Marters'. A further 10 maps were to be found in the Dining Room with 'a little picture of the pliarment'. (Parliament).

The whole house contained only 3 'glasse lanthornes' although subsidiary illumination would have been provided by rushlights. The only close stool was in one of the 'mayde's chambers', but garderobes (latrines) would have been built into the stone walls of the mansion. Weaponry was represented by 'a case of pistolls and a petronell (large horse pistol) in the garrett over the Nurserye', a Calliver (light musket) in the Kitchen and a sword. There were 'fower Corsletts' (cuirasses) in the garrett over the further chamber. These were upper body armour made chiefly of leather and pistol-proof. The only clock stood in the entry next to Mrs Rudstone's chamber. The family linen was worth £9.8s.8d., the pewter was valued at £4.1s.10d. and the plate at £6.8s.0d.

Soldiers and Smugglers

During the eighteenth century one of the most powerful influences upon the parish was the creation of Coxheath Army Camp. Even before the coming of the Spanish Armada in 1588 Coxheath, 'a wild and desolate spot', had played an important role as a mustering point for the county militia. In 1756 a semi-permanent camp was set up to house a large part of the 12,000 German mercenaries sent from Hanover during the Seven Year' War with France 1756-1763. Coxheath was only a day's march from the naval base at Chatham and a large encampment there could also be used to block any invasion force striking northwards towards London from the south-east coast. The Hanoverians, however, were unpopular locally and created such difficulties that they were returned to their homeland the following year. Fears of invasion were renewed when the American War of Independence, which had begun in 1775, intensified into a European conflict in which the fledgling United States was supported from 1778 by France and the following year by Spain – two naval powers who could possibly challenge British supremacy at sea.

High Jinks at Coxheath Camp.
Cruikshank's scurrilous print depicts the rigours of training whilst awaiting the French.

To counter this renewed invasion threat the militia was called up for active service and a series of military camps were established to concentrate militia and regulars at vital defensive points across southern England. The first camps were created to protect the naval bases at Portsmouth, Plymouth and Chatham. Others were set up further inland at Winchester, Salisbury and West Stow, near Bury St. Edmunds. Camps at Coxheath and at Warley Common, Brentwood were intended to block any advance on London from the south or east. Further camps subsequently appeared including Waterdown, Tunbridge Wells and Lenham Heath.

Coxheath and Warley were the most important of the camps. In 1778 Chatham held 1,400 men as opposed to Warley's 11,000 and the 17,000 housed in the camp at Coxheath. The latter was three and a half miles long and a quarter of a mile in depth. It held as many regular soldiers and militiamen as there were inhabitants in contemporary Leeds and dwarfed nearby Maidstone whose population in 1782 was a little over 5,000. If we add the accompanying wives, children and camp followers together with the children who were born in the camp, a comparison with larger contemporary urban centres such as Portsmouth or Plymouth is more appropriate. Further camp followers dwelt in the caves in the Quarries and plied their trade within the camp. In 1778 over three quarters of Coxheath Camp stood within Boughton Monchelsea parish extending as far eastward as the Cock Inn. The remainder stretched westward of the Turnpike to Cranbrook towards Coxheath. In 1756 it seems likely that the men were under canvas while the officers were billeted in the houses around Cock Street. In the later eighteenth century camps the officers and men of the regular army and milita were all housed in tents stretching along the line of what later became the B2163 from the Boughton Cock and the Knight's house. Each company had its own section identified by its colours. Mess tents, field kitchens, hospital and lavatory tents lay to the rear together with the tents of the rearguard and the old tents which housed the women. The parade ground for each regiment lay to the front. In 1804 the Artillery Park lay west of the turnpike together with the ammunition and baggage waggons. Camp Headquarters were situated at Linton Park. The Camp Bakehouse was built adjacent to the windmill at Haste Hill which ground the flour for the troops. The complex was surrounded by a wall to prevent soldiers stealing bread. Each soldier received 'a well baked 6lb loaf of good English wheat bread' every four days for which 4d. was deducted from his pay. Servants, batmen and the women received bread at the same price. A theatre and public room were constructed to entertain residents and visitors with concerts and similar performances. 'A Camp', stated Dr Johnson... 'is one of the great scenes of human life'.

View of the Grand
Encampment on Cox Heath.

Strict attention was paid to health and hygiene. These were the responsibility of the camp's medical officer who had command of the regimental surgeons. Each surgeon had a regimental medical chest and ten 'bits of bedding' for use in the regimental hospitals. No soldier, who could be cured in camp, was admitted to hospital. Patients with the 'itch' were encamped at the rear of their regiments and well-bathed before re-admission. Smallpox patients were attended by the camp medical officer in isolation at a general hospital. The medical officer also visited the regimental hospitals reporting to headquarters if they were not in good order. Streets and tents were kept clean by daily inspection and free from broken glass which could injure the horses. Conveniences were dug deep. Men who did no make use of them were punished. Any 'necessaries' at the rear of the camp, which were 'offensive', were immediately filled in by the quartermasters. 'The health of the Camp', read one order in July 1779, 'depends much upon the Cleanliness of it'.

The presence of a large body of soldiers drilling and practising their manoeuvres made the camp an obvious source of fascination and attracted huge crowds. Some came from the immediate neighbourhood and many from further afield. In August 1779 *The Morning Post* reported that 'a vast concourse of spectators' had watched a review of the Somerset militia. A trip to the camp made 'a good day out' for those who could afford it. On Sunday 15 August 1756 Thomas Turner of East Hoathley left Sussex to visit the first of the Camps:

In the morn we got up about 5 o'clock and breakfasted at my brother's. And then my wife, Sally, T. Davy and myself set out for the camp on Coxheath where we arrived about 11 o'clock, just as they were all got to their devotions, to wit, twelve congregations and a thousand in each congregation. They seemed to be very attentive at their devotions and the minister seemed to have a very fine delivery. I think the camp as fine a sight as I ever did see. We went from the camp to Maidstone (should it have been Coxheath?) where we dined at the 'Bird in Hand', together with many more, on a piece of fine boiled beef, carrots and cabbage and a fore-quarter of lamb roasted and French beans. We stayed till about 3 o'clock and came home by the camp and got to the Wells about 9 o'clock.

Not all visitors spent time watching the troops at their devotions. Others were attracted more by the prostitutes who the local authorities feared would become a health hazard to residents and visitors. London cartoonists had a field day celebrating the attractions of a camp whose very name provided immense scope for sexual allusions. In the end, however, it was bilious fever and poor sanitation rather than venereal complaints which struck the camp in 1778-79. The summer of 1778 was hot and dry. Twenty-two different regiments of regulars and militiamen were in camp throughout the summer months numbering almost 12,000 men. Six hundred were attacked by bilious fever and forty-two died together with some 'wives' and children. A year later the camp was still reported 'very sickly' as the soldiers began to march off Coxheath again in November 1779 carrying their infections with them to winter quarters or, in the case of militiamen, to their various home counties.

To some members of a fairly isolated local community of five to seven hundred people the arrival of the camps presented an unparalleled opportunity. Village wives took in officers' washing and received an allowance of wood accordingly. In 1779 Coxheath was said to have some 700 retail outlets giving it the appearance of a gigantic fairground. While some sutlers came from Maidstone or London a high proportion of those who ran booths and stalls inside the camp were locals supplying milk, meat, vegetables and fruit together with hot puddings and pies. Local brewers, distillers and publicans also enjoyed a few very profitable years. Boughton had some half dozen drinking houses including the Boughton Cock but there were many more which sold liquor without licence, with the tacit acquiescence of the military authorities, at the rear of the camp. Commanding officers were anxious to keep their men in camp as far as possible. General orders in 1779 stressed that 'there was no excuse... for any soldier being out of Camp' since 'almost everything they can want' was available within its boundaries. Patrols were stationed to prevent soldiers 'straggling out of the encampment'. Water details were not allowed to loiter but marched swiftly back to the kitchens. Troops discovered over a mile away from their regiments without a pass were treated as deserters. Frequent and unexpected roll calls were staged at night to catch absentees while sentries allowing soldiers to leave camp were severely punished. Ultimately patrols were operating in villages 'a considerable distance away' but still to no avail.

An Enraged farmer defends his wife's honour.
Duels and clashes like this with the local populace were the only serious martial activities witnessed on Coxheath.

In the summer of 1779, a year after the 15,000 troops at the Camp were reviewed by King George III, Coxheath was the temporary home of militiamen from Suffolk, Devon, Bucks., Monmouthshire, Norfolk, Somerset, Northamptonshire, Warwickshire, Lincolnshire, Gloucestershire, Yorkshire, Rutland, Caernarvon and Anglesey. Many were homesick. Almost all were thirsty.

Not only the publicans and sutlers benefited. There were the hordes of visitors to cater for as well. The Hon. Thomas Bruce reported in 1778 that 'The accommodations immediately about Camp are... always crowded' while 'The inns in Maidstone... from the great resort of people to this camp (are) generally full'. Since there were insufficient rooms in the Maidstone inns beds in private houses were hired out to deal with the overflow. While some gained others lost. A less desirable aspect of projecting a vast number of soldiers into a rural parish was the vandalism done to the locality. This ranged from poaching and the theft of produce from the fields and orchards to the stealing of wood, the killing of livestock and highway robbery. Soldiers were sporadically paid and invariably short of money. They were allowed 3lbs. of firewood a day. Two trusses of straw upon which to sleep were freshened by a new truss every eight days and completely replaced every twenty-four days when the old straw was passed to the 'wives'. In 1778 the troops were permitted to help with the harvesting but in 1779 the privilege was stopped. Soldiers were ordered to keep to the roads and footpaths; and to avoid damage to woodland, crops and hop poles. The incentives to theft and vandalism, however, were too great. 'The farmers about the country have for some time complained of a great deal of mischief being done them by the soldiers, I am afraid with too much truth', wrote Lord Althorp, a captain in the Northamptonshire militia, from Coxheath in September 1779.

For the local gentry and nobility the creation of the Camp meant, at first, a chance to widen their social circle. Officers with suitably aristocratic connections in the militia or the regulars were inundated with invitations to dine or take tea. Letters from the Camp were carried to Headquarters at Linton by the Drum Majors who brought back the incoming mail but inactivity inevitably brought boredom and frustration. At least two duels were fought between officers in 1778-79. When one officer was fatally wounded duels were ordered to cease. In the interests of safety the rank-and-file had also to be instructed to refrain from discharging their muskets either inside or outside the Camp when off duty. In a bid to capitalize upon the public fascination for the camps two London theatres staged entertainments in 1779 with the Camp as their subject. Sadler's Wells in July 1779 presented an entertainment of 'singing, dancing and decorations' entitled 'A Trip to Coxheath with a distant view of the Camp'. Next month the Theatre Royal, Richmond Green, not to be outdone, staged a 'New Pantomime Entertainment' called 'Harlequin Volunteer or A Trip to Coxheath' which included 'new Scenes and Machinery particularly a perspective view of the Camp at Coxheath'. In the same year an anonymous 'Lady' was inspired to produce a mediocre novel entitled 'Coxheath Camp'.

The last camp at Coxheath was established during the long French Revolutionary and Napoleonic Wars between 1793-1815. Again it became home to some 10,000 men for the same strategic and defensive reasons as before. The Camp closed for the last time in 1816. The following year finally saw the enclosure of the Heath. The only legacy of the Camp was the alteration to Boughton's road network which left Cock Street or Heath Road straightened and widened and ready to become the B2163 in the future.[65]

The presence of the Camps at Coxheath in the second half of the eighteenth century undoubtedly helped to make the area a target for smugglers who found a ready market for spirits and tobacco among the soldiery. One leading local critic of smuggling was George Bishop, a prominent Maidstone distiller. In his *Observations, Remarks and Means to Prevent Smuggling* published in 1783 Bishop maintained that:

> In the parishes of Barming, East and West Farleigh, Loose, Boughton, Linton
> and Hunton there are eleven licensed public houses and forty-one private
> retailers of smuggled spirits; the greatest quantity of which are sold by the
> unlicensed houses ...Country gentlemen and farmers have their spirits, teas,
> wines, etc much cheaper from the smuggler than they can of the fair trader...[66]

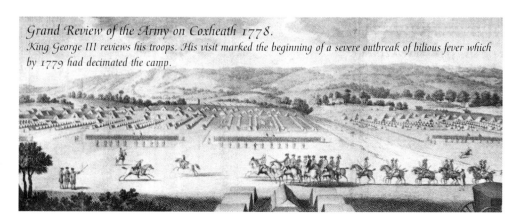

Grand Review of the Army on Coxheath 1778.
King George III reviews his troops. His visit marked the beginning of a severe outbreak of bilious fever which by 1779 had decimated the camp.

Not surprisingly details of a covert operation like smuggling are few. Oral information upon smuggling in the vicinity of Leeds during its last stages in the 1820s were given to a reporter of the *Kentish Express* in 1899 by John Milner. Milner had worked for a smuggling gang as a boy over seventy years before. The ringleaders were Wood of Leeds, Cook of Boughton Monchelsea; Munday of Linton and a man called Harris. They worked with the surviving members of the Aldington gang led by George Ransley until his arrest and transportation in 1826-1827.[67] Milner often saw Stephen Ransley in Leeds at that time. When the 'sea smugglers' had run their contraband cargo across the Channel, landing somewhere between Deal and Dover, it was transported overland by heavily-armed convoys of 'land smugglers' to the outskirts of Leeds where Wood had a shop. Some goods went to Boughton, Linton and other places. Before the contraband was finally transferred to its village destinations the smugglers secreted the Hollands, cognac, cigars and tobacco in 'holes' at Chartaway Street; on the outskirts of Leeds itself; or at Magpie Bank caves, Hollingbourne. The goods were then covered with brushwood and fern until their agents could be contacted. Milner, as the gang's messenger, then travelled from Leeds to Linton, Boughton and elsewhere with news that the contraband had arrived. He often saw thirty or forty kegs of brandy secreted in the 'holes' besides countless other illegal commodities.

The gang's success came to an end about 1839 when a smuggler was driving a large van, fully loaded, under cover of darkness towards Leeds. The night was dark and stormy. The driver blundered into the river Len. Next morning he was found drowned with his cart overturned, the horses dead and twenty or thirty casks floating in the river. Word was sent to Maidstone. Constables arrived to claim the contraband and Wood was arrested and sentenced to a long term of imprisonment at Maidstone Assizes. The 'Leeds gang' ended with his arrest. Old habits however, died hard. Shortly after Wood's capture a woman that Milner later married was sitting in Wood's cottage talking to his daughter who had a small keg of brandy under her chair. Preventive men suddenly entered the cottage and began to search for contraband. Wood's daughter tucked her skirt over the keg beneath her and continued her conversation in such a relaxed manner that after a while the officers abandoned their search and left empty handed.[68]

The Government of the Parish

English parishes until the nineteenth century largely governed themselves. As late as 1830 the only central government departments were the Home Office, the Foreign Office and the Treasury. During the Middle Ages local government was in the hands of the lords of the manor operating through their manorial courts. By Tudor times, however, with the decline of the manor and the encouragement of the Tudor monarchy, the parish gradually took over the work of local administration. Free from the control of the aristocracy and subject to the patronage of the new Tudor gentry the parish was a conveniently autonomous unit which could be supervised by the Established Church through bishop's visitations and by the Justices of the Peace at Quarter Sessions. The Tudors, therefore, revived the ancient manorial and parochial offices and gave their holders and the Justices who supervised them, power to administer parish affairs and operate the many laws which kept order and regulated economic welfare.

Authority came to rest largely with the parish vestry. This was originally an 'open' parish parliament which consisted theoretically of all parishioners. By the sixteenth century, however, the lower orders were excluded and it had become a closed oligarchy of the 'principal inhabitants'. Taking its name from its meeting place, the vestry of the parish church, it controlled the appointment of parish officers, granted rates for their expenditure and inspected and allowed their accounts. The rector, if present, was chairman of the vestry meeting by common law. The officers, who discharged the executive aspect of parochial government – the Churchwardens, Surveyors of the Highways, Borsholder and Overseers of the Poor – also had their functions defined by law. They were appointed from among the parishioners themselves and were obliged to serve unpaid for a year. All but the overseers of the poor are dealt with below. By the sixteenth century the officers of most rural parishes, like their vestries, were normally appointed from a ruling clique of substantial farmers. Between 1764-1792 two overseers of the poor were appointed annually at Boughton. Of these ten men were appointed twice and two others three times. By 1799-1811 an even tighter system had evolved whereby a man having served as second overseer for one year was appointed first overseer the next. Thus 11 men, including Thomas Rider, served for two consecutive years. Two others, Edward Hodges, who later became assistant overseer and Samuel Shirley, served for three. The same two men were also obliged to take their turn with another office. Samuel Cole, who farmed Wierton Hill, was overseer of the poor in 1804 and 1805 and surveyor of the highways in 1827 and 1828. During the 14 years 1822-1835 eight farmers were surveyors of the highways twice and two farmers three times. Elisa Beard of Wierton Street was unique in that she was a woman who acted as surveyor in 1832-33.

Of the two churchwardens one was normally appointed by the rector and the other by the vestry. The churchwardens were financed by the Church Rate which was the oldest of the parish rates. Their expenditure and duties were largely ecclesiastical although a small portion of the Church Rate was spent upon secular matters. Tudor statutes had given the wardens responsibility for pest control so that their accounts contain regular payments for the bodies of sparrows. Thomas Joy and Thomas Cull, Churchwardens from Easter 1831-1832, paid out £2.3s.0d. during their stewardship 'for Sparrows'. A sum was spent annually when the Bishop's ordinary visited the ecclesiastical court at Sittingbourne to hear from the churchwardens their report upon the moral state of their parishes. Joy and Cull expended £1.6s.0d. upon the visitation and a further £1.12s.0d. upon their own expenses! £5.4s.6d. was spent on 'Sacrament Wine and Ringers'. 'Tent' wine, a deep red Spanish wine, was used in the former. The Church bells were rung not only on Sundays but to commemorate special anniversaries such as notable military and naval victories and the failure of the Gunpowder Plot. Half a chaldron of coals (12¾ cwt) was bought for 18s.0d. as fuel for the stove which heated the Church and caused the great fire later that year. An annual salary was paid to John Beeching, the parish clerk, and to Thomas Wenham, the beadle, a minor parish officer whose variable duties included driving stray dogs from the Church. Four registers were bought to keep a record of parishioners' attendance at communion.

The principal duty of the Churchwardens was the upkeep of the church fabric and furnishings. During 1831-32 they met various unspecified bills including one for £5.11s.3d. from Richard Seager, the local stonemason and another from William Shadgett, the local carpenter, for £14.17s.11d.[69] The moral and religious control exercised by the Churchwardens could be quite formidable both before and after the Reformation. At Archdeacon Harpsfield's Visitation in 1557 the two wardens,

Edward Marten and Johanne Combe, and seven parishioners presented Thomas Walter for committing adultery with Jeroppa, wife of Nicholas Rabett. Walter was now living in Maidstone but the woman appeared in person and denied the charge in front of her accuser, John Garford. Jeroppa was ordered to purify herself under oath at Boughton on the following Sunday before the full congregation. At the same visitation another parishioner, John Master, who had left the parish and gone to Loose, was reported for failing to receive the Easter sacrament while the wife of John Rouse had also regularly neglected to attend church. In her case the borsholder was instructed to bring her before the archdeacon at Ulcombe the following day.[70]

The borsholder or petty constable was nominated by the vestry and 'sworn' by the magistrates. Descended from the manorial constable with his own levy but no salary the borsholder's chief functions were the prosecution of recusants and felons and maintenance of law and order. His powers of arrest were often exercised and his staff of office, a sign of his authority, was usually fixed to the door of his house. A prisoner might be held in the stocks or at the borsholder's dwelling until it was possible to bring him before a magistrate. In this event, he had to be guarded by 'tenders'. If a trial ensued witnesses and escorts had to be secured and their expenses paid. Convicted prisoners had then to be escorted to the House of Correction at Maidstone. Upon such occasions travelling and subsistence expenses only could be claimed. In addition the borsholder maintained the parish butts, arms and armour; organised its contribution to the County Militia in men and money; collected the county rate; assisted the churchwardens to find substitutes for married or sick soldiers and sailors who had been pressed; and paid relief to vagrants or soldiers travelling with passes from the Justices. He also whipped vagrants, cared for the stocks and whipping post; removed the indigent poor to their places of settlement; inspected and supervised all ale houses, weights and measures; and was empowered to raise the hue and cry. In some cases the borsholder was also responsible for maintenance of roads and bridges. His was the one parish office which was usually assigned to a parishioner outside the ranks of the ruling elite. All these amateur offices were time consuming and burdensome. The borsholder also needed to be active and physically fit. Help from his neighbours was often not forthcoming and he was always exposed to the danger of physical violence. Moreover he had to take care in the exercise of his office since someone he arrested in one year might be borsholder the next.

The...constables are usually village artisans totally unacquainted with the business of police... stated Ashurst Majendie in 1834. *They are changed every year and seldom willing to serve a second time. The state of the rural police is altogether inefficient...*[71]

This was perhaps too damning an indictment but the understandable reluctance of borsholders to exert their authority often led to their presentment for neglect of office.

A number of cases brought before Quarter Sessions around the turn of the sixteenth century give an idea of the crimes with which Boughton borsholders found themselves involved. Horse and sheep stealing were among the most serious offences and could be punishable by death. Laurence Roffe, husbandman, of Boughton Monchelsea on 24 December 1596/97 broke into John Culpepper's close with two other men and stole his sorrel horse worth 40 shillings. Roffe was found guilty and was fortunate to be sentenced to branding on the left hand. Butchers were often involved in sheep stealing although sheep stealers were also motivated by hunger, by personal profit or were farmers lacking the capital to start their own flock. In 1596 a Boughton butcher, Henry Blanchett, was bound over to give evidence against a Maidstone butcher, Gabriel Elson, who was in gaol on suspicion of committing a felony which was almost certainly sheep stealing. Two further butchers, one from Boughton and another from Loose, were bound over to be of good behaviour in 1600. Similarly a Marden labourer, Thomas Burden, on 25 September 1601 was charged in that he 'feloniously took, stole and drove off Coxheath' in Boughton Monchelsea 3 ewes, belonging to Levi Buskin, Esq., (worth 5s.), Nicholas Austin (worth 4s.) and Thomas Martin (worth 3s.)'. Grazing on the wasteland of the open Heath was obviously an invitation to theft. Even the Church, however, was not sacrosanct. In 1797 St. Peter's was robbed of a surplice and two window curtains together with some books. The real target was 'the strong chest' (parish chest) which the thieves attempted to force 'with Mr. Marten's Coulter' (the iron cutter in front of a ploughshare) which they had taken from the fields. Two or three other churches in the area were also broken open with 'a like instrument' on the same night.

Unlicensed or disorderly alehouses and illegal brewing and drunkards were a constant problem. 'Poor men tipple and families suffer' stated a Yalding petition urging restriction of unlicensed alehouses in 1653. Spasmodic drives for their suppression were made by the authorities. Edward Weare, a labourer of Boughton Monchelsea, was bound over 'for haunting alehouses' in 1599 while the following year Richard Browne of Boughton Monchelsea was ordered 'to keep victualling no longer'. When Thomas Gouldsmith, a Boughton Monchelsea tailor, applied for a licence in 1612 he wisely produced two respectable sureties in the form of Richard Webbe, gentleman and John Marten, yeoman, both of the same parish.

Major bridges, which were essential for civil and military communication, were ultimately the responsibility of the Justices but initially the borsholder was expected to draw attention to their need for repair. The 'great decay of Hersfilde bridge', between Boughton Monchelsea and Staplehurst parishes, which made it 'dangerous for her Majestye's subjects that way passinge' was first reported to Quarter Sessions in 1594. Six years later a Special Sessions ordered payment of £20 for its repair to be made with certain exceptions by parishes in the 'Seaven Hundreds of the lathe of Scraye and the hundreds of Marden and Eythorne'. The money from the rate raised was to be paid to four men (presumably borsholders) from the parishes which used the bridge most. Two were from Staplehurst, one was from Chart Sutton and the fourth was Thomas Rabbett 'of Boughton Monchelsey'. When the time came to collect the seventeenth century Hearth Tax the onerous task again fell to the unfortunate borsholder. The collector of the tax in 1664 was Richard Longman, Borsholder. Surviving borsholder's accounts in Kent are few and there are none for Boughton Monchelsea. Nevertheless it is not hard to imagine the difficulty with which the borsholder divided his time between his unpaid office and his regular job.[72]

Until 1555 care of the parish highways was in the hands of the manorial courts and their waywardens. Under the Highway Act 1555 the churchwardens and borsholders were required to appoint two Surveyors of the Highways annually to organise repair of the parish roads. Again the office holders were untrained and unpaid. Every labourer and ordinary householder had to perform four unpaid days of statute work on the roads each year at a time chosen by the borsholder and under the supervision of the highway surveyors. In the reign of Elizabeth this was increased to six days. Those who did not turn up were fined. Wealthier inhabitants provided carts, tools and able bodied labourers to perform their statute work for them. By the 1835 Highway Act, however, statute duty was replaced by a Highway Rate which paid for labour and materials. Statute labour was understandably unpopular and even before this many parishes, including Boughton, had begun to use road work and the breaking of stones as public works for the unemployed and underemployed whose numbers were increasing and becoming a burden on the parish ratepayers in the period after 1815.

Surveyors account books survive at Boughton from 1822-59.[73] They illustrate the most common methods of road repair which were to fill the holes with gravel or large stones. The gravel quickly sank or flew out with the passage of vehicles. The stones rendered the road surface uneven and a hazard to wheels passing over them. After 1835, as the account books show, methods remained little changed. The account book for 1836-37 shows that the money raised from the Highway Rate was spent under the various headings of Day Labour, Contract Work, Team Work and Materials. Day Labour consisted of scraping the roads, grubbing stones, stoning 'wheel tracts' to ease the passage of vehicles and general road work such as filling stone carts, laying stones, drainage, and levelling freshly laid stones. Labourers were paid 1s.2d. per day and Richard Wood, the supervisor, 2s.0d. Contract work was largely the breaking of enormous quantities of stones at 10d. per ton – work which was done by those unfortunates who were 'on the parish'. In May 1836, for example, John Crundall broke a total of 39 tons of stones for £1.12s.6d. Thomas Beale broke 17 tons for 14s.2d. during a fortnight of the same year. Local farmers clearing stones from their land sold them as materials to the Surveyors at 1s.4d. a ton. Thomas Rider in 1836 sold 41 tons while T.F. Best disposed of 34 tons. Even the smallest tonnage appears to have been acceptable. Thomas Cheeseman supplied a mere ton from his garden and John Pelham a ton and a half. If the stones of private individuals were insufficient they were picked from waste land by the roadside for the same rate by the unemployed or underemployed although technically this was illegal after 1834. Team work consisted of laying a certain tonnage of stones on a specified section of parish road. Two tons of stones, for example, were laid by George Lamb 'from Haste Hill to Bishop's Farm' and 'from Yew Trees to Bishop's Farm' in May 1836 at a cost of 1s.8d. per ton. Parishes continued to look after their own roads until the 1862 Highways Act permitted Quarter Sessions to establish Highway Boards for groups of parishes. Highway Boards survived until the new county councils, created in 1888, became responsible for rural Highway Authorities. This responsibility eventually passed in turn to Rural District Councils who took over the civil functions of the vestries although local areas retained at least a voice in road problems through the parish councils established in 1894.

The Maidstone to Cranbrook Turnpike

One factor which was influential in promoting the increased prosperity of the parish during the late eighteenth and early nineteenth centuries was the existence of the Maidstone-Cranbrook Turnpike or as it was known locally 'the Linton Road'. Turnpike roads were roads administered by Trusts which were authorized by Act of Parliament to levy tolls on road users in return for making and maintaining the road surfaces. Tolls were payable at turnpike gates manned by gatekeepers. The gates were surmounted by tall spikes to prevent a horse and rider jumping over them. When payment had been made the gatekeeper turned back the gate hence the name 'turnpike'. The trustees were usually local landowners anxious for a more efficient means of transport to serve their local agricultural or other needs. The Maidstone-Cranbrook Trust included the Mayors and Jurats of Maidstone, New Romney and Tenterden and Sir Edward Dering, MP for New Romney. All were doubtless anxious to enhance the commerce and agriculture of their respective townships or estates. The money to meet the cost of obtaining the Act was normally raised by a number of local dignitaries lending the cash. This was then converted into a mortgage on the tolls authorised. When the trusts were established it was commonly assumed that once the road had been widened, straightened and resurfaced there would be little more to be done and the tolls collected in the first twenty-one years or so would be sufficient to pay off the debt that had been incurred in the initial work and legal costs. It soon became apparent that this was not so. Instead the trusts found themselves burdened with liability for interest on the capital outlay and having to request Parliament for further Acts to increase their tolls.

The Maidstone to Cranbrook road was first begun by an Act of 1760. Eight years later the Trust required another Act to increase its tolls, terms and powers. The Wealden clay presented serious difficulties:

> *The turnpike road which leads over Cocksheath to Style Bridge,* wrote Hasted, *separates there at the 44th mile-stone from London, the left branch passing to Cranbrook and the right through this parish (Marden) to Goudhurst, the only parts of it which may be said to be above ground, the rest of it being so deep and miry as to be nearly impassable in wet weather.*[74]

THE GENIUS OF THE BROMPTON FOLD

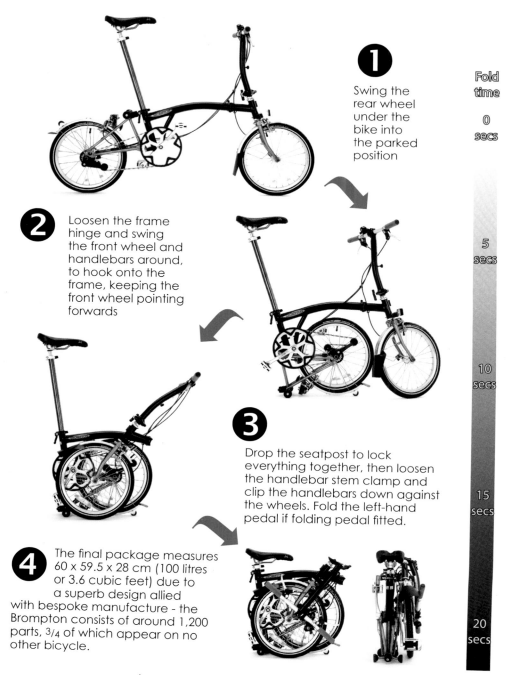

1 Swing the rear wheel under the bike into the parked position

2 Loosen the frame hinge and swing the front wheel and handlebars around, to hook onto the frame, keeping the front wheel pointing forwards

3 Drop the seatpost to lock everything together, then loosen the handlebar stem clamp and clip the handlebars down against the wheels. Fold the left-hand pedal if folding pedal fitted.

4 The final package measures 60 x 59.5 x 28 cm (100 litres or 3.6 cubic feet) due to a superb design allied with bespoke manufacture - the Brompton consists of around 1,200 parts, 3/4 of which appear on no other bicycle.

Fold time

0 secs

5 secs

10 secs

15 secs

20 secs

www.brompton.com Tel: 020 8232 8484

BROMPTON

BICYCLE

David Henshaw

with a foreword by Adam Hart-Davis

2nd Edition

NEW - Factory move, titanium manufacture & more

In 1802 a third Act was necessary 'for amending, widening and keeping in repair the road leading from the 29th milestone at the upper end of Stone Street in the Town of Maidstone...to Tubbs Lake in the parish of Cranbrook'. According to the Act 'the trustees had made great progress but had borrowed considerable sums on the Tolls the greater part of which still remained unpaid'. Since the tolls authorised by the previous Acts had been found insufficient to meet the costs they were again increased. Every horse, mare, gelding mule or other beast laden or unladen but not drawing a vehicle was charged 1¹/2d. If they were pulling any carriage the cost was 4d. Droves of oxen, cows or neat cattle cost 1s.3d per score. Calves, hogs, pigs, swine, sheep or lambs cost 8d. per score. There was a double toll on Sundays and also from 1 October to 1 April for any beast drawing a vehicle carrying hop poles, timber, wood, guns and iron from the Wealden iron industry. These were the autumn and winter months when most damage could be done to the road surface by heavy loads.

There were a number of exceptions. Persons, horses, cattle wagons or other carriages carrying or returning empty from carrying stones, bricks, timber, gravel or other materials for repairing the turnpike road or other parish roads in which any part of the turnpike lay were excused toll. So, too, were seed, hay, turnips, straw and 'corn in the straw' passing to be placed in outhouses, barns or on the lands of their owners. Similarly dung, compost and manure intended for use in local farming also travelled free with the exception of loads of chalk and lime. Animals going to ploughing, shoeing, water or pasture and persons attending divine service, funerals or visiting the sick similarly travelled toll free as did horses and carriages conveying the Royal Mail. Exemption was inevitably given to soldiers on horseback or on the march or those conveying the sick and wounded, ordnance or stores for His Majesty's Forces. While tolls were waived for officers travelling to and from Coxheath Camp and all military eventualities, the trustees were careful not to extend this privilege to the hordes of visitors who came to the Camp in its heyday. On a different level carts belonging to contractors returning vagrants to their rightful place of settlement by order of the magistrates, and persons journeying to vote on parliamentary election days were also spared the purchase of a turnpike ticket.[75]

This Act and another in 1813 appear to have brought some temporary improvement to the road. Dearn, writing in 1814, found that the road from Maidstone to Cranbrook

> with the exception of two miles between Staplehurst and Cranbrook is really a
> very good road... That it is passable by carriages is proved by the circumstances

of a stage coach passing to and fro three times a week for some years past without a singe accident that could be imputed to the road.[76]

Any improvement was short-lived. Further Acts, with their costly expenditure on legal fees, were required in 1834, 1835-36, 1836-37 and 1856. The real problem of the turnpikes was shortage of money. If there was insufficient income to pay the interest on the money borrowed, to pay the officers and also to pay for labour and materials for the road, the sole resource left was the statute labour of the parishioners. Initially this was determined locally by two JPs. Sometimes the parish was glad to compound with the turnpike surveyor for an annual lump sum. On other occasions parish overseers of the poor were glad of the statute labour on a local turnpike to provide work for unemployed parishioners. Statute labour was, however, abolished by the Highways Act 1835. Henceforth the turnpikes had to pay in full for all their labour. By the mid-nineteenth century their plight was intensified by the advent of cheap rail travel. The railway station at Maidstone was opened following the building of the Paddock Wood to Maidstone line. This linked up with the South-Eastern Railway's main line in 1844 whose stations included Headcorn, Staplehurst and Marden. Rail travel was still only for Boughton's wealthy few but it was the thing of the future. Between 1860-1880 the trusts were largely dis-turnpiked and handed over to the appropriate highway boards.[77]

Unbusinesslike and dilatory as the trusts often were they nevertheless gave Kent better roads than it had had before. The precise relationship between Boughton and the Maidstone & Cranbrook trust is not wholly clear since the road ran along the western edge of the parish. Boughton farmers may not have gained all the direct benefits in the form of freedom from toll but they undoubtedly gained indirectly in that they had a quicker and more efficient outlet to Maidstone and the Medway Navigation for their produce. Boughton overseers, too, sold loads of stones to the trustees in the 1820s at 10d. per ton. When the establishment of Coxheath Camp resulted in the upgrading of what had been a track across the Heath to become a stretch of essentially military road, Boughton also gained a direct and easy access to the turnpike and a far easier outlet for bulky heavy goods than by using the old parish roads to Maidstone which ran through the quarries. To the north of the parish a second turnpike, the Maidstone & Biddenden Turnpike, provided another outlet after its creation in 1805. Further east the Ashford & Maidstone Turnpike, opened in 1793, furnished, with its connections, an outlet to the coast. By 1836 daily coaching services linked Maidstone with Cranbrook, Tenterden and Ashford.[78]

The Relief of the Poor in the Eighteenth and Nineteenth Centuries

Two Acts of Parliament passed in 1597 and 1601 provided the basis for English poor law administration for the next 230 years. These laid down that in each parish 'substantial householders' were to be selected annually as overseers of the poor. Their task was to see that the sick, aged and impotent poor were given assistance according to their needs while those who were capable of it were set to work. The necessary funds were to be obtained by a poor rate levied on all inhabitants. Paupers unable to obtain relief or dissatisfied with their relief had the right to appeal to Quarter Sessions.

Further legislation in 1609-10 ordered the building of houses of correction and instructed constables to apprehend all rogues and vagrants and present them to the Justices who would commit them to the house of correction. The most important piece of poor law legislation between 1601 and 1834 was, however, the Act of Settlement 1662. This stipulated that any stranger coming to a parish could be removed by the Justices, upon application by the overseers, to the parish of his/her settlement unless he/she rented a tenement worth £10 a year or found other security to discharge his/her adopted parish from all expense if he/she became 'chargeable' to the poor rate. Determination of a person's settlement was a complex and often hotly-contested issue. A child took its father's settlement if known. Failing that it took its mother's and failing that its place of birth. Subsequently, if the person served an apprenticeship, was hired as a servant for a year, paid the rates of another parish or held a parochial office there it was possible to bring about a change of settlement. Marriage also altered a settlement in the case of a girl. An Act of 1697 made it illegal to remove a migrant until he/she became chargeable providing that a settlement certificate accepting responsibility in that event was brought from the parish of origin and deposited with the overseers. Nevertheless, despite this attempt to restore mobility and protect the labouring poor, illegal removals still took place.

The highest incidence of removals tended to be associated with years of economic difficulty when poor law expenditure was rising. The early 1780s were one such period. In 1781 the Boughton overseers paid 3s.1d. 'for an order to remove Marcy Gore'. Next year they paid James Bonkin (presumably the borsholder) 5s.0d. 'for removing Moore'. On 26 June 1786 the overseers paid 1s.0d. 'for a Warrant for Wm. Noble' and just over a fortnight later he was removed to nearby Leeds. A summons and order of removal 'to carry Martha Wolfe to Wilmington' cost £2.7s.0d. in 1806-07 and there was another flurry of removals in 1808-09 and 1810-11.[79] Large families, which could become a heavy burden upon the rates, and women upon their own, who might be widowed, pregnant or deserted by their husbands, and therefore more likely to become chargeable, were the two categories of pauper most liable to removal.

The earliest guide to the number of persons on or below the poverty line is provided by the Hearth Tax of 1664. Twenty-five (25.7%) of the 97 persons named are marked as 'Not chargeable'. These represented the poor. Since many would have been able bodied, however, they would have had to be found work and not supported out of parochial funds. Thus, while they may not have contributed towards the poor rate neither would they have been expected to draw upon it. Their substantial presence, however, is an indication of the way poverty was growing although it remained relatively small compared with things to come. The growth of poverty also often meant postponement or delay of marriage which, together with the prevalence of 'living in' for farm servants, brought a frightening increase in illegitimacy. Ecclesiastical sanctions against moral offenders were still humiliating and severe. In the eighteenth century parties found guilty of fornication could still be excommunicated. Women only could also be called upon to perform public penance. This involved a public confession during divine service clad only in a white sheet and carrying a white wand. By the seventeenth century moral misdemeanours increasingly involved the civil authorities. In 1665 Thomas Wildes, father of the illegitimate child of Elizabeth Cobducke of Boughton Monchelsea, was ordered at Quarter Sessions to pay 3s. outright to the Boughton overseers and a further 12d. a week for 'as long as the child continues as a charge to the parish'. This was a formidable sum. Nevertheless illegitimacy still increased and between 1814-60 just over one illegitimate child was born on average in Boughton every year. Maintenance of these fell on the parish if the father could not be traced. Boughton's overseers rejected the popular assertion that this system encouraged immorality and the increase of unmarried mothers but in 1834 no fewer than fifteen bastards were in receipt of weekly maintenance payments.

Detailed overseers' accounts have survived for Boughton for 1777-1789 and 1801-1817 only. They illustrate, however, the inexorable growth in expenditure at the close of the eighteenth century and the massive escalation at the beginning of the nineteenth century as the Old Poor Law began to break down. Expenditure began to rise in the severe winters of the 1780s and by 1788-89 exceeded £500 for the first time. We have no figures for the first great dearth of 1795-96 but by the second great dearth of 1799-1802 expenditure had more than doubled to reach £1353. It then fell somewhat until 1809 when it regained its massive proportions rising to £1712 during the harvest crisis of 1812 and remaining high during the post-war depression after 1815. No figures have survived but it was probably increasing again in the late 'twenties and early' thirties when the Old Poor Law came under increasing criticism and the Poor Law Commissioners began their enquiries.[80]

Analysis of the overseers' accounts shows clearly the working of what one historian has called 'a welfare state in miniature'. The largest part of the overseers' expenditure was upon regular payments which were made at first monthly and later weekly to the aged and incapacitated poor and to orphaned and illegitimate children. Recipients also included the heads of one-parent families such as widows, unmarried mothers and deserted wives. When the accounts begin in 1777 there were 24 such regular payments varying from 5s.0d. to 10s.0d. per month. This number of 'pensioners' was approximately the same eight years later. By 1805-06, however, 31 payments were costing the parish £132 regularly and by 1811-12 the figure had increased to 37. Next year, as poverty intensified, there were 48 monthly payments at a total cost of £190.

Apart from regular payments the overseers also distributed casual relief. Their purpose is not always specified but in general these payments were intended to tide the recipient over a personal or family illness, temporary unemployment or sudden need. In 1777 payments were made to 2 widows and to Benjamin Moore 'In need'. By 1833 37 widows were in receipt of fixed weekly payments. £466 was spent upon casual payments alone in 1811-12. Casual payments also included the cost of medical care and pauper funerals and the apprenticeship of pauper children. In 1779 the overseers paid 2s.6d. for a 'midwife' to attend Dame Simmons and in 1783 a boy was given 1s.6d. 'for going to the Doctors 3 times' in an emergency. In 1786 Mary Jenkins was given £1.16s.6d. 'to go to the Hospital'. Unlike some parishes

Boughton does not seem to have made an annual contract with a doctor to care for the poor although a number of paupers were referred to a Doctor Podmore in 1815. In 1835, perhaps as a safeguard after the 1834 Act, an annual subscription of 3 guineas was paid to Maidstone Infirmary and Dispensary. Full use seems to have been made of this facility by the cost-conscious overseers. Ann Town was 'at the Dispensary' for two weeks of that year at a cost of 5s.0d. in contrast to Mary Pierce whose bill from St. Thomas's hospital amounted to £2.13s.3d. the year before. Richard Wood 'going to the Dispensary' received 2s.0d. while a wooden leg was purchased for William Simmonds for an outlay of £2.0.0d. The overseers were obviously also interested in preventative medicine too. On 4 June 1824 William Startup was granted £1.0.0d 'towards smallpox' (inoculation). A fortnight later William May's child got 2s.6d. 'towards cowpox'. Startup was a lucky man. Two years later he was also given 7s.0d. in parochial aid 'towards a truss'. A regular nursing service was provided by the parish widows whose experience of life the overseers used to the full. In October 1777 Dame Barton was paid 'for nursing her own daughter 4 weeks with smallpox'. Dame Bromley received 1s.0d. 'for nursing' the same year. The following year Dame Ashby was granted £1.5s.0d. 'for nursing Bankeses children in smallpox'. Widowed elderly ladies were 'home helps' as well as nurses. Throughout 1786 Dame Ashby was paid regularly 'for doing for William Wenham'. When Wenham's wife, who had been ill for some time, died in August Widow Swift was paid 1s.0d. 'for laying Dame Wenham forth'. In the same way Dame Bromley was paid 'for doing for Joseph Banks' and laying him out upon death. Banks, like many others, received a pauper funeral with 6s.0d. paid by the overseers 'for carrying him to the ground'.

This seems to have been the standard payment for funerals at Boughton in the 1780s. By the nineteenth century the cost of dying had increased. Widow Frid was a woman with a Boughton settlement who was resident at Harrietsham with the blessing of both sets of overseers. When she became ill the Harrietsham overseers allowed her to stay there since Boughton had agreed to meet the expenditure. Her nursing at Harrietsham cost £2.17s.6d. 10s6d. was paid to her Harrietsham landlord, Mr. Shrubsal, for arrears of rent. 3s.0d. was paid for laying her out and 7s.6d. for bringing her 'household' from Boughton for the funeral. 'Beer and meet' for the wake cost 11s.7d. and her 'bering' 15s.8d.

Unless pauper children were helped to self-sufficiency they would be pauperised for life. The principal means of teaching skills to pauper children was apprenticeship.

In rural areas the tendency was to apprentice boys to farmers and girls to service with farmers and for them to be used as cheap labour rather than learn any genuine craft or skill. Few records of apprenticeship have survived at Boughton although we know that the overseers gave every assistance to pauper apprentices since the system could rid them of expensive mouths to feed in the future. In 1807-08, for example, the overseers 'Gave Widow Simmons for to binde her boy Prentice' £2.2s.0d. It was customary also to provide departing apprentices with a suit of clothing. In 1777, for example, Dame Fleet was given 10s.6d. 'for her girl's clothes'. Mrs Baker's boy was given 'two suites to go Apprentice' in 1814.

Since there was sometimes a tendency to spend monetary relief unwisely or upon drink, Boughton overseers, like many elsewhere, also furnished relief in kind in the form of fuel and clothing. Since coal was both scarce and expensive until the nineteenth century Boughton's overseers supplied the poor with winter wood. Large quantities were purchased for this purpose. In the 1780s the local farmers, William Sedgwick and John Tomkin, were the main suppliers sometimes providing between them as many as 700 faggots per year.

Very few Boughton labourers owned their own cottages. All cottages were 'generally exempt from rates' and from at least the second half of the eighteenth century the rents of some parish poor were being paid by the overseers. Ten shillings was paid to Dame Barton to cover Elizabeth Elliott's rent in 1777. £4.10s.0d. was paid to Mrs Simmons 'for Peter Drawbridge rent' in 1785. By 1805 at least 11 pauper rents were being met by the parish. Clothing and shoes were another popular form of practical help. In 1777 Dame Parker received 13s.0d. 'to buy clothes'. A 'paire of draws' for William Symons' cost 2s.8d. in 1785 and 'A pair of stayes for Elizabeth Cheeseman' cost 7s.6d. in 1786. 'A paire of shoes for Benjamin Moore' amounted to 6s.0d. the following year. Money was not spared. In 1805 Widow Sharp's two children were bought '1 round frock, 1 gown, 2 petticoats, 2 change and 2 paire of shoes'. Some 37 children were supplied with shoes and clothing between October and December 1805. A total of 82 children were supplied throughout 1806. On 27 March 1812 the Vestry resolved that:

> In future applications for clothes be rejected. Allowances for each child
> instead under 10 years according to the circumstances of the case.

Nevertheless, Boughton Overseers were keeping a special Clothing Account Book by 1814 and a Select Committee for Managing the Poor still made grants of shoes, stockings, clothing and flannel for shirts to adults and children alike from 1821-1834. In 1822 William Simmons was given a handkerchief and a hat while William Tett, a workhouse inmate, received 'a Roundfrock and a pair of trousers' in 1833. As late as 1842, although it was technically illegal, the Vestry agreed to give Richard Wood 'a suit of clothes for his better appearance at Church'.[81]

In addition to these basic forms of relief in kind parishioners were also given a host of other miscellaneous types of aid. The overseers paid for repairs to cottages and for purchase of furniture. Dame Bromley had 'a bed tick and cord' bought for her in 1777 while 10s.9d. was outlaid upon 'a quilt and sheets for John Bowin'. In 1781 five guineas was spent upon a substitute for William Mannering, who had been pressed into the army, otherwise the parish would become responsible for his wife and family. In 1822 £8.11s.3d. was paid for the discharge of Richard Wood who had enlisted in the Buffs leaving behind a wife and 3 children chargeable to the parish at 9s.0d. per week. Benjamin Banks's bill 'for Thatching' was paid in 1783 and a spinning wheel purchased for Widow Hernden to make her at least partly self-supporting. Benjamin Moore had his 'Poore Cess' (rate) of 3s.6d. paid by the parish since he was unable to meet it himself in 1785. If a parishioner was a member of a friendly society the overseers paid to keep up his membership if he was unable to do so since the club benefits would ultimately save the parish money. In 1821 John Lacy received 10s.0d. 'towards his club'. Four further payments were made towards men's clubs in 1830 and James Simmons was paid 8s.0d. 'towards his club' in 1835. No effort was spared to assist the poor and unemployed to help themselves and thus 'save the poor rate'. Humphrey Thomas was allowed 10s.0d. a week in 1821 'on the rode' (on tramp looking for work) while David Springett in 1830 received £1 'towards his hopping' (hop picking). Half acre allotments were let to the poor at a rent of 20s.0d. to 30s.0d. but free of tithe and tax. There was also a parish plot on what remained of Coxheath after enclosure. This the poor were first set to clear by 'grubbing the stones'. In 1823 10 sacks of potatoes were 'bought of Mr. Tomkin by the overseers at 4s.6d. to plant on the Heath Piece'.[82]

In 1812-13 'John Dadson, No work' was granted 11s.6d. This was unusual since the unemployed poor were generally set to work. Boughton's overseers used neither the Roundsman system, whereby unemployed labourers were sent round the parish farmers to do what work could be found for whatever they chose to pay, nor the Labour Rate system whereby ratepayers directly employed workless labourers in proportion to their rating or the acreage of their farms. An attempt was made to apportion the unemployed among the farmers but it was abandoned as unsuccessful. Boughton overseers, because they did not use these expedients which were widely employed elsewhere in Kent, were obliged to provide their own employment on the parish roads. In 1833 there were some 12 Boughton 'hard-core' unemployed in summer, including many aged and infirm, and as many as 30 workless in winter. Both groups were employed largely in grubbing and breaking stones. William Sunnick was paid 9s.0d. for grubbing 9 cord (a cord was usually 128 cubic feet) of stones and John Crundale 12s.0d. for breaking '18 cord of stones at 8d.' John Cook received only 4s.2d. for 'breaking 5 cord of rock stones at 10d.' Sometimes the men worked alone at stone breaking and sometimes in pairs. In 1834 William Sunnick broke 11 'tuns' in 10 days for 12s.0d. John Petham and John Cook, working in tandem, broke 21 'tuns' in 13 days but were paid only 15s.0d. Boughton overseers did not subsidise wages out of the poor rate through an 'allowance-in-aid-of-wages' as happened in many Kent parishes but an allowance was made on account of large families. It was considered that a labourer could support a wife and three children upon his average earnings if constantly employed. The sum of 1s.6d. per week was then given for every additional child in families above three. It was admitted that in the granting of any relief 'character is always taken into consideration' thus giving the overseers the opportunity to exercise a form of social control.[83]

Thomas Rider and Edward Hodges, who completed Boughton's submission to the Poor Law Commission in 1834, felt that it was 'the young and unmarried labourers who were the most idle and profligate'. Boughton, however, was comparatively slow compared with some Kent parishes, like Headcorn, Benenden and Tenterden, to turn to the solution of emigration. In March 1835 James Kingsnorth was granted £3.0s.0d. by the Vestry 'to go to America'. It was not until 1841 that the Vestry instructed the Churchwardens and Overseers to raise £58 'for the emigration of poor persons settled in the parish and being willing to emigrate'. This sum was to be paid out of the rates or raised for the relief of the poor and to comply with such regulations as the Poor Law Commissioners directed. Two families already wishing to emigrate were said to be William Waterman with his wife and 11 children and William Morris, his wife and 2 children. By this time the New Poor Law had already been in existence for seven years. It is not known whether the two families eventually went.[84]

Boughton by 1784 appears to have taken advantage of Knatchbull's Act 1722 to open a workhouse of its own in order to receive the benefit of 'the work, labour and service of its inmates'. In that year 2s.6d. was paid 'for an oven within the Poor House'. The location of the Boughton Poorhouse is unknown. In any event the building was probably little different from other cottages and the inmates it held were largely women, children, the aged and infirm who were small in number, without supervision, and catered for themselves. It is doubtful if the parish gained much from their labour. By 1790, however, Boughton had become part of the Coxheath Incorporation consisting of nine 'nearly adjacent' parishes with a United Workhouse at Coxheath. The nine parishes were Bearsted, Boughton Monchelsea, East Farleigh, Linton, Loose, Otham, West Farleigh, Hunton and Teston. Formed loosely as a result of Gilbert's Act 1782 the Incorporation was not a properly constituted union and the workhouse was built simply by agreement of the member parishes. Nevertheless it appears to have fulfilled the aims of a workhouse and acted as a deterrent more than many Old Poor Law workhouses did in Kent. In 1802-03 the inmates were employed in making hop sacks. Boughton spent £63.3s.1d.on materials for the workhouse in that year and £43.7s.3d. was recouped from their labour.[85] In 1806-07, Boughton overseers spent 6s.8d. 'Fetching 1 ton of hopbaggin from the workhouse'. When Ashurst Majendie, the Poor Law Commissioner, visited the workhouse in 1834 he was highly complimentary which was unusual:

At Coxheath...is a very well-regulated incorporated workhouse which is distinguished for good management. The good management is probably due to the superintendence of a principal proprietor of the neighbourhood, who acts as chairman at the meetings of the guardians. Formerly the articles of food were furnished by contract but, at present, the master farms the whole establishment at 3s.6d. per head with the profit of the labour; four acres of land are attached to the house and about 18 are hired by the master. The present number of inmates is 90; in winter, sometimes 160; those who are able are set to agricultural work, to quarry stone, which is sold to the (turnpike) commissioners, and to break stones into small pieces for gravel walks; the master is a wheelwright and employs some of the men on his business and as carpenters and sawyers; 2d. in the shilling is allowed to them; if they neglect their work they are taken before the magistrates who sentence them to the treadmill. A clergyman attends on Saturdays and all who are able go to church on Sunday; children are taught to read by a school-mistress who is boarded at the expense of the master. When a family is sent into the house, the man is placed in the male ward, the woman in the female ward and the children in the school; if the children are so young as to require the mother's care they are allowed to be with her at night; in consequence of this regulation families endeavour to get out and seldom remain beyond a few weeks, and many to whom the house is offered refuse to come in, and the confinement and restraint induces young men to find work for themselves. The governor has power of confinement for 24 hours; if any one runs off and is sent back he must undergo this punishment previously to being admitted on the establishment. The diet is the same to all except the sick, to whom tea and sugar are allowed and any food directed by the surgeon; nine parishes are incorporated, and so great has been found the advantage that several other parishes have joined as 'tenant parishes', some of which having small poor-houses, as asylums for the aged, subscribe to this as enabling them to resist the applications of troublesome paupers, the offer of a ticket of admission to the house being relief; the object is not the saving of expense on the individuals but the great efficacy of a well-ordered workhouse in keeping paupers from coming in.[86] (The 'principal proprietor' was Thomas Rider.)

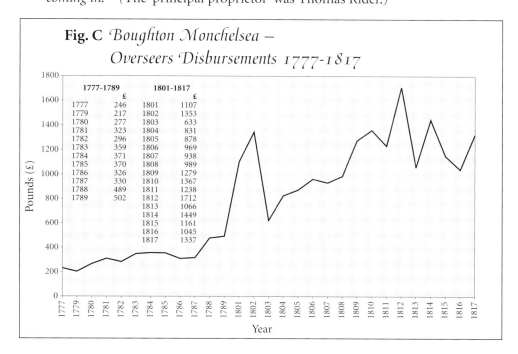

Fig. C *Boughton Monchelsea – Overseers Disbursements 1777-1817*

1777-1789	£	1801-1817	£
1777	246	1801	1107
1779	217	1802	1353
1780	277	1803	633
1781	323	1804	831
1782	296	1805	878
1783	359	1806	969
1784	371	1807	938
1785	370	1808	989
1786	326	1809	1279
1787	330	1810	1367
1788	489	1811	1238
1789	502	1812	1712
		1813	1066
		1814	1449
		1815	1161
		1816	1045
		1817	1337

The Old Poor Law was increasingly criticised nationally and locally for its over-generosity and because it was felt that it sapped the initiative of the poor as poor rates everywhere increased from the last decades of the eighteenth century. In a rural parish like Boughton, with little employment other than agriculture, unemployment and underemployment mounted with the rapid growth of population and the dislocation of farming which followed the French Wars 1793-1815. In a bid to arrest the rising post-war poor law expenditure Boughton had by 1821, like many parishes, decided to employ a paid, full-time Assistant Overseer, Edward Hodges, to keep the accounts and give help to the elected overseers. Hodges, himself, had been an Overseer in 1806, 1807 and 1810. The parish also took advantage of the Sturges Bourne Act 1819 to establish a select vestry or Select Committee for the Management of the Poor which took the decision-making over relief out of the hands of the overseers and was less susceptible to pressure from paupers. The committee consisted of twelve persons including Rev. James Andrews, the vicar; Thomas Rider; A.E. Douce, Esq.; the Overseers and Churchwardens and five Boughton farmers. Hodges attended and minuted the decisions. Meeting initially on Sundays at the Church it had changed its venue within three months to the more convivial surroundings of the Boughton Cock.[87]

At first there was a sharp decrease in expenditure. On 1 May 1815 32 families totalling 64 adults and 141 children had been in receipt of weekly parochial relief. In other words Boughton's 71 ratepayers were by this time maintaining 27% of the population of the entire parish. By March 1823 this had fallen to 18 families representing 36 adults and 82 children. Most of the latter came from large families of four to five children. Pauper numbers had been reduced to some 15% of the total parish population.[88] In the unfavourable economic climate of late 1820s, however, this improvement was difficult to sustain. In 1828 all cottages were assessed and revalued in a desperate attempt to raise more revenue while in 1833, with poor law reform likely to strip parishes of their autonomy, a series of panic measures were instituted by the Committee. Relief was barred for girls remaining at home with their parents at the age of fifteen and for boys at the age of twelve. Nor was relief to be awarded without first discovering the amount earned weekly from the applicant's master. No person was to be employed on the parish roads for a day rate except those who were too old and infirm to be capable of performing a day's work elsewhere. No man working for the parish was, in any event, to be paid more than 1s.6d a day. A maximum of 8d. a cord was to be paid for breaking stones. To try to raise funds from parish work the parish roads were to be scraped by the load and the scapings offered for their manure content at 6d. per cart load to the occupier of the adjoining land. If he refused they were to be offered to any other parishioner. There was also a drive to end fraudulent claims and the Assistant Overseer was ordered to investigate the amount earned by one Thomas May 'lately employed at cutting rags and at the paper mill who has made application constantly for relief'.[89]

It was all in vain. Despite widespread political opposition and direct action in the form of rioting and arson the Poor Law Amendment Act 1834 transferred responsibility for paupers from the parish overseers to elected Boards of Guardians who were directed by a central Poor Law Commission of three members in London. Throughout the country individual parishes were merged into poor law unions. To deter able-bodied paupers and reduce expenditure the 1834 Act stipulated that outdoor relief was to be given in only exceptional circumstances. Otherwise relief was to be provided only within a union workhouse which was made 'less eligible' than the least pleasant way of earning a living outside. There was no rioting or arson in Boughton although there was a considerable amount in Kent. This was possibly because Thomas Rider was one of the Kent Liberal MPs who fought the New Poor Law Bill in Parliament.[90] It was also perhaps because the Coxheath Workhouse was already in may ways a prototype of what the Commissioners intended the new workhouses to become.

The nine parishes of the Coxheath Incorporation became part of the Maidstone Union together with the parishes of Barming (East & West), Maidstone, Marden, Nettlestead, Staplehurst and Yalding. Urban Maidstone, which felt it should have constituted a union in its own right, continued to protest into the 1880s that it had nothing in common with the rural parishes. Its protests remained unheard. A new workhouse, intended to hold 600 paupers, was commenced in 1837 'on an elevated and healthy spot about four miles from Maidstone' at Coxheath. The 'large and substantial' brick building, costing over £7,000, opened for the reception of paupers in March 1838 and stood about a quarter of a mile from the old workhouse of the Coxheath Incorporation on the East Farleigh road.[91]

Meanwhile a new and much harsher regime began. Boughton in 1832 had only sent an average of 8 inmates into the United Workhouse at Coxheath during the year. By 1835 the parish had already committed 16 paupers as the procession to the old workhouse began even before the new workhouse building had been started. Four non-resident paupers were denied relief altogether. A fifth, Ann Town, was brought from Maidstone, where she had been living, in a horse and cart to be incarcerated in the workhouse the vestry having resolved that she be granted no further out-relief. Three other paupers had their relief terminated while it was decided that an old man employed in breaking stones should be found work as near as possible to the Quarries so that he could still help to earn his keep. Fourteen paupers, previously relieved in cash, were given instead between two and six gallons of flour each to comply with the new poor law regulations. All occasional relief was henceforth to be given in flour to persons with large families. The miller and the various Boughton grocer shops were instructed to supply flour in turn each quarter while the overseers were ordered to monitor total expenditure every six months and 'lay it before the parish meeting'. Social control was tightened by the resolution that future relief should be denied to persons 'who do not send their children...to Church regularly or to some other place of public worship'.[92]

These were the temporary regulations devised by Boughton until such time as the new workhouse was built and the newly-constituted Board of Guardians met. They nevertheless reflect the much more rigorous regime which the Commissioners required. The Guardians held their first meeting on 13 September 1835. Boughton's first guardian, Thomas Cull, was a farmer like most rural guardians although Thomas Rider, as a magistrate, also sat initially as an ex-officio guardian and presumably did his best to serve the interests of the poor as well as the ratepayer. Cull was succeeded in the 1840s by Edward Beard of Wierton Farm, Boughton Bottom, who gave way in his turn to Thomas Hayes of Charltons. In Kent's new workhouses cruelty tended to be psychological and insensitive rather than deliberate and physical. Maidstone union workhouse was involved in no major scandals and as time passed board and ratepayers were prepared to circumvent poor law regulations on behalf of their own poor. Nonetheless, workhouse life was far from pleasant and its stigma remained very real many years after the Poor Law ended in 1929.[93]

The 'Battle of Boughton Quarries' 1830

Unemployment, underemployment and low wages had been increasing at an alarming rate since the post-war depression of 1815. It was widespread throughout the parishes of rural Kent and was compounded by the rapid growth of population. Distress peaked when the bad harvest of 1829 combined with the severe winter of 1829-30. A wet summer followed and the hop crop failed. Maidstone was 'infested with radicals' prepared to take any opportunity to carry their message of parliamentary reform to the countryside. Some Kent labourers may have seen political reform as a prerequisite to improving their existence but the main motivating force which sparked off the arson, machine breaking and wage riots of 1830 was 'great and dire distress'. When asked in 1832 by the Poor Law Commissioners for the causes of 'the Agricultural Riots and Burning of 1830 and 1831', known as the Swing Riots, Thomas Rider and Edward Hodges, responded unhesitatingly 'in a great measure actual distress'.[94]

Boughton was one of many Kent rural parishes which admitted substantial winter unemployment intensified by the farmers' use of threshing machines which robbed the labourers of their only winter living. At the end of May 1830 the overseers and churchwardens of some 21 Kent parishes, including Boughton Monchelsea, Chart Sutton, Thurnham, Headcorn, Staplehurst and Marden met in the *Bell Inn*, Maidstone to appoint a deputation to the Lords of the Treasury to inform them of the overwhelming distress which farmers and their labourers were suffering and to request immediate assistance. Many parishes were without sufficient corn to feed the inhabitants until the next harvest while some ratepayers could no longer pay the poor rate.[95] There had already been sporadic outbreaks of rick burning since 1827. The summer of 1830 saw a series of alarming fires spreading from West Kent followed by the nightly destruction of threshing machines against which the authorities were powerless. In late October large bodies of labourers began to march from parish to parish exacting money from landowners and farmers and demanding work and increased wages. One large mob marched through Lenham, Hollingbourne, East Sutton and Langley. It was led by three Maidstone radicals. Adams and Patman were shoemakers while Halliwell was a journeyman tailor.[96]

At Langley, Adams told the son of the local rector that if they were not granted their rights they would 'bedew the country with blood...pull down the house...and build up the New with honest materials'. On 29 October the mob visited the Cornwallis and Rider estates while Thomas Rider and a second local magistrate, Major Best, were in Maidstone vainly trying to persuade an assembly of farmers to enrol as special constables. While the meeting was proceeding the magistrates were informed that 500-600 men were assembling at Boughton Monchelsea Quarries in order to march on Maidstone. Another band was marching from Thurnham to join them. Accordingly between two and three o'clock in the afternoon five county magistrates, including Best and Rider, left with the Mayor of Maidstone and a detachment of 30-40 soldiers headed by Colonel Middleton, commander of the cavalry depot.[97]

The party proceeded at a brisk pace towards Boughton; and on its arrival at the well-known quarries a large body of labourers was discovered about a quarter of a mile distant. The cavalry were then ordered to conceal themselves behind a little eminence in the neighbourhood lest their appearance should... contradict the conciliatory language by which the Magistrates hoped to bring about the dispersion of the mob. The Magistrates then advanced... and soon came up with the men. Mr Ryder, who was known to the greater number of them, spoke to them in the mildest possible manner and enquired the purpose of their assembling together. Three fellows, who appeared to direct the movements of the band... made use of the most inflammatory language. Some of their companions, less violently disposed, declared that their families were starving and they had taken that mode of proclaiming their suffering...[98] 'We want bread, we want work and to be paid sufficient to keep our families'. One of them stepped forward as spokesman... and being carried on the shoulders of his companions (to put him at the same level as the mounted magistrates) spoke about the difficulties of the poor in a very impressive manner. The company, he said, were honest and industrious men, desirous of providing for their families... but, finding it impossible, they met thus to draw the attention of the magistrates. These people want bread and not powder and shot; we blame not the farmers, they are oppressed with enormous taxes and cannot pay the labourer... The magistrates peremptorily asked them to disperse or the Riot Act would be read and the military called upon...[99] One of the ringleaders was then seized by W.H. Gambier, Esq.; our worthy

*Mayor,... acting as a special constable, immediately seized his companion.
The third ringleader was also taken into custody. This display of authority
surprised the mob; and it is probable that they might have made some use
of the heavy bludgeons they carried had not the cavalry, according to
previous concert, appeared at the top of the eminence. The cry of the 'Red
Coats are coming' had an electrical effect upon the mob and in about ten
minutes... they rapidly disappeared.*[100]

The three radicals were placed in a carriage and carried to the county gaol. On
Sunday evening about twelve o'clock two companies of Dragoon guards from
Epsom marched into Maidstone with two cannon and were followed next morning
by a detachment of two hundred of the 81st regiment of foot from Chatham. A
meeting of magistrates was held at the same time to provide measures to preserve
the public peace and 'for the employment of the labouring classes at full and
sufficient wages'. The Justices also ordered prompt relief to be administered to those
'poor persons who from age, sickness, accident, infirmity or the number of their
family' were in serious need. These measures were temporary and were
discontinued as soon as possible. The 'Battle of Boughton Quarries' did not end the
labourers' disturbances. Incendiarism and machine breaking continued in some
parts of Kent until 1832. The prompt action in the Quarries, however, quoshed a
potentially dangerous situation which could have become extremely serious in
Mid-Kent. Thomas Rider, caught in an invidious situation at Boughton Quarries,
continued to give his parliamentary support to the labourers' cause. Presenting a
petition from the agricultural labourers of Rolvenden in 1833 he again emphasised
that 'the cause of the distress... arises from want of employment and suitable
remuneration for their labour to enable them to obtain the necessaries of life...'
How many Boughton labourers were present at the Quarries it is impossible to tell.
Certainly the fact that Rider was so well-known among the crowd suggests that at
least there were some. Like many other Kent gentry Rider hired two watchmen
named Brooker and Ralph to watch over his mansion during the Swing
disturbances. He need not have bothered. The only trouble at Boughton
Monchelsea Place was created by two Maidstone men, who were apprehended
stealing Rider's apples from an oasthouse at Christmas 1830, one of whom
fractured Brooker's skull. While the surrounding parishes suffered from arson and
machine breaking the only fire at Boughton was the accidental destruction of a
large part of St. Peter's Church. [101]

Friendly Societies and Self-Help

Friendly societies were developed largely by working men to provide themselves with some security against the poverty created by illness and death. Whether a society existed in Boughton prior to 1834 is not known. Certainly Boughton's overseers thought it worthwhile to keep up the membership of those who belonged to a 'club' when they fell upon hard times since friendly society benefits were a valuable means of helping to relieve pressure on the poor rates.[102] The passing of the 1834 Poor Law Amendment Act saw the creation of many new friendly societies since the working classes feared that the effects of the new Act would be too awful to contemplate for the poor man obliged to seek parish relief. It was no coincidence that Boughton's first recorded benefit society – the Hand-in-Hand Benefit Society – was established in 1834. Like all societies it provided a strong element of conviviality and still existed in 1860 when it celebrated its annual feast with a church service followed by a parade through the parish and a dinner at the *Wheelwright's Arms*.[103]

The Albion Inn. In 1857 the landlady cleared the bar by discharging a pistol at a troublesome customer. Six years later it became the meeting place of the Boughton branch of the Ancient Order of Foresters friendly society.

Three years later it had been superseded by a Boughton branch of the national Ancient Order of Foresters, entitled the Court of 'Village Pride'. Founded with only three members by Thomas Boulden, landlord of the *Albion Inn* which became its Court House, the branch had swollen to 140 by 1866. To commemorate the Annual Festival the brethren gathered in the forenoon at the *Albion* and led by the 1st Kent Volunteer Band paraded to the *Cock* returning to their Court House to dine in the evening upon a meal provided by their host and first member. Three years later membership had risen yet again to 169 and the annual dinner was taken by kind permission of J. W. Braddick in the grounds of Boughton Mount. By 1910, when the Boughton Foresters celebrated their 47th anniversary at Linton Park, what had begun as their annual feast had become the principal bank holiday attraction of the district. On Sunday evening the members assembled with their banner in large numbers and full regalia for their church parade. They were joined by members of other branches from Leeds and Marden and headed by Maidstone Borough Band processed from the *Albion* through the village to the Church. Next morning the members and band assembled at the club house and spent the morning visiting their leading supporters including G. Foster Clark, W. Skinner, H.E. Tillman, M.A. Atkins, C. Smith, E.K. Corbett, and F.S.W. Cornwallis. The many attractions at Linton Park in the afternoon included a cricket match between Linton and Boughton and a goal-running match between Boughton and Smarden. The Kentish Bijou Concert Party gave three stage performances of songs and instrumental selections. The Maidstone Band played at intervals and there was dancing in the evening. The branch was in a good position financially with a membership of 298 at an average age of 42 years. A juvenile branch contained 22 members. Despite payment of £424 in sickness benefits and £93 in funeral benefits the Sick & Funeral Fund was £5,567 in credit. The branch had £2,724 invested in freehold property in Maidstone, Loose and Snodland.[104]

Initiation was at first heavily in favour of married men. Of the 48 members received into the branch between May and November 1863 75% were married. This preference was soon reversed, particularly after married men were required to produce a medical certificate regarding their spouse's health. When the initiation record ends in 1875 of an overall total of 183 members accepted 81.4% were single. Most, too, were young. 59.2% were aged 18-20 years as opposed to 29.6% who where between 21-29 years. Only 11.2% fell into the category of 30-39 years. Since the Ancient Order of Foresters was a national society members were accepted from outside Boughton. In the first intake 48% were from within the parish while 52% came from outside. As time went on the gap widened and by 1875 63.5% of all membership was drawn from beyond Boughton's boundaries as opposed to 36.5% from within. Most 'outsiders' were from nearby parishes. 19% were from Loose and 14.8% from Maidstone. Only 3.7% were from outside Kent. Most 'outsiders', apart from those from neighbouring parishes, had transferred their membership from another branch following a change of job P.C. John Wood of the Kent Constabulary, had already been taken by his work to Eastry, Boxley and Chatham before his initiation at Boughton. In the same way other members, anxious to keep up their membership, came from places as far as distant as Wandsworth and Warwickshire.[105]

The majority of members (58.6%) were labourers. The remaining 41.4% covered some 35 different occupations. 5.9% were gardeners and 5.3% were grooms. Bricklayers, blacksmiths, carpenters and wheelwrights together accounted for a further 12%. A coachman, two footmen, a grocer from the Quarries, a gamekeeper from Willington Street, a 'male domestic servant' and an engine driver were among the more unusual members. Approximately 30% of members were lost between 1863-76. 18.8% were suspended for non-payment of dues, a further 4.8% died, 2.8% were 'cleared' to join elsewhere and 1.7% withdrew. Four members emigrated and two, including the secretary, schoolmaster Thomas Gandy, were convicted of embezzlement.[105]

Interpretation of the rules was generous. In December 1905 William Roberts, three quarters in arrears through unemployment, was informed by the Committee that if he could pay his dues for one quarter they would meet them for two. Andrew Graves, another member unable 'to square the club', was re-instated and his fine paid. Assistance was given to members needing 'a little help' as late as 1907 but with the Old Age Pensions Act in August 1908 the society, fearing loss of members, began to interpret the rules in a much harsher fashion.[106]

The Management Committee was enlarged in August 1908 in order to put the claims of members living at a distance under closer supervision. In the same month members receiving sick pay were required to produce a certificate signed by their doctor each week and two committee members were chosen to visit them in doubtful cases. Two members – one living at Hastings and the other at Clerkenwell – were found to have infringed the rules whilst receiving sick pay and were fined and suspended until the fines were paid. Two unemployed members were refused relief because they were not believed to be deserving cases. Members who had achieved the age of 65 years had been relieved of paying further contributions to the sick and funeral fund in 1904, but owing to the decrease in funds the over 65s had to pay once more in 1909. Nevertheless, there was sufficient money available for 'a little black to be obtained to put on the club banner to show respect to the late King'. 1911, however, saw 14 members 'on the funds' increasing to 23 by 1912, and 29 by April 1913. At the same time the society had to contend with the impact of the introduction of compulsory, state-aided insurance against sickness and unemployment in a small number of trades by the Insurance Act 1911. This Act created such confusion that the secretary was granted additional pay for the extra work it involved. A Juvenile Section to provide additional members at the age of sixteen had been formed as early as 1904. This section now underwent a revision of its rules to induce young lads to join. Despite further pressure from the Unemployment Insurance Act 1920, which insured all workers against unemployment who were covered by the Health Insurance scheme, the Foresters were still in 1931 one of the most valued village institutions.[107] Their appeal, however, was not universal:

> My husband belonged to the club; but they 'shared out'... and it came to an end We wouldn't belong to the Foresters, you must be much grander to belong to those clubs,

stated a labourer's wife from Loose to the Commission on the Employment of Children, Young Persons and Women in Agriculture 1867.

Only about 12.2% of Boughton males were members in the 1870s and the remainder, when sick or unemployed, had to seek relief from the Thrift Club which met at the *Cock* in 1912 or the Slate Club which met at the *Albion* in 1921. The other alternatives were the Maidstone Poor Law Union Workhouse at Coxheath or charities like the Soup Kitchen on the Green, which was particularly useful in harsh winters when work was brought to a standstill. Started in 1853 this charity in 1886 was managed by James Wood and its funds maintained from public subscriptions collected by Albert Rolfe, the village schoolmaster.[108]

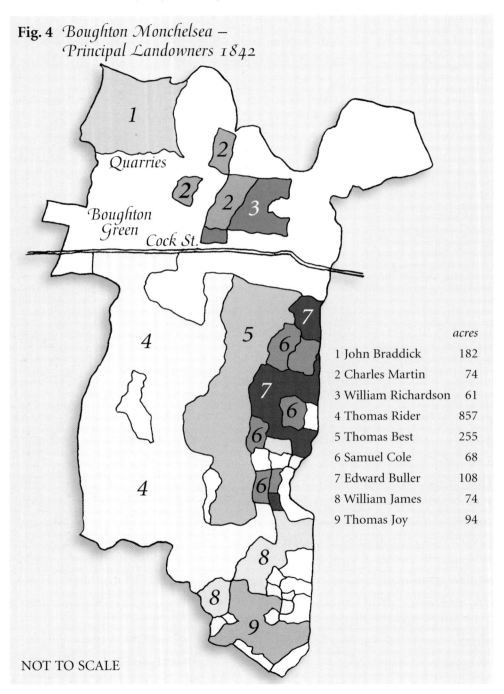

Fig. 4 Boughton Monchelsea –
Principal Landowners 1842

Quarries

Boughton
Green

Cock St.

		acres
1	John Braddick	182
2	Charles Martin	74
3	William Richardson	61
4	Thomas Rider	857
5	Thomas Best	255
6	Samuel Cole	68
7	Edward Buller	108
8	William James	74
9	Thomas Joy	94

NOT TO SCALE

Land Ownership, Occupation and Use in the Nineteenth Century

The common wasteland of Coxheath was finally enclosed in 1817 following an Act of Parliament in 1814. The heath covered land in Loose, Linton, Hunton, East and West Farleigh in addition to Boughton. At Boughton, piecemeal encroachment meant that only 128 acres remained for allocation between the 56 landowners concerned. William Murton of Tunstall and Robert Rugg of Detling were the two gentlemen selected to administer the enclosure assisted by Abraham Purshouse Driver, Land Surveyor, from Southwark. Their task was to resolve differences between the landowners and re-allocate the land which had to be viewed, surveyed and valued. The Commissioners were empowered to stop-up or divert roads and footways and since enclosure expenses were shared proportionately were authorised to levy a rate. By the time all this was satisfactorily completed some three years had elapsed.

Enclosure of the Heath paved the way for increased consolidation of the land into the hands of a few large landowners. Most of the land was shared between those who had previously held grazing rights. Sixty acres (46.8% of the total) went to Thomas Rider and Francis Hubble Douce of Boughton Mount. The former, as Lord of the Manor, received just over 34 acres. The latter got 25 acres. Six other landowners were awarded 35 acres in portions ranging between three and eleven acres and eleven received collectively some nineteen acres in parcels of one to two acres. Thirty-seven landowners lost their common grazing rights for pieces measuring under an acre each and totalling between them some fourteen acres.

By the time of the Tithe Apportionment 1842, nine landowners owned between them some 80% of the entire parish. Sixty-one other landowners held the remaining 20%. The biggest individual landowner was Thomas Rider of Boughton Monchelsea Place whose 851 acres represented 38.6% of the parish. Thomas Rider farmed 551 acres himself until his death in 1847. His successors were non-resident until 1902. This example was followed by John W. Braddick on his 182 acres at Boughton Mount while Thomas F. Best, who owned 255 acres at Wierton Place, farmed 113 of them. Smaller owner-occupiers were Samuel Cole (Wierton Hill), Thomas Joy (Coombe Garden) and William Tomkin (Tilts). The larger landowners also rented to tenant farmers. Rider leased 146 acres at Charltons Farm to Thomas Hayes and Best 142 acres at Boughton Bottom to Edward Beard while Thomas Joy leased 64 acres at River Farm to John Highwood. Edward Buller, who farmed no land himself in Boughton, leased his 108 acres at East Hall Farm to Stephen Tompkin.[109]

George Buckland, writing on Kent agriculture in 1845 when farming in general had recovered from the depression after the Napoleonic Wars, eulogised about the agricultural condition of Mid-Kent.

> More has been done to increase the fertility of the soil within these last ten years than within the other thirty...Draining has been done... On well-managed estates every yard of woodland and nooks and corners of fields are filled up and planted with wood, the hop grounds rendering the growth of poles a prime consideration. This part of the county stands unrivalled for hedge management... The beasts and immense productiveness of this district must be seen before it can be understood... There are some localities...in which a large proportion of the tillers of the soil are also its owners... Taking... altogether the range and variety of its products there cannot be found any spot to compare with it in the United Kingdom. It has been truly designated 'the garden of England'...[110]

Boughton Monchelsea answered this description in many respects. Both its landowners and its farmers were hailed for their agricultural improvement in the early Victorian period. Edward Beard of Boughton Bottom was noted for his stock breeding and the production of fine swine. Thomas Rider was renowned for his chestnut plantations, which made fine hop poles, while the late John Braddick of Boughton Mount was celebrated for his knowledge of fruit especially pears. His son, J.W. Braddick, stocked his estate at enormous expense 'with the rarest and choicest fruit trees' and 'scarcely ever fails to win prizes for pears at horticultural shows'. While Braddick was a member of the Horticultural Society, George Smith of Lyewood House, another of Boughton's improving farmers, was elected a member of the Royal Agricultural Society.[111] With the example of these agricultural reformers before them Boughton's farmers prospered during the decades of 'high farming' 1850-1870. Their principal crops were corn, hops and fruit. The hops were picked largely by transient 'hoppers' who came each year from London. By Buckland's time the mid-Kent parishes – among which Boughton, Linton, Loose, the Suttons and the Farleighs are mentioned as 'the best adapted localities' – were already supplying London as well as Maidstone with 'near two-thirds of home grown fruit', and it had become common to cultivate hops, apples and filberts on the same ground.[112]

In 1842 38.4% of Boughton's 2,200 acres were put to arable usage including some 220 acres of hop grounds. The latter represented just over a quarter of the area under arable cultivation. A further 28.9% of the land was meadow or pasture but only 156 acres or 7.2% was used for growing fruit. All the major farms were mixed and increasingly Boughton farmers began to grow larger amounts of hops and fruit, and later cob nuts, at the expense of corn.

In the 1870s depression conditions returned and in the years that followed farmers had to contend with an unusual number of poor seasons, several serious outbreaks of animal disease and much increased foreign competition in corn and wool. Commissioners who investigated the depression, however, drew a distinction between those farmers, dependent chiefly on sheep and corn and those who grew hops and fruit. 'Corn, I was told', reported the assistant commissioner who investigated the Maidstone district, 'pays no rent whilst hops and fruit have enabled many a man to weather the storm who might otherwise have gone under...On the corn-growing farms as distinguished from the hop farms the depression is sorely felt'.[113] Outside the hop and fruit districts the distress was severe. Inside these districts the impact of the depression, although still serious, nevertheless appears to have been lighter.

Significantly *Kelly's Directory 1867* lists 11 of Boughton's farmers as 'farmers and hop growers' as opposed to 3 who were just 'farmers'. Samuel Beadle of Lewis Court is described as 'farmer and fruit grower' and William Skinner, junior as 'farmer, hop and fruit grower'. In the *Post Office Directory 1878* the chief crops of the parish were listed as 'hops, fruit and corn' in that order. Eight of Boughton's farmers, were described as 'Farmers and hop growers' and a further four as 'Farmers and fruit growers'. By 1882 Edward Beard of Wierton Farm is listed as 'farmer, hop grower and fruit salesman at Covent Garden'. In the 1890s these crops were still dominant but by 1938 *Kelly's Directory* suggests that cob nuts, listed as Boughton's fourth crop as early as 1909, were beginning to challenge hops. Large areas of cob nut plantations disappeared, however, during World War II as part of the 'Dig for Victory' campaign and were never restored.

The Condition of the Agricultural Labourer in the Victorian Era

Throughout the Victorian Era Boughton Monchelsea was an agricultural parish. Seventy per cent of the local labour force was employed in agriculture in 1841 including 176 (59%) who were employed as agricultural labourers. 228 persons (nearly 55%) were employed in agriculture ten years later. One hundred and eighty-six (44%) were agricultural labourers who worked for the 21 landowners and farmers who cultivated the land. Farming remained the principal employer in 1871 and again in 1881, when it provided work for 230 persons or 48.5% of the total labour force. In both census years 32% of that labour force still consisted of agricultural labourers.[114] Not until 1891 did the number of agricultural labourers begin to show any significant decline with the advent of steam-driven machinery.

Until then farming was extremely labour intensive. In 1851, even with the use of horse power, a large force of agricultural labourers was still required and Boughton's 13 principal farmers hired 159 men and 22 'mates' (boys) to carry out the farm work. Among the big farmers Braddick hired 25 men and 7 boys and Beard at Wierton St. 21 men and 3 boys. Thomas Hayes of Charltons Farm kept the largest single labour force of 34 men and 6 boys although he also seems to have taken over the running of Boughton Place Farm as well after the death of Thomas Rider. In 1881 the same 13 farms gave work to 179 labourers and 39 boys. Although the steam age had begun, the demand for labour, in some cases, had increased. John Braddick, for example, now hired 41 men and 7 mates. The 1851 census recorded 186 agricultural labourers living in Boughton Monchelsea parish. In 1881 there were still more labourers than jobs although the margin was not as great. Throughout the century then Boughton had a constant pocket of labourers who were unemployed or underemployed. While the labourer in work lived always on the breadline those without work fell below it.

Steam power was in use at Boughton by the 1880s

but nevertheless horse power was still in widespread use in the 1930s.

The situation was compounded by the disappearance of the system of annually-hired farm servants, who 'lived in' the farmhouse with their masters, which had flourished in the previous century. These, by mid-century, had been replaced by day labourers who were unpaid in wet weather. They no longer lived with the farmer but instead were boarded out; housed in rented or tied cottages; or else lived in overcrowded dwellings in the various hamlets with their parents, even after marriage. Thirteen Boughton agricultural labourers lived in lodgings in 1851 and many more in parental homes. Eleven only 'lived in'. Thirty years later resident farm servants had all but disappeared completely. [115]

> *...In no district in England is the agricultural labourer better, if so well-paid as in the hop districts of Mid-Kent,* wrote Buckland in 1845. *Twelve shillings a week even in winter; while for the greater part of the rest of the year he has well-paid piece work which, with his double harvest* (corn together with hops and fruit*) for himself, wife and children, render his lot, with sobriety and good conduct, one of comparative comfort and happiness.*[116]

There were worse-paid areas but the case was overstated. The day labourer earned on average 14s.0d. a week. A man with a wife and four children spent this as follows:

6 gallons of flour x 1s.5d.	8s.6d
Rent	2s.0d
Fuel	2s.0d
Benefit Club	0s.6d
Money left for meat, cheese, soap, tea, candles, salt.	1s.0d
Total:	14s.0d

There was no margin for savings. A slight increase in prices or a reduction in wages could plunge a family into poverty overnight. In these circumstances fresh meat was virtually unknown and what little there was – usually pork – was eaten by the husband and older boys who were the bread winners. Bread was extremely coarse and baked in large loaves in the village baker's oven. The wife and younger children usually subsisted on a dish of potatoes surmounted by a lump of lard and with a pinch of salt; coarse porridge; or bread and treacle. It was not unusual for a man to go to work in the fields with a raw onion and a piece of dry bread as his only sustenance. The discovery of the emaciated corpse of a vagrant in a barn at Boughton in the winter of 1860 was a stark reminder that it was still possible to die of starvation in Victorian England. Petty theft of agricultural produce, therefore, was commonplace as was poaching despite the severity of the Game Laws. The latter only encouraged violent resistance to arrest. In 1861 Henry Collison, a member of a Boughton Monchelsea family, was involved in a poaching affray while in January 1870 Frederick and John Oliver, two Boughton labourers, were each fined 40s.0d. for poaching rabbits in the woodland of Boughton Monchelsea Place. As they left Maidstone Sessions House their father, Charles Oliver, who worked for the Boughton farmer, Mr. Whyman, promised Robert Gandy, the prosecuting gamekeeper, that 'he would wring his nose from his face before he got home that night'.[117] It is noticeable that each census from 1841-71 included a small number of aged paupers who were still described as 'agricultural labourers'. In 1841 three of the four, including a woman, were aged eighty. A similar group re-appeared ten years later. These octogenarians, fearful that they might have to enter the workhouse, with its dreaded stigma, were still trying desperately to eke out a living.

Nor was any consolation to be found in living conditions. Boughton's housing stock had failed to keep abreast of population growth. In 1758 Rev. Peter Wade reported that there were 'near 100 houses dispersed over the Parish'. Almost fifty years later in 1806 James Andrew, his successor, recorded an increase of only thirty dwellings. Boughton's farmers may have deliberately restricted the building of new cottages to prevent newcomers gaining settlements and becoming an increasing burden upon the Poor Law. The early decades of the nineteenth century, however, saw a rapid expansion of working class housing. By 1841 the parish had 220 dwellings but they were still insufficient to comfortably house the growing population and, thereafter, the expansion ceased. Only one additional house had been constructed by 1851 and a further 25 by 1871.[118] Many of the existing houses were timber-framed, as much as four hundred years old, and in a bad state of repair. This applied particularly to the cottages rented by the poor which were largely in Church Street and the Quarries.

> *Cottages in this part are bad generally,* stated Charles Whitehead in 1867.
> *The sanitary arrangements are horrible and the homes of the working man
> so contrived as to sap the foundation of morality, religion and health. In
> number insufficient,* confirmed the Rev. S. Shepherd, vicar of Boughton,
> *they mostly have two bedrooms...Rents 2s. to 3s. a week. Some of the men
> have to work a mile and a half from their homes.*[119]

Shortage of housing produced desperate overcrowding. In 1851 44 (42%) of the 104 households of farm labourers numbered six persons or more. Consequently adolescent males and females often shared bedrooms while their parents slept with the younger children. By 1841 housing shortage had even brought about the partition of some farmhouses into tenements. Holbrook Farm was occupied by William Daw, agricultural labourer, his wife and 6 children. Bessels Farm was subdivided among the families of 3 farm labourers while Tanyard Farmhouse was also split between 3 families. Rabbits Cross appears to have been divided between the farmer, Ralph Gibson, his household and the families of two agricultural labourers 'living in'. A third farm labourer and his family occupied a separate part of the dwelling. Knowlesden Farm, in 1851, was occupied by 2 agricultural labourers and their families of eight and nine respectively. A further two agricultural labourers' families were the occupants of Parsonage Farm.

The condition of the agricultural labourer worsened with the onset of the depression in agriculture which lasted from about 1870 to the First World War. In March 1866 a crowded meeting of agricultural labourers from the Maidstone district met at the *Castle Inn* in Week Street, Maidstone, to discuss their low wages. The 400-500 labourers present included among others, representatives from Bearsted, Otham, the Farleighs, Sutton Valence, Chart Sutton, Coxheath, Leeds and Boughton Monchelsea. Most of these villages established branches of the short-lived Farm Labourers' Protection Society. The Boughton branch met at the *Rose* beerhouse kept by Charlotte Mannering. Its secretary was Charles Oliver, father of the poachers mentioned earlier, who seems to have been something of a natural rebel. Proposals that there should be an increase of 2d. in the shilling on piece work and that work should end at 4.00pm. on Saturdays with 4d. per hour overtime thereafter were passed unanimously and a memorial to that effect sent to 150 farmers. The memorial was ignored and when some labourers were discharged for signing it the union collapsed.[120]

As the depression deepened landowners and farmers began to further reduce wages and labourers gave vent to their feelings in the Press.

> *...We are now getting our wages lowered to 12s.0d. a week, that is if it don't rain when we get stopped our time we lose,* (read a letter from a farm labourer at Loose). *The farmers say they can't 'ford to pay more so we must starve. I've got four children and my wife to keep and pay 1s.9d. rent per week which master always stops out of my wages so I got 10s.3d. to keep us upon. Does he expect us to work when we don't get enough to eat and I don't hear of him taking the horses' grub off when things don't pay.*

> *I can bear out the remarks of your correspondent last week as to the present distress among the agricultural labourers with every prospect of it getting worse* (stated another letter signed 'A sufferer Boughton Monchelsea). *During the past two or three weeks the labourers of Messrs. Hodsall of Loose and Braddick of Boughton Monchelsea and landowners of other districts have reduced their labourers' wages 2s.0d. per week. It is not long since the rents of labourers' cottages were increased 6d. per week and although they have reduced the wages they have refused to reduce the rents. When men are driven to the extremes of starvation can it be wondered that the labourers poach a rabbit or two? I would ask any person if my noble lord of Linton should have thousands of rabbits upon his grounds reared for the purposes of sport and no one to be permitted to shoot them – destroying as they do the food of the poor...It is evident that the landed interest and their farm holders are determined to starve the people into crime. The best plan*

would be for the whole of the labourers' families to throw themselves upon the (poor law) *union. We should then see what the farmers should do without the labourers. It wants more uniting among the labourers as the farmers could not allow the soil to remain untouched.*[121]

In 1872 Alfred Simmons, editor of the *Kent Messenger*, responded to the labourers' plea for unity by organising the Kent & Sussex Labourers' Association. A branch of the new union was established at Boughton by 1876 where it confronted a Boughton Monchelsea Farmers' Club established five years before. It was much more circumspect about its activities than the branch of the earlier Protection Society which suggests that its members may have feared victimisation. While other branches of the Kent & Sussex openly advertised their meetings, meeting places and the names of their secretaries in their newspaper, the *Kent & Sussex Times*, the Boughton branch did none of these things. A typical notice to members published in 1878 read as follows;

The Boughton Monchelsea secretary demands all members to attend at the meeting house on Saturday 2 March.

The branch, however, was much longer-lived than its predecessor surviving until at least 1884 when its members attended a franchise demonstration in Maidstone to secure the vote for agricultural labourers. One of Simmons' intentions was to secure both publicity and respectability for the union by means of a series of special church services for the membership of all branches. Members attended in full union regalia and collections were donated to charity. While the clergymen of Linton, Loose, Farleigh, and other parishes throughout Kent, refused to open their churches for this purpose, the vicars of Boughton Monchelsea and Sutton Valence agreed. After this it was no longer possible for the Boughton trade unionists to remain in any way concealed.[122]

The Ragstone Quarries

A band of ragstone about thirty miles from east to west runs through central Kent from Hythe to Westerham with its widest part in the Maidstone area. Although Boughton Monchelsea was predominately an agricultural parish its wealth was enhanced by the productivity of its ragstone quarries which were in use from Roman times. 'Providing the finest quality of stone' they were considered by John Whichcord, the Maidstone architect, to be 'the best ragstone quarries in Kent'. Their fifteen different varieties of stone had their own characteristics and uses. 'Kent Rag', second only to granite, is named from the way in which the stone breaks in a 'rough or ragged' fashion. The value of *hassock* and *whiteland bridge* as building materials, withstanding exposure to weather, has long been recognised. Other beds furnished paving kerbs, flagstones, headstones, 'chimney pieces' and roadstone or were used in the making of concrete and lime. 'Rag' from the 'Stone Hills' was probably an Imperial monopoly under the Romans who were the first to engage in large-scale quarrying in England. In Roman times stone was needed both for road-making and building. The native Britons supplied the labour force. Ragstone, the only hard stone to be found in the vicinity of the capital, was used in constructing the walls of Roman London and numerous villa and other sites. A highway for the laden barges was provided by the River Medway.

In medieval times ragstone quarrying became one of Kent's principal industries. Boughton's quarries furnished ragstone for the making of Westminster Abbey, Westminster Palace, Rochester, Cooling and Queenborough Castles, parts of the Tower of London and 'the edifices of the metropolis during the prevalence of the pointed style'. Nearer home it was used in the building of St. Peter's and other Kent churches and the sixteenth century re-building of Boughton Monchelsea Place. Ragstone also became an important provider for the medieval 'armaments industry'. In 1417, John Lough, clerk of the ordnance, and John Bennet, mason of Maidstone, were instructed to superintend the making of 7,000 cannon balls in the quarries around Maidstone and convey them to the 'Town Hithe' for the use of Henry V's army fighting in France. The stone was carried by cart to Maidstone for further conveyance to its destination by water. In 1434 a further 1,214 ragstone 'cannon shot' were supplied to the Tower armoury from Maidstone while in the reign of Henry VII John Baker, master mason, furnished another five tons of hard stone from Maidstone 'rough hewn for bombard shot'. These were not isolated orders. Henry VIII's ill-fated flagship the *Mary Rose* carried ragstone cannon balls and Whichcord in 1846 could still report that:[123]

> ...it is not at all uncommon even now for the workmen to find among the...rubbish in these quarries stones of different sizes sometimes as much as twelve inches diameter worked into a spherical shape such as were used for the artillery of the fourteenth and fifteenth centuries....

Fig. 5 *Boughton Monchelsea – Quarries*

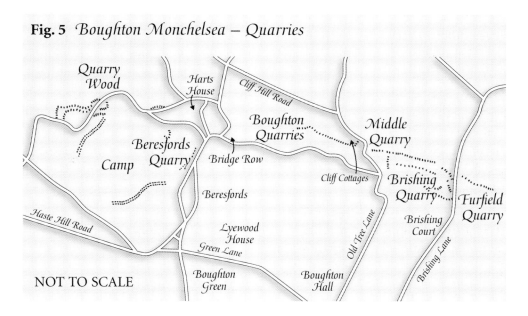

Towards the end of the fifteenth and during the sixteenth century there are indications that business in the quarries was booming and considerable sales of quarry land were taking place to enable the stone masons to respond to demand. In 1486 Richard Clerke of 'Bocton Monchensey', yeoman, sold two 'days workys' of quarry in 'the quarry called Bocton quarry' to William Crompe, the younger of Otham, mason. He also sold 'two daywerks' in the same place to Thomas Bettenham, an 'Otteham', mason. A 'days work' appears to have been a measurement of land covering almost three quarters of an acre. Ten years later Richard Clerke of Boughton sold Laurence Kyng of the same place a piece of quarry land in Boughton Quarry containing '5 daywerks and a half' in a place called

Henchaw. Henchaw was bounded by the land of the said Richard (Clerke) and the quarry of Thomas Hetnam to the east, land of Richard Clerke to the south and the quarry of William Crompe to the west. Thus there were at least three portions of the quarry in Boughton which, by this time, were in different ownership. One suspects that there were more. In 1532 Robert Bettenham of Boxley, smith, sold Thomas Yong of Boughton Monchensy 'the rest of two daywerks of quarry stone in Boughten' for thirty-five shillings. In the same year John Joce, a Boughton mason, sold his house and quarry lands 'in Boughton, Maydestan and Hunton' to Nicholas Ryche and Thomas Hunt. There were other transactions in quarry land involving quarry owners and masons in the mid-1530s and 1540s.[124] Boughton ragstone was used for paving Hampton Court in 1536 while 'acheles' stone from Boughton Monchelsea was sent in 1541 to repair the walls of Calais. An order to the Constables of Littlefield Hundred, issued in January 1600 by Henrie Jeninges, purveyor, who exacted materials for the use of the royal household, underlines the importance of Boughton's ragstone quarries.

> *Theis are in her Majesties name to chardge & command you presently... to provyde & appoynt sufficient carryages wythein your hundred to carry viii loades of stones (for the buyldinge of the Toower wharffe of London) from the Quarreys of Thomas Fyssher & William Yeomanson in Boughton Quarrey to the wharff of Thomas Parker in Maydstone. And that yt be carryed before the xth day of February...as you annswere to the contrary at your perill. And that (before the said date prefixed) you retourn me the names of those whoome you shall appoynt to carry to the howsse of the said Thomas Fyssher in Boughton aforesaid where I will geve attendance to see them carryed wherby I may knowe who they are that make default... And yf you cannot provyde sufficient carryages whereby the said stones may be carryed wytheout breakinge, yf you resort to howsses eyther of theforesaid Thomas Fyssher or William Yeomanson whoe dwell besydes the said Quarrey they will gett them carryed for you as reasonably as any other will carry them.[125]*

A further 290 loads of stone 'from ye great quarry at Boughton Monchelsea' were ordered to be despatched from 'the Towne Wharfe of Maidstone for the Quene's use' in April 1602.

The presence of freemasons in the parish registers and in the churchyard throughout the seventeenth and eighteenth centuries suggests that the ragstone industry continued uninterrupted during that time. Masons were normally members of a mobile profession travelling to wherever work was available. In the 15th century Kent masons went with their stone to Prittlewell, near Southend where they built a church with a tower similar to those at Ashford and Tenterden. At Boughton, however, it seems that sufficient work was always available to enable the masons to settle. Boughton quarries were deep. 'Very few quarries have been worked to the same depth as those at Boughton', commented Whichcord. As the stone was cleared the quarry owners, masons and quarry workers built their houses in the old quarry workings. While the cottages housed the quarry workers the high status 15th and 16th century dwellings Swiss Cottage, Harts House and Rock Cottage were the homes of the owners such as Fyssher and Yeomanson.

Early 20th century quarrymen pose at Beresfords Quarry. Rock Cottage, Hart's House and Swiss Cottage are in the foreground. Note the stone breakers' hammers and the narrow gauge track. One man (3rd from left) holds a powder flask. Another quarryman (5th from left) probably has a jumper bar.

Over 10,000 tons of stone, many of them undoubtedly from the quarries at Boughton, were exported from Maidstone between 1674 and 1700 as ragstone continued to be one of the county town's principal water-borne exports. About 1700, 10,856 feet of ashlar, the local name for the larger blocks of stone of superior quality, were despatched from Maidstone Waterside for paving the gun platforms at Cookham Wood Battery and a further 13,014 feet for similar use at the How Ness Battery. In 1719 John Harris remarked that 'a great quantity of good free stone' was still 'dug up and wrought' at Boughton Monchelsea while Edward Hasted at the end of the eighteenth century also referred to 'these large and noted quarries'. In the nineteenth century building boom the highest quality ragstone continued to be reserved for building. Local buildings of note included Maidstone Gaol (1818), Barming Asylum (1833) and Holy Trinity, St. Faith's, St. Philip's and St. Stephen's

Churches, Maidstone. No fewer than 33 ragstone churches were erected in London and its suburbs between 1841 and 1858. By mid-century it was also reported to 'be rapidly coming into use in the metropolis' for the construction of many types of building. Poorer quality Kent Rag was broken by hand in increasingly large amounts for use as roadstone.

Boughton Quarries c.1910.
Hart's House and Rock Cottage could have been the dwellings of Thomas Tyssher and William Yeomanson, the quarry owners mentioned in 1600. The walling is appropriately ragstone.

Even so the nineteenth century organisation of the industry remains something of a mystery. In 1841, when the Census Enumerators' Books begin in detail, there were 17 stone masons working in the parish but only 1 quarryman, Richard Baker. Ten years later the stonemasons numbered 15, including the 10 employed in the Quarries, by Master stone mason, John Seager, but there were still only 2 quarrymen. In 1861 there were 5 quarrymen and 12 masons including the 8 employed by Catherine Seager which included a statuary mason. The presence of a mere handful of quarrymen poses the question of how did they manage to cope in an extractive industry of considerable size without a larger work force? The answer seems to have been that these were the professional full-timers and that many farmers/quarry owners used their agricultural labourers in their 'quarry holes' or 'petts' when agricultural activity was slack or else drafted in additional quarrymen from neighbouring parishes like Loose. In the 1881 and 1891 censuses quarrymen increased to 9 while masons declined to 4 but the professional work force remained small.[126]

Roman quarrymen had used a tool called a jadd pick somewhat akin to a pickaxe. This, with frequent sharpening, enabled a quarryman to chop right through a block of stone. The process, however, was extremely slow and wasteful of material.

Increased demand in Norman times produced a change to a forerunner of the plug and feathers method whereby the stone was split by a sledge hammer which is still employed today. The introduction of gunpowder in the sixteenth century provided the quarryman with another important aid. 'Black powder', the name given to blasting powder, was carried in a copper can to avoid the danger arising from sparks. The can had a four and a half inch cap which served as an explosive measure. A description of ragstone quarrying is contained in 'The Topography of Maidstone and its Environs' published anonymously in 1839.

> *The operations of quarrying are peculiarly laborious and dangerous. The usual method is to undermine a portion of the cliff or face of the quarry which is supported by props until it is thrown in when it comes down with a severe concussion; there being sometimes as much as 2,000 tons in one of these falls. Notwithstanding every care accidents frequently happen and there are few of the old quarrymen but have been severely injured in their time. The large fragments of rock are then blasted into smaller pieces...and afterwards broken up and shaped by sledges and other tools.*

The Joys of Mechanisation. An overturned traction engine used to haul ragstone from the Quarries. The engine was preceded on public roads by a man carrying a red flag. It pulled three 7-ton trucks. The task had previously been performed by horse-drawn waggons and earlier by pack mules.

The nineteenth century quarrymen's tools were simple. Each was provided with an iron 'jumper bar' approximately four feet long sharpened at each end and about an inch in width with a wider part in the centre to provide weight. This was used to make holes for the gunpowder charges by 'jumping' the bar vertically up and down before the legs at a rate of some sixty strokes per minute. When several holes had been made and charged a 'touch paper' was applied. The workmen in the vicinity were warned to take cover by a blast on a whistle and the paper was lit exploding the charges and blowing up huge lumps of stone. The remaining work was accomplished with pick, hammer and shovel. The stone was broken up with a 16lb stone breaker's hammer and then wheeled away to be graded for quality and for 'skiffling' or roughly shaping to the required dimensions. This was for economy in transport and because the stone was easier to work when freshly quarried. The fragments were used for road chippings or burnt into lime. Even so some fifty per cent of stone excavated was waste. The quarries were worked in tiers. To get from one shelf to another temporary tracks, supported on posts, transversed the workings. Some quarrymen would race each other along the wooden planks pushing the heavily loaded stone barrows sometimes fifty feet above the excavated quarry. The large numbers of mule shoes still being discovered in the Quarries suggests that the seventeenth and eighteenth century quarrymen may have solved some of their transport problems, particularly over rough ground, by the use of mules.[127]

The pit-men or 'navvies' usually worked in pairs each pair having its own 'quarry hole'. Quarrymen were usually paid on a piece work basis by the cubic yard excavated. They were not normally paid for the removal of top soil by mattock unless the 'top' was very deep. Nevertheless they earned more than the agricultural labourer although their hours were as long. There was danger from the gunpowder but more so from the constant dust. Eye accidents, caused by flying stone, were frequent but fatal accidents were miraculously few.

> In 1848 a young man named Jenner, employed in Mr. Seager's stone quarry at Boughton Monchelsea, was undermining a face of stone and earth with a mattock contrary to regulations since such work was generally done with long crowbars. A mass of stone weighing about a ton and superincumbent earth fell on him. The man nearby had a narrow escape. Fifteen men got him out in a quarter of an hour but too late. His watch was crushed quite flat.[128]

The 'explosive cabins', roughly constructed from stone and protected by earthen mounds can still be seen in the quarries today as can the concrete tanks used in the washing of quarry stone. Blasting in Brishing Quarries was still taking place after World War II and there were complaints in 1954 that the explosions were damaging the ceilings of houses in Marlpit and Church Street. The need to reduce the strength of quarrying charges was again voiced strongly in 1963 when Furfield Quarry was being used by the British Quarrying Company of Borough Green.[129]

Boughton children in the early twentieth century regarded this labour 'aristocracy' with some awe:

> *The Quarriers walked in their working boots with...hobnails...Their dusty working clothes were leather-belted and 'dew-stringed' at waist and shin. Always they wore 'weskits', i.e. waistcoats, unbuttoned with shirt sleeves rolled and up and their jackets slung over their shoulders. This was unless the weather was wintry when they would have their jackets on...and a muffler covering their collarless striped shirts...Their clothes were shabby with a layer of white dust...Their strong legs and arms swung in easy rhythm as they walked. Caps or old trilby hats were invariably on the backs of their heads...Although they often stopped at the Bridge Tavern, which was also a small general shop, on their way to or from work, cold tea was the popular drink at the quarry face...*[130]

In medieval times and later the master masons were highly skilled craftsmen supervising the purchase and quarrying of stone in addition to acting as architects, organisers and supervisors on site. Many of the quarry owners seem to have been masons in their own right. The chisel, whose use as a tool was forgotten in Roman times, was not re-introduced until the thirteenth century. Norman stonework was, therefore, executed with an axe. Medieval masons were largely illiterate. Since each stone was the responsibility of the man who had worked it and errors had to be corrected, medieval and later masons cut their personal marks with a scriber on the stones they had worked for rapid identification. By the nineteenth century the emphasis upon apprenticeship had gone. George Shoebridge of Boughton served no apprenticeship but learned his trade from the older men among whom he worked.

The Cost of Ragstone in the 1920s.
Price list of W. Skinner & Sons.

Boughton Monchelsea's only other industry in the nineteenth century was the brewery in the Quarries built and then sold by James Wisenden in 1803. In 1847 this was in the hands of Randall & Newman, brewers. William Randall was the father-in-law of William Newman. Both originated in Middlesex. By the 1851 census Newman was still living in the Quarries and is still described as 'a brewer employing a clerk and 3 labourers'. Five years later Newman bought Randall out. Also present in Boughton by 1851 was William Baldwin of Quarry House listed as a master brewer employing 52 men and 4 boys. The relationship, if any, between the men is not clear. Baldwin was still in Boughton in 1861 when several brewer's draymen lived there too. In January 1864, however, the brewery, now converted to steam power, was sold to Messrs. Jutson & Rigden who were to give the village its only taste of nineteenth century industrialisation.[131]

John Seager, monumental master mason of Boughton Quarries, surveys his handiwork.
Ragstone was increasingly used for funeral monuments from Victorian times.

The pair planned to take waste material from Maidstone gasworks and use the brewery premises as a chemical works for its conversion to sulphate of ammonia. Within a short time the new factory was emitting clouds of toxic, offensive-smelling gas which hung over the village day and night. The gas seems to have descended principally upon the Boughton Mount Estate where the paint on the cottages of J.W. Braddick's tenants faded and the smell became unbearable. Worse still a white soapy substance covered the banks of the stream feeding Braddick's three ponds before running onward down the Loose valley. Braddick was a noted horticulturalist whose pear trees were legendary. When he discovered in November that great numbers of fish in his ponds were also dead or dying the battle lines were drawn. He employed Dr. Lettersby, an eminent London chemist, to inspect the works. He found that they were conducted with apparatus which allowed sulphurated gas to escape into the atmosphere 'almost at perfect freedom'. In the court case which followed Lettersby described the works as 'the worst conducted in the kingdom'. The activities of Messrs. Jutson & Rigden were brought to a close with damages granted to Braddick and Boughton Monchelsea ended its first encounter with industrial pollution. The village and its inhabitants were indeed fortunate that their best interests coincided with those of J.W. Braddick who purchased the offending buildings himself in 1868 to avoid any repetition.[132]

Population in the Nineteenth and Twentieth Centuries

The first decennial census was taken in 1801. From that date the graph records the population figure for each decade. The sole exception was 1941 when the census was cancelled because of the Second World War. The remarkable population increase in the second half of the eighteenth century continued into the nineteenth century. From 712 in 1801 Boughton's population rose steadily to 1190 in 1861. There was then a slight check until after the turn of the century occasioned, in part, by the agricultural depression. When Queen Victoria died in 1901 the parish had undergone comparatively few population changes since her accession in 1837. There were no great fluctuations since, although the Victorian Age was an era of population growth, Boughton's population was kept almost static by internal migration, particularly to the capital, and a small amount of emigration overseas. While America was the favourite spot for 'the pouring out of paupers' by parochial authorities in the 1830s and 1840s the Antipodes had become the preferred destination by the turn of the century. In 1909 a farewell smoking concert was staged at *The Albion* for the heads of five Boughton households who were bound for Australia.[133]

Population growth had resumed by 1911 but was again arrested by the slaughter of two world wars and the Depression of the 1930s. There was also a serious housing shortage in Boughton after World War II. On 26 March 1945 it was estimated that at least 25 new cottages were required for farm workers and aspiring young couples were invited to submit their names to the Parish Clerk. By March 1947 four pairs of Airey houses were under construction in Green Lane but in August 1955 the urgent need for more council houses was again reported since young people were being forced to leave the parish by the housing shortage. Not until the creation of a system of mains drainage ten years later was the most serious obstacle removed to major housing development. This paved the way for the building of the Lewis Court and Haste Hill housing estates in the 1970s which carried the population from 1,095 in 1961 to 1,704 by 1991. By 1974 the Lewis Court Estate contained approximately one-third of the total population of the parish and both the society and economy of Boughton Monchelsea had irrevocably changed.[134]

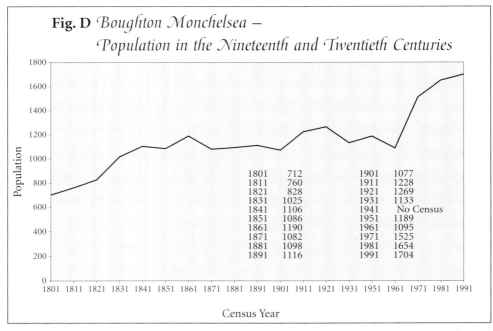

Fig. D *Boughton Monchelsea – Population in the Nineteenth and Twentieth Centuries*

1801	712	1901	1077
1811	760	1911	1228
1821	828	1921	1269
1831	1025	1931	1133
1841	1106	1941	No Census
1851	1086	1951	1189
1861	1190	1961	1095
1871	1082	1971	1525
1881	1098	1981	1654
1891	1116	1991	1704

Census Year

One factor which limited Boughton's population, despite a large eighteenth and nineteenth century rate of natural increase, was the high infant and child mortality rate. This had always been a demographic feature arising from the dangers of childbirth and the omnipresent battery of fatal childhood diseases. If a child could survive the latter and see out its first ten years there was a fair chance of it living for another three score years although general life expectancy was still much lower than in the twentieth century. In 1813-60 the average life span at Boughton was 31.5 years, increasing to 39.7 years in 1861-1898. However, five per cent of all deaths 1813-60 were of persons in their eighties, a percentage which doubled in the years 1861-98. The monumental inscriptions in St. Peter's churchyard illustrate graphically the perils of the early years. In the eighteenth century, for example, Edward Hadlow (d.1723 aged 55 years) and his wife (d.1761 aged 93 years) 'interred the bodies of 3 of their children' but 2 sons and 3 daughters survived. In the same way Alexander (d.1797 aged 67 years) and Jane Rimington (d.1784 aged 46 years) buried 4 children in infancy but 2 sons and 3 daughters survived. Four children of John and Mary Tomkin lived little longer. Their two daughters, Sarah aged 2 years 5 weeks and Mary aged 3 years 10 months, died in 1792. William passed on the following year aged 18 months and Thomas succumbed in 1796 aged 2 years 10 weeks.

The same doleful story continued throughout the next century. John and Elizabeth Webb buried 3 children in 1802-03 aged eight months, three months and thirteen months respectively. A fourth child died shortly afterwards. Mary, wife of Henry Loveless, who kept the beerhouse at the end of Bridge Row in the Quarries, lost six children before she, too, died in 1840 at the age of 37. William and Charles died in 1832 aged 15 months and 5 weeks respectively. Alfred and Charlotte followed in 1837. Their ages were 3 and 9 months. Jemima was 5 months old when she passed on in 1839 and Emma had reached 2 years when she passed away, like her mother, in 1840. A fourth girl, Ellen, born in 1834, lasted until she achieved her majority in 1855. Two children of the family survived their father who died in 1869 aged 73. John died in 1871, at the age of 43 years and Henry Jun., died in 1888 aged 58 years. Rich and poor suffered alike. J.W. Braddick of Boughton Mount, who died in 1896 leaving a personal fortune of £6,480, fathered 6 children by two wives. When his first wife, Emma, died in 1860 aged 41, 2 of her 5 children had already pre-deceased her in early childhood. In 1813-60 39.5% of all deaths in Boughton were of children under 10. The percentage for 1860-98 was 30.5%. Even in the early decades of the twentieth century infant and child mortality were factors to be reckoned with. Thirty-six children aged under one year and 25 aged below ten years still died between 1899-1918. The corresponding mortality figures for the period 1919-1945 were 15 children under one year and four children below ten years. It was not, therefore, until after the creation of the National Health Service that high infant and child mortality were finally conquered.

High infant and child mortality meant a reduction in family size. While many Victorian parents may have had ten or more children, in only a small proportion of these families did all members survive into adulthood. The belief that the very large Victorian family was the norm is a myth. For the period 1650-1749 work on household listings suggests a mean household size of around 4.4 and a mean conjugal group of about 3.4. In the mid-nineteenth century the work of Michael Anderson indicates a mean conjugal group of some 3.7 with a mean household size of 4.6. There were, of course, families whose hardiness or sheer good fortune enabled ten or more children to survive but these families were in the minority. In Boughton the Victorian family contained an average of 3.6 children in 1841 and 3.1 children forty years later.[135]

Table 1
Family Size in Boughton Monchelsea in 1841 and 1881

Families with	1841	1881
1 child	22 (15.0%)	34 (22.5%)
2 children	28 (19.0%)	34 (22.5%)
3 children	24 (16.3%)	27 (17.9%)
4 children	23 (15.7%)	21 (14.0%)
5 children	22 (15.0%)	14 (9.2%)
6 children	14 (9.6%)	12 (8.0%)
7 children	8 (5.4%)	2 (1.3%)
8 children	4 (2.8%)	4 (2.6%)
9 children	1 (0.6%)	3 (2.0%)
10 children	1 (0.6%)	0
Average Family Size	3.6 children	3.1 children

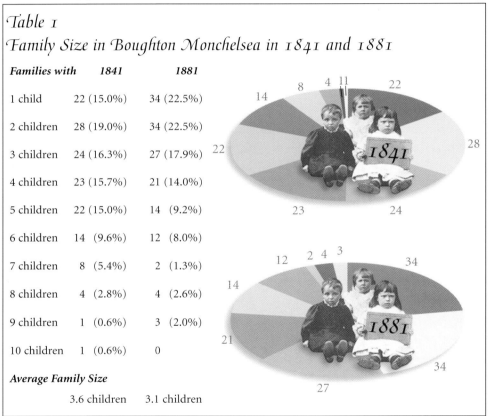

While the Census can provide only a crude guide, since not all children would have been living at home when it was taken, the point is nevertheless made. In 1841 roughly 66% of families had only 4 children or less. There was only one family with 10 children, 1 family with 9 children and 4 families with 8 children. Forty years later 76.9% of Boughton children lived in families of 4 or less. No families had 10 children, 3 families had 9 and there were 4 families with 8 children. John Craddock, who fathered the 10 children in 1841, was the blacksmith at Boughton Green. Anna, his wife, who was aged 41 years, had given birth to a child on alternate years for over twenty years. In 1881 one of the families with 9 children and one with 8 children were each fathered by quarrymen who, like blacksmiths, tended to regard their virility as an indication of physical strength.

Population growth was also influenced by the restricted nature of the marriage market. Before the transport revolution, few men were able to look for a wife outside their own immediate neighbourhood and only rarely did they marry someone from more than ten miles away. The marriage registers show that this was so at Boughton in the years both before and after 1754 when printed marriage registers were introduced for the first time. From 1754-1803 225 marriages took place at St. Peter's Church involving 450 men and women. Of these only 25 men and four women (6.4%) came from outside the parish. All save two of these were from Kent and all except six came from adjacent parishes to Boughton. In fact the 'incomers' remained a trickle until the 1860s when the pace began to quicken and more outsiders came from parishes further afield, particularly London. 1841 was also the year of the Census which confirms the very close nature of the community for the first time. Of Boughton's 1,106 inhabitants 96.8% were born within the county of Kent. The 35 (3.2%) 'strangers' included two from France and South Wales and the family of the vicar, John Haslewood. Ten years later the restricted nature of the marriage market showed some signs of easing. The parish had had access to the national railway network for seven years but of its 1,056 inhabitants 586 (55.5%) had still been born in Boughton Monchelsea and 421 (39.9%) had birthplaces elsewhere in Kent. Of the latter, 237 (56.2%) had been born in one of the nearby parishes of Staplehurst, Marden, Linton, Loose, Yalding, Chart Sutton, Sutton Valence, Langley and Maidstone. Only 46 (4.4%) came from other English counties such as Middlesex (11), Sussex (10), Surrey (4), Cambridgeshire, Essex, Yorkshire and Devon (3 each). Three persons (0.2%) were from Wales and Ireland.[136]

Thirty years later at the Census of 1881, 512 (47%) of the total Boughton population had still been born within the parish and the same percentage in other parishes in Kent. Again almost 58% of the latter gave their places of birth as the nine adjacent parishes to Boughton listed above. Slightly more inhabitants (63 or 5.7%) originated from other British counties while 10 (nine from Ireland and one from France) came from other countries. Only 32 'strangers' were involved in the

293 marriages at Boughton between 1841-1870. These consisted of 15 persons from the nine adjacent parishes, 10 from parishes elsewhere in Kent and seven from London Boroughs and Counties elsewhere. The pace quickened a little between 1871-1890. There were 55 'outsiders' involved in the 157 marriages. Twenty persons came from the 'adjacent parishes' and the same number from other Kent parishes. There were 15 persons involved from London and other counties but the 'Thames barrier' still remained a very real obstacle.[137]

The Victorian and Edwardian Village Community

Boughton, like most rural communities of the time, was not only a close community but also a self-sufficient one. In 1851 53 (12.7%) of the employed population were craftsmen. There were two builders, three wheelwrights, three blacksmiths, seven shoemakers, eight carpenters, a thatcher and a tailor. The local community was also serviced by a butcher, a baker, a grocer, two needlewomen, three dressmakers, three plumbers, a miller and a shopkeeper who sold 'candies'. Thirty years later the number of craftsmen had increased slightly. By 1881 there were four dressmakers, four seamstresses, two tailors, two bakers, two butchers and 12 carpenters. There were grocers' shops in Church Street, the Quarries and on the Green in addition to beerhouses in the Quarries and at marlpit. These also sold groceries. Seventy-five-year old widow, Susan Sunnock, still kept the village sweetshop on the Green. The expansion of most services was due to the growth of population. The increase of workers in the building industry owed much to the presence of James Wood, builder, who employed 48 men and four boys although not all lived in Boughton.

The thirst of the community was well-catered for. In 1841 William Peene, victualler at the *Cock Inn*, had competition from only William Spurgeon who ran a beershop in Church Street. By 1847 these two had been joined by two more beershops in the Quarries and a third conducted by Mary Barton on the Green. While an inn provided food and stabling as well as drink, the beerhouse owed its existence to the

1830 Beerhouse Act passed to try and reduce the high consumption of spirits which was a cause for government concern. Under this Act any householder could sell beer from their own house provided that they had paid the poor rate or purchased an excise licence for two guineas. After the Act beerhouses mushroomed. They were usually kept by local craftsmen or persons with some secondary form of employment. They soon gained an unsavoury reputation for temptations other than their beer such as gambling and radical politics. Some became notorious as brothels. At Boughton the two Quarry beerhouses were kept by octogenarian James Hart, and Henry Loveless who was a grocer and lime dealer as well as a purveyor of beer in his shop at the end of Bridge Row. Mary Barton was the proprietor of what may have been the forerunner of the *Oak Inn*. There was also a new landlord at the *Cock* in the person of John Stonham, a master blacksmith and widower, who also ran the nearby smithy at Cock Street.

The Forge on the Green c.1900.
One of the three village blacksmiths takes a 'breather' surrounded by admiring school children. The timber stockpile on the Green belonged to James Wood, the local builder. The 'Soup Kitchen' opened in 1853 lies in the background.

Edwardian Church Street.
Schoolboys survey an unexpected windfall. The headteacher, Mr. Forder, paid 1d. or 2d. for horse manure to put on his school house garden.

The *Albion Inn* is first mentioned in 1857 when Ann Rose, 'wife of the keeper' took the somewhat drastic step of discharging a pistol at a troublesome customer named 'Jack' Lamb. Not surprisingly by the next Census the second Inn in the parish had acquired a new keeper in the form of William Ancock! The keepers of the beerhouses had also changed with the exception of Henry Loveless. Richard Seager, a 48-year-old stonemason, had replaced James Hart in the Quarries. George Tomkin had not only taken the wheelwright's business from his 'in laws', William and Mary Barton, but the beerhouse on the Green as well. Two new beershops had also appeared in Wierton Lane run by Samuel Cole, a 57-year-old farmer, and Edward Daw, an agricultural labourer, bringing the parish total to five. A decade later the beerhouse on the Green had been redesignated the *Oak Inn* giving the parish three inns in all. By 1881 the beerhouses had fallen to four. The Loveless family still ran the beerhouse and grocer's shop in the Quarries and there was still a beerhouse in Church Street. At Marlpit, Edward Britcher was proprietor of a grocer's and beerseller's in addition to conducting the 12-acre Marlpit Farm. William Baker, farmer of six acres and beerhouse keeper of the *White Horse*, also catered for outlying drinkers.[138]

Keeping an inn, let alone a beershop, was no easy task. After the establishment of Kent County Constabulary in 1857 beershops became a target for magistrates who wished to exercise a tighter control over them for good reason. In 1864 Edward Daw was fined £3.0.0. for keeping unlawful hours on a Sunday. Charlotte Mannering, landlady of the *Rose* beershop, in 1868 was fined twice in four months for similar offences. On Xmas Day 1867 a police constable found five men drinking at 1.30a.m. with beer still on the table, yet she was again merely fined for remaining open after hours only three months later.[139] Violence from drunken customers was never far away. George Morris, a farm labourer living in Church Street, bit the landlord of the *Lamb* beershop so hard that he appeared in court 'with his arm in a sling and the marks of the prisoner's teeth plainly visible'. Morris also kicked and assaulted P.C. Little who was called to remove him. In 1869, in another drunken brawl, Isaac Sassons, a hop-picker, stabbed and seriously wounded Thomas Holcroft in the taproom of the *Oak*.[140]

Domestic service, apart from agricultural work, was one of the few accepted occupations for women and girls. In 1851 77 (18.5%) of the employed population were servants to the resident landowners and large farmers. Most were women acting as general servants, maidservants, cooks, housekeepers and nurses. The handful of male servants consisted of gardeners, grooms, a gamekeeper and three coachmen. The two butlers were reserved for the 'great households'. Most small farmers had at least one resident maid-of-all-work. At Boughton Place in 1841 Thomas Rider was cared for by four male servants and six female servants. Twenty years later his successor's household of eight included a footman, coachman and butler, a cook/housekeeper, a Lady's maid, an upper housemaid, under housemaid and kitchen maid. John Braddick in 1851 employed a butler, two nursemaids, a cook, a housemaid and a coachman. William Moore, magistrate, and his wife in 1881 lived at Wierton House surrounded by 80 acres of Parkland. Their household consisted of a housekeeper and six servants.

The Oak Inn c.1900. (Right) Locals pose outside the Oak. (Below) The Oak was patronised by local waggoners.

The hours of the domestic servants were long and tedious like those of the agricultural labourer. At Boughton, labour relations seem to have remained good in both spheres at least until the agricultural depression. In July 1863, for example, Capn. Moore gave a dinner to all his haymakers when the crop was safely gathered in.

Rev. Shepherd also gave a treat to his day labourers and over the years other farmers followed suite. At Boughton Mount, J.W. Braddick staged an annual servants' ball. In 1878 dancing began at 8.30p.m. with the Braddicks, their son and three daughters joining in. At 10.00p.m. all sat down in the Hall to a 'sumptuous supper' prepared by the cook. Toasts were drunk to the health and happiness of the Braddick family. After supper the dancing resumed and was kept up 'with great spirit' until 5.00 a.m.[141]

The Boughton agricultural labourer worked a 10-12 hour day for six days a week. There was consequently little time for leisure and recreation. The Boughton Monchelsea cricket club existed by 1856. It played in 1864 on the Pond field at Parsonage Farm by courtesy of farmer, William Skinner and held its meetings at the *Cock*. The licensee, John Stonham, who was the club's treasurer, provided the players and officials with dinners at 2s.6d. each following a match with Penshurst in 1856. Thirty-six sat down to eat in the Knight's House consuming about 100lbs. of meat. The players came largely from farming families. They included William Crittenden of Martin's Farm, William Tomkin of East Hall, Edward Beard, jun., of Wierton Street and the Britchers from Marlpit Farm. Only Thomas Gandy, presented in 1867 with a bat for making the highest score of 84 in a single innings, was a private schoolmaster and rate collector.[142] The labourer was much more likely to want to escape from his comfortless and overcrowded cottage to the warmth and companionship of the beerhouse where skittles, cards and cheap beer drunk from quart pots beckoned. A village football club, playing its games on the Recreation Ground, was not formed until January 1899 but by 1905 had made considerable progress.[143]

The Knight's House.
Built in 1689 and demolished as a road safety hazard in 1961. Its use is unknown except that it served as an overflow for the Cock. Here, in 1856, John Stonham served thirty diners at 2s.6d. per head after the Boughton v. Penshurst Cricket Match.

In the meantime those with more active tastes were perhaps attracted to the ancient Kent game of goal running. This was said to have been played in the county before cricket. By mid-Victorian times the last strongholds of the game were in the Weald and Romney Marsh. Biddenden, Tenterden, Pluckley, Dymchurch, New Romney and Ivychurch were among the most successful teams. Boughton had a team which played without overmuch success. The season lasted from May to August during which time the clubs played some 14 matches. The pitch was marked by flags in the form of a triangle with each side 45 yards in length. At the two bottom corners of the triangle the respective sides clustered beside their goal flags. Each team had a 'putter out' who sent players simultaneously in pairs to try to circle a point flag on the opposite side of the field and return to their own goal. A point was awarded to any who accomplished this. It was also the task of players to prevent their opponents from reaching the point flag. Once a player had set off he had to keep moving until he had either rounded the opposing point flag and returned home or had been tapped on the back by an opponent in which case he took no further part in the game. There were 22 players in a team. The average time for a game was 40 minutes. After 20 minutes the sides changed over. When two teams were well-matched there was often no score. Players played barefoot and often covered three to four miles in an afternoon. Much depended on knowing when to run although sprinters were seldom successful goal runners. Good players required plenty of stamina and the ability to keep jogging along. The Boughton team was still active in 1910 when it played against Marden at the Foresters' Annual Fete at Linton Park but shortly afterwards it seems to have disbanded and like the game itself became defunct.[144]

Since ordinary folk seldom went far from home, interest in their own village events was much stronger and a wide variety of activities were well-supported besides the sporting ones. The Boughton Monchelsea Cottage Gardeners' Society, first founded in 1871, by 1909 was 'one of the most prosperous societies in the neighbourhood'. Its 39th Annual Exhibition in 1910, held in conjunction with the Linton Cottage Gardeners' Society, attracted an attendance exceeding 4,000 and about 1,000 entries. Like the Cottage Gardeners' Society the Sparrow and Rat Club also had a strong practical purpose. Taking over the responsibility for pest control, formerly held by the churchwardens, it not only provided a 'sport' for its members but also kept down the pests which destroyed crops and fruit and were a menace to public health. Established in the 1870s the club was part of a county-wide organisation with a County Organising Officer based in Maidstone. His office was created by the Rats and Mice Destruction Act 1919. By 1921 he had responsibility for over 70 clubs throughout Kent. In 1909 the Boughton Club alone despatched 3,564 sparrows, 139 bullfinches and 2,366 rats.[145]

The White Horse Beershop.
In 1851 it was conducted by William Baker, a farmer of 6 acres. By the early twentieth century it had become the Red House. Some said this was because of the frequent brawls between 'home' and 'foreign' hop pickers in which blood was often spilt.

Entertainment of a more elevated nature was provided by Penny Readings which began in the village schoolroom in January 1869 and continued throughout the 'seventies and 'eighties. The readings were an attempt by the more 'well-to-do' and their sons and daughters to further the 'general instruction and entertainment' of 'ordinary people' by bringing to them readings in poetry and prose from the works of standard authors. These were interspersed with musical items and songs of an 'elevating and refining character'. Previously such entertainments had been limited to the drawing room. An admission charge of one penny served to defray expenses and make the readings self-supporting. Readings were strongly supported by the Anglican Church because of their high moral tone and since they enabled all classes to meet together to share the same pleasures. Boughton's first evening included readings from *Nicholas Nickleby* and *Pickwick Papers* together with pianoforte solos and songs. The chairman was William Moore of Wierton House. The performers included Moore himself; the son and daughter of Edward Beard, of Wierton Street and Thomas Hayes, farmer and poor law guardian from Charlton Farm and his daughters. The entertainment took place before a packed audience who loudly cheered those who took part in the programme. Similar to the Penny Readings was the Choral Society active at the turn of the century.[146]

Other attempts at self-improvement followed, encouraged and supported by a new generation of leading families in the parish. The Boughton Adult School Institute was established in 1908 largely due to the financial help of Hermann G. Kleinwort, merchant banker, the new occupant of Wierton Place and George Foster Clark who purchased Boughton Mount in 1902. Both were impressed with the valuable work of the Institute in the village. Meetings took the form of a bible reading and sometimes hymns followed by a lecture and discussion. Lectures were based upon a study course for the year, written centrally in London by experts of the Adult School Union. The target audience was 'adults lacking formal schooling'. The schools were described as '...groups which seek on the basis of friendship to learn together and to enrich life through study...social service and obedience to a religious ideal'. Social life, too, was considered important and while Kleinwort helped to write off the School's first deficit, Foster Clark presented it with a billiard table. A Women's Adult School was presided over by Mrs. George Smith of Lyewood House until her death in 1910.**147**

George Foster Clark.
A patron of Boughton's
Adult School Institute and
an active supporter of the
Liberal Party he
purchased Boughton
Mount in 1902.

The meeting place of the Adult Schools is not clear. The most likely venue was the Quarry Church or mission hall erected in the Quarries between 1874-1881. A piece of land in the Quarries was presented to the Church for building a mission hall for educational purposes in conjunction with the Anglican National Society for Promoting the Education of the Poor at approximately the same time that Walter Folliott Scott became vicar in 1873. Scott was an evangelical and champion of the poor. It was he who welcomed local trade unionists to a Church service in 1878 and who was probably the driving force behind the opening of 'a working men's club in the Quarries' in 1880 with a smoking and refreshment room 20 feet by 12 feet on the ground floor and a reading room and library above. Scott was the treasurer and William Moore of Wierton, who also chaired the first Penny Readings, was President. The house had been fitted out by members themselves and was open from 6.00p.m. until 10.00p.m. and during the daytime in winter when work on the land was impossible. There were 40 members enrolled when the club opened. Refreshments consisted of tea, coffee and bread and butter only. The first religious services were held in the mission church in 1881. Only part of the hall was regarded as consecrated so that the remainder could be used for secular events. It seems unlikely, however, because of its upper storey that this was the building used by the Working Men's Club which seems more likely to have been a converted private house.[148]

We hear nothing further of this Working Men's Club but in 1905 the reading room transferred to Frank Barton's house on the Green which was open from 7.00p.m. til 10.00p.m. every evening. The initial entrance fee was 6d. plus a subscription of 2d. per week. The daily papers were available and the vicar, now the Rev. Charles John Meade, made an appeal for gifts of books and periodicals. Meanwhile, other forms of adult education still continued. In 1896, a 10 lecture course on Plain Cookery was delivered in the Quarry Mission Room by Miss Parker of the South Kensington School of Cookery while fortnightly lessons in Wood Carving were held at the Vicarage. By now a Boughton Monchelsea Technical Education Committee existed with James Wood, the builder, as its President and a committee consisting of Edward Bowles, nurseryman, William Cole, jun., carpenter, W.H. Skinner, farmer and William Tree, wheelwright and blacksmith. This committee staged technical examinations such as the examination of the School of Domestic Economy. January 1898 also saw the creation of a Parochial Lending Library, formed by H.F.B. Archer, of Wierton Grange, which was open for the loan of books on Saturdays at 11.00a.m. Membership was 1d. per month.[149]

The new village hierarchy was divided in its politics in late Victorian and Edwardian times as it had never been before. Boughton Monchelsea was part of the Medway Parliamentary Division which was generally regarded as a safe Conservative seat. The parish, however, seems to have traditionally given its support to the Liberal Party since the days of its radical Lord of the Manor, Thomas Rider. H.G. Kleinwort of Wierton Place was President of Medway Divisional Liberal Association while

Alderman George Foster Clark, J.P., who had purchased Boughton Mount, and William Hewitt Skinner were also Liberals. In 1841 William Skinner was farming Olive House Farm, Pickering Street, Loose. The Skinners had also been in Boughton since at least 1842 when William was a tenant farmer at Tanyard. In 1861 his son, another William, occupied 120 acres of Boughton Hall. Twenty years later his 400-acre farm at Beresfords employed 31 men and four boys while Thomas Skinner farmed another 183 acres at Wierton Hall providing work for an additional 23 men and two boys. William Skinner of Beresfords died in 1896 but by 1905 William Skinner & Sons, farmers, hop and fruit growers and owners of Brishing Quarry were among the major landowners in Boughton. The company was headed by W.H. Skinner, William's son. When the 1909 election campaign began it was no surprise that the Liberal candidate for the Medway Division, Alexander Cairns, began his village campaign with a meeting in the club room at the *Cock*. Foster Clark presided. His deputy president was W.H. Skinner. 'The numerous audience was evidently in sympathy with the principles Mr. Cairns enunciated'. On the other hand there were 'signs of disorder' when the Conservative candidate, Colonel Warde, held a meeting in the village a few weeks later.[150] The Conservatives had powerful supporters too. A.W. Fulcher of Wierton Place was President of the Boughton Monchelsea Conservative and Unionist Association. His two vice-Presidents were F.S.W. Cornwallis of Linton and Mr. F. Smith of Elm House, Boughton Monchelsea.[151]

On village occasions, however, such political differences were forgotten. 1887 brought Queen Victoria's Golden Jubilee and a spontaneous outburst of local loyalty throughout the land. '...Such depths of local feeling', read an editorial in the local press, 'are one of the soundest characteristics of the British race'. At Boughton all the separate elements in the hierarchical life of rural England – gentry, farmers, shopkeepers, labourers, rich and poor – sat down together for a free tea and entertainment. Ten years later the celebrations were repeated to mark the sovereign's Diamond Jubilee. A meat tea for the elderly, widows and children at the School was again followed by children's sports. The harmony of the occasion was somewhat marred when the provision of three barrels of beer was opposed by an ever-vigilant local Temperance Society. In the end, however, Boughton secured a greater long-term benefit.[152]

When J.W. Braddick died in 1896 a portion of his estate was purchased at auction by R.J. Balston, the Maidstone papermaker. Next year the Parish Council leased from him the field which became the Recreation Ground and which the Council subsequently bought in 1919. On Saturday 21 May 1898 the villagers processed from the Green, headed by the Sutton Valence Silver Band, to hear Mr. H.F.B. Archer of Wierton Grange conduct the formal opening. Sports, a cricket and a football match followed. Thereafter until the First World War an annual sports day to commemorate the occasion was held for both adults and children. Events for adults included tilting on bicycles, a blindfold race and a pillow fight.[153]

'Hoppers' in Boughton hop gardens c.1900. (Right) 'Home' and London pickers.

(Below) 'Superior' peaceful pickers. Note the hop baskets and the bin.

The relative harmony of village life was disrupted, however, by the annual incursion of migrant hop-pickers who each year brought to the 'Garden of England' crime, poverty, violence and disease. Boughton, with 90 acres of hops in the parish, did not suffer as acutely as East Farleigh where Mr. Ellis of Court Lodge Farm was the largest hop grower in Kent. East Farleigh not only witnessed some of the worst scenes of disorder in the hop gardens throughout the nineteenth century but in 1849 the 'hoppers' were decimated by a cholera outbreak resulting from the insanitary condition in which they lived. At Boughton living conditions were little better:

> Half the pickers at least are lodged in old barns and lodges and some rough houses built of loam and thatch. The only partitions are hurdles put between the beds leaving them to twist straw in, if they like; they seldom do so.[154]

The 'pickers' may have escaped the cholera but the other danger amidst so much straw was fire. In 1864 a fire broke out in a barn housing drunken pickers working for Edward Beard. This time the hoppers avoided serious injury but in 1899 a seven-year old boy, whose parents were at work in Thirkell's hop gardens, was burnt to death and buried in St. Peter's churchyard.

The pickers' tendency to 'live off the land' was certainly not tolerated by the magistrates. Two little girls were each given 21 days' hard labour for stealing six shillings' worth of growing potatoes in 1868. George Jackson, who stole a quantity of apples from East Hall Farm, escaped more lightly with only 7 days' imprisonment. William Gregory, another hopper, who stole apples, plums and cobnuts from East Hall, received a month. Stephen Barnett, who stole Thomas Skinner's hop poles for fuel, was sentenced to a week's hard labour and twelve strokes of the whip.[155]

It was the hoppers' propensity for violence, inflamed by strong drink, which brought terror to the inns and beerhouses and fear to the communities which they visited. John Kenny, an Irish hopper picking for Mr. Beard, assaulted Mary Ryan, an elderly woman, in a Saturday night brawl at Linton in 1864. Michael White, another Irish picker, in 1875 treated his 'wife' 'as he would a football' during a drunken quarrel at Boughton. The woman, however, failed to appear at the court hearing and White was discharged. When there were no other opponents to fight the hoppers fought among themselves. In a general fight among hop pickers at Chart Sutton in 1869 Jeremiah Foley stabbed Richard Whitaker in the stomach. In 1878 a gang of hoppers even committed highway robbery on Boughton Green. Joseph Cook, chief stoker on board HMS Trent who was home on leave from Sheerness, was attacked by five men and his gold watch taken. Despite a severe blow on the back of the head he clung to one of his attackers until help arrived. William Morris, a quarryman who saw the assault, gave evidence leading to the arrest of a second picker but the others escaped. By the turn of the century the conditions among hoppers had improved but despite the good work of missionaries who held, for example, an open air service at

Boughton for London hop pickers in 1909, these troublesome but necessary visitors were still regarded with some suspicion by local people.

This Sporting Life.
Boughton Monchelsea Football and Cricket Teams. The Football team photo was taken in 1904-05. The cricket match was the first to be played on the Recreation Ground in 1905. 'Whites' were certainly not the order of the day.

By the 1840s Boughton had already increased its number of unpaid borsholders from one to eight under a High Constable, Edward Hodges, the former miller and assistant overseer, who lived on Boughton Green. This was due to the increasing population and the corresponding rise in crime. By 1861 Kent County Constabulary, established in 1857, had a resident police sergeant stationed at Boughton in accordance with Chief Constable Ruxton's policy of integrating his married policemen into local communities. Sergeant Jabez Bassett, his wife and family lived at Cliff Cottage which subsequently became known as 'Policeman's Cottage'. Also present by 1855 was John Thomas, postmaster and tailor, in the village's sub-post office in Church Street. The post arrived at 7.30a.m. and was despatched at 6.45p.m. by wagon to Loose and thence to the Post town, Staplehurst. These changes apart Boughton was relatively unaltered as it moved into the twentieth century.

Medical provision was one area which lagged seriously behind. In the seventeenth and eighteenth centuries self-medication had been the main form of treatment. Gardens supplied the plants and herbs which were administered by 'wise women' or used with the help of a herbal to treat illness at home. Even the rich resorted to practices of this kind in the absence of doctors. The eighteenth century recipe book of the wife of Sir Christopher Powell of Wierton Place makes fascinating reading. Instructions for making ginger bread, 'sillybub', rabbit sausages and roasting a pike are intermixed with procedures for the manufacture of balsam for 'A Rune in the Eyes after Small Pox', 'An Approved Drink to Cause an Easy Labour', 'Mrs. Ffloyds Recepe for an Asma', 'Lady Trisden ye Wound Drink' and 'An Excellent Oyle for a Straine or broken bone'. Some medical help for the parish poor was provided under the Old Poor Law as we have already seen. Under the New Poor Law doctors were employed by the guardians of every union but in a large and populous union like Maidstone Union they were very thinly spread. William Ayerst, a surgeon, was resident in the parish in 1847 but had disappeared by 1855. There was no other resident medical man until the twentieth century.[157]

The Parish Council 1894-1970

Parish councils were established by the Local Government Act 1894 which revived the dying parish vestries under another name. They were intended to act as a bulwark against the ancient authority of the vicar and the squire although their powers were rigidly circumscribed and their right to raise money was limited to a modest 3d. rate. Nevertheless, expectations in some quarters were high. A Liberal Party handbook for parish councillors claimed that the new councils would 'abolish patronage and banish privilege' and 'for the rule of the few it will substitute the responsibility and co-operation of the many'. At first it looked as if this might be the case at Boughton where the power vacuum created by the absentee Riders had been replaced by the influence of other landowners.

When the Annual Parish Meeting met for the first time at the Board School on 12 December 1894 to elect Boughton's nine councillors no fewer than 18 candidates had been nominated. The nominees included two agricultural labourers, two quarrymen and a gardener. Mr. George Smith of Lyewood House and vice-chairman of Maidstone Union Board of Guardians, was appointed to the chair. He read out the names of the candidates and a show of hands was taken for each. To the surprise of some but by no means all, John W. Braddick was not one of the nine returned. He was an unpopular employer and hard taskmaster who had reduced wages in the 'seventies'. When his daughter married in 1881 boys from the school had pelted the wedding carriages with mud. Albert Thorneycroft, a quarryman and another unsuccessful candidate, demanded a poll. Braddick supporters then had time to organise themselves and at the ensuing election by ballot Braddick came fourth securing 104 votes as opposed to the 33 votes he had obtained initially. Of the working class candidates only George Pike, agricultural labourer, was returned at the poll although Robert Duddy, a gardener, had been chosen at the show of hands as well. Pike was joined on the Council by five farmers or landowners, a builder, a stonemason and a shopkeeper. He was not returned at the next election. At the first meeting of the Parish Council Braddick was unanimously appointed Chairman. His reign was cut short by his death in November 1896 but from the moment of his election the parish council aroused little enthusiasm among the villagers until after World War II. No elections were necessary in 1897-99 or in 1901, 1904 or 1913. When elections were contested polls were low.[158]

The decade after 1890 saw a dramatic improvement in pure water provision in many Kent villages particularly after the Maidstone typhoid epidemic of 1897. A good supply of mains water was vital not only for public health but was also an important prerequisite for good drainage and fire fighting. Much of St. Peter's Church was destroyed in 1832 because of inadequate water supply. The Windmill at Haste Hill was consumed in 1858 for the same reason while in 1898 James Wood's builder's yard was burnt to the ground because the village pond was unable to hold water. Yet in the same year, when the mains of the Mid-Kent Water Company were spreading across central Kent, Boughton Parish Council decided to oppose the Mid-Kent Water Bill since, if passed, it would allow the Water Company to tap the springs in the village. Yet in August 1912 the *Kent Messenger* announced that piped water needed to be urgently extended to houses on the lower part of Church Hill and that from Boughton to the Staplehurst boundary 'almost every cottage was in urgent need of a water supply'. Three months later the water was pronounced polluted on East Hall Hill.[159]

While other communities enjoyed ample supplies of mains water some villagers at Boughton continued to rely on the parish wells in Church Street, Back Lane and the Quarries until the eve of World War II. 'We used to have shoulder yokes to carry two buckets at a time evenly balanced', stated Mrs. Nellie Pledger. Practically the whole of the parish was on piped water by 1941. Piped water came piecemeal, It seems to have reached the Green in the 1920s but it was not until 1935 that the Mid-Kent Water Company laid a main down Church Street and Green Lane, and to Haste Hill. [160]

> I remember the piped water being brought to Boughton and the pleasure to
> turn a tap on and get all the water we needed [reminisced one old
> inhabitant]. Before this my father had to draw all the water from the well
> for drinking, for washing we relied on a tank that caught the water from the
> roofs... The public wells that were used by small communities...were
> anything from 50 to 80 feet deep... [161]

Finally in 1945 water was carried to the Lewis Court area thus preparing the way for the later building of the Lewis Court estate.

In these early decades the Parish Council led a somewhat pedestrian existence providing some minor improvements for the parish without arousing much interest among the parishioners. Even the election of the first two women councillors – Brenda Jolly and Pauline Style – in 1937 made little difference. The period, however, was punctuated by a series of high profile events in whose organisation leading councillors played a major part. Edward VII's coronation in 1901 was followed by the coronation of George V in 1910. After this came the Peace Celebrations of 1919, the Coronation of George VI, V.E. Day and the Coronation and Silver Jubilee of Queen Elizabeth II in 1952 and 1977 respectively. The festivities followed a similar pattern. The coronation of Edward VII was celebrated by a Village Fete on the newly-established Recreation Ground with tea and coronation mugs for the children and a meat tea for adults and old people. At the coronation of George V eight years later the festivities began with a procession from the Green to the Church at 2.00p.m. headed by Marden Silver Band. After a short service the inhabitants adjourned to the Terrace Field, near the Church, lent by W.H. Skinner. The Union Jack was hoisted and saluted. A tea was taken by all inhabitants in a marquee lent by the Gardener's Society. Coronation mugs were presented to the children along with medals for school attendance and punctuality from Kent Education Committee. The presentations were followed by a Sports and Firework Display. The day was financed by a subscription amounting to £75 including the sum of £25 donated by H.G. Kleinwort. The balance of the subscription was given to the Recreation Ground Committee. The organising committee was headed by parish councillors W.H. Skinner and the builder James Wood who were Chair and Vice-Chair. Secretary to this committee was Councillor Philip Forder, the village schoolmaster. **162**

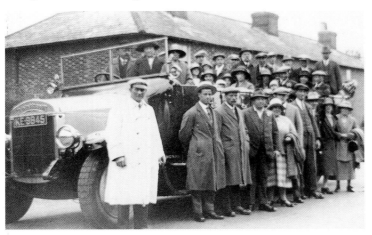

Village Institute Outing
Villagers gather for an outing outside Epsom Cottages, Church Street. Until the coming of the motor car they were heavily dependent upon community activities for entertainment.

Such celebrations made the national events which they commemorated not only enjoyable but also memorable for those who participated. They also continued to heighten the sense of community. The most lasting and perhaps most valuable memorial came, however, at the close of the Great War when it was decided to erect a Village Institute as a tribute to those who had perished in the conflict. A War Memorial Committee was formed. Two ex-army huts were bought and erected as Boughton Monchelsea Village Institute and Working Men's Club at the Recreation Ground in April 1921. At the official opening by W.G. Foster Clark tribute was paid to W.H. Skinner. 'the Duke of Boughton Monchelsea, without whose efforts the Institute would never have been established'. An enlarged photograph of Skinner was presented to him to hang in the club room. Dancing by the 200 persons present continued until 2.00a.m. to the music of Miss Whitehead's Jazz Band. By November it had 120 members and a successful programme of weekly dances and games evenings of dominoes, draughts, cribbage, quoits, whist and billiards. The Institute's debt had been cleared by H.G. Kleinwort and it supported cricket and football teams. A part of the Institute building was also set aside as a Village Hall. **163**

Throughout the 1930s the Parish Council met only three times a year and concerned itself with necessary but low-key matters such as the siting of the first public telephone box or the occurrence of holes in the road. By the end of World War II, however, life was imperceptibly changing. The influence of the large local landowners and the patronage of local farmers was declining. Farming and domestic service no longer totally dominated local employment while the slow spread of private and public transport began to break down rural isolation. Foster-Clark had died in 1932 and Lady Cornwallis in 1937. Their deaths marked the end of the Boughton Mount and Linton Park estates. The former, after requisition by the army in 1940, became Kent County Council property after the war. The upkeep of Boughton Monchelsea Place became so difficult that Mr. Michael Winch opened it to the public in 1955 while the death of H.G. Kleinwort in 1942 led to the partition and conversion of Wierton Place. Gone were the days when Kleinwort and Colonel Winch had occupied their own private pews in church. Nationally a new spirit was abroad. The men who had fought in World War II were more assertive and less deferential than their forebears particularly since the creation of the Welfare State by the post-war Labour Government released them from economic dependence. [164]

Feed the Cattle six times a day.
Clean out the troughs after each time of feeding.
Curry Comb & Rub twice a day.
Keep the Stalls clean and well litter'd.

Boughton Mount. Built by John Braddick in 1827 and inherited by John Wilbraham Braddick in 1844. The Braddicks aspired to replace the absentee Riders as lords-of-the-manor. The house was used by the army during World War II and was demolished in 1947. (Above) The Braddicks were hard taskmasters. Instructions to their stockman 'enshrined in a tablet of stone'.

This new spirit began to be reflected in village politics. In 1949 when the Borough of Maidstone was seeking to extend its boundaries by incorporating much of the surrounding rural parishes, including Boughton, which were then part of Maidstone Rural District Council, the proposal was emphatically rejected by the Annual Parish Meeting:

> *That this parish meeting resents the proposed appropriation of a large part of the parish by Maidstone Borough which is contrary to the wishes of the inhabitants of this rural parish and entirely approves of the action of Maidstone Rural District Council in resisting to the utmost.* **165**

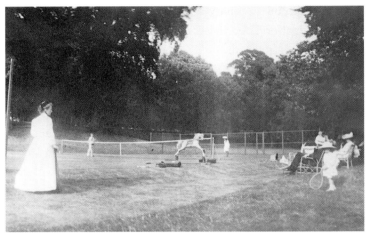

The End of an Era. Last scenes from an Age of Edwardian Elegance at Boughton Monchelsea Place. The social effects of two world wars were to create a very different society by the 1950s.(i) Children's tennis party under the watchful eye of a governess (ii) Madam, your carriage awaits.

Boughton's loyalty to Maidstone RDC was not rewarded. In 1956-57 the Parish Council was obliged to successfully oppose a proposal by Maidstone RDC to site a crematorium in Wierton Park. This was followed in 1959 by an epic struggle over the next six years to secure main drainage. Post-war Boughton was rapidly becoming 'a parish of old age pensioners'. By 1959 it was calculated that the number of pensioners had increased by 40% in the past five years yet because of housing shortage young people were increasingly being forced to drift to Maidstone and other nearby towns. No further building could be permitted without main drainage yet Maidstone RDC showed little inclination to install a service which was at least twenty years overdue. When public health issues had obliged main drains to be installed in many Kent villages at the turn of the century Boughton, like Loose, had considered it to be 'utterly unnecessary'. Now it was vital for the survival of the community. **166**

In January 1959 the RDC promised that when a drainage programme at Loose was finished Boughton would be next. By the end of the year, when there was no sign of the service being installed, the Parish Council was pressing for a date. In January 1960 the RDC promised completion within two years and the Parish Council, with all dwellings still on cesspools, threatened to take Boughton's drainage question to the BBC and the Press. Only when the local MP had raised the matter with the Minister and it had come before the House of Commons in 1961 was any serious progress made. Even so, with Staplehurst requesting further main drainage and residents complaining bitterly of the smell and the overflowing of cesspools, Ministry approval for the scheme was not secured until November 1963. Ultimately the drainage scheme was completed after a mammoth struggle in July 1965 and the way lay clear for Boughton's further development. **167**

Lewis Court Drive.
Without main drainage the modern centres of population at Lewis Court and Haste Hill could not have been built.

Boughton in Two World Wars

The declaration of war on Germany on 4 August 1914 found Boughton, like countless other British villages, almost totally unprepared. A letter from Kent County Council appealing for the appointment of special constables to protect life and property was only put to the annual parish meeting on 10 August and as a result 20 'specials' were sworn in. The Boughton contingent was headed by W.H. Skinner, chairman of the parish council. His second-in-command was C.S. Smith, a farmer from Elm House. All were under orders from the superintendent of the Maidstone Police Division. By 3 September 50 more parishioners had enrolled. Collections followed for the National Relief Fund and the Belgian Relief Fund and by the close of January 1915 70 parishioners had enlisted for the armed forces. Their names were

forwarded to the *Weekly Despatch* which, to boost recruitment, was offering a Bronze Medallion to what it termed the 'Bravest Village in the British Isles'. This 'most patriotic village' was to be 'the one which had contributed the greatest percentage of its manhood to the colours since the outbreak of war'. Boughton did not win but continued to send its young men to the slaughter for the next four years. A few joined the navy but the majority inevitably went to the army. **168**

Boughton's Contribution to World War I.
Many young men from the village, like George Potter, joined the Forces during the Great War. Twenty-nine perished in the slaughter. Their names were listed in the parish church and on the roll of honour at the School which was made by the boys in their Handicraft lessons.
(Left) The young George Potter 1918
(Right) Boughton Monchelsea Council School Roll of Honour.

Kent was subject to many hit-and-run attacks by air and sea but Boughton was too far from the coast and beyond the limited range of aerial bombardment to suffer in this respect. Most enemy activity was, of necessity, concentrated upon the East Kent coast, Thanet and the Thames. Maidstone was never even visited and the nearest the enemy came to Boughton was in air raids upon the Medway Towns. Boughton parishioners nevertheless found their lives changed in many ways by the impact of the Great War. Food was limited and its quality changed by government order. Publication of news was censored. Licensing hours were reduced. The clocks were changed and the state established a hold over its citizens which, although relaxed in peacetime, the Second World War was again to increase. For the time being, however, Boughton's contribution, in addition to helping towards the manpower requirements of a war of attrition, was to assist with the critical food shortages created by the German U-boat campaign of 1917.

BOUGHTON MONCHELSEA COUNCIL SCHOOL.

·ROLL OF HONOUR·

Old Boys of this School who gave their lives for their Country in the GREAT WAR ✦ 1914-1918.

"LEST WE FORGET."

JAMES ALLEN.	WILLIAM GILLINGHAM.
HARRY BARTON.	WILLIAM LAIGHT.
JOHN BOWLES.	JOSEPH LAMB.
HARRY BRIDGER.	WILLIAM LATTER.
WALLACE BURCHETT.	EDWARD NORRIS.
WILLIAM COLE.	GEORGE PAULEY.
EDWARD COLEMAN.	ALBERT PEARSON.
CHRISTOPHER DADSON.	SIDNEY ROLFE.
FREDERICK GATES.	CHARLES SHOEBRIDGE.
HERBERT GENN.	PERCY STEVENS.
JAMES GENN.	STANLEY WEAVER.
BRIDGE GILBERT.	CHARLES WELLARD.
WILLIAM GILBERT.	

The annual parish meeting of 1917 was convened to coincide with a visit to Maidstone by the President of the Board of Agriculture to address a large gathering of Kent farmers upon the need to increase food production. Cottage gardeners were urged by W.H. Skinner to grow as much as possible, particularly potatoes, and to help each other with the cultivation of allotments especially where men were away at the war. Since many agricultural labourers were also in the forces a Boughton branch of the Women's Land Army was established. Members did the work that would have been done before the War by men and were paid basically the same wages. Instructions to WLA members read as follows:

> *You are doing a man's work and so you are dressed rather like a man; but remember that...because you wear a smock and trousers you should take care to behave like an English girl who expects chivalry and respect from every one she meets. Noisy or ugly behaviour brings discredit not only on yourself but upon the uniform and the whole Women's Land Army. When people see you pass show them that an English girl who is working for her country on the land is the best sort of girl.*

Despite all efforts shortages of bread and potatoes continued and compulsory rationing started at the beginning of 1918 while even children at Boughton School cultivated much-needed vegetables in the school garden. The Armistice of November 1918 was signed not a moment too soon leaving the Allies victorious. Boughton, like every other British community, had made a sacrifice in blood. The names of 29 men were etched on the War Memorial in the parish church. Twenty-five of these young men had been educated at the village school. The loss of so many in their prime had a serious effect upon the size of the parish population between the wars.

Recruitment Drive in Maidstone.
Staged by the Boughton Monchelsea branch of the Women's Land Army during World War I. Mrs. Harling (Left) and Mrs. Munn carry the banner. Mrs. W.H. Skinner is on the latter's right.

The parish was little better prepared for the outbreak of World War II. In Britain, as in Europe, there was a heartfelt desire for peace and a shrinking from any repetition of the horrors of World War I. It was also believed in the 1930s that there was no adequate defence against air attack or poison gas. A lecture on 'Air Raid Precautions' was given for Maidstone RDC at the Corn Exchange as early as 17 September 1936 but the Parish Council tried in vain to secure the services of a volunteer Parish Air Raid Warden throughout the following year. Not until April 1938 did it finally enlist Mr. Pledger. Only then was the parish divided into five sections each with a sub-warden, three men and a messenger and the use of various private vehicles offered in the event of emergency. It was hoped to arrange a series of lectures and demonstrations on Air Raid Precautions involving all sections of the community but in February 1939 there was still no place where ARP equipment could be stored although in an emergency it was decided that the Village Hall and Institute would be commandeered as ARP Headquarters. **169**

On 23 March 1939 Colonel Scott, ARP organiser for Maidstone RDC, reversed this decision deciding instead that stores for individual parishes were unnecessary and that there should be one central store for all parishes situated at the Engine Sheds, Coxheath which would issue stretchers and protective clothing if an emergency arose. A scheme for the emergency billeting of evacuees was finalised in August but only on the eve of war on 17 August 1939 did the Parish Council respond to a Maidstone RDC request to conduct a survey of all parochial wells and springs which could be used for Civil Defence purposes if the piped water supply was put out of action by enemy attack. Boughton's clerk reported that there was an adequate supply of well and spring water available at Iden, White House and Church Farms together with the cottages at Iden Farm, the Cock, Wierton and Wierton Grange. Other wells were available at the Malthouse, Green Lane, Church Street, Loddington Lane, Marlpit, Wierton Hill Corner and the top of East Hall Hill. The clerk also stated that the ARP warning signals were inaudible to anyone indoors and requested that an adequate signal should be urgently installed. [170]

With the declaration of war on 1 September 1939 the main classroom in the school was commandeered as a First Aid and Cleansing Station. This, together with the arrival of a large party of evacuees from Timbercroft Junior School, Plumstead, necessitated the re-organisation of school classes and use of the village hall for additional school accommodation. The sudden evacuation of such a large number of London children into what was to become a major war zone can only be classified as a bureaucratic blunder. Some were sent to Wierton Grange and other large houses. The rest were billeted in smaller private dwellings. Their arrival brought a culture shock to Boughton's inhabitants. Four children, each under nine years old, were sent for example to Elm House.

We turned all the furniture out of the drawing room and put up camp beds with straw palliasses; they made a tremendous mess of that front room. They had very little in the way of clothes...so our mother had to go out and buy some. They were very much 'alive' so we had to treat their heads and cut off their hair. Their parents weren't very pleased the first time they came to visit...They also wet their beds...that's why we had the straw palliasses...I doubt if they had been in the country before...They threw all their rubbish out into the street...they said they always chucked things in the street when they were at home...Our aunts at Lyewood had two or three boys and...found them sleeping...under the bed because in their part of the world with families having so many in one room that's what they did...(Barbara and Rachel Smith).

The children of Timbercroft school gave the 'locals' an insight into social conditions in the poorer parts of London but by the end of 1940 the evacuees had mostly returned home just as the London 'blitz' was beginning.

If Boughton escaped direct involvement in World War I, during World War II Kent returned to its ancient role of 'Front Line County' and the village suffered accordingly. Not only was Boughton a mere thirty-four miles from the East Kent coast which was in imminent danger of invasion, but it also lay directly on the flight path taken by German bombers, and later flying bombs, towards London. The 'Phony War' ended with the German invasion of Denmark, Norway, Holland, Belgium and France in April-May 1940. By 24 May the sounds of battle could be clearly heard in East Kent as the British Expeditionary Force was driven back to the Channel coast and with the evacuation from Dunkirk German invasion seemed inevitable. A Radio Appeal by Anthony Eden on 14 May to join the Local Defence Volunteers (LDV), later re-designated the Home Guard, brought thousands flocking to join in the defence of their villages. At Boughton the local commander, Mr. Victor Skinner, had a leavening of First World War veterans such as Johnny Price, Bert Latham and Reuben Dann to help train an inexperienced assortment of amateur part-time soldiers both old and young. Known at first as 'The Parashots' because they expected to be confronted at any moment by German parachutists we do not know how the ill-armed and partially-training volunteers would have fared. One suspects they would have come off second best but fortunately they were never put to the test. [171]

The situation was extremely grave. In March 1940 the chairman, vice-chairman and clerk of the Parish Council were constituted an emergency committee with powers to act upon any directive of the RDC. The chairman, C.S. Smith, who had also been Boughton's elected representative on the RDC since 1924, became liaison officer between the civil and military authorities in the event of invasion. Victor Skinner, as LDV commander, was given a last ditch strongpoint which he was to defend demolishing a number of cottages around it to provide a clear field of fire. Following the Dunkirk evacuation in June the 'Parashots' were on high alert for a long period. There was a nightly curfew on the roads and anyone found travelling without very good reason was arrested. A keen lookout was kept on the Weald for German parachutists. [172]

During August and September, while the Battle of Britain raged overhead as the Germans endeavoured to destroy the RAF and prepare the way for invasion,

Boughton farm workers and hop pickers gathered in the harvest below. School children, on holiday, stood gazing skywards oblivious to the danger.

The planes went over in hundreds during the Battle of Britain...We used to count them and chalk up a hundred bombers. And then fighters and more fighters came up from the Weald. We used to get right excited. (Mrs. Dicker)

I remember coming out of church on a beautiful September Sunday morning and the sky was alive with dozens of 'dog fights' overhead. (Rachel Smith)

A Hurricane, 'wounded' in a dog fight, plunged into Furfield Quarry. The impact buried it deep in the ground where it remains until this day. The pilot baled out too late and was killed. As the battleground switched to the skies over London and the 'Blitz' began, an anti-aircraft battery was positioned on the corner of Park Lane and Heath Road to try and block the nightly armada of German aircraft. Air raid warnings were often twice daily throughout October. Children, now back at school, carried on normally taking cover only when aerial activity was directly overhead. The school, however, had no air raid shelters until February 1941 and because air raid precautions were thought unnecessary in rural schools, windows were at first unprotected against blast. During prolonged air raid warnings, therefore, school was frequently abandoned. On the Home Front by day Boughton parishioners collected scrap metal and waste paper. Mr. Skinner organised the scrap metal collection. There were dumps in Brishing Quarries and at Goodwin's stable yard on the Green where by July 1940 over two tons of scrap had been accumulated for the War effort. Mr. A.J. Gipps was Salvage Steward. Salvage collection was undertaken by the local Scouts. [173]

By March 1941 full or partially-filled sandbags had been issued to every house. Dumps of sand were also distributed at strategic points throughout the village to extinguish incendiary bombs while 42 volunteers took on the role of fire watchers. Two watches were on duty nightly in each sector in addition to the ARP Wardens and police patrols although even at this stage of the War the Wardens still lacked whistles and respirators. [174] With the approach of D-Day in June 1944 Boughton again took on the appearance which it had assumed in the eighteenth century during the heyday of Coxheath Camp. General Montgomery had his headquarters at Boughton Mount. His troops were stationed all around. Their encampments were in the field alongside Heath Road, once occupied by the tents of their eighteenth and early nineteenth century predecessors. Other tents stood in the grounds of Linton Park, Tilts Farm, The White House and Iden Farm extending almost to Chart Sutton, Wierton and Boughton Monchelsea Place. The field adjacent to Martins Farm became the temporary home for a contingent of Canadians also under Montgomery's command. [174]

Allied forces landed in Normandy on 6 June 1944. A week later the first of the 'doodlebugs' or flying bombs fell on Kent. These V1 [*Vergeltung* = revenge] weapons were aimed at London but many fell short of their target. By the end of the War 1,422 V1s had been shot down over Kent and another 1,000 or so had fallen in the Channel. To counter Hitler's strategy the Ministry of Defence introduced an elaborate pre-prepared plan. The 'doodlebugs' were first intercepted by patrols of daylight fighters or radar-controlled fighters at night. If they got past these they encountered an enormous barrage of heavy Ack-Ack fire mounted by almost all the AA guns in the land. These had been moved to Kent from all over England and spaced along the southern slopes of the North Downs. A last line of defence was provided by 480 barrage balloons anchored on higher ground. In this massive defensive system Boughton played a part. The Royal Observer Corps, situated at Goodwin's Chicken Farm between Heath Road and Haste Hill, upon sighting a flying bomb fired a flare into the air attached to a small parachute. This process continued along the pilotless missile's route enabling the fighter aircraft to intercept them more quickly. At one period they were said to be passing overhead every twenty minutes. 'Attendance poor owing to the attack of pilotless planes' read the school log book in June 1944. There was no answer, however, to the silent V2 rockets launched on 8 September 1944. These gave no warning of their approach and travelled too fast for radar or any AA gun to track. The mass assault by V1s ended on 1 September with the occupation of the Pas de Calais. It was another six months before the mobile launching pads of the V2s were overrun in the Netherlands and there was a voluntary and limited evacuation of some Boughton children to the safety of Mid-Wales. [175]

Two flying bombs fell on Boughton Monchelsea. The first dropped on Parkwood Farm causing no damage. The second fell near Cliff Cottage whose occupant, Tommy Reynolds, was killed by the blast. World War II was a very different conflict to World War I. The latter, a static war in the trenches, created far more casualties than a war of movement. In 1945 only 10 more names were added to the roll of honour in St. Peter's Church but this was of little consolation to the relatives and friends of those who had made the supreme sacrifice.

Schools

The earliest known educational provision appears at Boughton in 1806 when the vicar, James Andrew, referred to the presence of 'two or three small day schools' in the village. Previous vicars had made no reference to a school. Twelve years later there were still three unendowed day schools, holding between them 66 pupils, to which some of the poor sent their children at their own expense. There was also a recently-opened unendowed Sunday School catering for some 60 youngsters many of whom were unable to attend school during the week because of work or poverty. Some of

HYMN,

TO BE SUNG BY THE CHILDREN

OF THE

Boughton Monchelsea

PARISH SCHOOL,

ON SUNDAY, MAY 18, 1834.

I.
O would you wish on earth to know
In heavenly breasts what spirits glow;
'Tis Charity — whose sacred flame
From Heaven's eternal altar came.

II.
O would you wish on earth to view
God's holy Image, bright and true;
'Tis Charity — whose radiant vest
For Christ's own Banquet decks the guest.

III.
O would you live in hope serene,
And close in hope, life's transient scene;
Let Faith and Charity supply
The spring, and Hope shall never die.

IV.
Faith, Hope and Charity, "these Three,"
In heart unite, in toil agree;
One Spirit feeds, one Law defines,
One blessing cheers, one Soul combines.
HALLELUJAH ! AMEN.

PRINTED BY J BROWN, KENT ARMS OFFICE 87, WEEK STREET, MAIDSTONE.

Hymn Sheet of Boughton Monchelsea Parish School 1834. Possibly used at the re-opening of the church after the fire of 1832. The Parish School was probably the Day and Sunday School, supported by public subscription and parental pence, mentioned in the Parliamentary Enquiry 1833.

the pupils at the day schools and Sunday School, however, may have been the same. Nevertheless the poorer classes were reported to be 'desirous of possessing a better means of education'. Fifteen years later, despite an expansion of population, the situation remained unchanged. The Parliamentary Enquiry into Education 1833 reported the existence of three 'Daily Schools' containing about 75 children of both sexes, whose instruction was paid for by their parents, plus a Day and Sunday School attended by about 80 children which was supported by public subscription assisted by parental pence. **176**

Although no mention of a school occurs before 1806 it is difficult to believe that sound elementary instruction was not available to at least some Boughton children before this date. When printed marriage registers first came into use in 1754 brides and grooms were required to sign their names or alternatively, if unable to write, to make their marks. From then onwards the marriage register provides a crude yardstick for testing the state of literacy although the ability to sign one's name did not necessarily mean that one could either read or write fluently. Between 1754 and

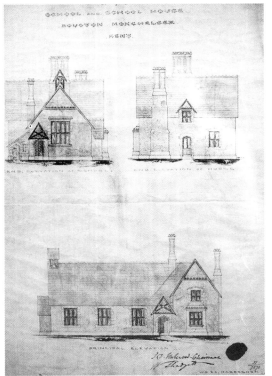

1799 214 or 53.2% of newly-weds signed their names at Boughton as opposed to 188 or 46.8% who were 'illiterate'. Sixty-three per cent of the latter were women for whom parents presumably considered 'literacy' less necessary than for men. In the years between 1800 and 1850, however, this quite impressive proportion was reversed. Whereas 463 or 45.7% of all persons marrying could sign the marriage register 550 or 54.3% could not. The majority of the 'illiterates' were still female. **177**

A School is Planned.
The plan for a National Society School and Schoolhouse at Boughton made by the architects W. & G. Habershon, Bloomsbury Square, London in 1850. The School consisted of 2 classrooms 22ft x 21ft holding a total of 75 boys and 75 girls and allowing 6 sq.ft. per child.

It was doubtless this situation which led Boughton's curate, the Rev. M. Jefferies, to approach the Anglican National Society in 1850 for help in erecting a school to replace the Day and Sunday School which had existed since at least 1818. The new school was to consist of two classrooms 22 feet by 21 feet which would hold 75 boys and 75 girls allowing 6 square feet per child. It was to be situated upon a site donated by the 4th Thomas Rider of Boughton Monchelsea Place whose uncle had acquired the land as part of the Enclosure in 1817. The total cost of the project, including a teacher's residence, was £609 of which £375 was raised locally. The Education Department grant was £114 while the Diocesan Office and the National Society gave £75 and £45 respectively. The school, which was built of Kent ragstone in the typical semi-ecclesiastical style of the mid-nineteenth century, had high windows to discourage 'distractions' which were of frosted glass protected by iron bars. The internal walls were bare and whitewashed and the paintwork dark brown to prevent over-stimulation or 'excitement'. There was a wood and glass partition between the infants' room which held Standard I and the main room holding Standards II, III and IV. The infants' room had a high gallery at the rear with tip-up wooden seats. It was near the window and bitterly cold in winter. The master's house was on the north side of the school with no damp course and rarely warmed by the sun. The children hung their coats in the lobbies and sat at iron-framed desks with bench seats which were still in use a century later. Children took their own lunch. Water was drawn by the boys from the well at the rear of the school. The school bell rang at five minutes to nine and the front door was locked at nine o'clock. On dark days the school was lit by oil lamps and heated by coal fires which constantly smoked and were 'injurious to health'.

The school building was complete by 1851. Teachers' salaries and other expenses were expected to cost £90 per annum. It was intended to charge 2d. per child per week for instruction and to rely upon subscriptions to cover the remaining cost. By 1852 125 children were attending and in the following year the first Master of the School, George Stevens, is mentioned in the parish register together with his wife, Anne. He did not last long and by the time of the first school inspection in 1855 had been succeeded by a master named Crook. He in turn gave way to George Goulding in April 1857.

The 1855 inspection described the school premises as 'very good'. Teaching was by means of the 'monitorial system' instituted by Andrew Bell, an Anglican clergyman, in India. This system involved the Master teaching a lesson to a handful of senior pupils or monitors who then re-taught the lesson to groups of younger children thus overcoming the scarcity and cost of qualified teachers. In 1862 Robert Lowe, secretary to the Committee of the Privy Council on Education, laid down that grants to schools would depend upon pupils' attendance at the school and success in an annual examination by an inspector of Reading, Writing and Arithmetic. This system, known as 'Payment by Results', placed heavy pressure on both pupils and teachers since the livelihood of the latter depended on grants which could only be earned by the children. Inevitably the curriculum was influenced, too, since there was a heavy emphasis on the basic subjects to be examined and upon rote learning. The Revised Code of 1862 also required that the Headteacher should keep a school diary or Log Book. William Lockyer Banks, the Boughton schoolmaster of the day, objected violently but nevertheless the Log was kept providing a gold-mine of information about the school, its staff, pupils, governors and its relationship to village life. [178]

The initial reports upon the school were good:

1864 Good building with excellent playground. A cheerful mixed school. Catechism fairly understood. Reading, Writing and Arithmetic fair. No home tasks. Needlework too much confined to one style. Singing very good.

1865 The school is in good order and is taught with creditable care and intelligence. Most splendid rewards were given this afternoon to all that passed the Inspector's examination.

1867 The examination has again been highly satisfactory.

Nevertheless local farmers were hesitant about extending education, particularly for boys, beyond the age of seven.

...We are not opposed to education, stated Thomas Hayes of Charlton Farm, Boughton's poor law guardian and subsequently Chairman of Boughton Monchelsea School Board, *Enlighten a labourer reasonably but don't let it be only book learning. If you prevent his being employed under a certain age you hinder his being taught to get a living...No limit should be put to the age at which boys are employed...A little chap of eight or even less may be useful. I have...from a dozen to thirty boys and girls...to pull 'kilk'* [ket locks or sharlocks] *and weed corn. I send a man with them...I pay them all by the day.*

Some were even more forthright. 'A child should have no education after the age of seven years', stated another Boughton farmer. 'From seven to fourteen should be the years of apprenticeship for an agricultural labourer'.[179] Until Education became compulsory, and frequently even afterwards, children's schooling was constantly interrupted, with the full agreement of their parents, by the demands of the agricultural year. In March 1868 William Roberts missed the Inspector's examination because he was absent bird-minding. 'Fruiting' in June and July often lasted two to three weeks and was closely followed by haymaking. At the end of August the 'Hopping holidays' began lasting for approximately a month. With the advent of cob nuts children were again absent 'nut picking' in October.[180] As if this was not enough senior boys were employed 'beating' for Mr. Skinner, Lord Cornwallis and their successors.[181]

William Lockyer Banks.
An early master of the National School. It fell to him to begin the first Log Book in July 1863. He resented the idea so much that he resigned in August and retired to Birchington. He was a prominent member of the Mid-Kent Schoolmasters' Association.

School attendance was not only affected by concessions to local agriculture but was also influenced by other factors such as inadequate clothing and footwear when children walked to school in all weathers; by epidemics, pressure to augment the family income and finally by plain truancy. Many children found the temptation of external attractions hard to resist. On 20 July 1863 a triple attraction in the form of a cricket match in Mr. Moore's Park, an auction at the Brewery and a Fair Day at Loose left only 70 children in school. Twenty boys were absent on 5 November 1890 'owing to the Guy Fawkes Celebrations' while attendance on May Day was always 'thin' as pupils 'kept up the May Day observations.' Very few children were present on the Foresters' Fete Day 1880 and the school was dismissed when the band had passed. 'Several' children were reported absent on 26 May 1875 when the Master supposed that they had gone to the annual demonstration of the Agricultural Labourers' Union at Maidstone. On other occasions the Master accepted the inevitable and declared a school holiday. The first Horticultural Show of the Cottage Gardeners' Society on the Pond Field in 1872 produced a holiday for the day as did the Flower Show in Linton Park on 20 July 1880.[182]

The incidence of epidemics also seriously affected school attendance. The epidemic diseases of the nineteenth century were frequently fatal and children were particularly vulnerable. Mr. Wilkin, a surgeon from Staplehurst, attended the school to vaccinate against smallpox in February 1866. Two years later scarlatina was reported to be spreading throughout the parish. In 1873 'a great many children were away with mumps' and on 25 June 1877:

> *One case of fever reported from Coxheath in the Chambers family. As the day was fixed for the Foresters' Fete I thought it was a fit opportunity to have the Schools thoroughly disinfected. Mr. Cleaver* [Sanitary Inspector] *called at 9 o'clock...all ventilation was stopped and the schools kept closed till the following morning. When the school was opened every place seemed sweet and healthy. I think with care and Mr. Cleaver's assistance we may prevent the spread of the disease in the parish which otherwise would necessitate the closing of school for weeks.*

In 1879 most of the children were sick with measles and several schools were reported closed since isolation was the only known preventative. Scarlet fever broke out again in 1882 at Coxheath and the services of Mr. Cleaver were again called upon at Boughton. Five tubs of carbolic powder were received on the evening of 6 January. Next day the Master disinfected the whole school, dusted the Coxheath children and ordered Mrs. Lamb, the caretaker, to sweep up the powder and throw it down the closets. In 1891 whooping cough was prevalent among the infants bringing many absences. Measles broke out in January 1892 while mumps and diptheria caused further poor attendances the following year. Infant attendance was decimated in December 1896 as whooping cough again passed through the 'babies' room to be followed by 'glass pox' [chicken pox] in April 1897. With scarlet fever and whooping cough prevalent for much of 1900 the Medical Officer advised that the school building should be 'thoroughly cleaned and whitewashed during the vacation'; but it was not until 1908 that the Managers decided to close the school for the first time for a fortnight on account of measles. A second school closure followed for the same reason in June 1911.[183]

Only too frequently epidemics were traceable to defective sanitary conditions in school. In 1873 the HMI Report complained that the cesspool was too close to the school. Two years later changes were made to the closets under the direction of Mr. Cleaver and a much relieved Master reported that 'It is to be hoped that the nuisance which has existed for years will be no more'. He was somewhat premature although admittedly over thirty years had elapsed before HMI again complained in 1908 of the offensive smell from the 'offices' and recommended more frequent emptying of the cesspits. The inspector was even more forthright in 1909:

> *The pits attached to the offices used by 200 children should be emptied more frequently than once a year. There is no apparent reason why proper apparatus for flushing should not be provided.*

Boughton Monchelsea School.

The village school which has served Boughton Monchelsea well for one hundred and fifty years. It was built in 1851 by the National Society on land allocated to Thomas Rider III at the Coxheath enclosure 1817, and donated by his nephew, Thomas Rider IV. At first it had to compete with the existing private and dame schools.

Alterations were made in 1911 and by 1912 Dr. Tew, the Medical Officer of Health, brought to the school by a diptheria scare, warmly praised the sanitary arrangements. Boughton school was fortunate, however, to escape any major nineteenth century epidemic.[184]

The 1870 Education Act enabled children aged 5-12 to attend school but made Education neither compulsory nor free. At Boughton, however, it also resulted in the highly unusual transfer of the school from the National Society to the care of a school board elected by the parish ratepayers. The reason for this step is unknown. Membership of the first school board consisted of two farmers, a retired miller, a malster and a butcher. The chairman was Thomas Hayes of Charlton farm. His vice-chairman was another farmer, John Hadlow. When the former died in 1879 he was replaced by the latter with the Malster, Mark Atkins, as vice-chair. Somewhat surprisingly in 1872 this Board, dominated by farmers, passed an enlightened bye-law anticipating Mundella's Act 1880 and making education compulsory between the ages of 5-13.[185]

Attendance, however, still remained a problem. Many parents could not afford to pay the school pence or needed their children as wage earners. When the school was under the National Society it was extremely difficult to get some parents to pay the 2d. per child per week. In 1865 two families which 'owed a week's schooling' were suspended and in 1868 a Mrs. Potter refused to pay the 2d. 'for her son's schooling'. In 1873 the newly-appointed board increased the fees to 4d. per week for the first child; 2d for the second child; and 1d. a week for the third child, for infants and the children of widows. Henceforth the Master 'had plenty of trouble with parents and children alike about the pence'. In 1875 Mrs. Noakes sent word that she could not pay more than 6d. for her four children. If the Master could not take them for that he was to send them home. In the same year Potter's children were admitted at a reduced rate on account of his death and the Chairman paid for John Lamb's schooling out of his own pocket.[186]

Only after an Act of 1891 enabled Boards to admit children free did attendance become less of a problem. At the same time the powers of the attendance officer became more formidable as did the readiness of the Board to prosecute offenders. The demand for child labour also slackened towards 1900 as many hop farms began the changeover to fruit although child workers were still in demand after World War II. Gradually the school roll began to climb from 130 in 1872 to 189 in 1875. By 1881 there were 223 pupils. Numbers stabilised around 250 between 1890-1921. The increase was created in part by the rise in parish population and partly by improved attendance. Moreover by the 1902 Act Boughton had become a Council School with premises expanded by 1906 and numbers swollen by the raising of the school leaving age to fourteen by 1918. In 1921 pupils fell, however, to 190 and declined yet further in 1936 when Boughton Monchelsea ceased to be an all age school.[187]

The school was always understaffed and the Master constantly overworked throughout its nineteenth century history. In 1872 Headmaster John Ares, with 131 children on roll, had only one monitor to assist him. Nine years later his successor had one assistant master and three pupil teachers to instruct 223 children. Pupil teachers had to be at least thirteen years of age and were annually examined by the

Inspectors. Queen's Scholarships, tenable at a training college, were competed for by pupil teachers and were intended to provide a flow of qualified recruits for elementary schools. An indenture was drawn up between the parents of the pupil teacher, the headteacher and the voluntary society or school board responsible for the school. The indenture was similar to that of an articled clerk in a legal practice. In it the headteacher agreed to give the pupil teacher daily opportunities to observe and practise teaching and to devote at least an hour and a half every morning or evening before or after school to the instruction of the pupil teacher 'in the several branches of learning taught in the school'. This placed a colossal burden upon a Boughton Master who also had monitors to instruct and a night school to run attended by tired and often reluctant early school leavers for a fee of 2d. per week.

In such circumstances, fatigued and overworked and often without qualified assistance, all Victorian schoolmasters had frequent recourse to the cane. 'G. Gilbert was very insolent to me this afternoon', recorded John Ares, 'I gave him a good caning'. Charles Rolfe in 1879 caned his own son for inattention as well as Henry Mortimore 'for not attending to his reading'. Mr. Rolfe's problems were not limited to the elementary school. In 1875 he reports 'I took my cane from my desk in the night school to keep order'. Three years previously he had taken the extraordinary step of announcing 'No talking allowed in future in school'. Two children who disobeyed were confined to school for a month and another was caned.[188] The regime of silence, however, did no last for long.

Rolfe's problems stemmed from his own lack of confidence in his disciplinary powers. He undoubtedly found rough and exuberant boys difficult to handle. His successor, P.R. 'Flick' Forder, who was Head from 1890-1923, was a more natural disciplinarian but his punishments verged upon the sadistic. A confrontation with Thomas Mathews led to his receipt of a £3.0.0d. fine plus costs for assault from Maidstone magistrates. Mathews, caned for throwing stones and injuring a fellow pupil, claimed incorrectly in the village that he had been caned ten times. Mathews was caned again and made to stand on a form from 9.30 a.m. till 1.00 p.m. holding a slate above his head indicating that he was a liar. Whenever, through fatigue, the boy allowed his chin to fall to this chest Forder jabbed him in the neck to make him hold his head up again.[189] Ultimately Forder was upheld by the Board but the whole affair, which dragged on until the end of the year, left behind an unpleasant taste.[190]

In 1870 the syllabus consisted of the 3Rs, scripture, needlework, singing and drill. Preparation for the annual examination, largely by rote learning, preoccupied teachers and pupils alike. After 1870 there was some relaxation of the Revised Code and schools could earn extra grants for 'specific subjects'. In 1871 a grant of three shillings was introduced for each child successful in an examination in not more than two such subjects including history, geography, algebra, geometry and the natural sciences. Few children were presented for 'specific subjects' in the 1870s but by the Code of 1875 grammar, geography and history became class subjects and grants were earned by the proficiency of the whole class and not by individual results.

> *How I am to get through all the work of the various standards since the*
> *Code adds geography, literature and grammar..., I am at a loss to know, was*
> *the despairing cry of Charles Rolfe.*[191]

Gradually, however, the curriculum widened. Singing first appeared as a curriculum subject in 1872. In the same year Mr. Rolfe also taught the pupil teachers history, geography, arithmetic, algebra and geometry. In 1875 he gave a model lesson in Grammar. The first references to recitation and model drawing occur in 1877. In 1881 visiting speakers first appeared in the person of Mr. Evans of the Staffordshire Potteries who made a cup, saucer and teapot in the presence of the children 'who expressed their satisfaction by the constant clapping of hands.' An innovation called the Object Lesson also materialised. Based upon the principle that children learn most readily from 'real' objects the Infants began Object Lessons in 1873. The first subject was 'The Table' followed by 'The Pin', 'The Window' and 'The Goat'. Subjects in the Syllabus of 1893 included 'Clock, Book, Coins, Slate, Lead Pencil and Railway train' closely followed by 'Apple, Orange, Horse, Camel, Sheep, Cow, Pig, Leopard, Seal, Beaver, Cat and Dog'. A museum case was recommended in 1898 and appeared within two months.[192]

The standards of the school fluctuated. In 1872, upon taking up appointment, Rolfe found two classes 'quite backward in everything' but by November 'of the 40 children neglected...by the last master 25 were fully up to standard'. To some extent criticism of the work bequeathed by a predecessor was standard practice but the HMI Report for 1876 was complimentary:

> *The school is in an efficient state and the results of the examination are*
> *highly creditable to Mr. Rolfe who is an energetic and skilful teacher.*

In 1881 the Inspector described the 'tone and order' of the school as 'very good'. By 1890, however, the situation had completely changed:

> *The examination...is again thoroughly disappointing...There is...much that calls for adverse comment. Having regard to...the previous low level of attainment I can recommend no Merit Grant. A school where so much of the attainment is so low as it is here is not doing the work for which a Public Elementary School exists...Unless HM Inspector can report more favourably next year upon the attainments of the scholars in the Mixed Schools the grant will be endangered.*[193]

The reaction of the Board was immediate and Rolfe was dismissed. His successor, Philip Robert Forder, was equally scathing in his criticism of Rolfe:

> *...It seems that although six months of the school year have passed the amount of work that has been done by standards II, III, IV is absolutely nil.*

During the next two and a half years Forder undoubtedly managed to pull the school round as the HMI Report for 1893 testified:

> *...The progress of the school during the last two years has been so marked, there are so many signs of intelligence, both in the class answering and in the composition and such ample evidence of hard and steady work on the part of the teacher that I have thought myself justified in recommending the grant on the highest scale...*[194]

By the time Forder arrived, however, the Marriage Registers 1850-1889 suggest that the struggle against basic illiteracy was already won. Of the 647 newly-weds between 1851-1889 472 or 73% were able to sign their names as opposed to 175 or 27% who still made their marks. After 1856 a majority of partners were able to sign in any given year. There were only two male illiterates in 1890 and two more in 1893 and 1895. Thereafter, apart from a man and a woman who could not sign in 1921, all parties were signatories.

Forder was plagued throughout his headship by the problems of inadequate staffing and overcrowding as the school roll rose with the population increase, enforced attendance and the abolition of the school pence.

The Staff works hard and well under great disadvantages, read the 1904 Report. *The main room is overcrowded and there is no space for the First Standard who are huddled into a corner without desk accommodation and cannot be well managed or taught...*

In 1905 Forder recorded the 'practical impossibility' of instructing pupil teachers and monitresses and also conducting the periodic examinations in the School. The following year he not only had to supervise the work of the school but had also to teach Standards IV-VII. Even the building of an additional classroom in 1906 made little difference.

The Best Years of their Lives.

Ill-shod and often clad in ancient family 'hand-me-downs' these early-20th century scholars walked to school in all weathers and were exposed to epidemics of all kinds. The Group 2 photo c.1912 was originally from Mr. and Mrs. George Potter who are pictured on the back row 5th and 6th from the left. The senior girls in the centre of Group 4, are probably monitresses.

After the 1902 Act the school leaving age increased and the School Board was replaced by a Management Committee appointed by the local authority. The personnel, however, remained essentially the same with a heavy emphasis on the local farming community. Only a handful of children went to the local boys' and girls' grammar schools before World War II. Few parents could afford the expense of uniform, books and travel apart from the loss of family income. In any event the expectations of parents, pupils and staff were low.[195]

> *One of the Colegate boys who lived in the cottage by the Albion...got through to the Grammar School but his parents couldn't afford it. The only ones I remember going were Harry Wood and one of the Pearson boys...The others didn't go because...as soon as it came to fruiting time you were gone for six weeks fruit picking to help get the money for the winter...I had to get up at five in the morning before school to pick fruit...* (Nellie Bolton).

During the period 1890-1923 rural life still remained comparatively unaltered. Yet in other respects changes were beginning. In 1900, influenced by the national outcry caused by poor physical fitness among recruits for the Boer War, greater emphasis began to be placed upon 'drill' as a curriculum subject. In 1900 the Management Committee agreed to arrange for a corporal from Maidstone Barracks to give drill to the pupils for 2s.6d. per week. By 1901 a former soldier from the Lincolns was drilling the children on Wednesday afternoons. In 1922 the upper standard boys spent thirty minutes in organised games (football) for the first time. The girls played rounders. Netball remained, as yet, unknown but a long tradition of sporting excellence in the school had begun. Similarly the arrival of the first gardening tools in 1910 heralded the start of a second longstanding tradition of rural science which, despite the depredations of rabbits, flourished during the inter-war years.

Early references by the Horticultural Superintendent to the correlation of gardening with other school subjects is another indication of the school being considered progressive.

> *Plans of the cropping and the garden are drawn to scale. A table showing the progress of the crops is kept. Notes are made of lessons given on insect pests propagating and general vegetable culture. Arithmetic is also correlated. The scholars are keen gardeners and get good results,* wrote W.P. Wright in 1923.

Nor was the experience purely theoretical. In December 1926 the boys of the gardening class spent the afternoon watching a demonstration of fruit tree pruning by W.H. Skinner in his orchard near the church. As the school garden was improved and extended so the plaudits and extra-mural activities multiplied and Boughton Monchelsea School's reputation grew. The Head and his gardening class made regular visits to the gardens of Wierton Place upon the invitation of H.G. Kleinwort. In 1932 the school was congratulated for its allotment plot at the County Agricultural Show. A year later HMI reported that 'Gardening is a particularly good feature...flower and vegetable culture are being successfully undertaken...' In 1934 the school won the Lady Colet Shield for gardening which was presented by Lord Northbourne and the Director of Education.[196]

A similar success in athletics brought the school a reputation and prestige which belied the smallness of its size. A grass athletics track was first cut on the Recreation Ground opposite the school in the 1920s. Thereafter hardly a year passed without its pupils achieving some success. The girls, excluded from gardening until Boughton became a primary school, were well to the fore. In 1925 Marjorie Bourne was a member of the Kent team in the 100 yards relay in the Inter-County Championships at Crystal Palace. Two years later Dorothy Skinner won the Foster Clark Cup awarded to the Champion girl in the Maidstone Elementary School Sports. A year later Nancy Offen won the Kent championship in the 75 yards hurdles and represented Kent at the SAA championships at Stamford Bridge. Gertie Marsh represented Maidstone in the Kent sports for four years and Kent in the All-England sports for two years in the 1930s.[197] The enthusiasm for physical education and for gardening continued unabated after Boughton's re-organisation from an all-age elementary school to a Junior Mixed and Infant School in 1936, with the transfer of the senior pupils to Loose Council School.

In 1936 the children staged a large display of Country and Maypole Dancing, Games, Gymnastics and Massed Physical Exercises while in 1937 the rose garden at the front of the school was planted to commemorate the Coronation of King George VI. During World War II poultry keeping by the older children played its part in the 'Grow More Food Campaign' and an additional 20 rods of land were rented adjacent to the school garden.[198] Even after the changes wrought by the 1944 Education Act HMI could still report in 1947 that:

The school is outstanding for its development of rural activities and the considerable part they play in the classwork of the older children. The result is a lively interest and sound practical approach to their lessons by both boys and girls...[199]

The 1944 Act produced many changes in both welfare and education. The most notable welfare development concerned free school milk. From September 1946 a one-third of a pint bottle was available daily for every child.[200] The most notable educational change was that grammar school places became 'free' to those who passed the 11+ examination. The remaining children attended the Cornwallis Secondary Modern School which opened on Heath Road in 1958.

In 1972 Kent County Council introduced the Thames-side System into the Maidstone Division in a bid to forestall the Labour Government's attempt to abolish grammar schools and make comprehensive schools universal. Under this system all pupils transferred from primary schools at 11+ to comprehensive high schools where they remained for two years. Following two years of continuous assessment approximately the top third of pupils then transferred to the Maidstone Division's four grammar schools to continue their education to 18+. The other two-thirds remained in the comprehensive high schools of which Cornwallis School became one. The system had its weaknesses and its critics. Nevertheless throughout the early and mid-1980s between 50% and 60% of ex-pupils from Boughton School secured grammar school places. With the restoration of the 11+ examination grammar school transfers fell to 30%-40% of Boughton children. By 1994, however, Cornwallis School had become a grant maintained comprehensive school as part of the myriad of educational changes which were taking place alongside the National Curriculum. Children, whose parents wished for it, could now receive a secondary education up to the age of eighteen within the parish but those who preferred a grammar school education could still attend a grammar school if they passed the 11+ exam. Compared with fifty years before a full secondary education to age 18+ and beyond was now in theory open to all.

During the 1970s, 1980s and 1990s the curriculum at Boughton Monchelsea Primary School widened and broadened with concerts, school drama, the development of school clubs and societies, school venture weeks, maypole dancing and educational visits. A Parents' Association, formed in the late 1960s,

Bringing Boughton School Sporting Success.

(Left) School Athletics Team 1930. One of the successful teams of the 'twenties and 'thirties when Boughton was an all-age school.

(Below) Their sporting counterparts over fifty years later.

(Right) Kent Primary Schools' County Netball Champions 1989.

(Left) The boys who won the Maidstone Seven-a-Side competition and the Maidstone Consolation Cup in 1983.

blossomed and developed with a phenomenal talent for fund raising and became itself a focal point for village social activity. A covered swimming pool, built by the Parents' Association in the late 1960s, ensured that by the 1980s few children left school without being able to swim while meaningful contact with schools in France, Italy and Finland added a necessary European dimension to children's horizons.

The 1980s and 1990s saw also a resurgence of sporting activity by both girls and boys which even bettered the achievements of the 1920s and 1930s. The school was still a small school with barely sufficient fourth year boys and girls to provide full football or netball teams. Yet coached by Olive Hastings and Peter Hirons the school teams enjoyed a period of outstanding success against numerically far larger rivals. The boys won the Maidstone Seven-A-Side Football Competition in 1983, 1986 and 1989 and were runners-up in 1987 and 1988. They also won the Maidstone Consolation Cup in 1983 and 1996 and were runners-up in 1989. Moreover between 1978-89 no fewer than nine boys were members of Maidstone District football teams while Paul Hobbs (Football) and Daniel Thirkell (Cricket) played for Kent Schools. The girls, not to be outdone, were runners-up in the Maidstone & District Area Netball Tournament in 1986, 1988 and 1989 and winners of the Maidstone & District 'A' and 'B' Tournaments in 1991 and 1992. The Boughton team became Kent Primary Schools' Netball Champions in 1989 and were semi-finalists in 1991. In the next year they won the prestigious Black Lion Tournament and were again semi-finalists in the County tournament. Boughton girls won the Maidstone & District Small Primary Schools Netball Tournament every year from 1985. Boys and girls combined to win the Maidstone Schools' Athletics championships in 1989 and 1990 after being runners-up in 1987 and 1988. Boughton won the Greta Bowles Invitation Athletics Championships for eight schools from 1988-92 and again in 1998.[201]

The Parish Council –
Towards the Millennium

From the late 1970s the role of the Parish Council began to change. Its responsibilities widened as it began to serve the needs of a changing village community which included the many newcomers upon the new estates of Lewis Court, Meadow View and Haste Hill Close, These often had very different aspirations to those of the old homogeneous population. Since the 1960s concerns had been expressed at the dilapidated state of the Village Hall which was owned by the Village Institute. Finally in the late 1970s a new Village Hall was built and £2,500 provided for furnishings by the Parish Council who became the custodian trustee.[202]

While the new Village Hall was of great benefit to the community two controversial planning decisions by Kent County Council gave warning that henceforth the Parish Council was to be heavily pre-occupied with issues concerning planning, the landscape, the environment and conservation generally. With Government directives increasingly favouring property developers it was inevitable that rural areas would come under pressure in the future. In November 1979 KCC authorised the use of Furfield Quarry as a waste disposal site despite loud protests from Boughton and Loose Parish Councils and Brishing Residents' Association. Such was the concern of the Parish Council that it conducted a survey to try to establish whether the proposed tip would pollute the Loose Stream. Nevertheless the project proceeded.[203] Four years later, when buildings at Monchelsea Farm were replaced by the giant fertiliser store of a haulage contractor with the approval of Maidstone Borough Council, there was further disquiet. The store was said to be three times the size of the original farm buildings. Over a hundred residents attended a protest meeting. Attempts were made to limit the number of vehicles using the yard and a further application by the contractor to extend the store, made five months later, was refused.[204]

The early 80s saw also increased Council involvement in other parish organisations. Authority in Recreation Ground matters had passed from the Parish Council to trustees in 1921. The trustees were replaced in 1980 by a Management Committee of users of the Recreation Ground. Children's playground equipment was purchased by a group of parishioners and installed on the Recreation Ground by the Council. A Summer Play Leadership Scheme was also commenced to occupy children during part of the school holidays. In 1983 it was decided at the Annual Parish Meeting to improve and extend the village green by the purchase of adjacent land thus furnishing the village with a clearly defined centre. Finance for these projects was obtained not only from parish precepts but by regular application to Maidstone Borough Council for grants and allowances from Concurrent Functions.

Councillor Ian Ellis, first elected as a parish councillor in 1980, was to the fore in these developments. Four years later he was returned as Boughton's ward member on Maidstone Borough Council with an overall majority of 179. At the same time in a double victory he topped Boughton's parish council elections with 515 votes. Thereafter he was regularly elected to both bodies where his enthusiasm, energy and expertise did much to promote parish interests. In July 1984 a village appraisal was launched 'to assess the needs of the parish and to create a working plan for its future'. Henceforth parish council activities gathered pace. As the Council moved towards the 21st century women came to play a more significant role in its affairs. From 1992-94 Olive Hastings became its first female chairman. Wendy Clarke was its first female vice-chairman from 1994 and the following year became chairman of Boughton Monchelsea Amenity Trust.[205]

Trust funds established in 1985 had by 1997 grown to become substantial permanent endowments for the village hall and recreation ground. Grants from Maidstone Borough Council Concurrent Functions supported the upkeep of the Green and the playground area of the recreation ground. Other financial support was provided by the parish council for the upkeep of the churchyard; a new water supply for the Recreation Ground; and re-furbishment of the Cricket pavilion and the tennis court. The Reiffgins charity, moribund for almost a century, had been resurrected by 1985 and its objects updated. William Reiffgins, 'a high borne German' had made his original bequest of 'one annuitie of 4 pounds by the year for 34 year's to come and 60 pounds of money to be bestowed in lands to the use of the poore for ever' in 1613. He left this bequest 'in gratitude for the Kindness he received when he came as a poor man in his youth to live in Boughton.' The investment income from the revived charity now allows grants to be made to parishioners in need such as students and the elderly.[206]

Two parts of the parish had been designated conservation areas in the mid-1960s. These were the area within the Quarries west of Bottlescrew Hill and the village green. To these the Council added the cluster of dwellings, including six listed properties, centred around the *Cock Inn* known as Cock Street. The Stonehouse (68, The Quarries) and 3, Park Lane were also added to the Department of the Environment's list of individual buildings of Special Architectural or Historic Interest in 1987. The Council itself was directly responsible for the restoration and refurbishment of the Soup Kitchen and Well on the Green in 1992 and for the Well House at Cock Street in 1993.[207]

A survey of parish housing in 1984 had shown a need for senior citizens to rent or purchase housing in the village. In conjunction with Gravesend Housing Association and using government funds, the Council erected Windmill Court which opened in 1994. In an entirely different sphere the village school was helped to obtain additional accommodation with a grant of £2,000 towards provision of a mobile classroom while in an attempt to weld the community more closely together the Council began to sponsor social and large-scale fund raising events for Charity such as a Garden Safari which raised in excess of £2,500 for aid to Leukemia in 1991, and a Bavarian Evening staged at *The Cock*.[208]

The Council was not always successful in resisting controversial planning applications. In 1993 a farm unit was converted into an industrial unit despite almost unanimous opposition from the village community while a second farm unit won an appeal to become a larger packing station. The Council, on occasions, was also in advance of its constituents with some of its planning. An overwhelming majority of residents were found to be opposed to footway lighting in 1992. Similarly a proposal to develop the 3.5 acres of land opposite the Village Hall in 1996 ran into serious difficulty. The scheme envisaged a small, mixed development of executive dwellings and houses for first-time buyers. Construction of the latter would be assisted financially by a housing association. The project also included a Millennium Garden and a doctor's surgery which would benefit the entire community in addition to meeting the need for a small amount of subsidised housing for young families and the elderly. The proposal met stiff opposition at a Parish Meeting arranged by the Council to discuss the issue. When a postal referendum, again organised by the Council, was conducted by the Electoral Reform Society 61% of the 1,400 papers posted were returned and the project was defeated by 452 votes to 384. The council was disappointed. Its decision, however, to seek residents' views illustrated its commitment to act as the agent of its constituents and not their master.[209]

If parish opinion was divided on this matter it was very much united over the other major controversial issues of the nineties. In 1994, as the use of Furfield Quarry for waste disposal came to an end, a planning application was made to fill in Quarry Wood, the site of the Iron Age Camp. Public opinion was rapidly mobilised by the Boughton Monchelsea Conservation Society to resist the application on the grounds of the damage which would be caused to the environment, wildlife and landscape of the area plus the dangers of the increased traffic levels. The County Planning Officer received 170 letters of objection to the application and over 850 signatures were collected on a petition. The Parish Council commissioned two reports by the Highway consultant, W.S. Atkins, on the implications of the proposal for Boughton's roads and ultimately the County Director of Highways and Transportation decided to object. A large number of residents attended a meeting in Cornwallis School with the KCC Planning Sub-Committee. At a very orderly meeting the latter were, nevertheless, left clear about the feelings of the public and ultimately rejected the application on the 21 June, 1994.[210]

The B2163 had been a cause for concern on safety grounds since the volume of traffic using it increased in the 1960s. Despite Parish Council attempts to restrict the use of minor parish roads by heavy traffic and to secure speed limits on the B2163 it continued to be the scene of serious, and sometimes fatal, accidents. In the 1980s concern was exacerbated by persistent rumours that with the development of the Channel Tunnel it could become the southern orbital road for Maidstone joining the new M20 extension at Leeds with all its possible implications. When a draft revision of the Kent Structure plan in 1988 suggested the provision of some 12,500 houses in the South Maidstone area before the end of the century there appeared to be an even more serious threat. Maidstone Borough Council could make provision for only 11,500 houses. Space for the remaining 1,000 houses seemed likely to extend into areas like Boughton Monchelsea where hitherto only infilling had been permitted within the village envelope. Unable to resist the urban sprawl it seemed likely that in the foreseeable future Boughton might, like Bearsted, lose its rural character and become a continuation of Maidstone.[211]

First Boughton's representatives attended a series of meetings with other representatives of a consortium of parish councils for South Maidstone. These met with members and officers of KCC and Maidstone Borough Council to devise a strategy to divert some of the proposed housing development elsewhere. Ultimately it was argued that because there were no plans for developing South Maidstone's roads the area would lack the infrastructure for so large a housing development and much housing went instead to Ashford. It was nevertheless accepted that Boughton would have to undergo some substantial development, especially as Government approval of the KCC Structure Plan suggested that much of the housing allocation for Maidstone should be accommodated to the south of the Town. This new dimension, which the Parish Council could not successfully resist, created the need for it to adopt very different policies than hitherto. Its approach in dealing with Maidstone's southern expansion was both novel and radical.

First the Council won acceptance that the Maidstone Local Plan should include specific policies for the creation of 'green wedges' to protect 'sensitive' rural areas adjoining the urban fringe, and a non-coalescing policy to prevent villages such as Boughton, Loose and Langley from joining up with each other. The Oldborough 'Green Corridor', which includes all of Boughton Mount Farm, has been established specifically to protect this 'sensitive' area from development as part of Maidstone's 'Green wedge' policy.

In 1994 the Parish Council formed the Boughton Monchelsea Amenity Trust 'to preserve open land and amenities for the benefit of the village'. The Trust, by endeavouring to negotiate realistic and legally binding option agreements with the landowners concerned is attempting to insure against further housing growth within certain areas of the parish. If, after successful negotiation, agreed development takes place, it is the intention of the Trust and Parish Council to see that 'green wedges' will be created. These should belong to the Parish free from the threat of further development and will help to resist urban sprawl. Among the areas which the Parish Council is trying to protect in this way are the earthworks and fortifications of Quarry Wood; all of the agricultural land consisting of Campfield Farm; and all of Furfield Quarry. The Council is also actively seeking to safeguard land running along the west side of Brishing Lane and south of the 'ridge' of Langley Park Farm. Where possible the Amenity Trust and the Parish Council will also attempt to acquire other 'sensitive' land in the parish as and when it may become available. Thus they have recently acquired some fourteen acres of land adjoining the south side of Cliff Hill.[212]

Upon
the
Quarry
Hills

A survey of buildings

Fig. 6 *Boughton Monchelsea – Buildings*

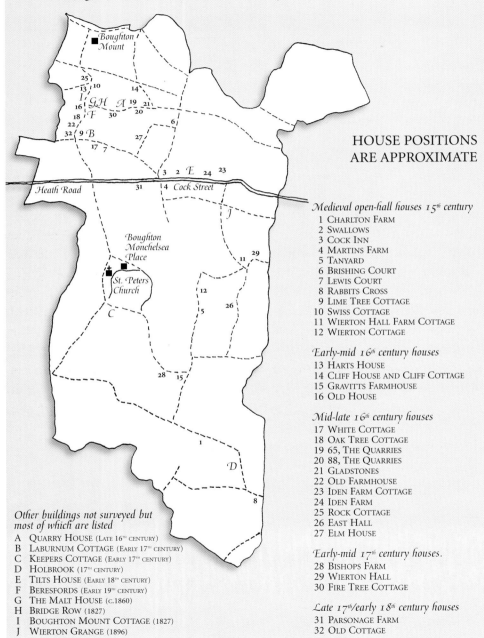

HOUSE POSITIONS
ARE APPROXIMATE

Medieval open-hall houses 15th *century*

1 CHARLTON FARM
2 SWALLOWS
3 COCK INN
4 MARTINS FARM
5 TANYARD
6 BRISHING COURT
7 LEWIS COURT
8 RABBITS CROSS
9 LIME TREE COTTAGE
10 SWISS COTTAGE
11 WIERTON HALL FARM COTTAGE
12 WIERTON COTTAGE

Early-mid 16th *century houses*

13 HARTS HOUSE
14 CLIFF HOUSE AND CLIFF COTTAGE
15 GRAVITTS FARMHOUSE
16 OLD HOUSE

Mid-late 16th *century houses*

17 WHITE COTTAGE
18 OAK TREE COTTAGE
19 65, THE QUARRIES
20 88, THE QUARRIES
21 GLADSTONES
22 OLD FARMHOUSE
23 IDEN FARM COTTAGE
24 IDEN FARM
25 ROCK COTTAGE
26 EAST HALL
27 ELM HOUSE

Early-mid 17th *century houses.*

28 BISHOPS FARM
29 WIERTON HALL
30 FIRE TREE COTTAGE

Late 17th/*early* 18th *century houses*

31 PARSONAGE FARM
32 OLD COTTAGE

*Other buildings not surveyed but
most of which are listed*

A QUARRY HOUSE (LATE 16ᵀᴴ CENTURY)
B LABURNUM COTTAGE (EARLY 17ᵀᴴ CENTURY)
C KEEPERS COTTAGE (EARLY 17ᵀᴴ CENTURY)
D HOLBROOK (17ᵀᴴ CENTURY)
E TILTS HOUSE (EARLY 18ᵀᴴ CENTURY)
F BERESFORDS (EARLY 19ᵀᴴ CENTURY)
G THE MALT HOUSE (c.1860)
H BRIDGE ROW (1827)
I BOUGHTON MOUNT COTTAGE (1827)
J WIERTON GRANGE (1896)

Boughton Monchelsea – Buildings

The two principal surviving buildings of the parish are Boughton Monchelsea Place (Grade 1) and St. Peter's Church (Grade 2). The nineteenth century Boughton Mount is largely demolished and Wierton Place much altered. Yet a wealth of historic houses survive as listed buildings. They, in themselves, constitute vital historical evidence although the many changes which they have undergone over the years often make interpretation difficult. Sarah Pearson, formerly of the Royal Commission on the Historical Monuments of England and an authority on the timber-framed buildings of Kent, visited the parish in 1998 and 1999 and conducted a buildings survey. In the course of five days she examined the interiors of 32 properties listed by the Department of the Environment as being of Special Architectural or Historic Interest. A further 10 properties were not examined although listed. Five were nineteenth century properties. The remainder consisted of 1 house constructed in the late sixteenth century; 3 houses built in the seventeenth century; and 1 house erected in the early 18th century.[213] The following is Sarah's table of building phases, established despite an almost complete dearth of documentary evidence. The table and its ensuing analysis together with the architectural histories of the 32 individual buildings are entirely her work and based upon her reports. Both Boughton Monchelsea Parish Council and myself are extremely grateful to her for the use of her time and expertise.

a) Medieval Open-hall Houses

There are 12 medieval open-hall houses plus a 'ghost' in the plan of the Old House, the Green. Numbers in brackets in this and other sections represent building phases.

1	Charlton Farm.	*Early 15th century Wealden house.*
2	Swallows.	*Mid 15th century end jetty.*
3	Cock Inn. (1)	*Mid 15th century end jetty.*
4	Martins Farm.	*Mid 15th century end jetty.*
5	Tanyard. (1)	*Mid 15th century end jetty.*

6	Brishing Court.	*Mid 15th century Wealden house.*
7	Lewis Court.	*Late 15th century Wealden house.*
8	Rabbits Cross.	*Late 15th century Wealden house.*
9	Lime Tree Cottage.	*Late 15th century cross wing.*
10	Swiss Cottage. (1)	*c.1500. No jetties.*
11	Wierton Hall Farm Cottage.	*c.1500. No jetties.*
12	Wierton Cottage.	*c.1500. No jetties.*

b) Early-mid 16th century houses

There are 5 houses with building work at this time consisting of 1 new house, 1 re-build and 3 houses with sections added.

13	Harts House.	*New Smoke Bay House.*
	Tanyard. (2)	*Second phase. Rebuilding of open hall with chimney stacks.*
14	Cliff House. (1)	*Single unheated bay. Probably addition to open hall.*
15	Gravitts Farmhouse. (1)	*Unheated wing. Probably addition to open hall.*
16	Old House. (1)	*Unheated wing. Probably addition to open hall (See above).*

c) Mid-late 16th century houses

Twelve houses show evidence of building work at the time. Ten are newly-built. Two are rebuilds.

17	White Cottage. (1)	*New 2-cell smoke bay house.*
18	Oak Tree Cottage. (1)	*New 2-cell smoke bay house.*
19	65, The Quarries.	*New 2-cell smoke bay house.*
20	88, The Quarries.	*Probably new 2-cell smoke bay house much altered.*
21	Gladstones. (1)	*Probably new 2-cell smoke bay house. (This is surmise).*
22	Old Farmhouse. (1)	*New 3-cell smoke bay house.*
23	Iden Farm Cottage.	*New 3-cell timber chimney house.*
24	Iden Farm. (1)	*Fragmentary remains of a building of this date.*
25	Rock Cottage.	*Third quarter. New chimney stack house.*
	Cock Inn. (2)	*New chimney stack house 1568.*
26	East Hall. (1)	*Chimney stack house 1597. Probably re-building medieval house.*
27	Elm House. (1)	*Date and form very unclear.*

d) Early-mid 17th century houses.

Six houses showed evidence of building during this period. Three were new builds and 3 were re-builds.

	East Hall. (2)	*Replacing the older range?*
28	Bishops Farm.	*New house.*
29	Wierton Hall.	*New house.*
30	Fire Tree Cottage.	*New house.*
	Swiss Cottage. (2)	*Re-build of one end.*
	Lime Tree Cottage. (2)	*Re-build of open hall.*

e) Late 17th/early 18th century houses

Seven houses had evidence of work of this period. One house was newly built, 3 were re-builds and 3 houses were new additions.

	Cliff House. (2)	*Re-build of part.*
	Gravitts. (2)	*Re-build of part.*
	Old House. (2)	*Re-build of part.*
	Oak Tree. (2)	*Addition.*
	White Cottage. (2)	*Addition 1670.*
	Old Farmhouse. (2)	*Addition.*
31	Parsonage Farm.	*New house.*

f) 18th century

Four houses of this date were seen.

	Elm House. (2)	*New front added to an older house.*
32	Old Cottage.	*New house.*
	Iden Farm. (2)	*Rebuild.*
	Gladstones. (2)	*Rebuild.*

This suggests there were two main periods for new building: the mid-late 15th century as the parish returned to more prosperous times after the recession at the beginning of the century: and the mid-late 16th century as the population began to climb. The first period was related to greater agricultural prosperity and is associated with the building of large and isolated farmhouses. The same prosperity is also reflected in the church with the insertion of the four perpendicular windows of the north aisle and the construction of the Lychgate. The second period, which saw the building of smaller dwellings at all four centres of population, may reflect the industrial development of the Quarries in addition to the general growth of population. Industrial wealth and population growth are also possibly related to the partial re-building of the north aisle and tower of St. Peter's. In both periods the problem of whether the new houses lie upon new sites or are total replacements of earlier dwellings is difficult to determine.

The principal period for enlarging earlier small houses or replacing portions of old buildings is the 17th century. The enlarged houses were usually 16th century and small in size to begin with. The replacements were made to parts of larger houses, some of which were probably medieval before, such as the Old House, Gravitts and Cliff House. The first two of these definitely have signs of medieval buildings on site.

Medieval Buildings

Date

None date from the 14th century or earlier. The earliest building is Charlton Farm in which the solid, two-centred doorheads and moulded cornice suggest a date in the early 15th century. Brishing Court, Swallows, the *Cock*, Martins Farm and Tanyard probably date to the mid-15th century. Lewis Court, Rabbits Cross and the early wing at Lime Tree Cottage are likely to be late 15th century. Swiss Cottage, Wierton Cottage and Wierton Hall Farm Cottage are much simpler, have collar-rafter roofs without crown posts and few dateable details. They were probably build around 1500.

Type

Charlton Farm, Brishing Court, Rabbits Cross and Lewis Court are Wealden houses. They have central halls and two, two-storeyed end bays jettied to the front, the whole being roofed over with a single, overall roof which necessitates a 'flying plate' across the front of the hall. The result is to make the hall seem recessed although at ground-floor level it is not. Charlton and Brishing are unusual in being jettied on both sides. Brishing Court is even more unusual in having double wall plates across each side. Lime Tree Cottage is the only house in the parish with a medieval cross wing. This may mean that it was attached to a much earlier hall than anything that survives. Martins and Swallows and the remaining ends of Tanyard and the *Cock* are end-jetty form with no overhang at the front, only at the ends. Such houses were often slightly less large and expensive than Wealden or cross-wing houses.

Swiss Cottage, Wierton Cottage and Wierton Hall Farm Cottage show no signs of jettying at all. This suggests, together with height, roof type and the lack of decorative features, that they may be slightly later, poorer, cousins of their medieval brethren in the parish.

Status

Some of the medieval houses have distinctive features. Charlton Farm and Brishing Court are double Wealdens – an expensive and unnecessary use of timber. Charlton has a decorated cornice in the hall. Rabbits Cross and Lewis Court have close-studded framing – a display of wealth typical of the later 15th century rather than earlier. Most of the medieval houses are spanned by crown-post roofs with a single decorative crown post over the two-bay hall. Good examples remain at Charlton, Swallows, Brishing Court, Lewis Court and Rabbits Cross. Charlton, Martins and Swallows have 'false' tie beams at the longer service end lying at right angles to the main roof; these are structurally unnecessary and seem to be done to create the illusion that the upper room lies in a cross wing; this is particularly marked at Swallows where the tie beam carries an extra decorative crown post. In contrast to these houses, Swiss Cottage, Wierton Cottage and Wierton Hall Farm Cottage have simple collar – rafter roofs with no crown posts above.

All the houses mentioned above were sizeable. All had two-bay open halls (except Swiss Cottage which may have had a single-bay open hall) and two end bays, indicating an arrangement with hall and screens passage, plus parlour and service ends, the latter containing two rooms, normally termed buttery and pantry (although it is not clear that this is exactly how these rooms were used). Most had clear evidence that the end bays were of two storeys which meant they each had to have their own ladder stair, usually sited against the rear wall (but sometimes placed elsewhere, as in the parlour ends of Swallows and Tanyard). However, in the cases of Wierton Cottage and Wierton Hall Farm Cottage it is possible that one of the two end bays was originally open to the roof like the hall. If so, it would be another indication of slightly lower status or quality and not necessarily indicative of date.

Early-mid 16th century

Some of the smaller, late medieval houses may not have been built until the beginning of the 16th century but during the first half of the century there were changes to what was required in the highest quality houses. Thus what appears to have been a new dwelling at Harts House was entirely different. Firstly the T-shaped plan is very unusual. The hall was of two storeys from the start, heated by a fire within an enclosed smoke bay. The house is jettied on three sides, the walls close studded and the details of high quality. All this suggests a builder with money to spend. By the mid-16th century other well-to-do houses or up-dates to older ones, with high quality doorways and windows, moulded beams and close-studded framing occur at Tanyard, Gravitts Farm and Cliff House and Cottage, all three being additions to earlier houses. It is interesting to note that Harts House, and Cliff House/Cottage, which were originally one dwelling, are closely associated with the Quarries, and Tanyard belonged, at least at a later date, to a tanner, perhaps suggesting that while good medieval houses were built from the profits of land the profits of industry may have become increasingly important at Boughton by the 16th century. We have already seen evidence which suggests that activity in the quarries showed signs of booming in the late 15th and early-mid 16th centuries.[214]

During the early 16th century several of the earlier open halls were updated by having half of the hall ceiled over. This clearly occurred at Brishing Court, Lewis Court, Martins Farm, Swallows and Wierton Hall Farm Cottage. Not only did the hall become a much more civilised room but an extra first-floor chamber was created, enlarging the amount of living or storage space. Only at Tanyard and Wierton Cottage, probably in the mid-16th century, was the move made directly from an open hall to a full-ceiled hall heated by an enclosed stack. This new method of heating is known elsewhere in Kent from around 1500.

Mid-late 16th century

By the middle of the 16th century smaller buildings start to survive for the first time. These are of two bays rather than the three or four bays of most earlier houses. An excellent example is White Cottage, which is a virtually complete house with a hall heated by a gable-end smoke bay, opposed entrances at the far end of the hall and two smaller rooms beyond, one set behind the other, probably used as a parlour and a service room, and two chambers above. The earlier part of Oak Tree and Oak Tree Cottage was probably identical and Numbers 65 and 88, the Quarries may have been the same to start with. In all of these there is no sign of an enclosed fireplace at ground-floor level. Instead, the bressumer of the fireplace was formed by a beam at ceiling height, even when the smoke was channelled into a narrower area on the first floor – as seems to have happened at Oak Tree Cottage where there was a first-floor window to one side of the smoke bay. Another point of interest about these houses is that they seem to cluster on the Green and in the Quarries suggesting that the population increase from the mid-16th century may have been concentrated there thus enlarging these older hamlets.

Slightly larger, new-build houses are probably contemporary or a little later. These were similar but had a further room behind the fireplace. The fire at Iden Farm Cottage seems to have been in a timber-framed chimney, in other words the flue was still of timber but was not a structural part of the house.

By the third quarter of the century larger, new houses were fully two-storeyed throughout, heated by fireplaces with stone jambs manufactured from local ragstone and brick stacks. In many cases their appearance marks the moment when houses began to have several heated rooms. The earliest dated stack in the parish seems to be that at the *Cock Inn* where the former open hall was rebuilt as a two-storey range with a continuous jetty. Plasterwork in the roof is dated 1568 and this may well indicate the date when the new range was built. A second stack was added to heat the kitchen at the rear which had been constructed from an old medieval service end. A more or less contemporary house is Rock Cottage, in which two ground and two first-floor rooms were heated and a newel stair curls up beside the stack, quite unlike the earlier straight flight stairs in sub-medieval houses. The next dated example is at East Hall, in which one of the fireplaces is dated 1597. This is surmounted by a highly decorative brick stack, of a type which was only erected in the best houses in the late 16th century.

The 17th century

By the 17th century all new houses were built with stone and brick chimneys rather than chimneys of timber and plaster. At the same time the old medieval arrangement of the house was giving way to a new design: the lobby entrance. This had been introduced in the mid-16th century and during the 17th century it became the norm for all but the smallest dwellings. In these houses the entrance was no longer into any kind of passage and it did not divide the hall from the service rooms. Instead the house was turned around with the entry giving direct access to the hall, or hall/kitchen as it had often become, and the parlour. Therefore, instead of the parlour being the innermost room in the house and furthest from the entrance, it was reached directly from the lobby, while the service rooms could only be reached by traversing the hall. In these houses both hall and parlour were heated by fireplaces within a single double stack – at this social level this was the first time that parlours were heated and used for sitting as well as for sleeping in. New lobby entry houses of the early 17th century in Boughton are Bishop's Farm and Wierton Hall, both of which have high-quality detailing. In both examples the new service rooms were placed at the rear, which was much more convenient than leaving them in a line at one end of the house. A slightly later and smaller example is Fir Tree Cottage.

At the end of the 17th and beginning of the 18th centuries Parsonage Farm, Gravitts Farm and the new build of Cliff Cottage were all of lobby entrance plan. If there was insufficient money for a rear wing then a single storey outshut was added at the back, as at Parsonage Farm. In fact, this kind of outshut, usually containing unheated service rooms, was being added to houses of all kinds by the early 18th century. A number, such as at Iden Farm Cottage, were built of ragstone.

When true chimney stacks and brick and stone fireplaces superseded smoke bays, the owners of medieval buildings had two choices. The conservative choice was to leave the medieval layout untouched and sacrifice being up-to-date. Thus at Rabbits Cross, Lewis Court, Brishing Court and Charlton, the old layout remained with the medieval entry continuing to form a cross passage behind the inserted stack. If more than one ground-floor fireplace was required in such houses, they had to be built in stacks on the rear or gable wall, as at Brishing, or in a new wing at the back as probably occurred at Charlton. However, in some cases far more radical alterations were made, as at Martins, Swallows and Wierton Cottage. Although the entrance remained in the old position, the passage was blocked and a lobby created by inserting a double stack with two fireplaces heating a hall/kitchen and a parlour. This meant demolishing the partition between the old passage and the service rooms, and the partition between the two service rooms themselves, and turning the old service end into a heated room. It also meant re-siting the stair which had lain at this end of the house. Sometimes this meant relegating the services to the far end of the house but in the Boughton examples the ends were long enough to contain both a new room and smaller service rooms beyond. This change took place at Swallows in 1616 and other examples are probably of much the same date. It is small wonder that in some cases, as at Swiss Cottage, the old service end was demolished rather than re-organised and a new parlour wing built instead.

Although some of the better quality houses, both old and new, had four heated rooms, two downstairs and two up, many only had three, and where this was the case the third fireplace often heated the chamber over the hall, marking a change in the use of this room from a badly lit storage or junk room, created when the hall was first floored over, to the best chamber in the house. This is almost certainly what happened at Swallows. Here the first enclosed fireplace was a smoke bay and the unheated chamber over the hall was probably nothing special. When the brick stack was inserted the hall chamber was completely renovated and given a smart, new window, set in its own gable, with the date of 1616 inscribed on it.

Some of the older, smaller houses were likewise updated by the end of the century. Although it had only one ground-floor fireplace, White Cottage was given an additional bay when the stack was built into the old smoke bay in 1670. We cannot be certain that the inscribed date actually dates the new stack but it seems likely that it does and that many other new chimney stacks were inserted into smoke bays at about this time. Oak Tree Cottage had an extra heated room added and its smoke bay rebuilt as a double stack while The Old Farmhouse, The Green got back-to-back fireplaces plus another for a kitchen at the far end of the house by the late 17th century.

While late 17th century building in the parish was quite considerable there was little *total* rebuilding at that time. On the other hand some of the earlier buildings were showing signs of age. They were not necessarily in a state of collapse. The re-use of medieval timbers at Gravitts suggests that the basic structure of that building was fine. They perhaps, however, could not be easily adapted to new requirements. Those that could be were partially updated. The surviving houses form 46% of those whose occupiers were charged in the Hearth Tax of 1664 (35 out of 76), and just over one-third of all the houses in the parish at that time (101 in all, 25% of whom were exempted from paying tax on the grounds of poverty).

The 18th and 19th centuries

The only houses which did not conform to the type discussed above are those which were too small to have double stacks. Gladstones and the Old Cottage, The Green, were small houses of this sort, originally with two rooms on the ground floor and a single gable end fireplace. Dating them is difficult. The former may have had a mid-late 16th century origin. The latter was probably not erected before the early 18th century. Later these small buildings were also given rear extensions.

Only one large 18th century house was seen. Elm House is unusual by any standards. It belongs not with the vernacular tradition of the rest of Boughton's buildings but makes an effort to be polite in county terms. Yet the aspirations of the owner hardly matched up to the result for he had to make do with an earlier rear range for all the service rooms and even the grand new stair was inserted into the older work. Also, in a world where symmetry was highly prized, the builder of Elm House committed the solecism of not placing the doorway centrally in the facade but putting it at one end in a most uncomfortable manner. Thus, although the brickwork of this house is of the highest quality, the design is provincial.

No buildings were examined conforming to the phase after the lobby entry plan: that is, with a central entry between two reception rooms heated by gable end stacks. This is the commonest plan for 18th and 19th century new-build farmhouses. Tilts House is described as such in the Department of the Environment List. The only other listed farmhouse in his period is Beresfords constructed in the early 19th century.

In the later 18th and the early 19th centuries, in response to a burgeoning population, many of the earlier farmhouses were split into cottages occupied by agricultural labourers and their families, as the system of annually-hired farm servants died out. This was partly due to the amalgamation of farms by large landowners, which left some farmhouses empty and ready for sub-division. In the first decades of the nineteenth century, prior to 1841, approximately ninety new cottages were also built, largely in Church Street and Haste Hill Road. These, too, became rapidly overcrowded as many labourers were obliged by poverty to take in lodgers as is clearly shown by the 19th century census enumerators' books.[215]

Descriptions of Individual Buildings

1 Charlton Farm

LOWER FARM ROAD, BOUGHTON MONCHELSEA. GRADE II.

The hall and service end of a high quality, Wealden hall-house only survive. Most of the hall has been encased in brick but the wide framing and downward braces of the end bay remain. This bay is jettied both to front and rear indicating that the Wealden was one of the small number of known examples in which there is a flying plate across both sides of the hall.

A small section of framing is exposed at the rear of the hall which includes a blocked doorway with a two-centred head and solid durns (door posts). This opened into the old screens passage at the lower end of the hall. Two similar doorways to the two service rooms also survive, together with evidence for the stair against the rear wall. The joists are wide and closely spaced. Upstairs this end bay is spanned by an arch-braced tie beam which has no structural function since the roof runs at right angles to it and its presence indicates a desire to give the chamber the appearance of a cross wing. A small doorway in the south-west corner, at the top of the stair, shows that the room was provided with a projecting latrine or garderobe serving the same function as a modern en-suite toilet. The main posts in the centre and lower end of the hall remain. All the features indicate both a high quality building and a date probably in the early 15th century.

Charlton Farmhouse

The upper end wall of the hall also remains and is constructed of close studded framing. There are traces of a dais bench at this 'high' end of the hall. Such a bench was normally fixed to the wall and used by the owner. A moulded, decorative beam lay above. Behind the owner's bench was his private room or parlour which has now gone. This upper-end wall would appear to be rather later than the rest of the medieval house dating perhaps to the second half of the 15th century or beyond. On the farther side of this wall the house is of 18th and 19th century date. The present brick fireplace, heating the hall, probably dates to the 17th century and it is likely that it was preceded by an enclosed fireplace area such as a smoke bay or timber chimney.

At the rear a two-bay, two-storey 16th or 17th century timber wing was added at right angles to the hall. This might have been a kitchen wing although there is now no sign of early heating. Otherwise it presumably housed the growing number of service rooms found on 17th century farms such as milk house, wash house or brewhouse.

In 1841 the farm was in the hands of Thomas Hope, a sixty-year-old farmer who lived there with his wife and family, two agricultural labourers and a female servant. By 1851 it had passed to Thomas Hayes, who lived there with his sister, a female house servant and three labourers. Hayes was joint occupier of 316 acres which were farmed by 34 men and 6 boys. By 1861 his 440 acres included Boughton Monchelsea Place Farm, in the absence of the Riders. His expanded work force consisted of 41 men, 5 women and 9 boys. Hayes was an influential member of the parish who was both poor law guardian and Chairman of the School Board.

2   Swallows
HEATH ROAD, BOUGHTON MONCHELSEA. GRADE II.

This is a medieval house with a two-bay open hall, flanked by two, two-storeyed, bays jettied at the ends. The open framing of the external walls and the internal details suggest the house was built in the middle of the fifteenth century.

The hall was originally entered at its west end by opposed doorways in the north and south walls. The long, two-storeyed service bay to the west was divided into two rooms, reached through two doorways whose heads are indicated by grooves in the centre of the north-south beam marking the hall partition. Mortices for the partition between the two rooms are visible on the central joist of the end bay. The arrangement of the joists shows that the ladder stair to the chamber above lay in the normal position against the rear wall. The upper-end of the hall is marked by a moulded 'dais' beam above the former upper-end bench. The doorway to the bay beyond lay to the north. The east end was divided into two rooms, one reached through the other and the stair was set at right angles against the hall partition. (See Tanyard for a similar arrangement.)

On the first floor, the service chamber, which was the largest of the two, was grander than that over the upper or parlour end. It is spanned by a false arch-braced tie beam set at right angles to the roof and carrying a decorative crown post. A similar crown post lies above the open hall itself. Smoke-blackened partitions remain at either end of the hall. In the early 16th century the open area of the hall was reduced in size by inserting a partition, again heavily smoke-blackened, on the line of the open truss: the open hearth was thereby confined to the lower or western bay. It is likely that at this time the eastern bay of the hall was ceiled over to create a new upper chamber. However, the present hall ceiling has a plainly chamfered spine beam and narrow joists which are more in keeping with the next updating of 1616.

Swallows

In 1616 a double brick stack was inserted with fireplaces heating the hall and a new room formed by moving the old screens passage partition westwards and adding the space, thus gained, to the screens passage itself. The original service end was long enough to make a reasonably sized room and still allow space for two service rooms beyond. New doorways to the two end rooms were made in the new partition. Probably the service end stairs were re-sited at the back of the stack. The new fireplaces have simply chamfered stone jambs and timber lintels. Although an upper chamber is likely to have been inserted above the hall when the smoke bay was created, this was probably nothing very special. The chamber over the hall was often used as a warm, dry storage area but when the hall was receiled, the chamber over became the best one in the house, heated by a stone fireplace and lit by a gabled oriel window which bears the date 1616 on the exterior.

Later the house was turned into cottages and was still known as Forge Cottages in the mid-20th century.

3 The Cock Inn

HEATH ROAD, BOUGHTON MONCHELSEA. GRADE II.

This house appears to have been built at two periods: in the 15th century and probably in 1568. The earliest part is the rear or north bay, which is of medieval date and probably formed part of a house which formerly ran north-south, facing onto Brishing Lane. The surviving bay is the two-storeyed service-end bay of an open hall house. On the interior, mortices in the central ceiling joist indicate the line of a partition which formerly divided the ground floor into two service rooms, and to the east the joists are pegged to allow for a stair trap for access to the first floor. On the exterior, the first-floor chamber was jettied to the north, beyond which an extra length of framing was added with a small doorway in the north-east corner. This must have been added soon after the initial construction, and is likely to have given access to a small projecting latrine or garderobe.

The Cock Inn

In the mid-late 16th century the earlier open hall was demolished and replaced by the present east-west range. This was jettied along the south front. It is entered at the rear of the fireplace heating the central hall, the entry allowing access to both the new range and the old wing, which was now turned into a kitchen: a large, plain kitchen fireplace was built beneath the jetty, its stack blocking the little, first-floor doorway on the west wall. The new hall was heated by a large fireplace with stone jambs and a timber lintel with hollow spandrels to its four-centred head. The beam and joists are simply chamfered. A small unheated room lay in the south-west corner, next to the entry, and another lay beyond the hall to the east.

The roof over the new range is of clasped side purlin construction with wind braces. The date 1568 has been inscribed high up in the plaster of one of the partitions above the hall and there seems no reason to doubt that this was the date when the front range was built.

The first written mention of the *Cock* was in 1623. It was still held from the Lord of the Manor in 1737. In 1799 the 'messuage (dwelling) and garden called the *Cock Alehouse*' was occupied by a Widow Cheeseman, In the 19th century it was the meeting place of the parish officers and the headquarters of Boughton Monchelsea cricket club. In 1841 it was held by fifty-year old William Peene, victualler, his wife and family and was still in his hands in 1847. By 1851 it had passed to John Stonham, master blacksmith and victualler who was a widower and owner of the Cock Street smithy which stood on the site of the present garage. By 1881 he had been succeeded by his son, George, who also combined the two businesses.[216]

4   Martins Farmhouse
HEATH ROAD, BOUGHTON MONCHELSEA, GRADE II.

This is a four-bay medieval open hall house consisting of a central two-bay hall, a jettied parlour bay to the west and a long, unjettied service bay to the east. At roof level the smoke-blackened rafters of the open hall survive although the central crown post has been destroyed by the insertion of the later chimney stack. The roof continues right across the east end although it is spanned by a 'false' north-south tie beam, set at right angles to the hall and therefore creating the appearance of a wing at first-floor level. On the ground floor, the west end of the hall is marked by a moulded dais beam with evidence for a doorway at its south end allowing access to the parlour. The east end of the hall is also marked by a beam which has mortices on its soffit for two doorways to two service rooms. There is no clear evidence for original external doorways in the north and south walls but all the internal evidence makes it certain that the screens passage lay within the body of the hall, to the west of the beam separating the hall from the service end.

Martins Farmhouse

When the hall was given its first enclosed fireplace this was, rather unusually, placed to the west or parlour side of the open truss rather than on the east or service side. This had the effect of reducing the hall to less than a single bay. At the same time the eastern or lower bay of the hall was ceiled over and the screens passage shifted westwards to the back of the new fireplace. A stair was then made at the north side. What happened to the old service end is unclear for it was now at some distance from the cross passage. Possibly it was turned to a kitchen heated by an external stack of which all trace has been removed. The first enclosed fireplace in the hall was a smoke bay. The inserted tie beam which formed its west face remains, as do a number of upright staves which carried the plaster walls. This second phase can be dated to the sixteenth century.

The third phase consisted of replacing the smoke bay by a stone stack and creating a second fireplace to the east. This meant that the 'new' passage across the house and new service end were replaced by a heated room, probably a kitchen. The main entrance was now into a lobby at the front of the stack. Again the use of the east end bay is uncertain.

The house was probably lived in by Martins from at least the late 17th century and perhaps long before. In 1664 three Martins paid the Hearth Tax; Alexander Martin and Widow Martin both occupied houses with two hearths, and John Martin had three. It is not clear which one lived here. In 1781, upon the death of William Martin who held 'one messuage (dwelling) and two acres in Boughton Monchelsea near the Sign of the Cock abutting to the highway towards the north and west and to other of his lands towards the east and south by service of fealty and suit of court', the premises passed to his brother. Daniel Martin attended the lord of the manor's court at Boughton Monchelsea Place, paid a heriot (death duty) of his brother's best living beast and agreed an annual rent of 2s.7d as his forebears had done before him. The days of the Martin family at Martins Farm were, however, numbered. By 1841 the farm had passed to William Crittenden as owner-occupier. He was succeeded by his son of the same name before 1861. Twenty years later, at the age of seventy-four, he was still farming 69 acres and employing 7 men and 2 boys.[217] The farm complex also housed a cordwainer (shoemaker) and his family in 1841 and a grocer's shop, which served the hamlet of Cock Street, in 1861. By 1942 its cultivated area had contracted to 32 acres of which some 28 acres were devoted to the growing of cob nuts.

5 Tanyard

WIERTON HILL, BOUGHTON MONCHELSEA. GRADE II.

The house was built in two periods. At the rear a 15th century range lies at right angles to the road. It contained a central open hall with a two storeyed end bay beyond, jettied to the east. It seems likely that this was actually the old parlour end and that the service end was rebuilt in the mid 16th century as a smart new front range with a continuous jetty to the road. The new range contains the main entrance, a staircase, a room which may have served as a new hall and has lost a further bay or bays which originally ran southwards from the entrance.

The upper part of the old hall has been replaced. On the ground floor the east wall of the hall has a moulded cross beam which looks like a simply cut 'dais' beam with evidence for a formerly projecting screen at its north end. This is a typical

Tanyard

arrangement at the upper or dais end of a medieval hall, the short screen separating the dais end bench from the doorway to the parlour behind. Mortices under the central joist show that the end was originally divided into two rooms. The southern room was formerly entered from the northern one. The stair to the chamber above always lay against the hall wall. The layout of rooms and stair is not the most common medieval arrangement for parlour ends but it occurs in other houses in Kent. Upstairs the partition between the former open hall and the chamber seems to have been rebuilt when the hall was ceiled over, a first-floor created and the hall re-roofed. The original chamber had a small doorway leading outwards from the east wall and this almost certainly opened into a projecting latrine or garderobe, a common feature of medieval buildings in this area.

In the mid 16th century the original service end was replaced by a new wing at right angles to the old range. Between the two, in the area of the original screens passage, a large stack was built with four fireplaces heating the old hall, the new main room and the chambers above them. No expense was spared on the new work, the main room having oriel windows with projecting sills, finely detailed fireplaces, a beam with clustered rolls, and leaf carvings in the spandrels of the doorways. At this time a new entrance was made in the centre of the new range. It now lies at the south end because one or more bays of the addition have been demolished. The new range is puzzling to interpret since there has been much alteration in this part of the building. The first-floor chambers in this range were ceiled from the start. Given the destruction of part of the new range it is difficult to determine how the house functioned in the 16th century.

The house name suggests the possibility that it was owned by a wealthy tanner in the 16th century, but so far this cannot be proved. In 1841 Tanyard farmhouse, as it was then called, was already subdivided between three households.

6 Brishing Court

BRISHING LANE, BOUGHTON MONCHELSEA. GRADE II.

This is a medieval open hall house of Wealden form and unusual sophistication. It is jettied both to the front and to the ends. The widely spaced studding of the exterior suggests it was built before close-studded framing became common in the late 15th century but the former presence of four-centred rather than pointed door heads and the very thin braces to the crown post are more likely to date to the middle of the 15th century than earlier. An unusual, if not unique, feature is the presence of a double wall-plate all round the exterior. Double wall plates are found on the gable walls of some late-14th century cross wings and occur on the long wall of a 15th century house in Headcorn. But in this example the second plate runs all the way round the house. Since this is a Wealden it means that there are three wall plates, across the area of the hall, thereby creating an immensely deep overhang.

Brishing Court

A wide doorway formerly opened into a screens passage which lay beneath the chamber at the service end. The doorways from the passage to the service rooms have gone but channels in the beam indicate that they had four-centred rather than the earlier two-centred heads. At the far end of the open hall a moulded dais beam with crenellation above marks the site of the partition between the hall and parlour beyond.

In the roof the open truss has a plain chamfered crown post with thin braces rising to soulaces. To the cross passage side of the crown post a narrow smoke bay was inserted in the mid 16th century when the hall was floored over. The smoke-blackened partitions of the smoke bay remain in the roof. In the 17th century it was made redundant by the insertion of a stone stack. This has a fireplace to the ground floor hall and another to the chamber over the service end. It is possible, but not certain, that there was also a fireplace to the chamber over the hall.

According to Hasted, Brishing Manor was in the hands of the Astry family from early in the reign of Edward IV (1461-1483). If so, the house might have been built by this family in the 1460s soon after they came into possession of this property.

7 Lewis Court

GREEN LANE, BOUGHTON MONCHELSEA. GRADE II.

This is a fine open hall house of Wealden form, jettied both at the front and the ends of the house. The exterior, with close-studded framing all round, and the interior with four-centred doorheads and thin braces to the crown post, suggest a construction date in the last quarter of the 15th century.

The main entrance opened into a screens passage lying beneath the chamber over the service end. The passage area remains behind the inserted stack, with high-quality panelling to the short screens set at either end to shield the hall from the draught of the external doorways. There is no sign of the rear doorway now, but almost certainly one existed originally. To the right of the passage the cross beam has mortices for two doorways to the service rooms and a gap at the back where the service-end stair was reached.

The open hall was of two bays, surmounted by a crown-post roof with a simple cap and thin braces set high up the post. Part of the moulded and crenellated dais beam at the upper end of the hall survives. The ceiling in the parlour end has been replaced by one at a higher level. Double mortices for the original joists remain along the back of the dais beam. Although the parlour itself may have been reached by a doorway at the end of the dais wall, there was also a second doorway opening from the back of the hall into what is now a later addition. It is possible that this opened into a small area containing the stair.

The first enclosed fireplace in the hall was a smoke bay and some of the staves of its partition remain in the roof. This was probably inserted in the 16th century and was replaced in the early 17th century by the present large fireplace with stone jambs and timber lintel. There is no evidence of a first-floor fireplace in the chamber over the hall.

Lewis Court

In 1861 the house was occupied by Samuel Beadle, his wife, nephew and a female domestic servant. Beadle farmed 23 acres with the aid of 7 labourers and 3 women. By 1867 he had become a farmer and fruit grower. His son, George, was the farmer and fruit grower by 1881 and still held the farm in 1905. Frederick Thomas Gilbert had the farm in 1938.

8 Rabbits Cross Farm

LOWER FARM ROAD, BOUGHTON MONCHELSEA. GRADE II.

This is a very fine Wealden house of late 15th century date. Apart from insertion of the hall ceiling and stack in c.1600 it has undergone very little alteration. The external framing is close studded and the main entrance, which lies within the hall, has a four-centred head with hollow spandrels and crenellation to the mid-rail above. Inside, the beams at either end of the hall are moulded and crenellated. A dais bench marks the superior end. Mortices beneath the beam between the screens passage and service end indicate two doorways to the service rooms. There is a space at the rear for entry to a stair against the back wall. In the upper or parlour end to the east the arrangement of joists shows that the stair lay behind the partition between the hall and parlour. The roof of the house is exceptionally tall and, as one would expect, it is heavily smoke-blackened in the two hall bays. The open truss has a crown post with a simple cap and thin braces.

All the details indicate a construction date in the 1480s or 1490s. This means it could be the house referred to in the will of William Rabett of Boughton Monchelsea dated 8 November 1497. He left his property to his wife but stipulated that his daughter-in-law, Marion, widow of his son Nicholas, should 'have and occupie all the chambers that be on the west ende of my hall, the whiche I now dwell in, with fre goyng in and owt to come to make fier in the hall and there to have hir easement as long as she is sole and unmarried so that she suffre Alice my wyff to have fre goyng and comyng through the chambre into the olde hall and garden...' This suggests that Marion was given the service rooms at the west end of the house, while Alice had the parlour and chamber above, at the east end. Both of them were to share the hall which had the only hearth and since Alice had no external doorway at her end of the house, she was to be allowed free access to the doorways of the screens passage. The reference to the 'old hall' may indicate that the house was new and that an older hall still survived at that time.

In the early 17th century the house was updated by the insertion of a chimney stack and a floor in the hall. The chamber over the hall was given a new, ovolo-moulded window and another window was placed in a small gable above to light a newly-created attic. Both the hall and the chamber over were provided with fireplaces. A new stair had to be inserted in the south-east corner of the first floor to reach the attic.

Rabbits Cross Farm

In 1847 the farm was occupied by Joseph Gibson, his wife and 5 children. Two agricultural labourers lived-in and a further five labourers occupied the cottages adjacent to the farm. The farm was only 40 acres. In 1867 Gibson is described as 'farmer and hop grower, and by 1881 he farmed 290 acres with the aid of 5 men and 2 boys.

9 Lime Tree Cottage

THE GREEN, BOUGHTON MONCHELSEA. GRADE II.

The earliest part of the house is a two-bay, two-storey cross wing at the north end. The details indicate a date in the late 15th century and the arrangement suggests this was an upper or parlour wing attached to an open hall which lay on the site of the present main range which dates to the early 17th century.

The earlier wing contains two rooms, a larger one to the west, jettied to the west front and a small one to the east. The first floor was likewise divided into two chambers spanned by a simple crown-post roof with narrow braces. The former end-of-hall wall is structurally part of the wing and, therefore, still survives. A lack of doorways in the centre indicates that this was the upper or dais end of the hall, the room behind almost certainly being the parlour reached by a doorway in a lobby at the back of the hall opening into the rear room of the wing. Caution should be exercised in interpreting some of the details since it is possible that some features have been moved.

Lime Tree Cottage

The end wall of the hall would still appear to have fragments of smoke blackening ingrained on it. This is the only piece of the medieval hall to survive. On the interior all the details suggest an early 17th century date but on the west front the close-studded framing underneath the jetty of the hall looks considerably earlier. By the early 17th century the hall range contained two rooms, heated by a double stack, and probably entered by a doorway opening into a lobby beside the stack although this is now blocked.

10 Swiss Cottage

BOTTLESCREW HILL, BOUGHTON MONCHELSEA. GRADE II.

The external appearance of the house suggests an early 17th century date but the facade hides a medieval core. Precise dating is not easy but it is possible that the open hall house was built in the years around 1500.

The medieval house was entered just to the right of the present lobby entry into a screens passage beneath a two-storeyed end or wing. The evidence for this lies in the roof and in the ground-floor beam just in front of the fireplace. A single-bay hall lay to the west. Above this section lies a heavily smoke-blackened crown-post roof. In the 'parlour' to the west of the hall, at either end, were doorways with shouldered heads and flat lintels above, an unusual design which occurs only rarely from the late 14th century onwards. These are probably medieval.

Swiss Cottage

In the early-mid 17th century the open hall was floored over and the new first-floor chamber provided with a window beneath a gable. At the same time the old medieval service end was replaced by a two-bay gabled wing of two storeys with a cellar beneath and an attic above. Both the floored hall and the new wing were heated by fireplaces within a double stack and the main entrance was moved to the left opening into a lobby against the axial stack. The stair was also probably moved to its present position behind the stack. The changes were profound, for the old service end became a smart new parlour and the old parlour, possibly extended at this time, was downgraded to services. This reversal of functions is common in the late 16th and 17th centuries. There were further alterations in the 19th century when the Braddicks, attempting to give an Alpine flavour to the Quarries, re-named the house Swiss Cottage.

11 Wierton Hall Farm Cottage
WIERTON HILL, BOUGHTON MONCHELSEA. GRADE II.

The eastern half of the building is a four bay open-hall house of medieval date. The east end was the service end, divided into two rooms as at present with a stair at the rear. Next to it, where the sill is lower, lay the front doorway of the screens passage. The open hall consisted of two bays, a short one containing the entrance and later stack and a longer one at the 'upper' or 'dais' end of the open hall. A further bay beyond the open hall remains but it is not possible to comment upon it since the ceiling joists are not visible and no timbers are revealed on the upper floor. On the ground floor a mullioned window in the west gable wall lit this inner room.

The main trusses have large arch braces to the tie beams and simple collared rafters with no evidence for crown posts or collar purlin above.   Smoke-blackened partitions remain at either end of the open hall. There is no evidence for jettying at either end of the house and the simple roof form and generally low proportions indicate a more modest medieval dwelling than the majority which survive in Boughton. It was probably built around 1500.

Wierton Hall Farm Cottage

In the 16th century the western half of the hall was ceiled over leaving the smaller eastern bay as a smoke bay. The smoke blackened, inserted central partition is still visible in the roof. At this date the old entry and screens passage remained in use behind the smoke bay. Around 1700 a stone and brick stack was inserted. This was oddly placed at the back of the smoke bay blocking the screens passage. In the late 18th and 19th centuries additions were made at the west end and the property was turned into cottages. It was still in multiple occupation in the 1930s.

12 *Wierton Cottage*

WIERTON HILL, BOUGHTON MONCHELSEA. GRADE II.

The house has been listed as 14th-15th century with a three-bay open hall and two two-storeyed bays, one to each end. This would make it an extremely unusual building and this interpretation is here considered to be unlikely. However, lack of visible evidence makes it impossible to prove an alternative interpretation.

Very little medieval work is visible below roof level but the roof, of simple collar-rafter construction, is smoke-blackened throughout the central three-bay section. On the ground floor, at the right hand end of the house, part of a shallow and simply moulded dais beam remains between the end bay and the former hall. Probably the presence of the moulded beam indicates that this is the dais or parlour end of the hall.

Wierton Cottage

The inserted stack lies in the lower or service end of the central bay of the hall. This is an odd position in a three-bay hall and, combined with the fact that the small area of ground-floor partition visible at the far end of the presumed three-bay hall shows no sign of normal service doorways, it begs the question of whether this was not in fact a two-bay hall with a screens passage at the left hand end, now blocked by the inserted stack and with a service bay beyond which was, like the hall, originally open to the roof. Open service bays are not common but they occur in a number of buildings throughout Kent, usually in ones which have simple collar-rafter roofs and few signs of sophisticated detailing. Certainly the roof structure suggests limited funds and this idea would also account for the fact that the smoke blackening tails away at this end with no evidence for a closed partition at roof level dividing the hall from the service end. There is very little by which to date the house. It is, perhaps, more likely to date from the late 15th century than from the late 14th or early 15th century when surviving buildings tend to be of higher quality.

The stack is likely to have been inserted in two phases. The stone fireplace of the first phase, heating the main part of the former open hall to the right, has a four-centred head and sunken spandrels. This is quite unlike other fireplaces in the district and suggests a rather earlier date, perhaps in the mid-later 16th century. The cross passage behind the stack remained in use and was only blocked when a second fireplace was added in the 17th century. The second fireplace has the normal 17th century chamfered, timber lintel and stone jambs found in nearly all listed houses in Boughton. If the house was extended, it is likely that it was done at this time to provide an unheated service room beyond the heated hall/kitchen, the old hall then becoming a parlour. It was at this time that the present lobby-entry plan was created.

In 1905 the cottage was occupied by Rev. William Smith, the curate.

sketch plans

Typical plans of three Boughton Houses of the 15th, 16th and 17th centuries showing some of the changes which they have undergone.

i Fifteenth Century

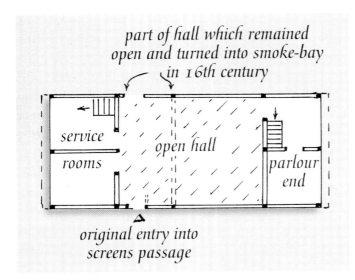

part of hall which remained
open and turned into smoke-bay
in 16th century

service rooms

open hall

parlour end

original entry into
screens passage

Swallows:

sketch plan, not to scale

15th century

Fig. E

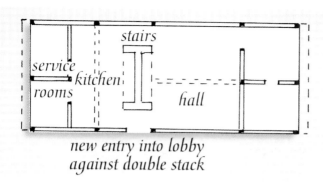

Swallows:
sketch plan, not to scale

1616

new entry into lobby
against double stack

ii Sixteenth Century

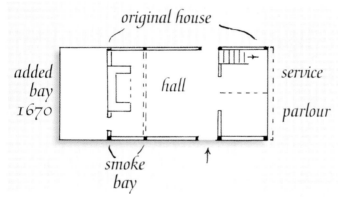

White Cottage:
sketch plan, not to scale

added bay 1670

iii Seventeenth Century

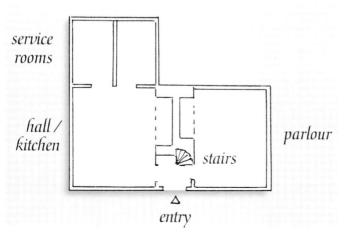

Bishops Farmhouse:
sketch plan, not to scale

Swallows: sketch sections to show changes

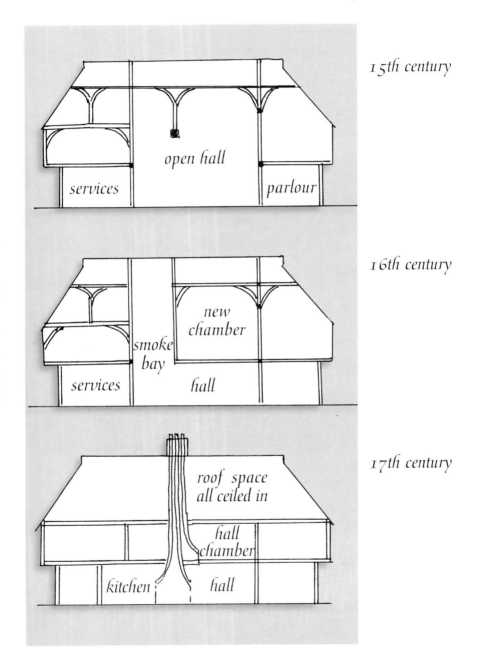

15th century

open hall

services

parlour

16th century

new chamber

smoke bay

services

hall

17th century

roof space all ceiled in

hall chamber

kitchen

hall

13 Harts House

BOTTLESCREW HILL, BOUGHTON MONCHELSEA. GRADE II.

This appears to have started life as a high quality T-plan house in the early 16th century, probably between c.1500 and 1540. It was always two storeys throughout, and was jettied on the west, south and north sides. The main front seems to have been to the west where a central entry opened into a cross passage which, most unusually, ran right back through the main range and the tail of the T. Evidence for the position of the former front doorway can be seen in the framing on the exterior. To the right of the entry lay a hall heated by a large smoke bay situated against the rear wall where the stack now lies. Behind the hall, in the tail of the T, there appears to have been an unheated parlour. To the left of the passage lay at least two unheated service rooms. A lean-to to the west of the south end of the hall seems to be integral with the original build, put there to house a stair to the first floor. The arrangement of joists suggests a second stair lay behind the service rooms.

The plan is highly unusual, perhaps because the building lies on a constricted site in the Quarries.

Harts House

The two parts of the house are contemporary.

A fully two-storeyed house is unlikely to date before c.1500 while the detailing with large, closely-spaced joists, close-studded walls, four-centred doorways with sunken spandrels, and a plain, crown post roof in the rear wing all suggest a date between c.1500 and c.1540. Secondly, and even more importantly, the smoke bay, which must be the original method of heating the hall, presupposes the existence of the rear wing. Although at ground-floor level the whole smoke bay area lies within the hall range, at roof level the large flue, some 10ft square, is partly constructed within the wing. It has heavily-sooted plaster walls remaining on all four sides and the smoke-blackened collar purlin of the rear crown post-roof runs a considerable distance into the flue.

In the later 16th century the smoke bay was replaced by a stone stack with fireplaces heating the hall and the parlour behind it. Only the parlour fireplace survives. In the 17th century the first stone stack was augmented by two brick flues serving fireplaces heating the north and south chambers in the front range. It was probably at this time that the cellar was dug out under the parlour and attics were created in the roof.

It has been speculated that a high status dwelling such as this may have housed Thomas Fyssher or William Yeomanson, the wealthy quarry owners who 'dwelt besyde' Boughton Quarry and supplied the stone for building Tower Wharf in 1600. By the 19th century, however, like so many Boughton houses, it was subject to multiple occupation.

14 Cliff House and Cliff Cottage
CLIFF HILL, BOUGHTON MONCHELSEA. GRADE II.

The present house is of several periods. The first periods date from the early-mid 16th century and the second half of the 17th century. The earliest bay, to the west, is of two storeys, timber-framed, close-studded and jettied on the north wall. Inside, the main ground-floor beam has clustered rolls typical of the first half of the 16th century (See Tanyard). On the first floor the west end wall has evidence for a mullioned window with sliding shutter. This bay was part of a larger house. Possibly it formed an up-to-date parlour added to an earlier building – but whatever was attached to it was re-built in the 17th century.

Cliff House and Cliff Cottage

In the 17th century all but this end bay was rebuilt in brick – although much of the wall was again rebuilt this century after damage from a flying bomb. Some earlier brickwork in Flemish bond survives and the wall plate, which is visible in a couple of places, shows no signs of posts or studding beneath. The new house had a lobby entry against a double stack serving both the remaining old bay and the new hall to the east. The beams in the hall are reminiscent of smoke-bay arrangements. Beyond the hall is an end bay containing one or two rooms. The new hall fireplace is built of high quality ragstone. There would appear to be an integral oven at the rear. The fireplace to the old end, which is likely to have been the parlour, was wholly of brick. The form of the stack on the inside suggests the first-floor fireplaces on each side may be later additions, perhaps of c.1700.

In the 19th century the house was divided into two, and additions were made to the rear of the west end. When the Kent County Constabulary was formed in 1857 it was decided to place married officers in the villages where they could integrate into the local communities. By 1881 one part of Cliff Cottage was occupied by John Froud, a local bricklayer and his family. The other portion was the home of Police Sergeant Jabez Bassett and his wife Eliza. To Boughton people Cliff Hill became known as 'Policeman's Hill' while Cliff Cottage became 'Policeman's Cottage'.

15 Gravitt's Farmhouse
BOUGHTON MONCHELSEA. GRADE II.

This is a complicated house in which the earliest remains are medieval but they have probably been re-used. The earliest part of the present building is the rear wing which is 16th century. When this was built at least part of the medieval house may have survived but it was re-built around 1700 and much of the earlier material was re-used.

The rear wing contains a large room jettied to the south. Close-studded framing remains on the first floor to the east. On the ground floor a

Gravitt's Farmhouse

medieval dais beam has been re-used on one wall but the main beam has cyma and hollow mouldings of a later period. On the first floor there is evidence for a mullioned window with sliding shutters.

The present front is of two tall storeys with brick below and tile hanging above. It has a central lobby entrance against a double fireplace. The exposed timber fireplace lintel in the hall is plain although the stone jambs are moulded. These are likely to have been re-used. The timber-framed rear wall of the house has been exposed and is clearly built of re-used timbers; among them are the heads of two windows with very large diamond-shaped mullions which must come from an open hall. Between the wing and the main range is a stair bay. The stair is modern but the beams separating the stair from the rear wing are chamfered. If these timbers have not been re-used they indicate that the stair was always in this bay, connecting the 16th century range with the later range at the front. Some of the roof timbers are probably re-used from a medieval open hall. It would appear that the rear wing was re-roofed when the front range was re-built.

16 The Old House
THE GREEN, BOUGHTON MONCHELSEA. GRADE II.

This is a puzzling house now consisting of a 16th century cross wing and a 17th century hall range but with the ghost of a medieval layout in the plan. The hall is heated by an axial stack and has a screens passage surviving behind it. Nothing remains beyond that point but it is likely that the hall lies on the site of a medieval open hall and that there was a service end beyond the passage which has been totally demolished.

The details of the present hall range suggest a 17th century date with deep and narrow joisting and a large stone stack with 17th century fireplaces heating the hall and chamber above. The roof is now modern

The Old House

but the rear wall plate has evidence on its soffit for a great eight light window with diamond mullions. Although this may be thought to remain from a medieval open hall, the presence of shutter grooves for sliding shutters indicates that the window always lit an upper floor. The upper section of the window in an open hall had to have hinged shutters so that they could be opened and closed at ground level.

The details of the wing are rather earlier with wide joists of 16th century character. The partition between the hall and wing is marked by a beam which is contemporary with the wing rather than the hall. It has evidence on its soffit for two doorways, a central one and one towards the front of the house. There is no evidence for the position of an original stair at this end of the house. On the first floor the main posts and tie beams remain but the roof has been replaced like that to the main range. Thus, despite its probable early origin, the sequence and layout of the house are not fully understood.

17 *White Cottage*

GREEN LANE, BOUGHTON MONCHELSEA. GRADE II.

The house seems to have been built in the mid 16th century as a two-bay, two-storey house heated by a smoke bay at one end. Although disguised by weather boarding on the front, the details survive exceptionally well. The layout of the building is still medieval, with the entry in the middle, at the west end of the hall, and an opposed doorway at the rear. Three doorways with straight heads and chamfered surrounds, remain in the central partition, opening into two small rooms and the stair. This end has plain joists and is jettied to the west.

The hall consists of a large main bay and a narrow bay to the west separated by a cross beam which carries the main spine beam. The main posts and cross beam are all still covered with a deposit of soot. The

White Cottage

roof is of clasped side-purlin construction with wind braces and the section above the fireplace is smoke-blackened. The evidence suggests not only that there was a smoke bay heating the hall but that there was no enclosed fireplace surround at ground-floor level; in other words one bay of the hall was simply left open to the roof.

In the 17th century a further bay was added to the east and the smoke bay was replaced by the present fireplace and brick stack. The date 1670 has been cut on one of the stones forming the back of the fireplace and it is possible that this dates the change from smoke bay to enclosed hearth. Later outshuts have been added all along the rear.

18 Oak Tree Cottage
THE GREEN, BOUGHTON MONCHELSEA. GRADE II.

The original house is split between Oak Tree Cottage and Oak Cottage [not seen]. When built in the 16th century it seems to have been of two bays only. Both the north and south ends of the present cottages were added later.

The original timber-framed building had a hall to the south, heated by a fireplace in a structural smoke bay at its south end, for which evidence remains in the roof. To the north there was another bay which was not seen but which was probably divided into two rooms. It is also likely that the stair lay in the rear of these two rooms. The position of the original entry is unclear but it is most likely that it would have been in the front wall of the hall. The hall joists are substantial and chamfered and these and other details suggest a construction date in the mid 16th century.

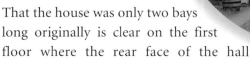

That the house was only two bays long originally is clear on the first floor where the rear face of the hall

Oak Tree Cottage

timbers are visible and heavily weathered. There was always a first-floor chamber over the hall and on the west wall the area beside the smoke bay was lit by a mullioned window with grooves for a vertical sliding shutter. The roof is of clasped side-purlin construction with wind braces. The bay continuing the later stack is not only partitioned from the rest but is smoke blackened indicating the former presence of a smoke bay rather than an enclosed stack.

In the 17th century a new bay was added at the south end. The new room has a central beam. At that time the smoke bay was replaced by a stack with two large fireplaces with stone jambs. The entry was probably shifted to the present position in front of the stack and the stair may have been moved from the north end to lie at the back of the hall as at present. On the first floor there is evidence for an unglazed mullioned window with horizontal shutter grooves. The attic was probably also created at this time.

In 1847 the building appears to have been a beerhouse on the Green conducted by Mary Barton. By 1881 it was designated the *Oak* and had become the third of Boughton's public houses. The licence was held by Mary Ann Bolton. Henry Arthur Bolton was the landlord by 1899 and remained 'mine host' in 1905. The premises were no longer licensed by 1938.

19 *No. 65, The Quarries*
BOUGHTON MONCHELSEA. GRADE II.

This is a small, two-bay house probably built in the mid-late 16th century. It has a hall to the right and two service rooms, and the stair to the left. The hall was heated by a fireplace set against the gable wall. It had stone jambs and a timber lintel. There is no evidence that the doorway, which opens into the hall in the centre of the house, was ever in a different position. The detailing and the arrangement of the secondary rooms and stair are basically sub-medieval.

No 65 The Quarries

On the first floor the space was divided into three by two cambered and formerly arched tie beams. Both beams have mortices for partitions beneath and it is probable that the right-hand room was not a room but a smoke bay channelling smoke from the hearth below. In the 17th century the brick stack and present fireplace were built, and later a second fireplace was added to heat the first-floor room. Evidence for two windows with diamond mullions remains on the back wall.

The roof is now a mixture of styles. Several of the timbers are heavily charred. Some of the rafters come from a simple collar-rafter roof but whether this could have been the original roof over this property is unclear.

20 No. 88, The Quarries
BOUGHTON MONCHELSEA. GRADE II.

This is a two-bay, timber-framed house with details suggesting a mid 16th century origin. The hall is divided by main posts and a cross beam into two sections; the larger area to the west has neatly-pegged north to south joists. The smaller section to the east has unpegged east to west joists. This end bay contains the stack which would appear to date only from the 17th century and is, therefore, later than the house itself. The fireplace must always have been in this area and the arrangement of joists and presence of main posts so near the end wall combine to suggest that the east bay began life as a smoke bay.

As in other small 16th century houses in the parish, the eastern half of the house was divided into two rooms. Pegs in the beam above the north-south partition also indicate the positions of the two central doorways

No 88 The Quarries

opening from the main hall to the two inner rooms. The stairs were almost certainly in the rear of the two rooms. It is likely that the house was entered by centrally-placed, opposed entrances into the hall next to the central partition. A front doorway, later used as a cottage doorway, remains in this position. In the late 18th or 19th century the house was turned into two cottages and the internal arrangement greatly altered.

21 *Gladstones*

THE QUARRIES, BOUGHTON MONCHELSEA. GRADE II.

This is a puzzling house. Most of it is built of local ragstone but the upper part of the rear wall and one gable are of timber. The earliest part of the building contains two rooms on the ground floor, one unheated, and one formerly heated by an internal stack. The lower part of the shell of the stone fireplace surround survives against the gable wall, although the present, much smaller, fireplace is served by a stack projecting beyond the gable wall. The earlier fireplace does not have the large stone jambs of most 17th century Boughton fireplaces but is made from a number of smaller stones.

Gladstones

The detail of the building suggests a mid-late 16th century origin for the construction. The stair is located in an original position against the rear wall. The plan is not a typical 17th century plan. Instead there are a number of oddities. The partition between the two rooms is not under the main beam. The central doorway opens directly under the same beam and into the minor room. Finally, all the beams are secured into the walls by iron ties. This must have occurred in the 18th or 19th century and is a strange thing to have been found necessary if the whole building was built at one time. These anomalies raise questions as to whether this dwelling may not have been a timber-framed house but with most of its walls replaced by ragstone in the 18th century when changes were made to its layout.

22 The Old Farmhouse

THE GREEN, BOUGHTON MONCHELSEA. GRADE II.

This is a house of complex development recorded in 1997 by David and Barbara Martin. The earliest part of the building, probably of the mid-16th century, seems to be the two bays at the south end. The building is of two storeys, with the hall to the north heated by a smoke bay separating the two rooms. This is an unusual plan. Further evidence suggests that originally the house ran further north. The width of the smoke bay suggests the house may have been entered by a cross passage behind the fireplace but no evidence was seen to prove this. It is possible that at first the stair lay in the presumed north bay and after the brick stack was built it was positioned east of that stack. The roof has clasped side purlins and wind braces and the timbers of the smoke bay are blackened.

This earliest phase was lit by a number of unglazed mullioned windows, those on the ground floor having vertical sliding shutters; those above having horizontal shutters.

In the 17th century the house was enlarged to the north. This took place in at least three stages. In the first place the presumed earlier north end bay seems to have been reconstructed with a narrow bay

The Old Farmhouse

beyond. A lack of partitioning between the new narrow bay and the area to its south at ground-floor level, and the smoke blackened timbers above, led the Martins to interpret this as the addition of a kitchen heated by a gable smoke bay. Shortly after, the end was enlarged yet again, the smoke bay destroyed and its area incorporated into a larger kitchen and chamber above, heated by fireplaces in a gable end stack. As both phases have very similar roofs to the original build, the whole process can have taken little more than 100 years. At much the same time a timber-framed rear wing was added behind the north end. Later still, brick outshuts were built along all remaining parts of the west wall and a cellar dug out beneath the hall. By the 19th century the property was known as 4, Wood Cottages and in multiple occupation.

23 Iden Farm Cottage
HEATH ROAD, BOUGHTON MONCHELSEA. GRADE II.

This is a timber framed house with jetties to either end. The ground floor was later re-built in ragstone and a ragstone outshut added at the rear. The original building is of 16th century date. It seems to have had three rooms and two storeys, with a separately framed bay which probably contained a timber stack where the fireplace heating the hall now lies. The evidence for the timber stack is slight and resides in four details. First the bay arrange-ment with a separate bay for the chimney; secondly the fact that the chamfered and stopped joists in the main bay of the hall and in the room which was formerly partitioned off at the south end do not occur in the stack bay, implying

Iden Farm Cottage

a larger fireplace than at present; thirdly, the stack had closed partitions to each side of it, which would have been rather unnecessary with a brick stack; and lastly the main tie beam on the first floor has a cut on its north face suggesting it formerly housed the sloping face of a chimney stack occupying a larger space than the present one at ground-floor level. Although very few timber stacks survive, evidence for them is not uncommon and in the mid or later 16th century it would not be surprising to find one in a medium-sized house of this sort. The roof trusses do not match the tie beams below and it is likely that the roof was re-built, perhaps in the 17th century when the present fireplace, with simply-chamfered, stone jambs and timber lintel, was inserted. Thus at roof level all evidence for original heating has gone.

Since the ground-floor walls were re-built in the 18th century it is not clear where the original entry lay. There is little space for it to have opened into a cross passage behind the fireplace and therefore more likely that it was into a lobby beside the fireplace. It is not known whether the north end bay was always divided into two rooms, as at present. The stair appears to have been in the west corner of this bay. The south end of the house must have been separated from the hall to start with although there is no sign of mortices to carry the partition. In the south end wall a mullioned window with sliding shutter lit the south end room, and further mullioned windows occur in the north gable wall.

24 Iden Farm

HEATH ROAD, BOUGHTON MONCHELSEA. GRADE II.

The present exterior of the house, built in Flemish bond brickwork with blue glazed headers, dates to mid-later 18th century, and it is to this period that most of the interior seems to belong. The house is of two storeys with attics in the main range and with rear wings at either end. The central hall area has clear signs, however, of a late 16th or early 17th century core of one and a half storeys, the upper floor being set partly within the roof.

The hall is ceiled with ovolo-moulded beams and neatly stopped joists. It is heated by a fireplace with stone jambs and a timber lintel. The present doorway opens into a lobby against the stack and this may be the original arrangement. On the first

Iden Farm

floor, above the hall, the rear wall plate of the original wall survives, set about 2ft.6ins, above floor level. This has rafter seatings for the original roof. Its low height indicates that the upper floor must have been set partly within the roof space and was probably lit by windows in small gables.

The front wall was re-built, and the rear wall heightened and became internal when the house was greatly enlarged in the 18th century. At this time whatever had formerly lain at either end of the earlier hall was replaced, rear wings were added at each end, and a corridor created between the wings. This later phase re-used a lot of earlier timbers, notably joists. The later work is not necessarily all of one phase.

25 Rock Cottage

ATKINS HILL, BOUGHTON MONCHELSEA. GRADE II.

This is a high quality house built in the mid-late 16th century. It still has echoes of a medieval layout in its plan but was well-heated from the start and no expense was spared on the details. On the exterior the south and east faces are jettied and the main rooms in the centre and to the east, had projecting oriel windows, which still survive on the east gable wall. The walls are in close-studded framing.

The entrance lies towards the west, originally opening into the hall which is heated by a fireplace in a large chimney stack at the east end. The main beam has a double cyma moulding and the fireplace has stone jambs and a timber four-centred head with hollow spandrels. The east room or parlour, reached by a passage beside the stack, has a similar fireplace with a wholly stone surround, and still retains its projecting mullioned and transomed window in the east wall. A small newel stair lay between the stack and the passage from hall to parlour. There may have been an entry into a lobby in front of the stair and stack although the date of the doorway here is

Rock Cottage

unclear, particularly as the house was later divided into cottages. Certainly there seems to be an original doorway at the west end of the hall, with another doorway on the rear wall opposite. Thus it seems likely that a cross entry was retained and this medieval arrangement is underlined by the presence of two doorways to two service rooms and a third doorway to a straight flight stair at the rear, very much in the medieval fashion.

On the first floor the chambers over the hall and parlour are heated and each appears to have been provided with a small closet on the north side of the stack. Access to the attic was not via the newel stair and must have been by a stair at the west end of the house which has now gone. The roof is of clasped side-purlin construction with wind braces. Like Harts House, Rock Cottage could also have been the home of one of the quarry owners, who 'dwelt beside Boughton Quarry', in 1600.

26 East Hall

EAST HALL HILL, BOUGHTON MONCHELSEA. GRADE II.

This complex building is of higher status than most in the parish. It consists of two ranges of late 16th and early 17th century date, probably erected on the site of a medieval building, of which traces survive in the present kitchen (north) range, in the plan, the re-use of smoke-blackened roof timbers, and in foundations to the west of the house. The earlier building is likely to have been up-dated in the mid 16th century, which is the date of two beams and a doorway in the kitchen range. But everything earlier was otherwise wholly reconstructed when the present house was built. This probably took place from about 1597, the date being incised on a first-floor fireplace in the kitchen range, which lies at right-angles to the south, dating to the early 17th century. The date of 1604 occurs on a stone garden gateway.

The new front range was of two storeys and an attic with a cellar beneath, and of two storeys only in the kitchen range. There are a number of puzzling features about the plan, and Edwardian alterations make it difficult to sort out exactly how the house functioned originally. Nonetheless, the large rooms, high-quality detailing in the form of carved surrounds to the stone fireplaces and clustered, corbelled

East Hall

and filletted flues to the brick stacks; ovolo-mouldings and decorative stops to windows, doorway and beams; a good dog-leg stair, and well-made side purlin roofs all testify to an unusually wealthy owner around 1600.

The re-construction around 1600 was carried out by Thomas Barham using the considerable fortune which his father, also Thomas Barham, an ironfounder from Wadhurst, had left him. Thomas Barham was 'Comptroller of the Pipe', a very lucrative office which gave him a monopoly of wine selling. In 1620 Robert, Thomas Barham's son, married one of the nine daughters of Sir Edward Filmer of East Sutton Park. One of their sons went to Virginia where his great uncle, Sir

Samuel Argoll, was governor.[219] Stephen Tomkin, his wife and seven children occupied the farmhouse in 1841 together with 4 female servants and 3 agricultural labourers. Tomkin farmed 158 acres in 1851 for which he employed 9 agricultural labourers. Ten years later he is described as a 'farmer and hop grower' employing 10 men and 3 boys.

27 Elm House
OLD TREE LANE, BOUGHTON MONCHELSEA. GRADE II.

The front of the house is a fine brick range of early 18th century date built to a similar design as Bradbourne Manor, Larkfield which was completed 1713-15. It is only five bays (two rooms) wide and one room deep. It was added to, and partially built within, an earlier timber-framed building which lies parallel at the rear.

The earlier range is of four timber-framed bays. The main posts and tie beams, some of the wall framing and clasped side-purlin roof with wind braces remain. It is not possible to date this with any accuracy, although the surviving details indicate that it must have been constructed in the 16th or early 17th centuries. The ground-floor arrangement is no longer discernible for walls have been moved and a new

Elm House

staircase and the stack serving both the old range and the new, have been built inside it. The height of the ground-floor ceilings in this section suggest that the floor level was dropped when the new range was added.

The early 18th century brick range is of two storeys and attic above a cellar. The facade has finely detailed brickwork on a stone plinth, with projecting giant pilasters at the ends and rubbed and cut bricks to the window heads. The oddity is that there is no central doorway as would normally be expected in a house of this sort. Instead the doorway is into a single-storey porch at one end. This destroys the symmetry of the facade and one may wonder whether the entrance originally opened directly into the north gable end, the porch being quickly added because this is the weather end of the house. The entrance opens into a square stair hall, the rest of the front being taken up by a reception room. Both rooms are panelled. The stairs, which are set within the old building, have twisted balusters and a moulded handrail. On the first floor, the cornices indicate that there was originally only one large room in the front range. The front rooms are both heated by a rear stack, which also has an angled fireplace to the ground-floor room behind. A service stair is contrived beside the stack. Behind the north side of the rear range lies a further wing which has some early timber framing in it. It is not possible to say when this was built. An icehouse lies to the south. Ice was collected in winter and packed in straw to insulate and preserve it for culinary use.

The identity of the 18th century owner who endeavoured to improve the status of the building is unknown. His efforts appear to have been comparatively short-lived. The interior improvement is incomplete and may well have bankrupted him or his successors. At the beginning of the 19th century and possibly much earlier, the farmhouse with impressive brick facade bore the name, Boughton Hall, although it never possessed the land to accompany the title. In 1841 it was occupied by Sarah Edmeads, a fifty-five year old 'farmer', her four sisters and a female servant. An agricultural labourer, his wife and child occupied the nearby Boughton Hall Cottage. Ten years later Sarah and her relatives were still there farming 25 acres. By 1861, she had been replaced by William Sturmer, who farmed 120 acres with 8 men. The revival was brief. Twenty years later it was occupied by an 84-year old widow, Elizabeth Smith. About this time the house suffered a serious fire and was repaired by the local builder, James Wood. It was also rented for a while by the Victorian artist, Thomas Joy. In 1908 the owner decided that the title 'Boughton Hall' was too grand for a farmhouse and re-named it 'Elm House'.[220]

28 Bishops Farmhouse

PEENS LANE, BOUGHTON MONCHELSEA. GRADE II.

This is a good quality house of two storeys and an attic, with a more or less central entry opening into a lobby in front of the double stack. To the rear of the larger southern section there is a contemporary rear wing. The detailing, with close studding, bay windows and ovolo mouldings, suggests a date in the first half of the 17th century.

The main entrance is now into a narrow lobby because a vertical brick wall has been built in front of the stack; however, the much larger area on the first floor, which forms a large closet, suggests that originally there would have been room for a stair in front of the stack. To the right lay the parlour and to the left a larger room which probably served as a hall/kitchen. Both are heated by fireplaces with stone jambs and timber lintels. At the back of the hall/kitchen the frames of two original doorways remain, indicating that on the ground-floor the rear wing was divided into two unheated service rooms.

Bishops Farmhouse

On the first floor the same pattern is repeated, although the wing probably only contained a single chamber. The roofs above the attic are constructed of clasped side purlins with butt purlins below; there is no evidence that the latter are insertions, and it is possible that both were thought necessary in order to cope with the openings for the gables towards the front. On the north side of the house the ground and first-floor windows are set into a projecting bay and the presence of symmetrical gables at attic level suggests there was a balancing bay on the south side which has been removed.

In 1851 the farm was occupied by William Ralph who farmed 122 acres with the aid of 4 men. It was held by Thomas Peen in 1861. His surname has passed to the lane in which the farm stands.

29 Wierton Hall

WIERTON, BOUGHTON MONCHELSEA. GRADE II.

Despite its Georgian facade, this is a much earlier building, probably dating to the early-mid 17th century. It is of two storeys and an attic and has always had a sophisticated lobby-entrance plan. It is timber-framed and has never had a jetty on the front wall.

The entry is into a lobby against a double axial stack, with a hall/kitchen to the right and a parlour to the left. There is a cellar beneath the parlour. A ceiling beam at the rear of the parlour indicates that another, unheated room lay behind it projecting at the rear. There was a newel stair at the back of the stack. This area has been considerably altered, although the final section up to the attic remains more or less intact. Beyond the stair and reached from the hall, lay another unheated room in a rear wing. This now has a gable-end stack but the presence in the gable wall of now-blocked mullioned windows indicates that the fireplace is a later addition.

Wierton Hall

The Listing Description suggests that the unheated bay in the re-entrant angle behind the parlour is a later addition but the wall at the rear of the parlour bay is exposed on the first floor and has timbers set in from the exterior, proving that this was always an internal wall and therefore that the small wing is integral.

The central stack in the front range contains five fireplaces. Four heat the main rooms and chambers over.

30 Fir Tree Cottage

THE QUARRIES, BOUGHTON MONCHELSEA. GRADE II.

This is a small, two-bay, two-storey timber-framed house with a lobby or central entry opening against the stack. The form and details of the house suggest a date in the 17th century. The larger hall/kitchen lay to the right, with a parlour to the left. The stair is likely always to have been in its present position at the rear of the stack. Both rooms had fireplaces from the start and the chamber over the parlour was also heated.

Fir Tree Cottage

It seems likely that a house with three heated rooms would also have had an unheated service room from the beginning but no evidence for such accommodation was found. Precise dating of the house is not easy. The fireplaces suggest a date in the first half of the 17th century but the fact that the lobby entry plan is so fully developed in so small a house may indicate a date more towards mid century.

31 Parsonage Farm

HEATH ROAD, BOUGHTON MONCHELSEA. GRADE II.

Although much of the timber is of 16th century date this seems to be a new house erected about 1700 with ragstone walls to the ground floor and timber framing above. The house is of two storeys and an attic and has two main rooms on each floor, probably always with a single-storey outshut at the rear. The central entrance opens into a lobby against the double stack. A newel stair is at the rear of the stack. Both ground-floor fireplaces are small, with little evidence of cooking, so there may always, as at present, have been a kitchen with another fireplace in the outshut.

The north room has a boarded floor and cellar beneath, and is likely to have been the parlour. The central chimney has four flues which suggests the upper rooms were heated from the start. The 16th century chamfered joists in the hall, to the south, and in the cellar, are earlier than the building itself. The roof, which is largely hidden, also re-uses earlier timbers. The re-use of old timbers which takes place in several of Boughton's listed houses is a clear indication of the growing timber shortage in the Weald by this date.

The earliest written mention of the farm is in a survey of 'one part of the Church of Rochester' taken in 1623. Whether the farm was the Parsonage before the two later vicarages were built on Church Hill or whether it was simply Glebe land for the maintenance of St. Peter's and its incumbent is not wholly clear. Nonetheless it is clearly the earlier Parsonage Farm buildings which are described consisting of 'One messuage tiled, one homestall, 2 barnes thatched, one stable adjoining the barn, one garden, one orchard conteyning by Estimation one Acre together with eight peeces of land'. Some of the outbuildings were already showing signs of wear and tear. The enclosures about the house were 'sufficient and well Paled and the Grounds well fenced' but one of the Barns was 'in dacay and very old, and a hovell in the yard ready to fall for repairing whereof warning was...given to the Archdeacon.'

Parsonage Farm

Twenty-six years later, at the beginning of the Commonwealth period, the Rectory of Boughton Monchelsea together with the tithes and the Parsonage House was up for sale. The latter consisted of Hall, Parler, Kitchen, Buttery, 2 cellers and one brewhouse, 6 chambers, 3 garretts and one outhouse, 2 Barns, one stable, another necessary outhouse, and a large court with 'the several peeces of Glebe land immediately following.' A final, but unfortunately brief, description of the buildings was made in 1776 after the present buildings were erected. 'One mansion house built with good Oak Timber and Tiled. Tiles require mending – now in occupation of Robt. Cheeseman. Wheat Barn in good repair – except a little Daubing or Boarding at the East End. Lent Corn Barn with two Threshing places:

a Cart Lodge and Stable connected under one roof Thatched – in moderate repair, some Thatch required very soon...'

By 1851 the Farmhouse had fallen upon hard times and was occupied as two cottages by Elisha Mills and Thomas Conway, both farm labourers, together with their wives and families. By 1861, Mills had become a farm bailiff. He and his family were the sole occupants and remained so in 1881.

32 The Old Cottage
THE GREEN, BOUGHTON MONCHELSEA. GRADE II.

This is a two-bay, two-storeyed timber-framed and tile-hung cottage. On 25 June 1739 William Roberts, senior and his wife, Mary, sold for £10 on a 99-year lease 'all that **newly created** messuage, tenement and cottage with land situate and lying near the Alms houses at Cocks Heath in Boughton Monchelsea' to John Meriam. George Meriam of Boughton Monchelsea, heir of John Meriam, in 1755 sold the property in turn to William Roberts, junior, Victualler, of East Malling.

The cottage consists of two rooms on each floor, the main ground-floor room heated by a large, brick, gable stack. The entry was originally in the centre of the house, opening into the main hall/kitchen. The stair now lies at the back of the secondary room and may always have occupied this position. Most of the timbers have been re-used.

The Old Cottage

Fig. F *Some architectural features in Boughton's timber-framed houses.*

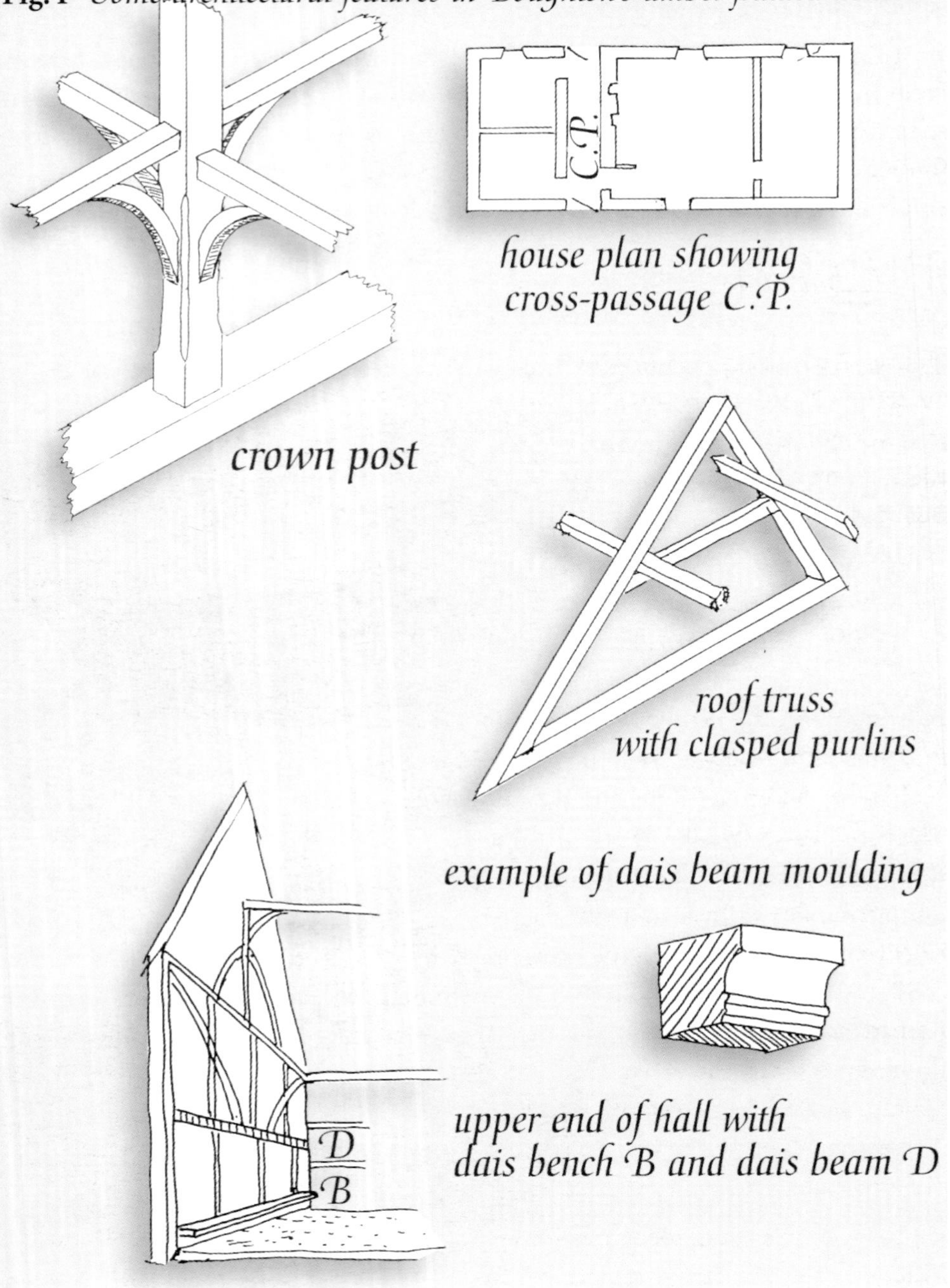

crown post

house plan showing
cross-passage C.P.

roof truss
with clasped purlins

example of dais beam moulding

upper end of hall with
dais bench B and dais beam D

Other Houses which were not surveyed but are largely listed buildings.

A Quarry House – GRADE II.

Late 16th century with early 17th century additions and considerable 20th century alterations. Mid-to-late 16th century lobby entrance plan. House of three timber framed bays. In 1851 it was occupied by William Baldwin, master brewer, employing 52 men and 4 boys. By the early 20th century it had become cottages.

B Laburnum Cottage – GRADE II.

House. Early 17th century or before. Timber framed, weather boarded, with plain tiled roof. Two storeys. Boarded door.

C Keeper's Cottage,
PEENS LANE – GRADE II.

Laburnum Cottage

Formerly the gamekeeper's cottage of the Boughton Monchelsea Estate it was well-placed for keeping an eye upon Brick Kiln Wood, Darnold Wood and River Wood to the south and the Deer Park and Tilt's Wood to the north. The cottage is early 17th century with a facade of 1842. It has two timber-framed bays. The ground-floor is of red brick in Flemish bond. The first floor is weather boarded with a plain tile roof.

In 1851 it was described as 'Mr. Rider's cottage' and occupied by his

Keeper's Cottage

gamekeeper, John Croucher. Poaching was not widely perceived as criminal either by poachers or the public. Nevertheless the Game Laws of the 18th and 19th centuries were extremely harsh and served only to intensify the long and bitter war between poachers and gamekeepers.

D Holbrook – GRADE II.

17th century with early 19th century addition and facade. Ground-floor red brick in Flemish bond. Two storeys with plain tile roof. Converted to cottages but now restored to a house.

Holbrook

E Tilts House – GRADE II.

Formerly Tilts Farmhouse. The farmhouse was re-built for William Musgrove c.1715, with red and grey brick in Flemish bond. It has a plain tile roof, is built in double depth and is of two storeys. There is a stone-flagged entrance hall with 18th century dog-leg staircase rising towards the rear of the front range. An iron range to the rear stack is dated 1720. The 19th century iron railings and the stone mounting block to the front of the house are also listed.

Tilts House

In 1851 the farm of 28 acres was farmed by William Tomkin who lived there with his wife and three children and one female general servant. Thirty years later the farm had grown to fifty acres. It was still farmed by Tomkin who was also a hop grower. He employed eight men and a boy.

F Beresfords – GRADE II.

Early nineteenth century house with tiled roof consisting of two storeys and a cellar. It has a central, half-glazed door with a rectangular fanlight up four steps. In 1881 it was held by William Skinner, who farmed 400 acres and employed 31 men and 4 boys.

Beresfords

G. The Malt House – GRADE II.

Maltings with integral warehousing built about 1860 of random ragstone with quoins and red brick dressing. The Building is south facing, of two low storeys with a plain tile roof. At the maltings barley was steeped in water, allowed to sprout and dried in a kiln. The resulting malt was used in brewing ale. In

The Malt House

1892 the premises were rented by Mark Abraham Atkins, a licensed malster living at Swiss Cottage, for the sum of £145 per year. He employed 4 men. When J.W. Braddick's Boughton Mount Estate was auctioned in 1896 there were two malthouses on this site. One had a 25-Quarter Steep, 2 cemented floors, a cistern, a kiln with tiled floor together with barley and malt rooms. The other had a 14-Quarter Steep, 2 cement floors, cistern, kiln with tiled floor, barley and malt rooms together with all accessories. 'An inexhaustible supply of excellent water' was provided by Brishing Stream which ran underground from Coombe Bank to the Old Malt Houses, and by a well on the premises.

The relationship between the Maltings and the brewery in the Quarry is unclear. These were probably the premises which were briefly used for the highly controversial chemical works of Jutson & Rigden in 1864 and may have become Maltings after the brewery and subsequently the chemical works, ceased to function. The Maltings are now converted into private dwellings.

H Bridge Row, The Quarries – GRADE II.

This row of six cottages formerly incorporated the beer house and grocer's shop, known locally as the Bridge Tavern, at its one end. The beer shop, much-patronised by quarrymen, belonged to Henry Loveless, grocer, beer retailer and lime dealer. The Row, was built in 1827 by John Braddick, It is constructed of small blocks of evenly-coursed stone with a slate roof.

Bridge Row

The cottages are of two storeys and rendered on the ground floor. There is a slate-roofed penthouse supported on rustic poles across the whole front elevation. This is said to have been an idea which Braddick adapted from the verandahs he had met during his stay in the West Indies. A plaque beneath the central stack is a constant reminder to his tenants of Braddick's Victorian values: *'With Industry, Economy, Honesty, Civility and Cleanliness a poor man may be happy and respectable 1827.'*

I Boughton Mount Cottage, The Quarries. NO LISTING.

Cottage traditionally built by the Braddicks for the overseer in the Quarries. Note again the rustic 'verandah' which was a characteristic of Braddick houses. The plaque above the front door shows the name of the cottage and its probably date of construction. The family group is the Potter family outside Boughton Mount Cottage in 1874. The tricycle had wooden wheels and iron tyres.

Boughton Mount Cottage

J Wierton Grange – GRADE II.

House built 1896 after the style of R. Norman Shaw. The ground-floor is of red brick in English bond. The first floor is hung with fishscale tiles. The house has a plain tile roof.

The interior is said to contain a two storey hall and fine joinery. In 1899 it was the residence of Henry Fairfax Best Archer and by 1905 the home of John Bazley-White. More recently it has become the temporary residence for Assize Judges during their visits to Maidstone.

Wierton Grange

Suggestions for further reading

The study of vernacular buildings is a highly specialised discipline. For further information about vernacular houses in Kent and the South East the reader is recommended to use the following books:

M.W. Barley,
The English Farmhouse and Cottage,
(London, 1961).

P.S. Barnwell, and A.T. Adams,
The House Within: interpreting medieval houses in Kent,
(Royal Commission on the Historical Monuments of England, HMSO, 1994).

R.T. Mason,
Framed Buildings of the Weald,
(Horsham, 1969).

E.W. Mercer,
English Vernacular Houses: a study of traditional farmhouses and cottages,
(Royal Commission on Historical Monuments, HMSO 1975)

A. Quiney,
Kent Houses,
(Woodbridge, 1993)

S. Pearson,
The Medieval Houses of Kent: an historical analysis,
(Royal Commission on the Historical Monuments of England, HMSO 1994).

A visit is also recommended to the Weald and Downland Open Air Museum, Singleton, Chichester, West Sussex, PO18 0EU.

References

1. Samuel Bagshaw, *History Gazeteer and Directory of Kent. Vol.1*. Sheffield, 1847. pp.168-9. *Kelly's Directory 1938*. p.96.

2. Frank W. Jessup. *Kent History Illustrated*, Maidstone, 1973. pp.52-3.

3. *Victoria County History. Kent. Vol.3*. Table of Population 1801-1921. p.361. Directorate of Planning and Development. Maidstone Borough Council, *Factfile Maidstone. Population Density and Electorate 1991 Census*, Maidstone 1994.

4. Bagshaw, *op.cit.*, p.169. S.C.L., *Historical and Descriptive Account of Maidstone and its Environs*, Maidstone, 1834. p.90. See Fig.1. Alan Everitt, *Continuity and Colonisation; the evolution of Kentish Settlement*, Leicester, 1986. p.50.

5. Everitt, *op.cit.*, pp.199-201

6. (C)entre for (K)entish (S)tudies P39/1/2 Boughton Monchelsea Boundary Perambulation 1720. Boughton Monchelsea Parish Council. Minutes of Annual Parish Meetings 1894-1993. 1907 Meeting.

7. Bagshaw, *op.cit.*, 168-9. *Kelly's Directory 1892*, p.71, 1905 p.88. Edward Hasted, *History and Topographical Survey of the County of Kent.* 12 vols. Canterbury, 1797-1801. p.337.

8. CKS P39/27/1-2. Boughton Monchelsea Tithe Map and Award 1842. Everitt, *op.cit.*, pp.50-51, 199.

9. Maidstone Museum Record Cards.

10. D.B. Kelly, *Quarry Wood Camp, Loose; A Belgic oppidum* in *Archaeologia Cantiana. Vol. 86.* 1971. pp.55-64.

11. *Ibid.* pp.69-73. I am indebted to Brian Philp, Director of the Kent Archaeological Rescue Unit, for comments on Boughton's archaeological sites.

12. Alec Detsicas, *The Cantiaci*, Gloucester, 1987. p.2.

13. Kelly, *op.cit.*, pp.68-69, 74-75,

14. *Ibid.* p.74.

15. *Ibid.* p.75.

16. Everitt, *op.cit.*, pp.86-87.

17. Detsicas, *op.cit.*, p.9.

18. Barri Jones and David Mattingly, *An Atlas of Roman Britain*, Oxford, 1990. p.217.

19 Detsicas, *op.cit.*, pp.140, 142. Victoria County History. Vol.3. p.106. Maidstone Museum Record Cards.

20 Victoria County History Vol.3. pp.158-59. Maidstone Museum Record Cards.

21 See Fig.1.

22 Detsicas, *op.cit.*, p.183. Peter Hunter Blair, *Anglo Saxon England*, Cambridge, 1956. pp.13-18.

23 Alan Everitt, *The making of the Agrarian Landscape of Kent* in *Archaeologia Cantiana*. Vol. 92. 1977. pp.7, 21-2.

24 Everitt, *Continuity and Colonisation...*p.51. Judith Glover, *The Place Names of Kent*, London, 1976. pp.25, 207. P.H. Reaney, *Place Names and Early Settlement in Kent* in *Archaeologia Cantiana*. Vol. 76. pp.66-7.

25 Jessup, *op.cit.*, p.25. D.W. Smithers, *Castles in Kent*, Chatham, 1980. p.87. F.W. Jessup, *A History of Kent*, Chichester, 1974. p.47. Some scholars now believe that the Domesday inquisition of 1086 was not finalised until 1089-90 when William was already dead.

26 Hasted, *op.cit.*, p.338.

27 Everitt, *Continuity and Colonisation...*pp.15, 86, 199.

28 Glover, *op.cit.*, p.25. Hasted, *op.cit.*, pp.338-341. *Guide to Boughton Monchelsea Place. n.d.*

29 CKS P39/12/1 Boughton Monchelsea Overseers Accounts 1777-1790. List of overseers 1799-1811. CKS P39/8/3 Boughton Monchelsea Vestry Minute Book 1821-1834. (P)arliamentary (P)apers 1834(44) Vol. XXVIII. Appendix A. Part 1. p.216A.

30 (P)ublic (R)ecord (O)ffice. MH 12. 5195. Maidstone Union 1834-37. First Meeting of the Coxheath Union 13.9.1835. (M)aidstone (G)azette 17.8.1847.

31 MG 17.8.1847, (M)aidstone (J)ournal 17.8.1847.

32 MG 17.8.1847.

33 *Guide to Boughton Monchelsea Place.*

34 Hasted, *op.cit.*, pp.342-43, 350. 'Brishing' in Old English meant 'Breosa's People'. Brishing Lane was originally so named because it led to Brishing Manor House. Later because of its shape and since it gave access to Park Wood and Brishing Woods, the lane came to be associated perhaps with the long-handled Brishing Hook used in Kent for cutting brushwood.

35 *Ibid pp.341-42.* C.W. Chalkin, *Seventeenth Century Kent*, Rochester, 1965. pp.196-97.

36 Hasted. *op.cit.*, p.343. MG 15.10.1830. (K)ent (M)essenger 21.9.1866, 21.7.1869. See Braddick Memorial in St. Peter's Church, Boughton Monchelsea. CKS PRC/27/42/23 Inventory of John Savage, Esq., Late of Boughton Monchelsea 21 May 1726. Particulars of Sale of the Boughton Mount Estate at Star Hotel. Maidstone, 7 May 1896.

37 See Calendar of Ancient Deeds presented by Charles Marchant in July 1904 to Kent Archaeological Society in *Archaeologia Cantiana.* Vol. 27. 1904. pp.167-176.

38 A.R.H. Baker, *Some fields and farms in Medieval Kent* in *Archaeologia Cantiana. Vol. 80.* 1965, pp.152-174. Jessup, *op.cit.*, pp.36-7. CKS P39/27/1-2 Boughton Monchelsea Tithe Map and Award 1842. J. Boys, *A General View of the Agriculture of Kent,* 1st Edition 1796, 2nd Edition 1813, p.61.

39 Calendar of Ancient Deeds, *loc.cit.*, pp.168.170. Ed. Elizabeth Melling. *Some Kentish Houses,* Maidstone, 1965. p.8.

40 CKS BX 93060609 C15 Transcribed Mary Wigan, Boughton Monchelsea Parish Registers 1559-1812,1990. CC RC E1-E5 Surveys of Parsonage Farm 1623-1861. Catholic Record Society. Vol. 2. *Archdeacon Harpsfield's Visitation Returns. 1557.* p.199.

41 See E.B. Fryde, *The Great Revolt of 1381,* London, 1981 for background.

42 *Sequel to the Great Rebellion in Kent 1381* in *Archaeologia Cantiana. Vol. 4.* 1861. R.M. Filmer, *Chronicle of Kent 1250-1760,* p.23. Calendar of Patent Rolls 1381-85. pp.237, 264-65.

43 Compiled by Linda Darling, *Guide to St. Peter's Church, Boughton Monchelsea,* 1996. John Newman, *The Buildings of England: West Kent and the Weald,* Harmondsworth, 2nd Edition 1980. pp.175-76. Department of the Environment, *Seventy-third List of Buildings of Special Architectural or Historic Interest,* 1987, pp.10-11.

44 *Calendar of Charter Rolls 1285.*

45 This is an indication of the state which the medieval church had reached by the beginning of the fifteenth century although the Reformation was still a century away.

46 Rev. J.H. Warren, *Short Guide to the Church of St. Peter, Boughton Monchelsea.*

47 Catholic Record Society. Vol. 2. *Archdeacon Harpsfield's Visitation 1557,* 1950-51, pp.45-6,199-200.

48 Peter Clark, *English Provincial Society from the Reformation to the Revolution: Religion. Politics and Society in Kent 1500-1640,* Sussex, 1979. pp.168,172.

49 *Archaeologia Cantiana. Vol. 80.* 1965. p237.

50 Ed. Ann Whiteman assisted by Mary Clapinson, *Diocese of Canterbury. The Compton Census of 1676: A Critical Edition,* London, 1986. p.30. Footnote 184.

51 CKS. Bishops' Visitations 1716,1720, 1724, 1728, 1758, 1786, 1806.

52 *Ibid.* 1720, 1728, 1758, 1786, 1806.

53 MG 1.1.1833.

54 *Ibid.* Guide to St. Peter's Church 1996. Department of the Environment, *op.cit.,* pp.10-11.

55 Sarah Pearson, *The Medieval Houses of Kent: an Historical Analysis,* London, 1994. pp.14-15.

56 Mary Dobson, *Population 1640-1831* in Ed. Alan Armstrong, *The Economy of Kent 1640-1914,* Woodbridge, 1995. pp.9-13.

57 Stephen Conway, *Locality, Metropolis and Nation: The Impact of the Military Camps in England during the American War* in History. Vol. 82. No. 268. October 1997...p.551.

58 CKS. Probate Inventories. 11/51/53,149,152. 11/55/120. 11/56/58,194. 11/57/2,48. 11/58/9. 11/59/166,177. 11/160/131. 11/62/277. 11/63/36. 11/65/91. 11/71/87,120. 11/74/3,204. 11/76/189. 11/77/65. 11/81/62. 11/82/228.

59 Chalkin, *op.cit.,* p.108.

60 *Ibid.* pp.103-4.

61 (M)edway (R)ecord (O)ffice. CCRC E1-E5. Parsonage Farm.

62 MRO U 1323/24 T49. Brishing Court Farm. Indenture of Lease 1726. John Martin to Richard Wembon.

63 CKS PRC/27/42/23. Inventory of John Savage 21 May 1726.

64 See Peter Eden, *Small Houses in England 1520-1820,* London, 1969. pp.3-6,9. Ed. Elizabeth Melling. *Some Kentish Houses,* Maidstone, 1965. pp.1-6, 11-13. Chalkin, *op.cit.,* pp.236-240. W.G. Hoskins, *The Rebuilding of Rural England 1570-1640* in *Past and Present. No. 4. November 1953.* M.W. Barley, *The English Farmhouse and Cottage,* London, 1961. pp.134-185. Department of the Environment, *op.cit.,* I am also indebted to Sarah Pearson for a recent update on vernacular buildings in Kent.

65 I have drawn heavily for information in this section upon the excellent article by Stephen Conway, *op.cit.,* pp.547-562 and CKS U333 Z1. *General Orders and Administrative Instructions issued for Coxheath Camp. Whitehall 1779.* See also Beryl Bush. *St. Augustine's Alphabet, 1992.* pp.43-46 and Julia Page, *Coxheath Camp 1756-57* in *Loose Threads. No.1. 1988.* pp.25-31. I am also indebted to

Fergus Wilson for first drawing my attention to the maps of the Camp at Maidstone Museum.

66 George Bishop, *Observations, Remarks and Means to Prevent Smuggling,* Maidstone, 1783. pp.11-12.

67 See John Douch, *Smuggling; The Wicked Trade,* Dover, 1980. pp.35-83.

68 (K)entish (E)xpress 19.8.1899.

69 CKS P39/5/2 Boughton Monchelsea Churchwardens' Accounts 1831-1889.

70 Catholic Record Society. Vol. 2. *Archdeacon Harpsfield's Visitation 1557.* pp.194, 200.

71 PP 1834. Vol. XXVIII Select Committee on the Poor Laws pp.175, 211.

72 Ed. Louis A. Knafla, *Kent at Law 1602: The County Jurisdiction, Assizes and Sessions of the Peace,* London, 1994. p.120. No. 860. Beryl Bush, *op.cit.,* pp.61-63. Ed. Elizabeth Melling, *Kentish Sources. Some Roads and Bridges,* Maidstone, 1959. pp.46-47. CKS Hearth Tax 1664. P39/1/2 Boughton Monchelsea Parish Register.

73 CKS P39/21/1-3, P39/21/16 Boughton Monchelsea Surveyors of the Highways Accounts 1822-25, 1835-36, 1836-37, 1858-59.

74 Hasted, *op.cit., 2nd. Edn. Vol. VII 1797-1801.* p.52.

75 CKS Q/RVO3 Anno 42 Geo 3. c.65. 1802. Conway, *op.cit.,* p.554.

76 C.C.R. Pile, *Cranbrook: A Wealden Town,* Cranbrook, 1980. pp.57-8.

77 B. Keith Lucas, *Kentish Turnpikes* in *Archaeologia Cantiana Vol. C.* 1984. pp.364-65. F.H. Panton, *Turnpike Roads in the Canterbury Area* in *Archaeologia Cantiana. Vol. CII.* 1985. p.184. B. Keith Lucas, *Parish Affairs; The Government of Kent under George III.* Maidstone, 1986. pp.83-99.

78 B. Keith Lucas, *op.cit.,* pp.367-69. Terence Paul Smith, *The Geographical Pattern of Coaching Services in Kent 1836* in *Archaeologia Cantiana Vol. XCVIII.* 1982. p.201.

79 CKS P39/12/1-2 Boughton Monchelsea Overseers of the Poor Accounts 1777-1790, 1805-13.

80 CKS P39/12/1-2 Boughton Monchelsea Overseers of the Poor Accounts 1777-1790, 1805-13. CKS QCR Poor Relief Returns 1801-17. See also Royal Commission on the Poor Laws. Answers to Rural Queries. PP1834(44) XXX-XXXIV. Appendix B. Boughton Monchelsea. Answer 47. pp.238 e. CKS QSB 10/58q Michaelmas 1665.

81 CKS P39/12/4 Boughton Monchelsea Overseers' Clothing Account Book. CKS P39/8/3-4 Boughton Monchelsea Vestry Minute Books 1821-34, 1833-58.

82 P39/12/1-3 Boughton Monchelsea Overseers' Accounts 1777-90, 1805-13,1833-35. PP 1834(44) Appendix B. Answers to Rural Queries 19, 20.

83 Boughton Monchelsea Overseers' Accounts *loc.cit.*, and Answers to Rural Queries 6, 23-28, 39.

84 Answer to Rural Query 37. Boughton Monchelsea Vestry Minutes 1833-58. See also Paul Hastings, *The Old Poor Law in Kent* in *Religion and Society in Kent 1640-1914*, Woodbridge, 1994. pp.117-18.

85 Boughton Monchelsea Overseers' Accounts. Answer to Rural Query 22. CKS U310 T19 Boughton Monchelsea share in Coxheath Workhouse. PRO 5195 Maidstone Union 1834-37 31 January 1835. Vicar of East Farleigh to Poor Law Commission. PP 1802-3 Abstract of Answers and Returns relative to the expense and maintenance of the Poor 1802-03 pp.220-21.

86 PP 1834(44) XXVII. Appendix A. Part 1. p.216A.

87 CKS P39/8/3 Boughton Monchelsea Vestry Minute Book 1821-34.

88 CKS P39/12/3 List of Boughton Monchelsea Families in receipt of parochial relief 1 May 1815 and P39/8/4 10 March 1823. Census Returns 1811, 1821.

89 CKS P39/8/3-4 Boughton Monchelsea Vestry Minute Books 1821-34, 1833-58.

90 Paul Hastings, *The New Poor Law* in *Religion and Society in Kent 1640-1914*, Woodbridge, 1994. pp.154-163.

91 *A Topography of Maidstone 1839*, p.81. C. Igglesden, *A Saunter Through Kent. Vol. 9.* 1920, p.57.

92 CKS P39/12/3 Boughton Monchelsea Overseers' Accounts 1833-35. P39/8/4 Boughton Monchelsea Vestry Minute Book 15 October 1834.

93 Paul Hastings, *New Poor Law...op.cit.*, p.174. MH 12.5195. Maidstone Union 1834-37, 13.9.1835.

94 Answer to Rural Query 53.

95 (K)entish (G)azette 3.6.1830.

96 E.J. Hobsbawn and George Rude, *Captain Swing*, Harmondsworth, 1973. pp.46, 58, 184-85.

97 W. Carpenter, *Political Letters and Pamphlets 1830-31.* (K)ent (H)erald 4.11.1830. MG 2.11.1830.

98 MG 2.11.1830.

99 W. Carpenter *op.cit.*

100 MG 2.11.1830.

101 MG 14.12.1830, 25.6.1833.

102 See Section on Relief of the Poor in the Eighteenth and Nineteenth Centuries.

103 (S)outh (E)astern (G)azette 5.9.1860.

104 KM 21.7.1866, 12.7.1869, 21.5.1910.

105 Ancient Order of Foresters. Court of the Village Pride. No.4168. Boughton Monchelsea. Initiation Book 1863-75. Sick and Funeral Fund Cashbook 1888-1907. Register Book.

106 Ancient Order of Foresters. Court of the Village Pride. Boughton Monchelsea. Minute Book. 1904-21. 12.12.1905, 12.11.1907, 11.8.1908.

107 Minute Book 9.2.1904, 9.8.1904, 11.8.1908, 13.10.1908, 28.10.1908, 9.11.1908, 16.3.1909, 9.11.1909, 10.5.1909, 14.3.1911, 10.12.1912, 8.4.1913, 13.4.1920. KM 30.5.1931.

108 SEG 18.1.1886.

109 CKS P39/27/1-2 Boughton Monchelsea Tithe Map and Award 1842. Census 1841, 1851.

110 George Buckland, *On the Farming of Kent,* 1845. pp.271-73.

111 *Ibid.* pp.274, 278-80. KE 13.3.1897.

112 *Ibid.* p.278.

113 PP 1894 Royal Commission on Agriculture. Minutes of Evidence taken before Her Majesty's Commission appointed to Inquire into the Agricultural Depression. PP 1894-95. Vol. XVII. Part.1. On the Andover District of Hampshire and the Maidstone District of Kent.

114 Census 1841-1881.

115 *Ibid.*

116 Buckland, *op.cit.,* p.273.

117 SEG 15.1.1861, KE 8.1.1870, 22.1.1870.

118 Census Abstracts 1841-71. CKS Archbishop's Visitation Returns 1758, 1806.

119 PP 1868-69. XIII. Report of Royal Commission on Employment of Children, Young Persons and Women in Agriculture 1867.

120 KE 17.3.1866, 31.3.1866.

121 KM 30.10.1869, 6.11.1869.

122 (K)ent & (S)ussex (T)imes 7.2.1871, 6.7.1876, 19.1.1878, 2.3.1878, SEG 28.7.1884.

123 Richard Filmer, *Kentish Rural Crafts and Industries,* Rainham, 1981. p.29. John

Whichcord, Jun. *Observations on Kentish Ragstone as a Building Material,* London, 1846. pp.5, 8-9, 12. Alec Clifton-Taylor and A.S. Ireson, *English Stone Building,* London, 1994. pp.63-64. L.R.A. Grove, *Kentish Bygones: Quarrying Tools,* in *Kent Life, July 1963* p.62. Anne Creasey, *A Walk Through Boughton's Quarries* in *Loose Threads, No.1.* 1988. Records of Assize. Kent. 30.1.1600-01, April 1602. 1989-90.

124 Calendar of Ancient Deeds presented by Charles Marchant to Kent Archaeological Society July 1904. *loc.cit.,* pp.171-75.

125 CKS QM/S Bp. 27.

126 Census 1841-91. Richard Filmer, *op.cit.,* L.R.A. Grove, *op.cit.,* p.62. John Whichcord, Jun., *op.cit.,* pp.11,18.

127 Ed. D. Tye, *A Village Remembered 1900-1940,* Maidstone, 1980 pp.19-20. Filmer, *op.cit.,* Clifton-Taylor, *op.cit.,* p.65. Grove, o*p.cit.,* p.62. Whichcord, *op.cit.,* p.14. Anne Creasey, *Ragstone Quarries,* pp.6-8.

128 MG 8.8.1848.

129 Ed. D. Tye, *op.cit.,* p.21. Boughton Monchelsea Parish Council Minutes 18.3.1954, 25.8.1954, 14.1.1963, Boughton Monchelsea Parish Meeting 14.4.1955.

130 Ed. D. Tye, *op.cit.,* p.21. Mrs G. Bowles on the 'Quarriers'.

131 Census 1841-61. Creasey, *op.cit.,* p.8. Bagshaw, *op.cit.,* MJ 20.12.1803. U1327 T9/8. Deed of Conveyance 1856. KJ 1863. Information from Mike Newman descendant of William Newman. 1997. I am indebted for much of the data in this paragraph to Mrs. Beryl Bush.

132 SEG 11.4.1865.

133 KE 5.6.1909.

134 Boughton Monchelsea Parish Meeting 26.3.1945. Boughton Monchelsea Parish Council Minutes 18.3.1947, 29.8.1955, 13.7.1965, 27.2.1978.

135 CKS P39/1/12 Boughton Monchelsea Burials Registers 1813-1945. V.H.T. Skipp and R.P. Hastings, *Discovering Bickenhill,* Birmingham, 1963. pp.78-79. Michael Anderson, *What is new about the Modern Family?* in Ed. M. Drake, *Time, Family and Community,* Oxford, 1994. p.69.

136 Census 1841-81. Boughton Monchelsea Marriage Registers 1754-1841. *loc.cit.*

137 Census 1841-1891. Boughton Monchelsea Marriage Registers 1841-1890.

138 Census 1841-1881. SEG 3.3.1857.

139 KE 15.10.1864, 11.1.1868, 11.4.1868

140 KE 16.1.1869, 22.10.1869. SEG 11.1.1869.

141 KE 25.7.1863. SEG 9.2.1878.

142 SEG 3.5.1864, 26.2.1867, 23.3.1867. D.F. Tye, *op.cit.,* p.5.

143 Boughton Monchelsea Parish Magazine January 1899, February 1905.

144 KM 21.1.1933.

145 KE 13.2.1909. KM 6.8.1910, 19.3.1921.

146 SEG 7.2.1871. KE 8.5.1909. CKS C/ES 39/1/1, 39/1/2, 39/1/3. Boughton Monchelsea School Log Book (henceforth referred to as 'Log Book') 12.1.1869.

147 KE 23.1.1909. KM 5.2.1910, 5.10.1912.

148 Beryl Bush, *op.cit.,* pp.3-4. SEG 3.11.1880. 28.7.1884.

149 Parish Magazine 1896, 1898, 1905.

150 *Kelly's Directory* 1905. Boughton Monchelsea Tithe Award 1842. Census 1861-81. Parish Magazine June 1897. KE 16.10.1909. KM 15.1.1910.

151 KE 28.3.1896.

152 KE 22.5.1897.

153 Parish Meeting 1897. KE 1.8.1908, 24.7.1909. Parish Magazine July 1898. Recreation Ground Lease 29.12.1897. Recreation Ground Correspondence 11, 17.11.1919.

154 Paul Hastings, *Epidemics and Public Health* in Yates, Hume and Hastings, *Religion and Society in Kent 1640-1914.* pp.192-98. See also Paul Hastings, *Crime and Public Order* in Ed. H.F.C. Lansberry, *The Government of Kent 1640-1914.* PP 1868-89. XIII. Report on the Employment of Children, Young Persons and Women in Agriculture 1867. Part II. p.62.

155 KE 1.10.1864. SEG 17.8.1868, 24.8.1868, 31.8.1868. Parish Magazine October 1899.

156 KE 19.9.1864, 2.10.1869, 2.10.1909. SEG 25.9.1875, 16.9.1878.

157 CKS P39/8/4 Boughton Monchelsea Vestry Minutes 8.2.1847. Bagshaw, *op.cit.,* Census 1841, 1861. CKS U1121 E1, E9. 18th Century Accounts of Sir Christopher Powell of Wierton.

158 The Parish Councillors' Handbook 1894 pp.4-5. Boughton Monchelsea Parish Meeting 1894, 1897-99, 1901, 1904, 1913. Parish Magazine 1895, 1896. Log Book 29.11.1881.

159 See Paul Hastings, Epidemics...pp.219,223-24. Parish Magazine July 1898. KE 19.2.1898, 24.8.1912, 16.11.1912.

160 D.E. Tye, *op.cit.,* p.15 Boughton Monchelsea Parish Council Minutes 21.3.1941. Information from Mid Kent Water PLC.

161 D.F. Tye, *op.cit.,* p.49.

162 Boughton Monchelsea Parish Meeting 1902, 1911, 1937, 1953, 1977.

163 KM 30.4.1921, 9.7.1921, 5.11.1921, 26.11.1921.

164 D.F. Tye, *op.cit.,* pp.47, 55.

165 Boughton Monchelsea Parish Meeting 1949.

166 D.F. Tye, *op.cit.,* pp.55-56. Boughton Monchelsea Parish Council Minutes 29.8.1955, 12.1.1959, 25.5.1959, 14.5.1959. KE 28.5.1932.

167 Boughton Monchelsea Parish Council Minutes 16.1.1959, 14.9.1959, 9.5.1960, 14.11.1960, 9.1.1961, 13.3.1961, 13.11.1961, 12.3.1962, 13.6.1962, 14.1.1963, 11.11.1963, 24.5.1965, 13.7.1965.

168 Boughton Monchelsea Parish Meetings 1914-1919.

169 Boughton Monchelsea Parish Meeting 1938. Boughton Monchelsea Parish Council Minutes 26.8.1936, 21.1.1937, 12.4.1938, 16.2.1939.

170 Boughton Monchelsea Parish Council Minutes 23.3.1939, 20.4.1939, 17.8.1939.

171 D.F. Tye, *op.cit.,* pp.52-3. Log Book 19.9.1939.

172 *Ibid.* Boughton Monchelsea Parish Council Minutes 14.3.1940, 24.3.1942, 30.4.1942.

173 Boughton Monchelsea Conservation Society Newsletter. No.2. August 1994. Boughton Monchelsea Parish Meeting 11.7.1940, 29.4.1941. Boughton Monchelsea Parish Council Minutes 14.3.1940. Tye Archive, University of Kent Library. Log Book 5.8.1940.

174 Boughton Monchelsea Parish Council Minutes 21.3.1941. D.F. Tye, *op.cit.,* p.53.

175 *Ibid.* Log Book 21, 22.8.1944.

176 Visitation Return 1806. PP 1819 IX..2.HC 224. Digest of Parochial Returns to Select Committee on the Education of the Lower Orders pp.382, 414. PP 1835. XLIII. HC 62. Abstract of Answers and Returns relating to the State of Education in England and Wales 1833. p.385.

177 CKS P39/1/6, 1/7 Boughton Monchelsea Marriage Registers 1754-1850.

178 Ed. D.F. Tye, *Boughton Monchelsea School: Extracts from the School Log Books,* 2nd Edtn, Boughton Monchelsea, 1976. Introduction pp.1-3.

179 PP 1868-69. XIII. Report on Royal Commission on the Employment of Children, Young Persons and Women in Agriculture 1867. p.46. Sharlocks

were tall, yellow-flowered weeds which grew among the wheat and were pulled with difficulty in mid-summer. Information kindly supplied by Mr. Tommy Thompson who pulled sharlocks himself as a boy.

180 Log 2.7.1863, 26.8.1864, 19.3.1868, 22.6.1869, 25.8.1875, 13.7.1878, 19.8.1890, 24.10.1890, 12.11.1890, 5.10.1896.

181 Log Book 20.12.1897, 29.1.1903.

182 Log Book 20.7.1863, 24.7.1872, 26.5.1875, 28.6.1880, 20.7.1880, 5.11.1890.

183 Paul Hastings, *Epidemics...*pp.206-07. Log Book 7.2.1866, 7.2.1868, 25.6.1877, 16.8.1879, 11.6.1891, 8.1.1892, 16.3.,18.9., 4.12.1893, 4.12.1896, 26.4.1897, 7.7., 31.7., 16.8., 18.10., 22.10., 20.12.1900, 17.1.1908, 2.6.1911.

184 Log Book 18.6.1873, 12.4., 24.5.1875, 2.10.1908, 7.6.1909, 29.3.1912. KE 27.4.1911.

185 Log Book 13.5.1871. KE 14.4.1879. SEG 17.8.1872.

186 Log Book 20.3.1865, 25.5.1868, 17.6.1873, 8.2.1875.

187 Ed. D.F. Tye, *Boughton Monchelsea School.*

188 Log Book 29.1.1867, 30.10.1872, 6.11.1872.

189 KE 20.8.1892.

190 Log Book 28.7., 29.7., 26.8., 23.12.1892.

191 Log Book 16.3.1875.

192 Log Book 16.3.1893, 12.4., 11.6.1898.

193 Log Book 14.6.1876, 4.7.1890.

194 Log Book 1.5.1893.

195 CKS P39/1/11 Boughton Monchelsea Marriage Registers 1850-Present. Tye Archive.

196 Log Book December 1926, April 1929, July 1931, November 1933, May 1934.

197 Log Book 1925, 1927, 1928, 1930, June 1936.

198 Log Book July 1936, March 1937, January 1941, June 1941, November 1944.

199 HMI Report 1947.

200 Log Book 1946.

201 Information supplied by Peter Hirons, Deputy Headmaster, Boughton Monchelsea County Primary School.

202 Boughton Monchelsea Parish Council Minutes 11.11.1963, 20.6.1977, 14.11.1977.

203 *Ibid.* 27.2.1978, 25.6.1979, 12.11.1979, 9.3.1987. Boughton Monchelsea Parish Meeting 12.3.1979.

204 Boughton Monchelsea Parish Council Minutes 27.7.1984. Boughton Monchelsea Parish Meeting 2.2.1984. Kent Messenger 10.2.1984.

205 Boughton Monchelsea Parish Meetings 10.9.1980, 20.5.1983. Boughton Monchelsea Parish Council Minutes 3.7.1984. *Boughton Monchelsea Explored,* Maidstone, 1989 p.3., Boughton Monchelsea Amenity Trust Minutes 14.11.1995.

206 Boughton Monchelsea Parish Meeting 13.5.1997. Boughton Monchelsea Parish Council Minutes 11.2.1986.

207 *Boughton Monchelsea Explored...*p.18. Department of the Environment, *op.cit.* Boughton Monchelsea Parish Council Minutes 14.7.1992, 30.3.1993, 15.3.1994. Boughton Monchelsea Parish Meeting 25.5.1993.

208 Boughton Monchelsea Parish Council Minutes and Parish Meetings 9.7.1991, 15.9.1992, 30.3.1993, 15.11.1994, 13.5.1997.

209 *Ibid.* 15.9.1992, 30.3.1993, 13.5.1997.

210 Boughton Monchelsea Conservation Society Newsletter No.2. August 1994.

211 Boughton Monchelsea Parish Council Minutes and Parish Meetings 29.10.1985, 8.3.1988, 29.9.92.

212 Boughton Monchelsea Parish Council 29.9.1992, 14.6.1994, 17.5.1994. Boughton Monchelsea Amenity Trust Minutes 19.7.1994,10.11.1994, 17.1.1995, 14.2.1995, 24.2.1998. Boughton Monchelsea Parish Meeting 1996. I am much indebted to Councillor Ian Ellis for information and explanation about this subject and upon the nature of Maidstone Borough Council Local Plan 2001-2006.

213 See Fig. 6.

214 See p.213-217.

215 See Census Abstract 1841. County of Kent. p.129.

216 U80. M1. Manor of Boughton Monchelsea. Court Book. 1683-1799. Kindly loaned by Charles Gooch. The occupiers of all individual houses are taken from Trade Directories and the Census Enumerators' Books 1841-1881.

217 *Ibid.*

218 Ed. Elizabeth Melling, *Some Kentish Houses: Kentish Sources V.* Maidstone, 1965. p.8.

219 I am indebted to Capn. and Mrs. Roome of East Hall for these details.

220 I am indebted to Miss Rachel Smith for some of these details.

221 CKS Chatham. CCRC E3/108188. Survey of one Part of the Church of Rochester taken 1623.